I'll never forget hearing Helen Roseveare speak: immediate authority; convincing clarity; relentless passion. Now her three classic works have been brought together for a new generation of readers. Prepare to be challenged, moved, and inspired!

COLIN S SMITH
Senior Pastor, The Orchard
Arlington, Illinois

I've lost count of how many times I've recommended Helen's writings to people. Not only does Helen tell an amazing story, but, just as in life, she's more interested in talking about Jesus than herself. She was a woman in love with her Saviour. Anytime she talked of Jesus her face would light up with a warm glow of delight. You'll see that delight as you turn these pages. *Helen Roseveare: A Life in Her Own Words* is an amazing autobiography that I'd encourage any Christian to read. You'll learn of Helen and her adventures for the Lord, but greater than that, you'll see the beauty of Jesus in her life, even in the most difficult of circumstances.

JONATHAN CARSWELL
Founder, 10ofthose.com

We shouldn't live in the past but it is a good place to visit now and again. And what better way to do that than by rereading books that have been a foundational influence on your life. So I'm delighted to see these Christian classics together in one volume. Helen Roseveare's story is a frank and honest account of her time as a missionary in Africa and beyond. There is no other biography that covers the ups, downs and heartaches of life better than Helen's. Rudyard Kipling wrote about meeting triumph and disasters head on – Helen writes about facing the joys and travails of life with her beloved Lord and Saviour Jesus Christ. She was in her eighties when I first met her in Northern Ireland, still the focussed and faithful follower that I had first read about as a young teenager. The words she said to me as we waved goodbye at the Belfast City airport are some of the most encouraging and challenging words ever said to me. The Helen you meet through these pages is the real deal. No pretence or enhancement. The only one she built up was Jesus.

CATHERINE MACKENZIE
Children's books editor and author

Helen Roseveare

A Life in Her Own Words

Introduced by Betsy Childs Howard
Foreword by John & Noël Piper

CHRISTIAN
FOCUS

Give Me This Mountain by Helen Roseveare was first published by Christian Focus in 2006: 978-1-84550-189-1.

He Gave us a Valley by Helen Roseveare was first published by Christian Focus in 2006: 978-1-84550-190-7.

Digging Ditches by Helen Roseveare was first published by Christian Focus in 2005: 978-1-84550-058-0.

Unless otherwise noted, Scripture quotations from The Authorized (King James) Version. Rights in the Authorized Version in the United Kingdom are vested in the Crown. Reproduced by permission of the Crown's patentee, Cambridge University Press

Scripture quotations marked ESV are from The Holy Bible, English Standard Version, copyright © 2001 by Crossway Bibles, a publishing ministry of Good News Publishers. Used by permission. All rights reserved. ESV Text Edition: 2011.

Scripture quotations marked NIV are taken from the THE HOLY BIBLE, NEW INTERNATIONAL VERSION®, NIV® Copyright © 1973, 1978, 1984, 2011 by Biblica, Inc.™ Used by permission. All rights reserved worldwide.

The map on page sixteen was modelled after the map "DR of the Congo" found at d-maps.com/carte.php?num_car=25932&lang=en, last accessed 27 January, 2025.

hardback ISBN 978-1-5271-1139-4

ebook ISBN 978-1-5271-1313-8

10 9 8 7 6 5 4 3 2 1

Published in 2025 by
Christian Focus Publications,
Geanies House, Fearn, Ross-shire,
IV20 1TW, Scotland, UK
www.christianfocus.com

Cover design by James Amour

Printed and bound by
Bell & Bain, Glasgow

MIX
Paper | Supporting responsible forestry
FSC® C007785

CONTENTS

Foreword

In 1989, 120 young people sat cross-legged, covering nearly every square inch of our living and dining rooms. They had accepted our invitation to anyone who thought missions might be in his or her future.

As Helen Roseveare stood by our fireplace and looked into their faces, she reached back toward the mantel and eased a long-stemmed red rose bud from its vase. While she spoke, she used a small knife to remove thorns, leaves, petals, the green outer layer of stem—every element that makes a rose a rose. What remained was a sleek, straight shaft. The pieces that lay on the floor were not bad things. But, she explained, they had to be removed if she were going to make an arrow. God does this, she said. He cuts away everything—even innocent, good things—that hinders us from being arrows that he will shoot for his purposes at his intended target.

Outwardly, Helen Roseveare's life may be different than ours. She served for twenty years as a medical doctor and missionary in war-torn Congo. But her inner battles were similar to ours. And as we know, inner battles don't stay in. They may spill over, injuring even the people that we care about most. The three books in this volume give us a window into a great and embattled soul.

Seeing another's battles gives us perspective on our own struggles. For one thing, there is seldom only one cause.

We realise how tangled the causes of spiritual dryness are as Helen describes a period during medical training:

> The joy and excitement of the first three years suddenly seemed to drain away. . . . Work began to get on top of me; unhappiness, loneliness, fear, inferiority, all began to be acutely present. At the same time Bible study and prayer became perfunctory instead of joyous .... Witness continued, but with no real faith or expectation of seeing results. Looking back it is easy to realise that at least part of the explanation lies in the fact that ... I was suffering from overwork and strain resulting from a very full programme ... I ... thought this exhaustion meant spiritual failure.[1]

She felt like a spiritual failure. She forced herself to her Bible and prayer. It seemed pointless to talk about Christ. But that deadness didn't come from nowhere. She was working and studying too many hours in a day, not getting enough sleep. Her vulnerability to "unhappiness, loneliness, fear, inferiority" came from two directions: her physical exhaustion and her spiritual depletion. Her spiritual life dragged because she was exhausted, and she was exhausted because her spiritual life dragged—a tangled circle.

That is a good lesson. Given a choice, we need wise decisions about sleeping, eating, and other things that affect our health, so we don't open ourselves to sin that undermines spiritual well-being. From the spiritual side, we must work to keep our connection with God strong through his Word and prayer, so we have eyes to see when we are sliding into bad attitudes and glossing over our sin.

God often uses other people to retrieve us when we're easing into sin that flourishes in spiritual dryness. It's humbling when others point out our weaknesses, our *sins*. It was especially encouraging to see Helen turning to her

---

1 See later in this volume: *Give Me This Mountain*, pp. 72-73.

African pastor and co-workers and receiving their correction. It can be hard to believe that someone from another culture understands or has the right to admonish us.

It is a gift when God gives a mind and heart to know and feel that brothers and sisters come in every ethnicity—that "in Christ Jesus [we] are all sons of God, through faith ... one in Christ Jesus" (Gal. 3:26-28 ESV). That realization was a gift and a lesson Helen received with thanks and humble wonder. To think, she wrote later, "I had gone out to them as the missionary-teacher!"[2]

When things were going badly at Nebobongo, Helen knew she needed a change: "Suddenly I knew that I had to get away from it all *and sort myself out and seek God's forgiveness and restoration*, if I was to continue in the work."[3] When things are bad, we do try to take a break and relax. But is relaxing all we do? Taking a break will do little good unless it turns us toward God. She learned this truth so well that her ministry extended years beyond her crises.

One deep personal factor in Helen's early struggles was her felt need to do and be her very best. But God called her to Africa where the "best" often looked very different than back home. At every turn, there were unforeseen challenges: learning to treat malaria by symptoms rather than with prescribed lab tests, needing to do surgery without having the training, having to make bricks rather than working with patients. Perhaps some of us struggle with the reality that God has called us to less than what we believe is our best. That can happen in any setting. Maybe our problem is that we think more highly of ourselves than we ought.

---

2 *Living Sacrifice: Willing to be Whittled as an Arrow* (Fearn, Ross-shire: Christian Focus, 2007), p. 48.

3 *Living Holiness: Willing to be the Legs of a Galloping Horse* (Fearn, Ross-shire: Christian Focus, 2008), p. 67 (emphasis added).

Helen Roseveare was humbled by her Savior. She was cut down from a rose stem to a sharp and penetrating arrow in the hand of her Master. She learned that no one is too great to be spared such humbling. If anyone was too good to die, it was Jesus. If anyone should have done greater things than walking dusty roads and talking with people too dense to understand, it was Jesus. In Philippians 3, the passage that headlines Helen's story, is verse 10: "... that I may know him and the power of his resurrection, and may share his sufferings, becoming like him in his death" (ESV). When God called Helen to less than she expected, he was helping her become like Christ, rather than becoming like the best doctor or missionary she knew. Not surprisingly, as we learned from Jesus, this humbling catapulted Helen Roseveare into a life of global fruitfulness that was not "less than she expected" but rather exceeded all her dreams. We are thrilled to see the impact of her life and ministry carried forward with this publication of her work.

JOHN & NOËL PIPER
Minneapolis, Minnesota

INTRODUCTION

I don't remember how old I was when I first heard of Helen Roseveare, but I'll never forget the story my childhood pastor told in a sermon. It was the sort of story that will make a young girl's ears prick up!

In an African mission hospital, a mother died in childbirth, leaving behind a premature baby and a two-year-old daughter. The hospital had no incubator or even electricity to keep the baby warm. A midwife warmed water on the fire and filled up a hot water bottle to warm the baby, but to her great dismay, it burst. There was no other hot water bottle in the hospital, and nowhere to buy one. The best they could do to warm the baby was to let it sleep close to the fire.

The next day, the hospital's missionary doctor, Helen Roseveare, met to pray with the children living at the mission orphanage. She told them about the burst hot water bottle, the tiny baby, and the two-year-old sister who was missing her mother. Although she asked the children to pray, she was unsettled by the boldness of ten-year-old Ruth's prayer: "Please God, send us a hot water bottle. It'll be no good tomorrow, God, as the baby'll be dead; so please send it this afternoon. And while you are at it, would you please send a dolly for the little girl, so she'll know you really love her?"[1]

1 Helen Roseveare, *Living Faith* (Fearn, Ross-shire: Christian Focus, 2016), p. 56–58.

Helen considered this request impossible. She thought to herself, "The only way God could answer this particular prayer would be by sending me a parcel from the homeland. I had been in Africa almost four years at that time, and I had never, never received a parcel from home; anyway, if anyone did send me a parcel, who would put in a hot water bottle? I lived on the equator."

To Helen's great surprise, a large package from England—the first she had ever received—arrived on her doorstep that very afternoon. She called to her the orphans who had prayed that morning, and they opened the box together. Carefully, she untied the string and removed the paper while the children's anticipation grew.

The parcel contained colourful knitted jerseys and bandages for hospital patients. There was soap and a box of raisins. Then Helen reached in and pulled out a hot water bottle. She couldn't help crying as she realised how small her faith had been. Little Ruth immediately announced, "If God has sent the bottle, He must have sent the dolly too!" Sure enough, the last thing in the box was a beautiful baby doll.

The package had been on its way for five months before Ruth prayed her prayer. This was not the first time that God surprised Helen Roseveare, and it would not be the last.

* * *

Helen Roseveare was born in 1925 in Hertfordshire, England, the second of Martin and Edith Roseveare's five children. The family was nominally religious and well-educated, but not especially well-off. Martin bounced around between teaching and civil service jobs. Helen and her siblings were sent to excellent British boarding schools, but she often found herself without adequate pocket money to enjoy the amusements her fellow classmates took for granted.

In 1939, when Helen was fourteen years old, Great Britain declared war on Germany. The Roseveare family was fully involved in the war effort. Bob, Helen's older brother, worked as a codebreaker at Bletchley Park. Her father, Martin, worked for the Ministry of Food, where he played a key role in developing and implementing the fraud-proof ration system. (In fact, he was later knighted by the Crown for his wartime service.)

In 1944, Helen matriculated at Cambridge University. Although she had long been religious, while at college she was truly converted through the ministry of some Christian students. Helen worked hard and qualified as a doctor via an accelerated wartime course, but, by the time she finished her studies, the war was over.

Helen chose to become a medical missionary by joining the World Evangelization Crusade (WEC), a missions agency founded in 1913 by missionary C. T. Studd. Although Studd had started the WEC mission in the Congo thirty years before Helen arrived, it still had no doctor. After spending time in Belgium learning French, Helen Roseveare set sail for Africa on February 13, 1953.

Helen's mission work in the Congo took place against a backdrop of great political and civil unrest. The country that is now known as the Democratic Republic of Congo was a Belgian colony from 1908 until 1960. The Belgian government resisted giving the people of Congo any form of self-governance until 1960, at which point the international and internal pressure became too great. Independence didn't end Belgian or Western interference; it merely rerouted it through back channels.

The new republic lacked a stable chain of command. In the first year as an independent nation, the president, Joseph Kasavubu, and the prime minister, Patrice Lumumba, each tried to fire the other. The country's wealthiest province,

Katanga, tried to secede under a third leader. The army chief of staff, Joseph Mobutu (later known as Mobutu Sese Seko), staged a coup d'état. And Lumumba was brutally assassinated barely six months after taking office.

The political instability of the Congo brought with it ever-changing, ever-complexifying systems and regulations. Throughout her life, Helen Roseveare believed that missionary doctors in Africa had an obligation to train Africans in medical work. Her call to medical missions was thus also a call to a teaching ministry, and, over the course of her career, Helen started two hospitals and established numerous training programs and clinics. This work meant Helen developed an unwanted side ministry of bureaucratic slogging.

Helen loathed spending precious time filling in forms and writing reports that might never be read, but she accepted that her time was the Lord's. She could have moved on to a country where medical ministry involved more medicine and less placation of low-level government officials, but she didn't. Because of Helen's perseverance, her medical ministry didn't end when she left Africa. She left behind institutions and training programs that exist to this day.

In her later life, Helen developed an illustration she called "the stripping of the rose." As she spoke about what God requires of his servants, she would hold a rose and cut off thorns, branches, and leaves. She would even remove the beautiful petals and talk about how the good things in our life can keep us from usefulness if they are not surrendered to the Lord. After she had a bare stem in her hand, she used a knife to strip away the bark until she had a smooth, polished shaft, ready to be used as an arrow.

As you will see, this illustration came out of Helen's own experience. God stripped her of everything that interfered with his purposes. Over and over again, she was stripped of her pride. This was no less painful for Helen than it is for any one of us. But she willingly submitted again and again to God's sanctifying work, and consequently was used mightily for his kingdom.

—BETSY CHILDS HOWARD

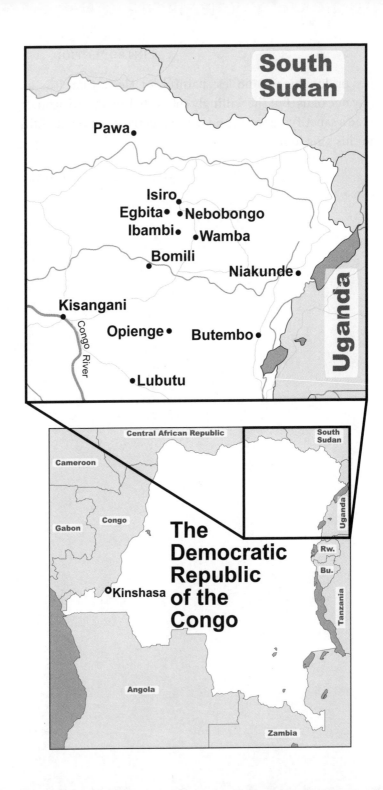

A Timeline of Helen Roseveare's Life

1925 Born at Haileybury, Herts, England.

1931 Primary and secondary school education.

1944 Left school and began studying medicine at Cambridge.

1945 Converted while a medical student at Newnham College, Cambridge.

1951 Became a missionary candidate with the Worldwide Evangelization Crusade (WEC).

1953 Sailed to Africa under the auspices of WEC to the Belgian Congo. Spent eighteen months establishing medical services at Ibambi, NE Congo.

1955 Moved seven miles to establish WEC medical centre at Nebobongo, comprising: 100-bed hospital and maternity services; leprosy-care centre and children's home; 48 rural health clinics in immediate vicinity; training school for national paramedical workers, that is, male and female assistant nurses and midwives.

1958 Two years of furlough with further medical training in UK.

1960 Independence: formation of the Republic of Congo.

1964 Rebellion and Simba uprising (civil war): spent five months in captivity.

1965 Rescued by National Army: one year's furlough in the UK.

1966 Returned to Africa, under the auspices of WEC to Congo/Zaire, to give seven years' service in an inter-mission (comprising five missions and churches) medical project at the Evangelical Medical Centre of Nyan-kunde, NE Zaire.

He Gave Me This Mountain first published.

1973 Home to the UK after twenty years of African service.

1976 Spoke at a missionary conference in the United States of America.

1977 *He Gave Us A Valley* first published.

1988 Returned to Nebobongo to make a video for missionary societies.

1989 Life is portrayed in the film *Mama Luka Comes Home*.

2004 Returned to Nebobongo to open a new surgical unit.

2005 *Digging Ditches* first published.

2007 Worldwide speaking and teaching ministry continued while settling in Northern Ireland.

2016 Died at 91 in Northern Ireland.

Give Me This Mountain

CONTENTS

And Caleb said: Now therefore give me this mountain, whereof the Lord spake in that day; for thou heardest in that day how the Anakims were there, and that the cities were great and fenced: if so be the Lord will be with me, then I shall be able to drive them out, as the Lord said. And Joshua gave unto Caleb Hebron for an inheritance.

Joshua 14:12–13

INTRODUCTION

In the following pages I have tried to write an honest, unadorned story of my somewhat tempestuous life. Except in the Epilogue, I have not tried to draw any morals. But neither have I wanted to pull any punches. I have tried honestly to thank those who have helped me along the way and to be careful not to criticise unkindly others with whom I disagreed. At times, this may have made the story a little lopsided since occasionally I have felt unable to give publicly all the facts that influenced me at certain periods. I do not think, however, that this materially alters the basic story.

I have only once in my life kept a diary, and that was under the special stress of the five months in rebel captivity from August to December, 1964. All the rest of the story comes as my memory prompts me. There may be some chronological discrepancies. Many episodes are excluded, either because they have been forgotten or else because I did not consider that they helped forward the main theme. Other episodes are mentioned and then never referred to again. They were there, but did not substantially alter the course of the journey.

My life has possibly included more dramatic episodes than many another, but this is not the impression I wish to leave with any reader. Rather, it has been for me a journey towards one definite and glorious goal, 'that I may know him…', our God, revealed to us in his Son, the Lord Jesus Christ. I have often felt that my life was akin to mountaineering, with a clear goal to reach the highest peak. There may be a fairly long journey to reach the foothills before the real climb begins. On the way up, clouds or lesser peaks often hide the goal from view, but the original sight of the summit keeps us pressing on, despite weariness and even discouragement.

I found frequently that I climbed in glorious sunshine, warm and invigorating, my face set determinedly for the nearest peak I could see. As I reached it, I revelled in the sense of achievement and victory and in the glorious view. I did all I could to encourage others to join me and to help them up over the difficult parts. Then, slowly, my imagination would be caught by the next peak ahead, higher, steeper, but again bathed in sunlight, and eventually the resolve would form to set off upwards again.

Here I made a mistake, many times, as the story shows. As I went down from the present peak into the valley between the mountains, I was often shadowed by the very peak I had been enjoying. This I interpreted in a sense of failure and this often led to despair. I felt I was going down into the 'slough of despond'. I see now that I was wrong in this 'feeling'. The going down was merely an initial moving forward towards the next higher ground, never a going back to base level. The shadow was only relative after the brightness of the sun; the valley could provide rest for working out the experiences previously learnt, a time for refreshment before the next hard climb. Had I understood this meaning of the sunshine and shadow in my life rather than interpreting my experiences along life's way as 'up' and 'down', I might have saved myself many deep heartaches.

I trust, despite this failure, that readers will be able to enter into the joy of this wonderful pilgrimage and the satisfaction of a life spent seeking to know the One who alone gives life. I am in no way offering my story as an example for others to follow. There are many mistakes that I hope may warn others. There are streaks in my nature that I am glad to see the Lord is dealing with, and I should hate others to think that they ought to emulate them. I think especially of the tremendous ambition to be a success in anything I undertook, which so often drove me to set myself standards which, under all the circumstances, were not required and which, if I had been more perceptive, I should have known I had no chance of achieving. No, it is not an example; but maybe it will be an encouragement to some on the journey to realise that others have passed the same way.

Events in Africa move quickly. Already some of the place-names are out of date. Leopoldville in the following pages should now be Kinshasa, Paulis is now Isiro and Stanleyville is Kisangani.

1

GETTING TO THE START

'Either you join us, or you go down by yourself: it's your own affair.'

The nursemaid moved away. I swallowed hard, my eyes misting with tears. Five minutes before, everything had been so different as I had run and scrambled up the wooded pathway with my elder brother, gathering wild flowers, happy in the flickering sunlight, chattering and unconcerned. I had noticed Bob's face set in a quiet determination and had wondered. Then we came out from the trees at the top of the ghyll and stood on the flat rock overlooking the rushing stream, silenced, as always, by the noise of the waters and a sense of power and awe at its depth. Suddenly, quietly, so unexpectedly, Bob drew back a few paces, ran and jumped the ghyll. My eyes followed him with silent admiration, and yet with horror glancing down at the fury below. He had done it—our much-discussed exploit of jumping the raging torrent from the rock. Determinedly I drew back, clenched my fists, closed my eyes, ran up to it, and stopped dead!

Bob had run on into the woods, suddenly a man, alone, successful. Then the nursemaid struggled up, carrying my four-year-old younger sister. She stepped over the narrow channel with one easy stride, and told me to hurry up and join them; they couldn't wait all day. Then she moved on, to follow Bob down the pathway the other side.

Despair, loneliness, tears. I could not do what Bob had done, and jump across. The more I longed, the greater the noise and depth and width and horror. I was terrified of that water. With a wild sense of defeat, I turned and rushed back down the hill, burning tears of shame choking me. What would he think? Would he play with me again? I was just a sissy, a girl, afraid—yes, that was it—afraid of water and height.

This longing to be accepted, this need to be loved, to be wanted, so often a part of childhood, came early to me. There was that day in Cornwall two years before, when suddenly a hush fell on the crowded beach, and Mother noticed all eyes being drawn in one direction. Way up the sheer face of the cliff on a narrow ledge, unable to go up or down, she saw the round, diminutive figure of her four-year-old, trying to defeat this sense of inferiority, longing to shine in the eyes of her adored six-year-old brother.

As a child I was endlessly active, restless with animal spirits, always in mischief, with an urge to excel, to be noticed, to be the centre of the group, with an inner need to be admired—and life often seemed very hard and unsympathetic. Often blamed for trouble that was not of my making, I would despise the others in my heart for not owning up to clear me of the accusation.

School soon absorbed much of my excess energy, but the work came easily. Books were a fascination, so much so that, when my younger sister whispered, 'Read to me, Peggy', in the dark of an evening, I could forget the whipping I had earlier suffered unjustly. Lying side by side, by torch light, under the blankets, we devoured many of the thrills of Long John Silver, the White Rabbit, Pooh, and Henry Esmond, and the world took on new silvery lights of happiness and mystery.

This air of mystery laid the foundation of Sundays. I loved this day and the sense of difference—dressed tidily, walking up the steep, narrow road past the curio shop, where two white stone cherub bookends smiled at me each Sunday as I ran ahead of the family, till I had saved enough to make them my mother's birthday present. The cool, dim building, with high, carved wood pews; the thin, tall candles flickering below the amazing coloured east window; the vases of austere white lilies; the choirboys in surplice and ruff, the acolytes and servers, the cross and incense; the priest in his beautifully embroidered linen vestments; the pealing organ and rich strange music that filled the building right up to the great carved dome; the long, difficult words folded into the lilting chants; the sermon with its grave cadences; all these I loved, absorbing almost unconsciously a lasting impression of beauty and solemnity. Then home we would go to a family dinner, so often the only day Dad was with us, and after that off to Sunday school, held locally at the teacher's home. I vividly remember that wonderful day (my eighth birthday) when she talked to us of India, and we cut out pictures of Indian children and stuck them in our 'Missionary Prayer Book'. It was then that the quiet resolve was made. When I grow up, I will go to tell other boys and girls about the Lord Jesus—a child's determination that never faded.

Odd incidents stand out clearly like beacons, all pointing to the absorbing necessity of being loved and wanted. There was the day I had a new dress, in velveteen, plain, dark, with three silver buttons set obliquely on each side of the chest, just what I longed for, quite different, smart, commanding. I recall a visit from an American cousin to my school when I was ten and my being sent for by the headmistress who introduced me as 'an exceptional pupil with a brilliant mind'! I had to look up 'exceptional' in a dictionary afterwards, and was very puzzled to know if it was complimentary or not, but it had obviously impressed these important relatives!

The following year, exam-time came round and I woke up feeling ill one morning. Despite it, I struggled to school, starting on a glorious, straightforward maths exam, and then was violently sick after completing only one of the ten questions. I shall never forget the bitter disappointment of having only 10 out of 100 for my best subject, or the subsequent radiant joy when it was not included in the averages and I once again received the form prize for the year. These little things mattered so much.

During these years three memorable summer holidays added to the scenic background of life. The first—through France and Switzerland, then south to Pompeii—had the added joy that my beloved godfather, 'Uncle Ray', accompanied us in his own car. I glowed with happiness at being specially 'his', sometimes travelling on my own with him. The second, with family car and camping equipment, took us through Germany (where we joined the crowds in Berlin to watch the Olympic Games), Hungary (and the Budapest Music festival, with everyone in national costume), Bulgaria (with its back-to-front writing, and nods for nos), to Istanbul (all minarets and tramcars). But it left less impression. The third stands out clear in my memory—the majestic beauty of Norwegian fjords girded by mighty mountains; the deep clear depths; the coastal steamer. Up and on we journeyed through to the far north, where we saw the aurora borealis, splendid in all its magnificence of heavenly colours. There were reindeers and moose; Laplanders, shy and colourful; and the sharp cold of the Arctic. Then back again, through festoons of lakes and stately crimson pines, reflected in glory in the evening sun. Last of all came a few days in Leningrad, travelling by train; guarded by soldiers, sight-seeing by permission!

Then it was my twelfth birthday—and boarding school.
I insisted on changing from my pet name, Peggy, to my real
name, Helen. The former now seemed childish, an obstacle to
my determination to be a success, to grow up, to be popular.
For here at boarding-school, too, the urgent 'need' was to
impress, to be loved, to be wanted—a need that grew steadily
stronger through these formative years. My vivid imagination
found plenty of food for exaggeration in all the experiences
of recent holidays, magnifying out of all proportion the
happenings and personalities. I boasted of my introduction
to Hitler at the Olympic Games in Berlin—weaving truth
(that we saw Hitler at the lighting of the torch) and fiction
(that I was introduced to him) so cleverly that I myself failed
to remember where one ended and the other started. Linked
with all this, there was a funny sort of feeling in the back of my
mind that I had been sent to boarding school because I wasn't
wanted at home. I do not now think this was true, or fair to
my parents, but these are the things that eat their way into
a child's mind. It became a must to be popular, to impress;
I was hungry to be loved and wanted, yet I just wasn't that
type. And so I lied, and magnified still further my fabulous
stories. It didn't work. In fact, it had precisely the opposite
effect, and I found myself more 'unwanted' than ever.

There were growing needs at other levels too, not least the
demands of a quick mind. I found a great urge in me to lead,
and there just had to be an outlet for this. Even as a child
I could see in a flash a possible line of action—how it could
be accomplished—and its consequences! This led me into
endless mischief, a scheme for 'escaping from the school block
if a fire broke out in the basement cloakroom', for example.
Needless to say, the route—through the gymnasium window,
across the tiles behind the sewing-room, down a drain-
pipe, on to a small flat roof over the music wing—had to be
demonstrated; and the severe reprimand that followed when

we were found halfway was well merited! I wanted to lead in 'good things', too, but seemed to lack the opportunity and outlet for the healthy, buoyant energy of youth.

Then, again, the urge to learn began to burn in my heart. I would have learnt anything they put in front of me! I longed to grasp knowledge, particularly proven facts, mathematical and scientific, with their orderly reasoning and accurate method. I wasn't, at that stage, interested in the 'end', or the out-working; I just longed to assimilate knowledge for its own sake. With this went a 'need' to win, to dominate, not others, but the facts themselves, to get a 100 per cent not in order to defeat other pupils, but simply for the satisfaction of knowing I had mastered the subject. If I didn't succeed, if I didn't gain the form prize, I'd failed—failed myself. And I probably also felt, deep down, that if I didn't do well I would fail to win the love and respect of my parents and brother, always so deeply important to me.

I joined the school dramatic society. As a youngster at home I had always been fascinated by acting and had organised productions of various plays which were performed in an oasthouse loft with footlights, curtains, stage props and everything else all meticulously correct. The actors were my sisters and any local friends I could inveigle to join us. Proceeds were in aid of mission funds. The school dramatic society, however, was a very different kettle of fish. But still I must be good at everything; I must succeed and be in the limelight. Even though I dreaded every moment of every rehearsal and, when it came to the actual performance, dreaded being in front of people, scared that I would make a fool of myself, this inner sense of need drove me on.

Somehow, in the middle of this, I became conscious of God. I've no idea what I thought of God, or who I thought He was; but there was Somebody, God, who was bigger than everything around me, and I needed Him. I needed something big. I needed Someone who was so big He could be bigger than me! And so God came in, and I was confirmed, along with the rest of the Upper Fourths. It may not have meant very much. I'm sure I didn't understand the real meaning or full significance of it. But it was a sincere intimation that I realised my need for God. In a stumbling way, it was the conscious start of my search for Him. I had to take hold of this God. Confirmation appeared to be the way people got God, so I was confirmed. God knew, and accepted, and leant towards me to draw me steadily nearer Himself. I wasn't 'converted', it's true. But I'm not sure that God is as interested as we sometimes seem to be in the precise order of the steps that lead to true conversion. At any rate God drew near to me in it all, because He knew that my decision to be confirmed indicated a search for Him, for Someone bigger than myself, Someone I could draw on and depend upon, Someone to deal with all my complicated 'needs', all the complexes and worries that burdened my heart.

Sure enough, shortly afterwards I began to get guilt-stricken about the everlasting troubles I was in—talking in prep., talking in corridors, talking after lights-out—all necessitating a journey to the headmistress on Monday morning. Mounting that dreaded flight of stairs from hall to platform before the assembled school was a weekly affair for me! Not that I was really so much worse than the others. It was just that, when asked, I had to own up. Our school was run on a principle of trust and honour, with no staff supervision, particularly of prep. periods. The form monitor, a girl appointed each term from her own class, was responsible for maintaining discipline. I didn't even need to think when the inevitable question came; I knew perfectly well I must have talked, because I always talked. My great friend Kath and I used to sit together in class. The Monday came when Kath was ill and mine was the only hand that responded to the Form Mistress's 'Anyone talk in prep. on Saturday?' Oh, she said, so you're talking to yourself now, are you? But at break she sent for me, and over a cup of hot milk and a slice of marvellous currant cake in her little study, she had a heart-to-heart talk with me about the stupidity of breaking rules, the value of hard work, and above all, the preciousness of strict honesty. She taught maths, and from then on I was her star pupil!

There was a growing hunger for honesty from this time on. I had to have Someone big enough, above it all, outside, so to speak, who could cope. And I gradually became conscious that I could reach Him only if I were absolutely honest.

At this time, too, came a hunger for beauty. It was wartime, and everything was rather drab—plain white china, blacked-out streets, school uniform clothes, and the tragedy of war. My school was in North Wales, but my home was in Kent. I used to travel through London, and many times saw the blitz and its awful horrors that, along with the poverty and filth, shocked me bitterly. I remember travelling back to school one day, crossing from south to north London in a bus, when an air raid occurred and panic broke out. Before we could even halt, women leapt from the moving bus, running for shelter in the nearest building. Suddenly a bomb fell on that very house, which crashed in a blazing mass. I watched with horror as Civil Defence men tried to reach the screaming women.

Young though I was, I was deeply upset by the meaning-lessness of it all, feeling that something was fundamentally wrong. Surely Somebody was big enough to get all this into focus. I didn't then know who this Someone was. It was just a search going on inside me for Someone who could cope with all the world's needs, as well as with mine. There was a growing consciousness that everything seemed so useless, so pointless. One went on talking in prep. and reporting to the Head. And on the larger scale, bombs fell and men and women were being killed. Others were hungry and nobody was really bothering to provide them with food. People in other lands had so little, and no-one seemed to care. We read the newspapers, we discussed in school current-events lessons, and through it all was this growing impression that life was meaningless. Where was it all leading? As I tried to probe deeper, I became scared. There was no-one to turn to, no-one to guide one through the rocks.

All this led to an intense reaching out after the Unseen, a developing perfectionist attitude that shrank alike from the sight or sound of destructive suffering, unalleviated poverty, and superficial insincerity. In the summer of 1941, I cycled from school to attend a Society for the Propagation of the Gospel summer school.

Shyness kept me from joining in many of the activities, but I'll never forget the short, daily, devotional sessions led by the chaplain, Father Charles Preston, a 'brown' monk of the Anglican Franciscan order. His face shone with an inner light. His words were always quiet and kindly, never tinged with sarcasm or frivolity, obviously utterly sincere and quietly satisfied. He drew me. He was never hurried or impatient. We sat in the still hush of the chapel and he talked of God, and my heart was filled with longing. Our surroundings melted and he carried me away into the great mysterious Presence of God, and showed me the nail-pierced hands and the out-poured love and the wooing heart of the Saviour.

One evening, with an inexplicable hunger after God, in absolute simplicity and forthright honesty, I made my first 'confession'. An overwhelming sense of release poured into my heart that now God knew all. He knew the very worst about me, and it was now up to Him. The burden of sin and failure and shame rolled away. I went back into the nave of the chapel walking on air. In the dim light, I knelt and read that lovely hymn:

> 'Take my life, and let it be
>   Consecrated, Lord, to Thee …
> Take myself, and I will be
>   Ever, only, all for Thee.'

I meant every word. I walked out quietly into the moonlight, across the grounds, and a great joy flooded my whole being. I felt I could have jumped over the rooftops!

Home I went again, to put much right, with apologies and a real effort to be useful and part of the family. Then back to school, to pull with authority instead of against, to apologise for past wrongs, and, above all, to make an all-out attack against the spirit of lying, driving myself to confess every time to the one concerned, till very shame began to close my lips against the fantasies. I became a school prefect, and the head of my house. I longed to lead, and to lead well and rightly. I longed to be respected, not now for myself, exactly, but that I might lead others to put God first.

I tried earnestly to help others, to be kindly, to be sincere. I was an ardent Anglo-Catholic, regular at the confessional and the mass, every part of me stretching out after the Unseen Power who could meet all needs. And yet I was acutely conscious that He was not doing so. The needs were getting bigger; the hopelessness was more hopeless; the futility of life itself at times became almost unbearable. Whilst in church, I could lose myself to all the problems, bathed in the strange mysticism and pious ritualism but, on leaving the service, I had nothing—no power, no companion, no help to answer the daily needs and meet the daily problems.

It was this sense of emptiness and futility which led me to become a cinema fan in my holidays, to try to escape from the pointlessness of life. Every week-night and twice on Saturdays, if there were seven different films, I would try to lose myself in a make-believe world—anything to drown reality. Sometimes I would even go twice to the same film rather than suffer the boredom of an empty evening. There was a great emptiness, a great void in my life.

I helped at times at the Franciscans' headquarters in Peckham. Because of the blitz, there were no Sisters living in that area, but I loved to stay in the guest-room of the Order's Home. There was a lovely church opposite, very still and quiet, in the midst of the rush of traffic, the whine of the air-raid warnings, the sufferings and poverty of the people around. Flickering lights burned in the red crucibles in front of each altar. All else was dim, with a vague sense of the unreal. I would creep in, and upstairs to the gallery, along to the Lady Chapel, many times in a day, seeking an explanation, a companion, a comfort to my heart's loneliness. Every three hours, the Franciscan monks had prayers there, and I knelt in the shadows, and drank in their piety. Then back I would go to the poor tenement building opposite, with its rickety stairs, uncarpeted floors, peeling paint, and its many and varied visitors—mothers in distress for sons missing in the war; mothers in dire need of coal or food or clothing; mothers in depravity, in immorality and loose living—all came, and were helped, and went away comforted. In the evenings, there was the 'Club' for young people, teenagers who had been turned away from the Civic Centre Club for one reason or another, young men and women often from most unsavoury backgrounds. The dancing, endless records, and open rottenness; the weakness and weariness and emptiness of life—I saw it all, but took no part. I had no interest, no awakened desires, just an apathy.

And all the while, God was driving me to see that in myself there was nothing, absolutely nothing of any worth. It became at moments almost a desperate fight—the knowledge that God held the key, the answer; that He could make sense of it all; that without Him, it was a weary, stupid, empty, pointless, useless life. The burden of the world's need was crushing, overwhelming. Only God could meet it, could answer it; and yet, where was He? How could I find Him? How could I become part of His pattern, and lose myself in Him?

2

CLIMBING TO THE TOP

I left school a few weeks before the end of the summer term 1944, in order to have a short holiday and prepare to go to Cambridge for the 'long vac' term. This was a war emergency measure, enabling doctors to complete their nine-term university course in two years by making compulsory the fourth term from July to September each year, during the long vacation. My father met me in London and took me to a show—one of the Gilbert and Sullivan operas.

It was the time of the V1 'doodle-bugs' and everyone was tense and fearful. There was little chattering in the streets and shops. When the siren alerted us of an approaching raid, everyone hurried quickly on their own business. Then someone caught the high whine of a V1 and stood still, looking up. The action was infectious. We almost felt the very traffic stand still and draw in its breath, and all London waited. The whine grew; faces were strained. Each one knew we should make for shelters, but we had done it too often, and even shelters were not proof against these new weapons. A fascination was on us. Suddenly, there was a sharp silence—a great pause hung in the air, then an explosion, a rumble, and a gentle sigh caught up and multiplied, as each walker hurried on his way, secretly ashamed of the first thought, 'I'm safe this time'. The urgency of self-preservation amidst all the fear and uncertainty, almost pushed into second place the thought, 'Poor beggars, I wonder who got that one?'

And so I reached Newnham College, Cambridge, at the end of July, found my way to Clough Hall, and discovered from a list on the noticeboard that I had been allocated room 8a, a small room, usually the bedroom attached to the larger sitting-room. The latter was to be a bedsitter for this extra term, to enable the new 'freshers' to be accommodated. The place seemed vast and empty and silent. A cold fear of loneliness clutched at my throat. Why had I come? I felt that I would never fit into college life. I knew no-one. My trunk was pushed against the communicating door and, to try and calm my yearning to run away and leave it all, I started urgently to unstrap and unpack. Having piled everything on the small bed, and pushed books on the two small shelves over its head, I turned to place things in the drawers of the chest. I glanced at my pale sallow face in the mirror, and the untidy plaits hanging down over my shoulders—and noticed a card stuck in the frame. Leaning forward, with my arms full of clothes, I read, 'If you don't know anyone, and have nowhere to go after supper, come and have coffee in my room, no. 12, at 8 p.m.' It was signed 'Dorothy'. My eyes blurred, and a lump filled my throat. I quickly finished unpacking, my mind excited, homesick, and fearful by turns.

A bell sounded, and I slipped into the corridor and watched and waited. Others walked by, chatting and nonchalant, and I joined the stream towards the 'hall'. It was still war days, and food rationing was strict, yet a good meal was served us at the serving-tables, each one collecting what they wished individually. The other students were friendly and would have drawn me into their conversation, but an overwhelming shyness (from a sense of inferiority, or a fear of not being able to hold my own) kept me a grim prisoner.

Soon their conversation drifted into their own channels, and my monosyllabic replies became unnecessary. Tears pricked my eyes—my very first day, and I had raised up a barrier that I had vowed should never stand again! I wasn't hungry, yet didn't dare to leave, not knowing the rules. So I made a mockery of eating, following the lead of others.

Back in my room after supper, my loneliness and fear of this vast place with its swarms of intellectual students became so intense, the feeling of being submerged and lost in it all so real, that I lay numbly on my bed and planned how to write home and ask them to let me leave.

I must have dozed from sheer weariness of mental strain. Wasn't that a clock striking ? Glancing quickly at my watch, I remembered the invitation—8 p.m. at no. 12. I ran to the bathroom, washed my face, and made my way along the corridor. Knocking at the door of no. 12, I entered, and Dorothy glanced up, her face red, smoke swirling around her, as she knelt by the hearth, trying to coax a fire into existence! 'Can you make a fire?' The straight forward, urgent appeal, the complete acceptance of a total stranger in her room, the absurdity of the smoking pile in the grate on a hot, sticky, July evening, and the barriers were gone! We soon had a kettle on a cheerful blaze, and a group of about eight of us, I think, sat around on chairs, sofa, bed, and floor, chatting about everything and nothing. I never quite knew who were newcomers like myself, and who were 'old stagers'. I don't remember much of all the chatter. I believe the coffee tasted a good deal of smoke and paraffin, but I know I slept well that night, with a quiet feeling of security that I had a friend.

Next day Dot called for me for breakfast, and later took me down town, showing me the quickest way to the Anatomy block, then on to the shopping centre to see which shops were the cheapest, and which the most reliable for books, equipment, stationery, and so on. Home we went to lunch, then back again to sign on for afternoon lectures and to arrange about tutorials. She was with me all through that day. That was Dorothy. I am glad to say she eventually got her own degree, as well as helping crowds of us to settle in and to get ours.

The Anatomy Dissection Room! Never will I forget the first day, and my sense of unutterable horror. The very smell of formalin today brings back a wave of memories. The crowds, the noise of chatter and instruments, the growing silence through the morning as concentration mounted, the greasy books propped open on the benches to show their brightly coloured, tidy diagrams of the pale mess we were handling—and to me, always a sense of unreality, of horror, almost of foreboding. I developed a deep sense of revulsion that almost paralyzed my thinking capacity. A demonstrator coming round, neatly sorting out one strand from the higgledy-piggledy mass in front of me, and demanding name, description, origin, was one of the daily nightmares of the next three years that began to crush my hopes.

A paralysis seemed to settle over my mind each day at 9 a.m. as I entered the lecture theatre. All I had studied the night before seemed wiped out, like a clean slate. The lecturer's words never penetrated, owing to the gnawing fear that he might ask me a question and reveal my ignorance to all. And by 5 p.m., as I stumbled out of the block and found my bicycle, joining the stream of humanity, I felt bowed and unable to face any more study. Fortunately, that first term, there were no tutorials, or I really might have given up and gone home!

Then came the first Saturday. What a wonderful sense of freedom! I lay in bed late in the morning, and wandered to the notice-boards after breakfast. Pinned up was a list for any to sign who would like to play cricket in the afternoon. Dare I? I loved it, but I hadn't been any good at school—and here they were probably all excellent. 'Hallo', said a voice behind me. 'Do you play?' and there was a tall broad girl, with a beaming smile and thick wavy hair. 'I'd like to try', I replied diffidently. And that was the beginning of another friendship—with the cricket captain for the coming year. I was assured somewhat jokingly that if I knew which end of the bat to hold I'd be in the team! We had a wonderful afternoon, about fourteen of us. I wasn't good, by any stretch of imagination, but I was far from being the worst!

After tea, we went on the river in a punt. I was thrilled, not only by the actual novelty of the experience and the loveliness of the countryside from Cambridge to Grantchester, but above all by the natural friendliness of the other girls, the very fact that they appeared to want me to join them. We went bathing together in the Grantchester pool. It was all wonderful and new, and I determinedly set about forgetting the past misgivings and fears, my insecurity and need.

On Sunday, I got up early and went down town to Little St Mary to early mass. The quiet reverence, the sense of mystery, the peace was all as I knew it, and yet no-one spoke to me as I entered or as I left. I went again at eleven and saw several students there, but again there was no gesture of friendliness or welcome—and none of my little group of new friends was there. The day dragged on, but without the usual happiness of a Sunday. In the evening, I went to St Benedict's Church, where the Franciscans worshipped. I spoke to one at the close of the service, mentioning my friendship with Father Charles. He was courteous, but distant—certainly not welcoming, nor proffering any invitation of friendship. I felt hurt and puzzled as I cycled home and went to bed supperless, since I had missed 'hall'. I didn't see any of my new friends about and realised anew the old pangs of loneliness.

And so a pattern began to set in, and with it a sense of belonging, and thus security: a pattern of work, and study, mingled with friendships and Saturday outings. On certain days, however, Dorothy and the others didn't join us after hall. When I asked about this one week, she told me they had a prayer-meeting daily between early and late hall, and a Bible study together, once a week after halls. Would I care to go? Certainly! And so I went to my first Bible study and sat amazed as someone unfolded the mysteries of Ephesians 3, and even more amazed as they discussed it afterwards and freely quoted other parts of Scripture to support their arguments. Going back to our rooms later on, after a cup of cocoa and biscuits, I shared with Dot my amazement at their knowledge of the Bible and understanding of its contents. With a kindly smile, she suggested that I should go regularly.

The following Sunday we met at late hall, and she asked what I was doing afterwards. Would I care to go with her to a Christian address? I had cut evening service and was feeling a little guilty at having been caught out, but she made no comment (doubtless having been praying that she might meet me there). And so together we went to the sermon arranged by the Cambridge Inter-Collegiate Christian Union (CICCU), a regular Sunday evening activity during University terms. We left our bicycles in the small courtyard outside and they were stolen during the service, which rather effaced any memory I might have had of the sermon's subject-matter!

And so my first term passed. I was still closely bound to the Anglo-Catholics, sensing a need of the protection of organised religion and imposed discipline to control the hungry urges of spirit and soul, and possibly also to carry the ultimate responsibility for solutions for the world's great needs without involving me. I went regularly to confessional and mass, found peace of mind in formal obedience, but lacked any friendship or encouragement there. Alongside this, were the happy, free friendships with Dorothy, Sylvia, and other members of the Christian Union—games and outings together, sitting together for meals and, later, for the Bible studies and Sunday evening services—friendships that were open and clean and healthy. Their lives and faces radiated a happiness and peace that was very nearly infectious, and quite obviously satisfying. It was thrilling, just tasting the wonder of this level of friendship and of communion. Yet some inner fear, or reserve, kept me back from definitely identifying myself with them, so that I always remained just a little apart.

Four weeks' holiday followed, back with the family in our new home in south-east London—a lovely big house and a marvellous garden. And yet I missed my new friends and longed for the next term to start. My school-girl sisters all seemed very young and immature. And I don't doubt that to them I seemed stand-offish and a prig! The first 'V2s' fell at this stage, and there were sufferings and shortages on all sides. The parish church had been badly bombed and we now met in a hall behind the Methodist church. But I did not appreciate the way the Vicar took the service, and missed so much the elaborate ritualism to which I was accustomed that I was not over-bothered about going regularly.

My second term began with mixed feelings, joy in renewed friendship and dread of the growing pressure of work, augmented by the fear of tutorials. Slowly, I began to slip into the habit of joining the CU for the prayer meetings as well as for Bible studies. Then on Sundays, I began going to church with them, sometimes Congregational, sometimes Brethren, sometimes Evangelical Church of England. Mr Kenneth Hooker, I remember, preached the Freshers' Sermon on 1 Timothy 2:5-6. I was stirred and challenged. I learned new hymns and choruses, and enjoyed the bright, alert singing. Even now I can remember the first time I sang, 'More about Jesus would I know....' My whole being was deeply stirred. We were sitting round the fire in Sylvia's room for a Bible study one evening, late in October. I don't remember the study—the words of the hymn kept repeating in my mind. When the others dispersed, I stayed sitting on the rug, gazing into the fire, with a great longing stirring in my innermost soul. 'More about Jesus would I know....' As we sat, the two of us, in complete, unbroken stillness, it was as though a window opened and slowly, amazedly, in stunned awe, I glimpsed through—a twig sputtered on the fire, and it was lost. Again, urgently, holding on to the moment, willing the very presence of Jesus to become real to my soul, the glory seemed to shine, a light of great brightness. I hardly dared to breathe; it felt as though life was suspended, caught up, breathless. My heart filled with joy and wonder—and it passed. With a sigh, I turned to Sylvia. She was praying. It was already the early hours of a new day. We did not talk; I slipped away to my room.

During that Christmas term, I think I reached a mental assent that the presentation of the gospel offered by the CU members was true, though I remained unconvinced that this need clash with ritualistic practice in church worship. I was tremendously intrigued by their love of Scripture, and I began to read avidly. I started at Matthew and slogged through to the end of the New Testament that term. Slowly, I became gripped by it. First I read with them, then I read on my own, with a growing hunger to know what it was all about and to know the One who had written it. Everything began to fit into a pattern. I could see that they had something that I did not, and a great desire to have it myself was born. I stopped going to other meetings and other churches. I went to all the CU activities I could—Bible studies, prayer meetings, missionary study groups, open-airs, church meetings. I agreed to it all in my mind. And the joy of new friends, the great happiness of being an accepted one of this new crowd, made life seem very good. As far as they were concerned, they believed

I was truly 'converted', and told me so. But as yet I had no peace, no heart satisfaction. The sense of need was still there, with the niggling question, 'Are you sure this is real?' I was sure it was real and the truth; but I was also conscious that I lacked something.

Then two other demands entered into fierce competition. One of the SPG home workers came on a visit to Cambridge for a long weekend in late November and especially asked to see me. I did not want to meet her; I did not want to face again the conflicting loyalties. But I could not politely refuse. The evening's talk left me unsettled, unhappy, yet completely unconvinced. Her argument about the sacraments, the mass and the confessional in particular, no longer rang with authority as in the past. Her plea seemed to rest only on the historical symbolism of the church and not on scriptural reality. She stressed that in the church, symbolised by the priest, was stored all truth and the only means of salvation. The accent was on works, regular attendance at church, full confession, implicit obedience to all church discipline, and the receiving of grace only by the divinely appointed means of the sacraments in the hands of the priest. There was so much I did not understand. I felt so weak and helpless, like a baby, unable to answer her, or to give a reasoned explanation of my newly-awakening faith. Why did I no longer need the doctrine of consubstantiation, the real presence of Christ in the elements at the mass? How dare I ignore the church's recognised means of grace? I did not know the answer then. All I had was an indefinable realization that something was missing, something wrong. 1 Timothy 2:5-6, the text of the Freshers' Sermon, came back vividly: 'There is…one mediator between God and men, the man Christ Jesus.' Nowhere in the New Testament had I read of the priesthood being invested in a human priest who could act as a go-between between myself and God.

The following weekend Father Charles came, and I loved him, simply and sincerely. I went to confessional on the Saturday evening, and to services all day Sunday where he was ministering and preaching. Again the old mystical attraction drew me and enfolded me, and my newly-awakening soul cried out for fear of being submerged once more.

The other interest which competed for my support at this time was Communism. One Saturday, that same term, I was asked to 'help out' by playing goal-keeper for the Newnham hockey team—and my luck was in! Having practically no previous interest in hockey, I became goal-keeper overnight for the Cambridge University Women's team! Here I met the captain for the year, the quiet, efficient, outspoken leader of the Cambridge University Women's Communist Party! Our rapidly flourishing friendship involved many party meetings, and the learning of the fundamentals of dialectical materialism, and of the ideology that they said could answer all the crying needs of our poverty-stricken and suffering world.

Sundays became a three-cornered battle: Anglo-Catholicism in the mornings; Communism in the afternoons; Evangelicalism in the evenings. The CU made no criticism, neither did they retract the offered friendship. They did not argue, nor seek to persuade; they just went further out of their way to draw me out and help me.

As Christmas approached, news came from home that one of my younger sisters had mumps. We had all had chickenpox together several years before and I had been very ill with it. Later, we all had measles and my eyesight was permanently damaged. So it was felt best that I should avoid the mumps if possible, and therefore not go home till January. Where then for Christmas? Two kindly Methodist friends, Jean and Mary, each invited me for a week to their homes, and I had a lovely holiday with each, in keen Methodist families. But there were ten more days before the quarantine would be ended.

Dorothy and Sylvia arranged for me to go to a houseparty. They even filled in the forms, looked up the trains, and handed me the timetable of events! So, on December 27th, I arrived at Mount Hermon Bible College, Ealing, with a suitcase and my fears, to join what turned out to be a gathering of keen Christian women training as officers for young people's camps and houseparties for the coming Easter and summer. I was like a duck out of water! I shared a dormitory with other girls of my own age—including a bright, red-headed girl of nineteen next to me, whose brother was a medical student in my year at Cambridge. I remember they all seemed to have plenty of money, and I had practically none! Afternoons were free, and they all went sightseeing, or to the ice-rink-and I stayed at home, ostensibly to study, unwilling to let them know that I could not afford it! It was cold—the last winter of the war, and coal rationing was severe. We huddled eiderdowns over our knees as we sat in the study room for morning Bible study and discussion groups. I bought a lovely new Bible complete with a commentary.

On the second day, we were led in a study through the book of Genesis, shown how to summarise it, get hold of it, divide it up, and then share it with others. I was fascinated and took detailed notes. My ignorance of Scripture was appalling. Our leader told us that the day after tomorrow we would do the same with the book of Romans and suggested that we each try to read through it beforehand. I bought the IVF Search the Scriptures (a Bible study course prepared to help students). The next evening, after supper, I curled up by the fire in the sitting-room, and started out into Romans. I read. I studied each suggested question. I wrote the answer in the margin of my lovely new Bible. Time ticked on. I reached the end. With a satisfied sigh, I closed my Bible, uncurled my stiff and cold legs, and slipped quietly upstairs to bed. On the landing I met two girls coming from the bathroom. 'You're late', I said. 'You're early', they rejoined with a grin. I slipped into my bedroom, to find that it was 6.30 a.m. and these girls were getting up for kitchen duty! Later that morning, in Bible study, I fell asleep and missed the very session for which I had spent all night preparing! But Romans has remained one of my 'favourite' books of Scripture ever since. Through its orderly array of facts, its clear systematic presentation of doctrine, I gripped the essential basic truth of man's need in his lost state of sin and depravity, and of God's provision to meet that need through the substitutionary death of Christ, of His wonderful power to make this provision real and vital to each individual by the work of the Holy Spirit, and, even more, of His amazing desire for fellowship and communion with us, His adopted children, by the daily indwelling and outworking of His same Spirit.

I sat through meeting after meeting and filled an exercise book with notes. I talked things over with many of the staff. I heard the different doctrines being carefully and accurately expounded, supported by Scripture. My mind could grasp it, and begin to take in the tremendousness of its import. I was beginning to get the 'jargon', yet I knew in my heart that I hadn't got Him.

The last evening of the houseparty there had been a bit of a row at the supper table and some sharp disagreements, largely revolving around denominational practices, particularly differing ways of celebrating the Holy Communion service. I had spoken up, albeit diffidently, in defence of the doctrine of consubstantiation, the 'real' presence of Christ in the elements of bread and wine. Had not Jesus said, 'This is my body.. .this is my blood'? But I became heated when laughed at. They asked if I could be truly converted if I was such a Romanist at heart?

I left the room and rushed upstairs, bitterly ashamed of having been drawn into the argument and losing control of myself. I gazed out of the window, and heard the happy chattering of the others down below. My mind went back through that week and all its teachings, through the past term and the multitudes of new influences and new friendships, back to my home and family and childhood. Suddenly, I flung myself on my bed, in a flood of tears and loneliness. With an overwhelming sense of failure and helplessness, I cried out to God (if there was a God) to meet with me and to make utterly real and vital to me Himself. I raised my eyes, and through my tears read a text on the wall: 'Be still, and know that I am God' (Ps. 46:10). That was all. Immediately the whole burden fell away in a moment. Be still and know God, whose name is 'I am'. Be still and know Him. Stop going to this one and that; stop striving to understand with the intellect. Just be still, and know Him. In that moment, a great flood of peace and joy and unutterable happiness flooded in, and I knew that He and I had entered into a new relationship. I knew God, and I knew in that moment that all the theories were true, and somehow He would work them out for me. The steady reading of Scripture in the previous months, the careful listening to doctrinal teaching both at the houseparty and in Christian Union meetings, had prepared the way. For years the Holy Spirit had been opening my eyes to a sense of sin, convicting me of my unworthiness before a Holy God. But now came the wonderful gift of repentance. God poured out His grace in forgiveness, in cleansing from all the uncleanness of sin, and in revealing, at this time, the amazing wonder of the friendship of Christ.

I went downstairs walking on air. Some of the other campers said afterwards, 'Your face was absolutely shining and we knew something had happened.' I went into the sitting-room and joined the rest for the final meeting. We sang a few choruses (I remember that I didn't know any of them!) and then our leader opened the meeting for testimonies. I didn't know what she meant by a 'testimony', so I waited. Silence reigned! She made another attempt to get us talking by pointing out what a blessing it could be to testify to others. Still dead silence! 'Well, hasn't anyone anything to tell of what God has done for her during the week?' I understood that and opened my mouth—and suddenly found I'd nothing to say! I who had been accustomed to speaking at any time, on any subject, found I was tongue-tied with an intense helplessness. I just didn't know what to say. I knew something had happened, and as I sat there with my mouth open, I eventually somehow blurted out that I had met with God, and He had forgiven me and...that was all! Dr Graham Scroggie, a veteran Christian and much-loved Bible teacher, was there. He wrote in my new Bible Philippians 3:10, 'That I may know him, and the power of his resurrection, and the fellowship of his sufferings, being made conformable unto his death.' He said to me, 'Tonight you've entered into the first part of the verse, "That I may know him". This is only the beginning, and there's a long journey ahead. My prayer for you is that you will go on through the verse to know "the power of his resurrection" and also, God willing, one day perhaps, "the fellowship of his sufferings, being made conformable unto his death."' And so started for me the thrilling journey of the Christian pilgrimage through this earthly life towards the heavenly eternity.

3

Enjoying the View

I went home the next day wearing a bright new Scripture Union badge and carrying a shiny new Bible. In the crowded compartment of the slow Victoria–Bromley train a man diagonally across the carriage from me asked what my badge stood for. A little embarrassed, I explained that members of the Scripture Union undertook to read a set passage from the Bible each day, believing that it was God's book and that it would help them to live good lives. He asked for further explanations. Raising my voice against the noise of the engine and the wheels, I sought to reply, very conscious of the curious, rather antagonistic, looks of the other ten passengers, disturbed in their happy solitude. Red in the face, but determined not to run from the challenge, I told him of my conversion the day before, and of the battle that led up to it, including my real longing to know God and to obey Him. Our conversation continued until Shortlands where, with a sigh of relief, I stumbled out, only to find myself followed by my questioner! Quietly, he placed a hand on my shoulder and wished me God's richest blessing in my new life. The surprised look on my face made him smile. Then he explained that my brand-new badge and Bible had told their own story and he had deliberately drawn me out to testify in public to help me start out in the way I should go on! I later found that he was a keen member of Christ Church, Bromley, whose fellowship I myself soon joined.

Now began a period of great joy. Everything was wonderful. I loved every moment, every meeting, every opportunity for testimony. I had the inestimable joy of knowing that Christ was my Saviour. I joined the Cambridge Women's Inter-Collegiate Christian Union, and enjoyed fellowship with many new friends. I revelled in the security of being publicly committed. I had, as it were, burned my boats. I gave up going to the cinema and lost my desire to join in many of the activities which were merely the done thing—drink, smoking, make-up, and dancing—none of which had ever held any very real attraction for me personally. I wrote to my father and to the board of directors of my school who were paying my college fees, to tell them that I was now studying medicine to be a missionary. In all honesty, I felt I must let them know just in case it affected their desire to continue paying for my education. Both wrote back and assured me that they were delighted and would continue to support me.

To be a missionary? I had known for years that I was going to be a missionary. Would my conversion change this? Did I need some further specific call? I had already, however, signified my intention of serving God abroad by joining the Inter-Varsity Missionary Fellowship, and the urge in my heart towards overseas missionary service was growing greater, not diminishing. It began to seem to me the obvious Christian duty of one and all. I was puzzled by others' lack of interest in missionary service, their lack of concern for the millions who were in darkness, who had never heard of the love of God.

Bible study was an excitement in those early days. I remember being fascinated by a series of ten Bible readings on the Song of Solomon. Next term we were going to study Hebrews 11 for ourselves, and Sylvia, our Christian Union leader, said that I was to lead the third study on verse 3: 'Through faith we understand that the worlds were framed by the word of God….' I spent hours with her preparing that study, and I learnt more perhaps in its preparation than in all I heard others teach in the following weeks. It set for me the pattern for the future, of thorough, accurate Bible searching and digging. It impressed me with my appalling ignorance of Scripture. All I had was a vague rudimentary knowledge of some well-known children's stories, but with no real idea of where they came from, nor of their context. Sylvia was studying Psalm 119 in the early mornings of each day and had made a beautiful and exquisitely neat chart of it, on one huge sheet, in all its sections. On this chart she was underlining in different colours each line of thought throughout the Psalm, and one could see a pattern emerging. To watch her studying the Bible in this way, to see her obvious love of it, stirred up in me a great desire to know more. Since my conversion, I had also started Dr Graham Scroggie's four-year Bible Correspondence Course, which meant, roughly speaking, studying a book a month. From seven to eight each morning was one of the happiest hours of the day, reading, studying, underlining, comparing, learning Scripture. And slowly it was taking possession, the new affection replacing the old.

Then there was a growing realization of the possibilities of prayer. In April 1945, I went to the IVF Student Conference in Oxford. Again, the old shyness of meeting new faces and the fear of being asked things I did not know, tended to shut me up within myself. Everything was a bit high-powered. Open discussion groups tended to depress me as everybody else seemed to know much more than I did! But the prayer sessions were the great moments of each day. God drew near in those seasons of prayer, and I began to learn the liberty of the outpoured heart. Mildred Mitchell, daughter of the Home Director of the China Inland Mission, was there, and was a great help to me. She and I, and another friend with whom I was sharing a room, had a discussion late into the night about guidance. How, we asked, can one be sure of knowing God's will? I remember her summarizing on her fingers in the following order:

1. Daily Bible reading, when He can speak to us through a passage, an example or a warning;
2. Daily private prayer, when we talk the problem over with the Lord; as we wait on Him in quietness, He can speak directly to our hearts;
3. The advice of Christian friends and those of greater experience, who may have had to make a similar decision in the past;
4. One's circumstances, including family or business commitments, health, or even finance.

Then she moved her thumb to and fro in front of her fingers and said, 'Peace—in each one, in turn, individually and together. Let the peace of God umpire in your heart; if He is speaking He will give peace and silence other voices.' I still use the same basic principles in guidance today.

Then came the problem of sport. I had played in goal for the hockey team that season, and now the cricket season was starting. I loved the exercise, and perhaps again I was influenced by the feeling that I could achieve something, gain my blue, prove to myself that I wasn't useless! But it all took time—daily practices down at the nets, and games or matches every Saturday. So I, and other Christians involved, began to pray about it and God challenged us to use our sport as a medium of evangelism, and to seek the captain of the team for Himself. That summer our cricket captain was a Christian Scientist. She and I were great friends and enjoyed being together. As a result, I began going to many meetings with her to learn what she believed and, in exchange, she came to a few of ours. Slowly, the warmth of friendship offered in the Christian Union, and the obvious sincerity and warmth of conviction, backed up so solidly with scriptural accuracy, began to win her towards our faith. But in particular, she was influenced by our growing friendship and intimacy. For me, it was a wonderful day in the summer of 1945 when she openly declared herself for Christ and broke away from the Christian Scientists. I believed she was my first 'convert', and it was with a deep sense of grief that I came to realise a few years later that she was won by my persuasiveness and personality, rather than by the beauty and power of Christ. The former could not hold her, nor establish her, nor satisfy her, except along a fleshly level of human friendship. Only the latter could have given her new life, and strength and joy and courage. Many times since I have had to be careful not to over-persuade folk, nor to draw them only by the strength of my own rather dominant personality.

In the summer of 1945 I went to my first camp as a junior medical officer. What an exciting, wonderful fortnight! There were some six Christian women as Camp Officers, and fifty or so junior teenage girls. We had hired a lovely boarding school at Chumleigh, Devon, to give the girls a first-rate country holiday for a fortnight. I remember so clearly VJ Day which celebrated the defeat of Japan and the end of those six long years of war. One of my jobs at camp was seeing to the cleanliness of the toilets—and we had a mild epidemic of summer diarrhoea! At the 8 a.m. staff meeting, I mentioned our urgent need of toilet paper to our Commandant so that she could add it to her shopping list. Just then the telephone rang. It was the local Vicar giving us the news of Japan's surrender and warmly inviting us all to a united service of thanksgiving in the village. 'Oh', I exclaimed in horror, 'the shops will all be shut. Whatever shall we do for toilet paper?' The group got down to praise and prayer for all the events of the day and the spiritual wellbeing of each young camper. Then the Commandant, in her closing prayer, reminded the Lord of our need of toilet paper. I think I was shocked! Certainly I was amazed that one could dare bring such a topic to the Almighty!

Later in the morning, we all walked down to the church and attended the united thanksgiving. As we left afterwards, one pleasant-faced man came up to me, and said how very pleased they all were to welcome us to their village and to their fellowship, adding with a smile that he was the local grocer and would be delighted to do anything he could to help us. I blurted out my tale of woe, our need of toilet paper! And in half an hour, twelve rolls were delivered to the school where we were staying. Truly God had answered prayer.

Near the end of camp, we had an 'object-service'. The youngsters all went out, two by two, to collect or make some object mentioned in the Bible. These objects were all gathered on the table in the meeting-room, each with a small label giving the Scripture reference of where this object could be found. There was a piece of bread: 'I am the bread of life'; a wild flower: 'even Solomon in all his glory was not arrayed like one of these'; a bunch of grapes referring to those brought back by the twelve spies of Moses' time; a jaw-bone calling to mind one of Samson's exploits. There were many others, among them a lovely plaited ring of thorns. The text attached to this was Mark 15:17, 'And they…platted a crown of thorns, and put it about his head.' At prayers that evening each leader in turn spoke a few words on one of the objects. I was terribly nervous. I had never tried to speak before without hours of careful preparation! I gazed at the table in a sort of numb horror, and the crown of thorns stood out so clearly, I could not see anything else. I was number four to speak— and I willed the others not to choose the crown of thorns! Eventually I stood up to take my turn, lifted up the carefully plaited ring, and then closed my eyes in a sudden wave of nausea from sheer panic. My heart was pounding; my mouth felt dry. Somehow I pulled myself together, and spoke of His suffering in my place, His receiving my condemnation. At last it was all over. One of the staff mentioned afterwards how touched she had been to see my earnest prayer before I spoke—and my heart lurched! Yet in the years ahead, I was to learn that she had been more accurate than I then dared to believe, as I discovered new avenues of prayer, when, as Paul puts it in Romans 8, the Spirit groans within us and our hearts go out to God in wordless prayer as we do battle with the unseen powers of darkness, knowing nothing but a horror and fear of failure.

During the next Christmas term life continued to be very full and wonderful and worthwhile. I was asked to become an executive member of the Christian Union for the coming year. When reading the doctrinal basis which I would need to sign, I was struck by the statement that I believed the whole Bible to be the inspired word of God. I had not yet read it all, and felt I could not honestly sign this until I had read it right through. This stiffened me to a concentrated effort to complete my first reading of the Old Testament by Christmas, before the end of my first exciting year as a newly born-again Christian. I was deeply stirred at the thought of being trusted with leadership. I had always longed to lead, and now strangely I feared it. I felt so unable, yet knew that I could rely on His enabling.

During the term I was asked to go to the home of Dr Joyce Goodchild at Nottingham to give my testimony at an informal Saturday evening meeting. This was another milestone; my first public speaking engagement! I remember preparing with such infinite care and practising in the bath, speaking to the taps, timing myself exactly to the limits I had been given. What a thrilling and wonderful weekend that was! Every new experience seemed to be just one more part of this new mountain-top of joy, one more view over the glorious surrounding peaks. It was to be the start of a precious friendship, and forerunner of several such meetings in the coming year.

I was chosen to play goalkeeper not only for the University Women's team, but also for Cambridge County Ladies hockey team, along with Olga, the University captain, and Jessie, another Newnham undergraduate. Together we set out for Colchester in the week after Christmas for the week's tournament of Eastern Counties at Clacton. We lived at the Girls' Friendly Society Hostel at Colchester, sharing together an attic dormitory, since Clacton was out of reach of our student allowances! The first night there, I fought, as many others have done, the brief battle with pride and self-consciousness, and then got down on my knees by my bedside for prayer. They were both quiet till I climbed into bed. Then in the dark, Olga (the leader of the University Women's Communist Party!) bluntly demanded the point of what I had done. What benefit did I think prayer was? I knew so little how to explain, but I tried to share my assurance of the truths I had learned during the past year. Throughout the week, at meals, on buses, in the evening round the sitting-room fire, we argued Communism versus Christianity. I felt very helpless and seemed to make no impact on Olga at all. Jessie just listened and watched, but during next term she quietly joined the Christian Union. She was never very dramatic, just quietly sure of Christ's love for her and her love for Him. What a joy and encouragement this was to me, even as I saw Olga slipping away from us and apparently hardening against us.

In July I went to Keswick with Dr Goodchild. We were to be a mixed bunch, about eighteen of us, in three big bell-tents. Three were girls from Nottingham University, Mary and myself from Newnham, and the rest were factory and shop girls, many of whom had been converted during the previous year at Dr Goodchild's Saturday night At Homes. It was a memorable Keswick for me. Dr Goodchild, Mary, and I went a day earlier than the rest to set up camp. First we had to scythe the long grass! It was blisteringly hot, the end of a heatwave, and it was exciting pitching the tents and preparing. Food rationing was still severe. That week, bread, cake, and flour rationing commenced. We managed to procure all necessary permits and bought the week's stores—a tongue, the week's butter ration, etc. These were placed in large basins in the small stream at the bottom of the field. We went to the station to meet the other campers and returned to find the butter gone, basin and all! We reported our grievous loss to the police, and set about helping everyone to unpack, to make palliasses and to settle in. I felt sure the thief would return for the tongue! As dark fell, I slipped from our tent and sat on the running board of the car, facing a hole in the hedge the other side of the stream, with a large mallet on my knees—my one urgent prayer that the Lord would not let me kill him! I heard him approach; I raised the mallet; he neared the hole; I sneezed! And he fled!

The camp presented great difficulties. Despite sincere efforts on the part of the student element to prevent it, we found ourselves divided into two groups, university and others. Friendliness was interpreted as patronage; squabbling and petty unkindnesses started and it looked as though the whole purpose of the camp would be wrecked. Then the rain came—and it poured steadily for three days! The field was a quagmire, the stream a rushing torrent; everything was soaking and there was no way of drying it. Then I became ill. Frantically, Dr Goodchild sought for a solution. The Convention secretary came to our aid, and arranged for us to have the loan of the local drill-hall. The IVF men came over and cleaned it out for us, loaned us camp beds and dry blankets, and started a shuttle service to move us in. Now we were all together in one big room around a central table, except for Dr Goodchild in a little side room. And I lay ill on her bed with a mild attack of pneumonia. When everyone was settled in, she joined them for a short prayer meeting. Together they praised God for everyone's kindness to us and His provision for us, and prayed for His outpoured blessing and especially for my speedy recovery. Immediately, He began to work. Apologies were made, new friendships began as they all mixed together. I recovered quickly. We were all deeply conscious of the Lord being vitally in our midst.

There followed in the summer another, and longer, camp at Weston-super-Mare, to which secondary schoolgirls from all over England came. Again, it was far from easy. To begin with, there were divisions among the leaders, some of them denominational in their origin, others arising from differences in their approach to the whole question of discipline. The campers were quick to sense the lack of unity among the officers. Rules were broken continuously and, at one stage, near-anarchy reigned! Instead of the usual harmless ragging and fun, we were faced with vicious and spiteful gang warfare. During that camp, however, I began to sense clearly His hand upon me for leadership. There was a new sense of dignity, a great assurance of His will, a fresh vision of what I believed He yearned to do for us and through us. I was conscious that the girls responded to me and appeared to respect me, and this gave me a deeper desire to help them. I was not myself deeply involved in the staff difficulties, since I was a relative outsider. This gave me more time to be quiet and on my own. It was at these times that different girls came to me with their problems, and I was amazed to see how the Lord gave me the words to help them. Then I found a great longing to take a series of Bible studies with any who wanted to come, and I readily obtained permission for this from the other staff. In those meetings I 'found my feet' and began to realise that He was giving me a gift of imparting to others that which was precious to me.

The following Christmas term, at the start of my third year, a member of the CU executive with a great desire to win other students for Christ, I faced up to His demand for complete, unquestioning obedience. I felt that this involved me in Believer's Baptism as a public testimony to my faith. Asking the advice of certain spiritual leaders at Cambridge, I was shaken by their apparent antagonism, one of them even quoting Galatians 3:1-3 to me. I became convinced in my own mind, however, that my spiritual advancement towards maturity in Christ demanded this step of obedience, even though it might lose me Christian friends and valued fellowship. Possibly this was for me the first touch, the first hint, of the years of loneliness that lay ahead, though I knew nothing of this then. I went to Nottingham to stay with Dr Goodchild for a weekend in November, and I was baptised at her church. It did not mean anything definite so far as a new experience in grace was concerned, but for me it was a definite step of obedience.

Every third year, the Christian Union in Cambridge organised a Mission to the whole university. The time for this was now upon us. We had been preparing for weeks. Every day had meetings arranged. We had given out leaflets and personal invitations and it was easily our greatest concerted effort of evangelism of my three years at the university. On the Saturday previously, Olga had arrived at my room to borrow my hockey tackle (I wasn't playing that year because of the Mission, and also because of my tripos!).[1] In the evening she returned and I offered her a bath—a luxury to

---

1 Editor's note: 'tripos' are the undergraduate examinations for a BA degree at the University of Cambridge.

her as she now lived in very poor digs as a research student in nuclear physics. She accepted gratefully after a little pressure. Because of the shortage of coal, baths were still rationed. She then joined me round the fire for hot buttered crumpets! We had been praying hard; it was a long time since we had had any contact with her. She was friendly and open, obviously lonely, and enjoying being with us. We invited her to the Mission and she agreed to come.

An amazing week followed. I seemed to live for Olga's conversion. I was round at her digs all hours. I waited for her for meetings. We discussed and argued; I prayed and wept. For the first time since I entered Newnham, I incurred late gate fines, and Miss Chrystal, my hall tutor, was so thrilled to think I was coming out of my shell, she paid them for me! And, on the last day of the Mission, Olga acknowledged a mental assent to the truth of the gospel. Then a fight began. We read and studied, prayed and discussed together till all hours. I obtained leave to stay up in Cambridge for the first week of our vacation to stay with her in her digs. I yearned over her in a way I had never previously experienced. At last, she said that unless God Himself revealed to her heart the assurance of her salvation, she would not go on believing. Doubts poured into my soul; I nearly lost my own faith. Could God fail her? Was it possibly not true? To me, this was just a glimpse of the great agony of identification to which we are called. I held on, almost in blind faith, almost in despair. And just before Christmas, peace came. Olga quietly knew a tremendous assurance and depth of reality. She was hungry for fellowship, Bible study, knowledge, everything she could receive. In January we went together to Nottingham and she, too, was baptised.

A few weeks later, at the beginning of the Lent term, Princess Aida Desta of Ethiopia came into my room and said that she had just received a letter from the Headmistress of Clarendon, her old school, telling of their urgent need of a matron as their own had suddenly taken ill. We got down on our knees and laid this need before the Lord. As we arose, there was a knock at the door. Olga came in and blurted out: 'I've given up my job; it seems inconsistent with my faith as a Christian. Pray for me that God will show me what he wants me to do now.' Within ten minutes we were on the phone to Clarendon to ask if Olga would be suitable as assistant matron. That weekend she went to take up her new duties! It was there that she assisted at the annual China Inland Mission Conference and received her clear call to missionary service; and for many years now she and her husband, Douglas Abrahams, have been preaching and teaching the gospel in Japan.

In March, I had two amazing dreams on consecutive nights, all the more extraordinary as I very rarely dream. The first was a walk alone across snow-covered fields, very white and dazzling. There was a road up the hill, with a fork, leading down through dark sombre pines. Suddenly a garish farm-wagon, in gaudy red and green, came roaring down the hill, skidded, slewed down into the pine forest, and was soon lost to view. Then the deep impenetrable silence fell again. I drew my eyes away from watching the empty track where the lurching wagon had passed, and turning, climbed the stile and started across the white waste, climbing, climbing. My breath hurt, the cold was cruel, the pure white burned my eyes, the lonely silence weighted the frosty air. I neared the top, strangely fearful, suddenly conscious of a great destiny. Each step ached; each gasping breath tore at my chest. There was a sense of foreboding, of death. To reach the top was essential, yet it spelt death. Then came the final struggle—tremendous brightness, clarity, purity, far distant views. I felt caught away from myself, apart, separate, and I seemed to die, shrivelled in the icy cold, yet reaching out into the blazing light. I woke in a sweat of fear, and yet a sense of tremendous triumph, as though I had been vouchsafed a glimpse into the future. I reached for my Bible, opened at my daily reading, and Obadiah 17 shone out with joy, 'Upon mount Zion shall be deliverance, and there shall be holiness; and the house of Jacob shall possess their possessions.' It was a call to an utter dedication, a going forward to possess my possessions in Him, my Deliverer, my Sanctifier.

The next night again I was caught up, as it were, in a dream of great vividness and horror. It was a dream of big crowds and pressures and fear. I found myself in the streets of London, being hunted, driven, threatened by evil men, surrounded and impeded by endless traffic. All was noise and bustle and colours, confused and terrifying. Again I woke in fear, in horror, pleading Him to deliver me. And clearly a voice seemed to ring in my ears, 'They need Him!', and my life's task was unmistakably clear. He was calling me to seek and to save the lost, to be identified with them as He was, in all that wretchedness and humanity, to snatch some from the burning, the fear, the hysteria, and draw them into His peace and grace.

Finals came and went. The last weeks were a frantic rush of study, continuing late into each night. I remember as we entered our Biochemistry practicals, my best subject, the one on which I was relying to pull me up to 2nd class honours—a slip of paper was passed to me. My brother Bob, it said, who was a student at St John's College, was very ill with angina. Everything went from my thoughts. The invigilator, Dr Baldwin, came round to see our prepared notes as to what we intended to do to work out the problem set, in order to give each one permission to use the delicate apparatus, but my paper was blank. He looked at me astonished, knowing my keenness for the subject. I silently passed him the scrap of paper. Immediately seeking permission from the other examiners, he hurried me out, got me into his car, and drove off to the hospital named on the slip. There we learnt that Bob had a mild attack of Vincent's angina and would like a bottle of lemonade! With my heart at rest, we flew back to the labs and I was given the full three hours from then, and managed to pull off the desired 2nd class honours degree!

July found me travelling once again to Keswick, just two of us, on bicycles with tents, to camp under Speaker's Rock. It was a wonderful week. On the Tuesday I went up to the mountains alone and spent all night before the Lord—Miss Ruth Paxson had spoken to a women's meeting on 'That great big capital "I"' and my heart yearned to know full surrender, that it might truly be 'Not I, but Christ'; that I might fully enter into the experience and understanding of the crucified life, identified with my Saviour. Once again, I became ill at Keswick with a sort of gastric flu. After two days in bed, others kindly made it possible for me to go home by train instead of bicycle.

Camp followed, an exciting and enjoyable fortnight. But just at the close, the sickness caught up with me again. I managed to get home, and arrived on the day my family had left to go abroad for five weeks' holiday. I was to look after the place in their absence! For two weeks I was really ill. The doctor wanted to move me to hospital and to send for my parents, but I dissuaded him, not wishing to spoil their holiday. He then told me that I had poliomyelitis. Slowly the pains and stiffness wore off and I got better. But a great spiritual battle began to rage. During the illness, I found I didn't want to die; and now that I was getting better, I didn't want to be a missionary! This shook my faith—my faith in myself, perhaps; my faith in my experience of salvation and, since it followed so hard on the time spent at Keswick, my faith in the validity of my consecration. Yes, He began to shake everything that was shakeable, to get me free for Himself. But I wasn't sure any longer what I wanted, nor where to turn.

4

Down into the Valley

Slowly, painfully, there had been growing within me during this past year a sense of incompleteness, a gnawing fear that possibly I wasn't being absolutely honest. Outwardly everything was fine! I was a leader of the Christian Union, a keen promoter of missionary interest, an ardent student of the Bible, as well as being a third-year undergraduate with hockey and cricket blues. Yet there was a feeling of cloaking something over, that somewhere there was a higher level of thinking that I hadn't yet reached, that perhaps I wasn't even looking for as yet.

I was conscious of 'explaining away' certain texts of Scripture, such as 'He that committeth sin is of the devil.... Whosoever is born of God doth not commit sin ... he cannot sin, because he is born of God' (1 John 3:8-10). I feared this chapter, with a strange kind of horror. I remember going to a series of Bible studies on the letters of John, and hearing what was no doubt an excellent and scholarly explanation of such passages based on the tenses of the verbs in the original Greek, and so on. Though the interpretation was completely satisfying for the one who taught us, deep inside myself I was not personally convinced. I was frightened of indulging in spiritual dishonesty, of accepting explanations just because they suited me, suited what I wanted to believe, and in this way quieted the qualms of my conscience.

Then again, there were 'expressions' of our faith, certain words and phrases used to express conservative evangelical thought, which doubtless were perfectly accurate and scriptural, but which I suddenly realised had no definite spiritual content for me. I remember so clearly with Olga, in the days which led up to her conversion, how precise she was. 'How do you know it is true?' she would query. 'He is in my heart; He has changed my life', I would reply. 'But how?' 'I received Him as my Saviour; I am cleansed in His blood.' Slowly there entered a gnawing doubt. Was this just evangelical jargon? Was there a reality behind the shadow of words? Olga's conversion became desperately important to me, not only for her own sake, but for mine also. Should she be truly convinced of Him in her head as well as her heart, I would be sure, because I knew that she would not be converted merely through an emotional need (as possibly I had been). And yet at the same time I felt ashamed of this mental attitude of clutching at a straw to convince myself.

It was a method of 'establishing assurance'. Assurance is one of the great glorious truths of the evangelical faith, one of God's great gifts to us from Calvary. Scripture assures us that we may know Him, that we may know that we have eternal life (1 John 5:13). I lacked this assurance as a permanent reality in my life. At one moment I lived in it and enjoyed it, testified to it and taught it to others. Then would come a wave of depression and fears and doubts 'lest that by any means, when I have preached to others, I myself should be a castaway' (1 Cor. 9:27). I had to persuade myself. I had to encourage others to persuade me. I had been baptised as a public committal and testimony, a burning-of-my-boats. It was to me an act of obedience, but it was all part of my effort to receive assurance. I claimed the promises of Scripture,

'He that hath the Son, hath life', 'Lo, I am with you always.' I underlined them in my Bible. These were the facts on which my assurance stood, and still I lacked it as a consistent permanent experience. I accused myself of trying to work up what could only come down from above.

Again there was a certain 'exclusiveness' in the outlook of many Christians I knew that an inner voice urged me to question, the attitude that this was the truth and there was no other. One part of me accepted this utterly. I was deeply convinced mentally of the absolute reality of the truth and value of the Scriptures. But beyond this, I was not so sure. How much was tradition? The phraseology that we used to express the truth—was it not too small to include the whole greatness of truth? Was it not possible that others, though using such different phraseology, were actually describing the same truth? I had experienced a tremendous sense of liberation when He revealed Himself to me. I left the Anglo-Catholic way of worship. I felt the terminology of the mass and of consubstantiation was unscriptural and sadly misleading for hungry souls who were seeking Him who by His own blood 'entered in once into the holy place, having obtained eternal redemption for us' (Heb. 9:12). And yet, as I looked at the life of Father Charles, humble, gracious, consistent, severe and yet withal gentle, he revealed Christ to me. How was this reconcilable?

Another growing fear was that of excusing behaviour with which I knew I ought to be dissatisfied. I suppose this was the outcome of various conflicting doctrines. On the one hand, there was the grand sublime teaching of our eternal security, of our assurance that He who had undoubtedly saved me on Calvary would equally certainly perfect the work and bring me into His eternal presence; that He who had caused me to be born again, adopting me into His family, had promised never to forsake me, never to cast me out, never to loose me from His hand. All this was of grace, infinite wonderful grace, received by faith but never won by works. Yet on the other hand equally, I read that to him who overcame to the end would be given power (Rev. 2:26). To him also was the promise given that his name would not be blotted out of the Book of Life (Rev. 3:5). I read also that there shall in no wise enter into heaven anything that maketh a lie (Rev. 21:27). And there was the story of the unforgiving servant who, although previously forgiven his debt, was delivered over to his tormentors till he should pay every penny (Matt. 18:23-35). Much of the teaching of Scripture was undoubtedly conditional. There were great 'if' passages.

In the mental strain which resulted from all this, I tended to call certain sins weaknesses, or human frailties, and thereby to excuse them. It was nicer to speak of exaggeration, probably due to over-enthusiasm in a good cause, than to speak of lying. Yet I felt I was practising mental dishonesty in making such excuses for myself, and trying to establish assurance. Again, it was nicer to speak of 'warm friendship' than 'inordinate affection', and thus to vindicate the over-exclusiveness of affection between two of us that shut out a third, or at least made her feel uncomfortable and unwanted. It was easy to excuse myself in my own heart with such arguments as 'Surely the friendship could not be sin? Were we not being blessed in witness to others?' Or again, 'Was I not a Christian Union leader, respected and honest, and no-one appeared to criticise my behaviour?'

Then slowly there dawned a sense of exhaustion. The joy and excitement of the first three years suddenly seemed to drain away. When I left Cambridge and started at West London Hospital there was not the same fellowship. There were new temptations and difficulties. Working in a small group instead of in huge classes, I could no longer hide in the crowd and avoid the questions I so dreaded. Work began to get on top of me; unhappiness, loneliness, fear, inferiority, all began to be acutely present. At the same time Bible study and prayer became perfunctory instead of joyous. I no longer wanted Christian fellowship, but had to stir up the desire. Witness continued, but with no real faith or expectation of seeing results. Looking back, it is easy to realise that at least part of the explanation lies in the fact that, like many of my fellow medical students, I was suffering from overwork and strain, resulting from a very full programme. I did not understand this at the time, however, and so thought that this exhaustion meant spiritual failure.

Throughout this difficult period—a coming-down from a mountaintop in order to strike out for another peak, as I could see later—I had a horror of being thought inconsistent. I'll never forget going to Oxford in June 1945 for the Varsity Cricket match. It was to be played on Saturday, but rain caused the match to be postponed. On Sunday morning, on our way to the cricket field, Mary and I met the Rev. W. H. Rowdon, our own vicar from St Paul's, Cambridge, who was the visiting preacher at St Ebbe's that morning! We were carrying our cricket bats over our shoulders. When he stopped to speak to us, asking where we were going, I remember the surprised tone of his voice when he said, 'Playing cricket on a Sunday?' We continued to the match in sober silence. We had given it no thought! We were part of a team, away from home. Could we have let them down overnight? The match started with no joy for us. Oxford women batted first and made 173 for 8. Then Cambridge, believe it or not, were all out for under 30. I was opening batsman and carried my bat for a duck! But my heaviness and dissatisfaction of heart had nothing to do with the score. Were we wrong? Others inferred we were. I must be personally convinced. Was God telling me not to play games on a Sunday? Ironically, I remembered my school days when, as an Anglo-Catholic, I refused to take part in

House sports on Ascension Day, taking a lone stand against much determined opposition. Was I not willing to take the same stand now for love of my Saviour as I then took out of reverence for my God?

All these gnawing problems, and the sense of possible dishonesty, led to an almost desperate effort to convince myself. Olga's conversion had been a tremendous buttress to my faith, but could it still be possible that it was all emotionalism, a myth, a soporific? Could it all be untrue? I was urgently aware that I must know the answer, one way or another. I daren't ask openly. I was afraid others might think as I thought, and my questioning might undermine their faith. If one started to question, might it be the start of a snowball, till the whole fabric of faith was shaken?

So the determination grew to teach others, and in this way to convince myself! I threw myself wholeheartedly into summer camps: Varsity and Public Schools in 1947, Inter-Schools 1948, Barbican Mission to Jews 1949, and so on. On Sundays I became a Girl Crusader leader. I loved it. We had our class at home where I was living while studying at the West London Hospital, in a room behind the garage. Two boy Crusaders came in one week to help me cement the floor and clean the place up. Next week, two or three of the thirteen-year-old girls came and helped me paint the doors and windows. Then we made forms and a table, using sawn logs for the legs. We drew and painted big thermometer-charts for our inter-group class competitions. Days were full and the girls were as keen as I was. The preparation involved for the regular weekly class was good for me.

One Sunday, arriving a quarter of an hour before class, I overheard two twelve-year-olds earnestly discussing the pros and cons of cinema-going. A great yearning grew in my heart not to fail these youngsters, and so our 'Keenite Class' came into being. My only free afternoon was Saturday, so it was given out that any twelve to fourteen-year olds who would like to do regular Bible study could come to my home on Saturday from 3 to 4 p.m. Some of the other leaders were sceptical—Saturday afternoon for a Bible study? But they came! They crowded our small room! I can see them now. The twins, the one thin and wiry, the other round and cosy; Jean, bright-eyed and keen; two little scraps, probably only eleven years old. Each week anything from eight to sixteen of them would turn up. We set out on the Minor Prophets! I have never learnt so much about the prophets as through those weekly classes—their historical order and setting, spiritual content and purpose, personal application and reality. I loved teaching those youngsters. And yet there was still a haunting fear that I was not willing to be weighed up by my own standards.

Ward services in the West London Hospital were another outlet. There was no nurses' Christian Union at the hospital then—we started one a year later—and there was little fellowship in witness. I obtained permission from the Board and Matron and the Chaplain to conduct these services, covering three or four wards each Sunday. I didn't really believe I would see conversions. It was an act of duty, the kind of thing a Christian medical student should do. I carried a little portable harmonium, set it up in a ward and gave out hymn sheets I had bought. Then, playing with two fingers as best I could, I sang a solo (because no-one sang with me!), I led in prayer, read from the Bible and preached a short message. Then gathering up the hymn sheets and folding up the harmonium, I would move on to another ward. I spent two hours doing this every Sunday evening for almost three years, constrained by a 'must', a deep personal challenge to fulfil this duty even though at times it was an unpleasant one. Others joined me in this service: a fellow student, Pauline Bousquet; our Casualty Officer, Derek Rose; and at times people from my home church.

There came the day when I accepted the challenge to go to the men's wards as well as the women's. I started in the men's orthopaedic ward. What a mistake! The occupants were sixteen: fit and healthy young fellows, some with their legs strapped up in the air following a motor-cycle accident, and others of similar kind. 'What hymn shall we start with?' I never made that mistake again! 'Roll out the barrel', from the far end of the ward! I gallantly plodded through No. 7, 'Fight the good fight', whilst they lustily roared 'Roll out the barrel'. In the second verse, a boot landed on the harmonium. Through the third verse I prayed earnestly what I should do, especially with regard to the boot! At the end of the verse, I picked up the boot and hurled it back down the ward. I didn't play cricket for Cambridge for nothing! The fellows were so impressed that a mere girl could chuck straight, I had no further trouble at all. They all listened quietly, even intently. And then the thrill; after the service one young lad in his early twenties gave his heart to the Lord! My first known convert in those ward services. It challenged me deeply. Why had I not seen others? Why did I not expect conversions? My coward heart answered hesitatingly: because your life does not measure up to Scripture, 'Be ye holy; for I am holy.'

It didn't really matter what people thought. It didn't matter what it cost. One just had to be all out for Him. Sometimes there was a sense of desperation in my heart that days were closing in, and it was our responsibility to tell the heedless and careless, the indifferent and the sarcastic, or else their blood might be demanded at our hands. With it all came this tremendous challenge to holiness. We must be holy. I fought against the apparent cost involved, the realization that I must give up anything that got in the way of 'Jesus only'.

In the wards and in front of other doctors I was very conscious of inferiority, or rather a fear of what others thought. This crippling shyness just had to be subdued and overcome by a daily dying to self, by a vigorous painful effort. Yet there was very little success. Almost crushed, and deeply discouraged, I was invited one day by a nurse to accompany her to see a film. I asked no questions. Coming off duty from casualty at 6 p.m. I joined her and we travelled together to Richmond. We arrived at the theatre late and found it packed out. We stood at one of the doors craning our necks and, taking turns to be in front, were able to watch a little. The film was *Three Miles High*, an amazing record of courage and endurance, of magnificence and beauty, of challenge and determination, filmed in the Himalayas on the Tibetan border. It told the story of twenty years of missionary endeavour against tremendous odds. Immediately, something deep within me stretched out to join this team, to throw in my lot with such people. Major Leonard Moules of the Worldwide Evangelization Crusade was showing the film and was at the bookstall afterwards. I hung around till most people had left, and then went to speak to him. We talked and my heart thrilled. He gave me literature and he invited me to his Mission Headquarters. At last we parted and I returned to hospital, but with a new joy, a new certainty, a new challenge.

Then the struggles redoubled! I had been twice to the Keswick Convention. The addresses I heard there had offered me just what I wanted, all that I was striving after, but they didn't show me how to enter into this wonderful full life. It was all there, the challenging ideal of this glorious life of holiness and victory, of purity and of power. But there seemed no way of bridging the gap from my despair to this liberation. I agreed to all that Keswick had offered me. I agreed to all the teaching of Scripture. My whole being acknowledged that this was the truth, but—there was always that 'but'—my heart wasn't involved in it all. Every part of me cried out that there must be heart involvement, communion within this truth. It was quite plain that mental assent without heart involvement was ultimately impossible.

I was filled with a tremendous desire, a great hunger after Him. I must go on at any cost. I no longer cared what it would mean, or what it might involve. I was willing even to leave my home and join in mission life at WEC Headquarters while still a medical student at the West London Hospital. There at Headquarters I lived in a hot-house of spirituality. Students from Emmanuel College, Birkenhead, from Cliff College, from Swansea, Redcliffe, and Mount Hermon Bible Colleges surrounded me, all keenly devoted to His service. Talk at meals was largely of the Lord. I listened in also to organised discussions on different doctrinal and theological matters such as the difference between Arminianism and Calvinism, pre- and post-millennialism, foreign and indigenous missionary strategy, and found myself profoundly ignorant. I joined prayer meetings for revival which went on into the small hours, alive and on fire with a passion for souls and the zeal of the Holy Ghost. I watched lives that were real, earnest, separated, that radiated light and warmth and truth. I longed to be fully one of them. I pleaded with the Lord. I trusted and stepped out in faith, claiming the promises. I tried to fulfil every formula that each one testified to in their own experience. And still my heart felt cold. Sin in my life seemed to mock at my endeavour.

Looking back, it is easy to smile at the intensity of feeling and also the excessive introspection. Yet how extremely real it was at the time. I readily grant that chronic introspection of this type can become very unhealthy, mentally as well as spiritually. As has often been said, a carrot cannot grow if it is continually dug up to see how it is getting on. Nervous individuals can make themselves chronically ill by taking their temperature four times a day and noting each little rise and fall. Likewise, persistent introspection can work one up into a highly tense state of spiritual sickness.

I fell into most of the traps possible. I made myself almost ill through my preoccupation with my own holiness, or rather lack of it! It took a long time to recover from that mistake, which need never have been made. Of course, I never can be holy! How simple, when one realises that the Lord knows me as I am in all my weakness, loves me, and waits to impart Himself, His own holiness, His life, living in me.

Each conviction of sin was good in so far as it led me to trust the only One who can deal with sin. But if the sense of failure only made me more acutely conscious of my own miserable state, it had achieved nothing. The Lord allowed a growing realization of failure in each of the different realms mentioned, in order that He Himself might fill the vacuum. He longed that I would become more preoccupied with Him and less with myself.

5

TRUDGING ON

For four years I had known that there was something wrong with my voice, some trouble in my throat. Where previously I had been a member of various choirs, I was now no longer able to sing in tune. There was a growing huskiness, a feeling of a 'potato in my throat', accompanied by a slight difficulty in swallowing. I was vaguely afraid, but did not seek advice. Now rapidly the condition worsened, and it became virtually impossible to speak above a strained hoarse whisper. At times I was reduced to using a pencil and paper when I wanted to converse. In March 1950, I entered my own hospital where I was a student for an operation under the ENT specialist for 'benign nodes on the vocal chords'. I was given a small single room adjoining the women's ward. When I came round from the anaesthetic that Friday evening, the walls were cheerfully panelled with large amusing diagrams of the war-time celebrity and such slogans as, 'Wot! No talking?'

An attendant nurse hastened to impress on me that on no account must I make any attempt to speak. Anything I wanted must be written down. The vocal chords must be completely at rest for four days following the operation.

The Tuesday following, while I was alone and resting, a wonderful thing happened. Slowly, an intense awareness developed. Someone was with me. My heart thrilled; the room seemed charged with His presence; a great sense of light was borne in upon me. For two or three hours I was deeply aware of a wonderful companion spirit, not hearing anything, nor seeing anything, but just knowing.

Later, lunch was brought in. The vision dimmed, and yet something had occurred, a new start had been made. From that morning, a hatred of sin was born. Till then I had hated the consequence of sin, the shame of failure, the fear of exposure. But somehow I lacked a hatred for the sin itself. In fact there was a curious liking for it; in its way it was pleasurable. I wished to be freed, and yet I wanted to enjoy it. Suddenly I now knew an intense hatred of all that had crucified my Lord. It was the turning-point for me. The downward path from the peak of happiness, with its puzzlements and questionings, was arrested. Suddenly the next peak stood out clearly ahead. The encircling mist had lifted and left the way clear and inviting. He who was calling me on to service overseas was standing there, gently smiling, promising His presence and companionship and enabling, telling me to look forward and upward, not backward or inward. Suddenly the months of struggle and longing were over; I was satisfied. Not that my doubts were exactly explained; they no longer seemed to need explanation.

The next day the surgeon visited me. He stood at the foot of the bed and commanded me to speak. I had been longing to do so for five days but now found nothing to say! The moment was deeply important to me. Could I speak? At last, fearfully, expectantly, I tried. A deep wave of disappointment and nausea swept over me as I made a noise like the barking of a dog. He examined me carefully, and then curtly said that the operation appeared to have been a failure, but that if I liked to come back in six months he would see if he could help me. With that he left the room; the sister and nurse followed him. I was alone, deeply alone. A wave of giddiness, darkness, heart-ache, came over me. My medical career, let alone my missionary career, was in the balance. My head reeled under the cruel blow. Stunned, miserable, I just lay, tasting the bitterness of the empty future, the mockery of all that had led up to that moment.

Slowly another voice began to force itself through the night in my heart. 'Can you not trust Me?' it seemed to whisper. 'Did I not meet with you only yesterday, beckoning you on to Myself? Why are you so fearful?'

My heart rebelled. Was I not crushed, unable?

'Have you not used your voice for your own ends, for your own glorification, for years? I will give you a new voice for use in My service.'

I just lay there quietly, and slowly peace filtered back into my heart. I felt that His promise was not only with regard to my natural voice; that was just a kind of token. It was to be my whole life, my inability to be holy, my longing after Him—all this He was promising to indwell and fulfil.

That Friday I went home. It was Good Friday, and my mother's birthday. Roughly speaking, my condition was much the same as when I entered hospital. When I spoke it was in a strained hoarse whisper. On the evening of Easter Sunday I went to church with my sister. The Rev. Tom Darlington (who was a missionary in China during the Boxer Revolution) was preaching. It was a powerful sermon, appealing to us to let God the Holy Spirit have His way in our lives, taking possession, infilling, making holy with His holiness. Afterwards a group of my old friends gathered outside the church, discontented and unsatisfied. One challenged me directly: 'Helen, do you know what Mr Darlington was preaching about in your own experience? Is this really something for us now, or only in old age after years of suffering and trial, such as he himself has gone through?' Clearly, without a moment's hesitation,

I said a joyous 'Yes!' ringing with assurance. And suddenly I realised He had healed! An amazed hush entered my heart, a tremendous feeling of awe. He had touched me. I looked forward, upward to Him from that moment, and knew that I must always go upwards and onwards, whatever happened in the world around. His call was to live always unto Him.

Six months later I went to see the specialist in outpatients. He was honestly amazed when he first examined me and asked if I had been treated elsewhere. I assured him that I had not sought help at any other hospital, and I tried to testify to him of the power of God to heal. However he merely commented that such cases were known, on occasion, to show considerable regression, and the matter was closed.

Finals followed in three months. What a grind it was! Parts I and II of my final MB comprised some twenty examinations—papers, practicals, orals—a fortnight's gruelling nightmare. The results were read out a short while after I had left my last oral, and though I had passed Part I, I had failed Part II. It was a blow and disappointment, and yet there was the certainty that in six months I would try again and by His grace succeed. So I began a six months' 'trial of endurance', studying all hours, from an early 6 a.m. rise until after midnight. Harry and Gladys Jones came home from Congo that autumn. Mr Jones needed immediate surgery for a large gastric ulcer and came back to us at Mission Headquarters for post-operative care. About this time, his wife developed bilateral pneumonia. I had the privilege of caring for them and spent many hours in their room. We talked much about the work which they had to leave—and that was the start of my knowledge of the need of the Congolese.

The day came to go again to Cambridge for Part II finals. We read Isaiah 58 in the early morning, the chapter of my missionary call, especially verses 6-11. I remember Harry taking up verses 13 and 14 and praying that I would keep holy the Sabbath day in the coming week, and that He would cause me to rejoice in Him as a result. This time He crowned the effort with success. What a thrill, ringing home to say I was through! A doctor!

There followed ten days' wonderful holiday at a Christian guest house near Bournemouth where the Joneses were now recuperating. There was a Salvationist there, an elderly man, I remember, and he had no jersey! I knitted him one, incorporating the Salvation Army badge of Blood and Fire. I gave it to him as a New Year gift, but really it was a 'thank-you' to the Lord for seeing me thus far.

Harry, Gladys, and I had wonderful times of prayer and Bible study together, as well as many walks and discussions. It was a time when I could think over many questions that had been shelved during the years of intensive study. Gladys Jones was a trained church worker. Together we discussed and prayed over many problems, particularly such matters as hurtful friendships, inordinate affections, the loneliness of the single woman missionary, and the battles involved in this loneliness.

On 15th January 1951, I returned to WEC Headquarters as a candidate! I really felt I was getting somewhere at last. It was Monday when I arrived, and I moved into one of the rooms on the first floor of the hostel, sharing it with another candidate, a girl from Sweden. On Tuesday, after breakfast and washing up, I was told to go and wash the cement floor of the toilets and bathroom on the women candidates' floor. I found a bucket and brush, and set to. Strange as it may sound, it was almost the first time in my life that I had done a household chore. I was always the trainee-doctor till that moment! I scrubbed out the first toilet and started on the second. A candidate entered the first with muddy shoes. The floor was still wet. When she left, I returned and did the first again. Meanwhile, someone else entered the second. This continued for some little time with a rising sense of frustration. I'd never get them clean! I'd fail, my very first day in training, to achieve the task I was set. Tears pricked at my eyes. I scrubbed on, muttering, 'Devil, get out of here! Devil, get out of here!'

Someone came in, and standing still a moment watching me, heard my muttered comments. She laughed and startled me. 'Now I understand why our cakes are all burnt today!' she exclaimed. 'We're in the kitchen underneath, and you're sending the devil down to us!' She left amused. But there was another quiet spectator, Elizabeth, who was in charge of the candidates and who had given me this task. After a short pause, she gently asked me why I was so upset. I explained the cause of my frustration. 'For whom are you scrubbing this floor?' she replied. 'Why, for you, of course; you sent me here.' I've never forgotten her answer: 'No, my dear. If you are doing it for me, you may as well go home. You'll never satisfy me. You're doing it for the Lord, and He saw the first time you cleaned it. That now is tomorrow's dirt.' It was quiet, godly wisdom that has followed me through many years in Congo.

My six months at Mission Headquarters were wonderful days! Early morning rising at 6 a.m.; serving tea to missionaries on furlough; a quiet hour of prayer and Bible study; breakfast and washing up; family devotions, worship and prayer until 10.30 a.m.; coffee; then 'chores' till high tea at 5.30 p.m.; and those amazing thrilling evening meetings when I learnt what prayer meant, labouring, believing, claiming, rejoicing—all across the world from Colombia to the Philippines, holding on for missionaries and nationals, governments and projects, in persecutions and triumphs. They were tremendous meetings! And so to bed by 9.30 p.m., worn-out and happy.

Chores! What memories there are! I was put in the laundry for most of my six months with Ruth, a grand girl who had just completed her course at the WEC Missionary Training College in Glasgow. Elizabeth showed me the first day what was expected—through the bath (soaking), to the boiler (boiling), to a tub (rinsing), up through the mangle (beware of your fingers!), out on the lines (beware of the mud!), back through the rollers, and so, neatly piled, into the airing cupboards—some thirty-six sheets, pillowcases, and towels plus white overalls and the men's shirts for the first day. Starching of collars was an interesting extra! Somewhat fearfully, yet believing for the best, I made a start (merely adding my own personal laundry to the vast pile, to save time) and went through the exercise exactly as instructed. A distracted Elizabeth arrived somewhere around 3 p.m. when all the sheets, etc., were nicely out on the lines in the back garden. 'What have you done?' I glanced round fearfully wondering if I'd set the house on fire inadvertently. 'Everything is green!' I learnt that you don't mix coloureds and whites—the only white articles at the end of my first day were my green ankle socks, shrunk to child's size with happy boiling!

Ruth and I soon discovered how to work the rollers with a minimum of effort. She fed the clean sheets in, and they passed out on to a board balanced on my outstretched legs as I perched on the table, reading aloud to her—always from the very best books in the WEC library!

I was tried for one week in the kitchen, but that was disastrous. Saltless solid lumps floated in a tasteless soup served up as porridge; Welsh rarebit came out like chewing gum surmounted by a sickly yellow sauce. The male candidates could stand no more, and despite grumbles of a 'stiff-necked people' (from over-starched collars) I was duly returned to the laundry.

Norman Grubb, our home-base leader, had recently visited Ruanda and the work of the Church Missionary Society and came home deeply moved of the Spirit at the work of revival he had witnessed there. He spoke many times in morning prayers of the way of the cross, not only for conversion, for the start of our walk, but also for the daily continuance of that walk: 'keeping short accounts with God', the immediate confession of sin, as soon as the conviction registered, listening to the still small voice of the Spirit; the quick claiming of the cleansing of Christ's blood and renewal through forgiveness; the restitution to any offended brother; the joy and happiness of 'walking in the light'. My heart was stirred. I wanted all God had for me. With this renewed desire for close, continuous fellowship with the Lord came an increased sensitiveness towards sin. I began to feel the sinfulness of pride and selfishness and lack of prayer burden, as well as of exaggeration, or deceit, or quick-temperedness. The open way of sharing and fellowship became precious and vital. The candidates were brought into an even deeper unity and joy.

Whilst staying as a student at Headquarters I had made a deep friendship with another girl candidate. We were drawn very close to one another. The urge of affection grew. I found myself hurrying home from hospital to be with her. Then slowly I knew that I was on a slippery path that I had walked before; a demanding friendship that did not want a third person to share it with us. I can thank God now that there were faithful senior friends on the staff who understood, and who separated us. Then the other left for the Far East. I saw her off, and a great blank filled my life for weeks.

Now that I was a candidate my face was set to join her in her missionary sphere. I had been at Headquarters only ten weeks when the staff clearly and firmly told me I could not be accepted for that field. I understood, and thank God, by His loving grace, I agreed and knew that they were right. Then where was it to be? I was a qualified doctor. I was living in a missionary training school. But so far I had no knowledge of where He wished me to serve. Every week missionaries on furlough from any of thirty different countries pleaded for more workers, and almost all of them added, 'specially we need a doctor'. The need was on every side. I could see it clearly! I longed to serve, in turn, in at least six different places. But how could I be sure which it should be?

Daily I asked the Lord for clear guidance, for a definite word from Himself. One Tuesday in April 1951, I tore off the block calendar in the dining-hall and was puzzled by the text there: 'Repair the house of the Lord' (2 Chron. 24:4; 34:8). Why had this been chosen? I pushed the slip of paper in my pocket and forgot it. On Thursday I received a letter from an old school friend (who had been converted in recent years, a fact of which I was unaware). She enclosed that same tear-off calendar slip saying that the Lord had urged her to send it to me. Amazed, I went and read carefully through those relevant chapters but still could not see what the Lord was saying to me. On the Friday at morning Prayers, the leader of the leprosy crusade of our Mission read that same verse, from the same calendar slip, telling us how the Lord had burdened her through it in special prayer for Congo, our oldest field in the Mission, with over 1,500 leprosy patients in our care, and over a quarter of a million Congolese looking to us as a Mission for their medical care, as well as for spiritual and educational help. And yet, after thirty years of pioneer work and earnest prayer, we still had no doctor to offer them. Surely this lack was as a 'breach' in the wall of the church of God in Congo, and He needed us to be burdened to 'repair the house of the Lord'.

I could not get away from it. Three times in one week the Lord had spoken. But I did not want to hear. Not Congo, Lord!

Anywhere else but there. But I'm an evangelist, a preacher, a pioneer. I want to go to a people who have never yet heard the message of salvation. Congo is an established church, a ministry to Christians.

On Sunday, as I made my way to my own home church, I prayed again earnestly that He would speak so certainly that I could not be mistaken. The vicar read the story of Balaam and his ass (Num. 22) and he preached on verses 31 to 33! 'Three times the Lord has clearly spoken to you', he said. 'But you do not want to heed. You want something special and dramatic. Beware! He may not be patient for ever. Heed his voice in His thrice-repeated message and obey, and He will bless.' I went home very soberly, but completely convinced that He would have me to serve in Congo.

On 27th June the Mission quarterly staff meeting was taking place. Amongst much other business five candidates were being considered for acceptance into the Mission. I was called to the kitchen, and asked to carry some fifty cups and saucers to the hall next to the library where they were meeting. The swing door into the hall was stiff and heavy. Gingerly I leant on it, pressing, balancing the heavy tray. Very slowly I edged my way in, and carefully along the narrow hall. Suddenly I realised that I was overhearing the staff meeting. I could not hurry! I tried to close my ears, but inevitably I listened for two long agonised minutes to myself being discussed. Lowering the tray on to the table, I fled-back down to my beloved laundry, my face scarlet with shame as I realised what others thought of me—proud, always knowing better than others, unable to be told things or warned or criticised difficult to live with, and so on.

I carried a basket of sixteen sheets upstairs and hung them on the eight lines criss-crossing the garden. Turning to walk back for another load, I heard a sharp twang. Swinging round dismayed, I saw my precious day's work lying bedraggled in the mud. Suddenly the Lord showed me the funny side of it, and with a rush of laughter, I said aloud, 'Hallelujah!' Those in the staff meeting had seen the disaster from the library windows and had come hurrying out to help. They were suddenly arrested and puzzled, as they heard my exclamation followed by a chuckle of dry humour. It was infectious, and grins slowly spread from face to face. When they returned to their discussions my fate was sealed. I was accepted, a sense of humour being considered heavier in the positive balance than all else in the negative!

That morning my Scripture Union reading had been Psalm 60. Verse 2 had gone straight to my heart, 'heal the breaches thereof'. It was the same phrase! Called into the august presence (the meeting consisted of all missionaries who were then on furlough, together with the home staff, about forty of them all told) I was asked if I had any special Scripture to read first. Asking for Isaiah 58:1-11, I was suddenly shaken, as the reader went on and read also verse 12, 'Thou shalt be called, The repairer of the breach.' After various questions, and loving exhortations and warning, I was given the right hand of fellowship to become a member of the mission.

I had a short holiday, and in September sailed for Belgium to learn French at the Colonial School in Brussels to be followed by a course in tropical medicine at the Medical School in Antwerp. They were eight memorable months. The very first day, knowing practically no French at all, I attended a dictation, with about 140 other missionaries, designed to divide the class into two groups. I understood nothing at all of what was read to us, but wrote down the sounds as best I could. We duly heard the results, and I was listed in the 'forte' class (the strong ones!), presumably because seventy folk, wishing to be in the 'faible' class, had handed in blank sheets. I attended our first lecture without understanding a single word, till suddenly I heard my own name! My neighbour told me to stand up, and then everything seemed to happen till I was in tears, the lecturer shouting in fury, and the class torn between sympathy and amusement! Never mind; that Professor taught me French in four gruelling months, and I can never be too thankful.

In Antwerp, there were more lessons to be learnt. I lived with our missionaries, Mr and Mrs Boerop, and what an atmosphere of sacrificial love there was! I had three weeks in bed with jaundice, following a savage dog-bite when cycling home from school one day. They couldn't do too much for me. Then I followed it with mumps! Their kindly concern knew no bounds. Their teenage daughter Joke and I shared a room, which by day became dining-cum-sitting room. Their boy, now a missionary in Europe, helped his Dad in a hundred and one jobs about the house, and in the Bible shop in the front room.

Then Joke became very ill. There was no extra money available. They trusted me to care for her. Two other missionary doctors on the tropical course kindly came and visited her also, giving their services freely. It was an anxious ten days of high, swinging fever, interludes of delirium, much pain, and increasing weakness. She needed penicillin, but we had no ready money available. All extra money had been spent on me during my four weeks of sickness. We were down to 'brown bread and sugar' meals. Urgently, importunate prayer was made. Each injection of penicillin was 'prayed-in' individually, being provided by the local chemist only as we produced the necessary francs. Yet all the time there was money in the shop from the sale of Bibles. I was puzzled; my faith was sorely tried. Their radiant quiet confidence and unswerving loyalty to principle, and through this, to their Lord and Saviour, was a tremendous lesson to me. Joke got better. My course ended. I left their home deeply-blessed spiritually by their faithful sacrificial fellowship throughout those six months.

Deputation work followed for three months, then a round of farewells to friends and family. There had been a most generous response in many meetings that enabled me to buy the necessary personal needs and medical equipment for the years ahead. Shopping, packing, labelling; visits to consul and shipping agents; vaccination and inoculations; the time passed all too quickly.

And so the great day dawned! I remember at the evening fellowship at Headquarters, Thursday, 12th February 1953, giving my testimony and thanking the staff for 'putting up with me' for the past three and a half years. This was greeted with a resounding 'So you should!' which put me right off, so that I couldn't say any more. The following morning, Friday the 13th, saw me off at Liverpool Street Station at 9 a.m. to catch the boat train to the London docks. I recall the great crowd of staff and candidates on the platform, the last phone call to Mother to say goodbye, the accordions and hymn singing, the handshakes and tears. Then the whistle, the green flag, and we're off!

6

MADE IT!

The Dunnottar Castle sailed late, leaving early next morning as dawn broke over the grey mist of the London dockyards. There were seven of us in our party which consisted of two returning missionary couples going out for their third or fourth term of service, an American and his wife from the home base setting off for a six-month tour of our African fields, and myself. With morning Bible studies and prayers, hours spent happily in language study, writing letters and reading, and informal Bible studies with interested passengers in the evenings (the newly-appointed Bishop of Kampala led us through the Epistle to the Romans), our days were happily full, as we steamed through the straits of Gibraltar, to Genoa, along the length of Italy, across the Mediterranean to the Suez Canal, in ever-growing heat to Aden, and at last to Mombasa, in Kenya.

The journey had various highlights—principally the excitement as we rounded the easternmost point of Africa. A radio message requested us to change course to due south, instead of south-west, following the coast. A sick sailor on an oil-tanker needed urgent medical care and we were the nearest ship carrying a doctor. We steamed steadily south to the Equator and next day met the tanker. We all watched the short, early-morning drama of the visit of our doctor in one of the lifeboats, and his return with the sick man suffering from appendicitis. Then our steamer began a large swing to steam westwards for Mombasa. Suddenly, the note of the engines changed, and there was another alteration of course. All on deck waited to know the reason. Eventually we spotted a white fleck on the horizon: we steamed slowly towards it and then watched, fascinated, the real drama as several men were rescued. Now in the last stages of despair and agonised thirst, they had been adrift from the Seychelles Islands in a small fishing boat with no stores, compass, or sail, for over nine days. Had we not gone off-course for the oil-tanker, no ship was likely to have seen that tiny distress-signal shirt, and those men must all have perished. How wonderful are the ways of God, directing a great liner carrying hundreds of passengers to the very spot in the ocean where nine pathetic men so urgently needed help! The hearts of all of us were strangely moved that day as once again we swung westward and steamed for Mombasa.

Africa! Customs formalities, unbearable heat, arguments and noise, flies and thirst and at last the train for Nairobi. We had a carriage to ourselves, three double-bunk bed compartments, and one large four-bunk compartment for me and all our luggage. Excitement? I couldn't eat or talk. I was barely able to think for it! I rushed from side to side of the compartment so as not to miss anything. At each station on the long slow climb up from sea-level to 5,000 feet, I leapt down to stand on African soil, to read the name of the station and its height, to sense the feeling of Africa, its smells, and ways, and moods.

We spent a week in Nairobi at the Church Missionary Society's guest house, and for the first time the realization of fear set in—in those days it was fear of the Mau-Mau. No-one was sure who was friend, who foe. Even a faithful, willing house-boy might have been forced to take the bloodoath, and your life might be in danger.

Up country again to Namasagali, then the lake steamer to Masindi. The heat and dust, the gorgeous frangipani flowers, the leisurely pace, and the horror of seeing someone's precious tea-chest containing a china dinner service haphazardly and unconcernedly tossed from the boat to quay, or quay to boat, with a resounding thud, remain indelibly imprinted on the mind. On again to the edge of Lake Albert. I recall the small steamer, the customs formalities, the happy, indiscriminate mixture of French and Swahili. And so we reached the last lap of the journey. It was stiflingly hot as we crossed the lake, not a breath of wind. Mosquitoes and flies owned the atmosphere, and I felt suffocated under my mosquito net. Out on deck at 5.30 a.m. I watched, straining, for the first glimpses of the Congo as a glorious sunrise broke across the lake, bathing the mountain range in golden crimson light. I was home! It was a deeply thrilling and moving moment, a climax to all that had gone before.

The Mission truck was there. Jack Scholes, my field leader, was at the jetty side, a distinguished-looking man with shining white hair. Beside him were two Africans, and Jim Grainger, his right-hand fellow-worker. They joined us on board for breakfast, everyone full of chatter and news. There were letters of welcome from all the missionaries—almost overwhelming to a newcomer! One from Jessie Scholes to me quoted Zechariah 2:5, 'For I, saith the Lord, will be unto her a wall of fire round about, and will be the glory in the midst of her.'

Customs formalities completed, we loaded up the truck and were off up that tremendous, breath-taking escarpment of countless hairpin bends and magnificent views back over the lake. We stopped at an Africa Inland Mission station for lunch, and what a welcome they gave us! Everyone made me feel I was coming home! Then on again to the Brethren station of Nyankunde, where we were to stay the weekend. There I met two missionaries who had been with me in Belgium. We played some strenuous tennis—not what I had expected in Congo! We arrived at 5 p.m. and that evening an urgent call came for the doctor, but he was away, and I was asked if I would care to go. As we approached the distant forest village we heard the awful death-wailing. We entered the round mud hut, circling between the outer and inner wall in growing darkness, our eyes smarting from the wood smoke, till we reached the centre. Slowly we became accustomed to the dark and the noise, and I knelt beside the still figure, stretched on the earthen floor, already chilling and stiffening, surrounded by naked women (his wives and relatives) rocking to and fro on their heels, wailing abysmally.

After a weekend of rest and fellowship, we set off again. Five of us went with Mr Scholes in the two-ton lorry, and two with Mr Grainger in a three-quarter-ton pick-up. Down from the mountains and wide-open grasslands we drove, into the endless forests, crossing rivers, passing village clearings, on and on, two days of travel, till we reached Ibambi as dusk fell on Tuesday evening, 17th March 1953. My reading that morning had been in Genesis 35: 'Arise… go up to Bethel and dwell there.' Truly I felt this was my Bethel and, like Jacob of old, my one desire was to make an altar there to God for worship and service.

Trees were decorated in welcome. There was even a floral arch as we approached the home up the long avenue of palms—a red banner with cotton-wool words 'Welcome to Ibambi'. We were surrounded by a great and growing crowd of Africans and whites. I remember the talk and noise, the laughter and singing. First to greet us came Jessie Scholes, with her 'Welcome home, dear'. Then Pasteur Ndugu, senior elder of the African church, stepped forward to welcome us all, and myself in particular as the 'new' missionary, in the name of the church.

'We, the church of Jesus Christ in Congo, and we, her elders, welcome you, our child, into our midst.' I never forgot that moment, or those words. What a privilege for a young missionary to be 'their child', one of them, to be cared for, nurtured, loved, and taught by them.

Everything was so new, so strange, so exciting. The early morning tea at 5.10 a.m. so as to be able to be ready to go over to the Bible School for morning prayers at 6.30 a.m.; those wonderful morning Bible studies (that term in Hebrews), and the struggle to get beyond the language barrier; breakfast and family prayers followed, and at 9 a.m. over to the dispensary—an empty room in the old Mission Office building, with cement floor, tin roof, wide verandah, and large windows. It had so little equipment, just a camp stool and table, some tea-chests with boards across as shelves, a handful of basic medicines, and a few slips of paper hurriedly torn up from an exercise book for report cards. We had no common language but made up for it with an abundance of goodwill. And suddenly there were swarms of patients! Noise, heat, smells, waves of nausea, everyone talking at once, crying babies, running sores…it was dusk before all had drifted away, and I was left cleaning the room, sorting out what there was of drugs, frantically making lists of what we urgently needed, almost overcome by waves of weariness and in the background a slight dread of inability to cope. Then came supper, family Bible study and prayers, cocoa, and so to bed about 10 p.m.

So began the routine, at first with no helper, Congolese or European. But it was a beginning. The Scholes were thrilled, as I was, in the vision the Lord began to unfold, even in those early days, and did all they could to help and encourage me in what seemed a monumental task, the creating of an official and efficient medical service for the church in our 'Heart of Africa Mission' area.

One day that first month there was an evening call to go to see a catechist, Abamangi. Jack Scholes kindly drove me out to the village, some twelve miles off the main road. As we went he talked to me of Mission ways, of the Lord's dealings, of the possibilities of success as a missionary. 'If you think you have come to the mission field because you are a little better than others, or as the cream of your church, or because of your medical degree, or for the service you can render the African church, or even for the souls you may see saved, you will fail. Remember, the Lord has only one purpose ultimately for each one of us, to make us more like Jesus. He is interested in your relationship with Himself. Let Him take you and mould you as He will; all the rest will take its rightful place.'

At Easter I went with the Scholes to Poko, 120 miles north, for the weekend conference. I gave my testimony in Swahili! It was my first public attempt to use my new language. After the service, I met Elizabeth Naganimi, a widow of about my own age, a sweet Christian woman with a great desire and longing to serve the Lord. He spoke to her that weekend, and she soon came to join me as my first helper and close friend. Oh, the laughs we had in those early days together as she spoke Bangala and I stumbled through Swahili, and neither of us understood a word of each other!

Following the conference came four weeks working at the Red Cross Hospital at Pawa, fourteen miles north of Ibambi, travelling to and fro daily, learning more of tropical diseases, their diagnosis and treatment, and the necessary laboratory work involved. One day, on the rounds, I noticed a teenage boy dying of tetanus. Dr Kadoner mentioned that he was from our Mission. I went back after the ward round and tried to speak to his parents, with my few halting words of Swahili.

When I felt they understood, I laid hands on the boy's head and prayed (in English!) in the name of our Lord Jesus Christ for his healing. As I prayed, I felt the fever leaving him. I was awed, and a little fearful. Next day, I asked Ida Grainger to go with me and talk to the parents in Swahili and to pray with them. She did, and learnt that the boy had slept peacefully all night, without another fit. He was, of course, receiving all possible treatment and serum, but it was clear that the Lord had chosen to heal him.

The following week one of our church catechists, an elderly faithful warrior, was taken to the Pawa hospital with an obstruction, for an urgent operation. The next day, when I arrived, I met his two teenage grand-daughters from our Ibambi girls' school, on the hospital verandah in tears. Slowly, there and in the ward, I heard their story.

The old man had not had an operation; he was merely written up for four-hourly sulfonamide therapy. When the local nurses arrived at 6 p.m. they offered him his pills in exchange for one of his grand-daughters for that night (almost all our Congolese nurses are men). 'I'd rather die', the old man exclaimed, sending his girls away. They had gone to a neighbouring village, to Christian relatives, and returned next morning to see their grandfather. I was shocked and deeply horrified. I called Dr Kadoner to the bedside, and tried to explain in excited muddled French; but he shrugged his shoulders as much as to say that he knew these things went on but had no power to prevent them. 'Is not this Africa?' Every part of me refused to accept this, and I vowed, God willing, to have a Christian hospital, run by Christian nurses, where all should see and know Christ's love and purity. The old man died next day.

In May, Mrs Scholes was taken ill. I woke at 2 a.m. and heard her husband moving about, and then heard vomiting. I called out quietly to see if he needed help. She was unconscious, with a fever of over 105°. We made up an injection of quinine from crushed tablets and did all we could. By 6 a.m. her temperature was only 96°, but her blood pressure had fallen to within dangerous levels. I stayed with her all through the next three days as we fought first cerebral malaria, then blackwater fever, with intense weakness, hours of semi-consciousness, vomiting, and feeding problems. How I longed for a nurse to help me! How very ignorant I felt as a mere doctor when it came to urgent nursing procedures. For two months we nursed her, and cared for her, and slowly watched the Lord heal her and restore her to us. It knit us together in a deep bond of love. From then on they treated me as one of their own children whom they had had to leave at school in England.

We went away together for a two-week period of rest and convalescence during Bible School vacation, south to Bomili (80 miles) and on to Opienge (a further 140 miles). There we met the Revival. How can one ever hope to explain what we saw and experienced of the mighty working of the Holy Spirit? Senior missionaries and African church elders had been praying earnestly for years that the Lord would graciously pour out upon the Congolese church floodwaters of revival in the Holy Spirit—and suddenly the answer was upon us.

At Opienge, we were at first spectators, puzzled, a little afraid and uncertain, as we saw and heard much that was unusual and foreign to us. Slowly He brought to our hearts the peace of conviction that this was of Him, that He was in control. Meetings were alive with a new power; the building was crowded out as never before. Some were shaking violently, others crying out for mercy, yet others singing and praising the Lord. There was much noise. Humanly speaking, we might have felt it was confusion, yet He revealed that it was Holy Spirit order. Hour after hour, in church, on the compound, at the home, to Africans or to Europeans, men and women were confessing sins, seeking forgiveness and cleansing, going away full of a mighty joy, their faces radiant with new-found peace. Jesus Christ was being glorified. Sin was being put away. Many were being burdened to pray for the unsaved, to go out in teams of witness preaching the gospel. Surely this was never of the devil! God forbid! Only the Holy Spirit glorifies Jesus.

We returned to Ibambi, arriving on Friday afternoon, 27th July. There we heard from the other missionaries that for two weeks an amazing work of repentance had been going on all over the station compound, many being convicted of hidden sin and seeking out Europeans and church elders for advice and counsel, for confession and restitution.

That evening we gathered in the Bible School for the Friday evening fellowship meeting at 7 p.m. Jack Scholes led the meeting. After some hymn singing and a time of prayer, he stood to minister the Word before opening the meeting for testimonies. Almost immediately, a mighty wave of Holy Spirit power swept through the hall. There was a great rush of noise. We looked around amazed, possibly shocked. Then we felt puzzled, even afraid, as we saw apparent confusion. Africans were on their feet, their arms raised above their heads, calling on the name of the Lord. Others were shaking violently and crying out in apparent pain where they sat. Yet others were thrown violently down, across the forms, on the cement floor, yet without physical hurt. Another rushed wildly to the front and threw himself on the ground, crying violently. Some just sat looking round, stupefied. Some children cried, clinging to their mothers. We prayed, and all felt the conviction that this was of God. The Holy Spirit was in control. We must keep our hands off, and let Him work.

Slowly the pattern changed—tears became laughter, crying became singing, shaking of conviction became trembling with joy, as sin was confessed, cleansing claimed through the blood of Christ, and the Spirit took possession. The singing! It was such singing as we had never heard! The whole congregation was slowly drawn into the rising crescendo of joy. In the small hours of the morning we began to make our ways home. On all sides the singing continued. Others drifted back, drawn to the fellowship, and worship and singing continued all night and all next day. The station was alive with a new thrill of His presence.

In the weeks, and even months, that followed, a great burden of prayer came upon the church, a yearning over sinners and unsaved loved ones. Many saw amazing visions, of heaven and all the glories of His presence, of hell and the great horror of His judgment. All were seized with a sense of urgency in witness. Schoolgirls would go out in small groups before dawn, to testify to Jesus in some outlying village before getting back again for school. Stories were legion of His power, dealing with backsliders, dealing with outsiders, convicting, cleansing, converting. All had a hunger to hear the teaching of the Word, and a joy in testimony. There was no waiting for people to arrive for services; they used to run to church ten minutes or more before time, and start singing! There was no waiting for people to testify; they queued up. Work on the station went ahead and everywhere there was singing. They were tremendously thrilling days.

At the start, the work was mainly amongst Christians who had hidden unconfessed sin in their hearts and lives, secret drinking, hasty tempers, adultery, impure thoughts, prayerlessness, or coldness of heart. Many times as these things were laid open and confessed, my own conscience smote me. Were not the same things, certainly coldness, prayerlessness, and impatience, present in my own life? Yet I did not then find release and joy. I joined in their joy, but I held myself largely apart from the work of the Spirit. One

African confessed to exaggeration leading to untruthfulness, and I left the meeting bewildered and unhappy. I spoke to the Scholes. I confessed my own fear that I too exaggerated, possibly unintentionally, maybe in circular letters, more by what was omitted than by what was actually written. But I did not find peace and joy. My fellow-worker, Elizabeth Naganimi, deeply involved in the Revival, was radiant. Her shining love often rebuked me and I almost feared to be with her. She walked very closely with the Lord.

One day during this time, as the work of the Spirit spread all over our mission field, station after station sending in wonderful reports of His mighty dealings, John Mangadima, a student nurse at the Red Cross Pawa Hospital, arrived at Ibambi. He said simply that God had sent him to work with me in the church medical service. Later we heard of the great blessing he had been in the camp of leprosy patients at Pawa and of his shining testimony to the doctors there that earned him his dismissal. We also learnt of his quiet acceptance of God's ways. Through his testimony at the Government post where he went to have his labour card stamped and endorsed, a woman, Mama Damaris, was converted and brought to repentance and faith in Jesus Christ. She arrived at Ibambi next day with a glowing face. Asked where she came from, she could only say 'Hell'. Who are you? 'A woman from hell.' Where are you going? 'Heaven.' And the woman from hell joined our ranks to become in the years ahead our chief midwife in charge of the Nebobongo maternity unit.

In the three months before Christmas seven other senior schoolboys joined me at Ibambi, all keen to train as nurses. So was born the vision of the nurses' training school. As I toured our large field area, visiting eleven of our fifteen stations, I became more and more convinced that my main ministry must be to train Congolese nurses to run dispensaries and clinics at each station. They would be nurse-evangelists, preaching the gospel to their own people, gathered through their need for medical care and aid. 'Repairer of the breach.' This seemed clearly the meaning of the phrase which had been so prominent in my missionary call, to supply a Congolese medical service to their own people, staffed by keen, well-trained church workers, of a similar standing to the church, Bible-school-trained, evangelists.

In January 1954, we held our missionaries' conference at Ibambi, when all gathered together for prayer, Bible teaching, and spiritual refreshment, and to discuss our programme for the coming three years. I looked forward immensely to this gathering, and to meeting all my fellow workers. Yet I was not unconscious of underground tensions and a sense of anxiety. There were those amongst us who were not in sympathy with the way He had chosen to send and reveal revival power in our midst. There were personality clashes and hidden jealousies. There were determined views on many subjects that seemed not to be in accordance with the general policy.

During the conference, both Dr John Harris, who had arrived in Congo only four months after myself, and I were asked to give some idea of our medical vision and proposed programme. John was keenly interested in the welfare of leprosy patients throughout our area of responsibility. I was keenly interested in the training of national workers to accept this medical responsibility. We outlined our plans; we sought permission to go ahead. Then came the question: Where should the nurses' school be located? It seemed obvious to me (and therefore subconsciously I expected it to be obvious to everyone else!) that it should be at the centre, at Ibambi, where we were already firmly established. So it was a shock to realise that some were strongly opposed to having the medical centre stationed at Ibambi—anywhere else, at all costs! After hours of discussion, it was eventually agreed that it should be in the Ibambi area, but not actually at the station.

It was suggested we move it to Nebobongo, seven miles north, where for many years we had had a large camp for leprosy patients and maternity work.

I was somewhat stunned. I felt so sure it was not His will to make the medical centre a separate work from the Mission, under separate administration with all the problems that my quick mind could see clearly following such a move. However, I was encouraged to wait quietly and let the Lord resolve the problem in His own way and time. There was no immediate hurry.

I remember at that conference the wonderful daily Bible studies led by Jack Scholes, from the first eleven chapters of Leviticus on the four 'basic tenets' of the Mission: faith, holiness, sacrifice, and fellowship, as revealed in the sacrifices, the types of Calvary. One illustration which he used about a carpenter stands out clearly in my mind today. The man had completed preparations to make a cupboard, each board cut accurately to size, planed and aligned. Now he gathered up nails of various sizes and different heads, for the final assembly. Holes were bored to receive the heads: the nails were placed in position in turn, and then hammered home, covered over with wood filling, and the whole varnished, so that in the completed article no nail was seen, only the cupboard as a whole. Were we willing to be nails, in the hands of the Master Carpenter? Would we grumble at the painful blows of the hammer, or would we remember that the hammer was held by the nail-pierced hands? It was He, not our circumstances, nor our fellow-missionaries, who was choosing us to take our hidden place in His church.

The conference ended; days of tidying up followed; station routine recommenced. Then, on 20th January 1954 our nurses' school started, with a membership of eight. It was a very humble start. I was not fluent at Swahili, and used no French. The boys were from all different standards, from John

Mangadima who had done one year post-primary school and was keen to go ahead, to Joseph who had only completed 4th grade primary and been out of school for some years with practically no desire for academic advancement. I had no notes to help me, no idea of what such a course should include, no indication from the Government as to official standards or syllabus.

We built our first two wards, a lovely whitewashed mud building with a thick thatch and large shuttered windows. On one side was a twenty-four-bed ward for women and children, a hall for consultations and drug cupboards, and three small rooms, for maternity, minor surgery, or special cases. All these were to the right of our dispensary. On the left, we built a small eight-bed men's ward. The church members did most of the work, helped by nurses and patients. Catechists and evangelists came in to roof it. It was officially opened, named 'Bethany', and dedicated to the Lord's service in September 1954.

One day in this same month I was sitting on my verandah during the lunch-hour rest period when I was presented with a whimpering six-month-old baby, sturdy, healthy, but hungry! The agitated aged relative, who almost threw her at me, told me that her mother had died that morning. They had tried to bring her to me, but were prevented by flood-waters. He pleaded with me to adopt the child, so that she might be brought up to love the Lord. If I refused, her other relatives would take her and she might never hear the gospel. So 'Fibi' (Swahili version of Phoebe, 'moonshine', light reflected from the sun) entered my home and, in a few days, my heart, to become my own little girl. The sudden weaning, linked with my own ignorance of milk mixtures and sugar measures, led us into three dreadful weeks of endless crying, diarrhoea, skin rash, losing weight, and frantic disturbed nights. But slowly we got to know each other, and to enter on our new life together.

I was ill in late November with a severe attack of malaria. Elizabeth Naganimi took little Fibi, and from then on became her nanny, her most precious friend, her faithful tutor in things temporal and spiritual. I had to be at Bomili for Christmas, to attend the confinement of one of our missionaries, although I was hardly fit for the journey. On arrival, I developed jaundice, and an unhappy three weeks followed. So many memories crowd those days. I recall eating a red-hot pepper by mistake; the birth of a white baby in a village surrounded by forest, seventy miles from the nearest hospital should aid be needed. I remember the love of our Ibambi evangelists and their wives, eight families who were working in the Bomili area as missionaries, to help this much smaller church to get established.

So back to Ibambi for another year of work. The nurses' training school was going ahead. Arthur Scott, one of our missionaries who had trained in Belgium as a Health Officer, had sent me the notes he had prepared over the years for training African nurses. These, with Dr Chesterman's textbook for African dispensers, made the basis of our new textbook, painstakingly typed out for each of our eight students each evening for the following day's lectures. Then Miss Roupell, another missionary, became very ill. I drove her to Stanleyville, along three hundred miles of Congo roads, to have an electro-cardiogram and to see a heart specialist. After that we had a tremendous epidemic of infective hepatitis; then another of a severe kind of measles. Days were always full. But God gave the ability to cope with ever-increasing responsibilities. Greek traders brought their children to me with tonsillitis, or for general check-up during their school holidays. Africans poured in from every side, demanding a surgical service, midwifery care, eye specialist work, plus the multitudinous stream of medical cases. The work grew and grew; the vision clarified; I was happy.

In October 1955 five of my nursing students were ready to go for their state examinations. We were all terribly nervous! I managed to provide each of them with new khaki shorts, a shirt, and a clean white apron. I drove them up to Pawa in my Chevrolet van. They were subdued—very strange for Congolese! We were ushered into one of the rooms at the back of the large laboratory buildings where the Red Cross nurses had their schooling. There we were joined by some twelve of their students who were all talking off-handedly in French. Our boys felt awkward, knowing only the local Swahili. But they were the better dressed (small comfort to my heart)! A government doctor came from Wamba, eighty miles to the east; the Red Cross doctors were there, and myself. For their oral examination the boys came in singly, my students politely being offered first place. Each one had from five to fifteen minutes' questioning (in Swahili, I was relieved to hear) while the doctors chatted casually amongst themselves, and seemed to give scant attention to the answers. I dared not look at my boys. I was frightfully anxious they should do well. At last it was over and the results were read out. Yokana of Ibambi was first with 95 per cent! Mangadima was third with 85 per cent; two other Ibambi boys had passed, and one was deferred till next year's exams. It was wonderful news! We set off home, singing triumphantly the whole journey, wild with excitement.

Our medical service for the Congolese church was launched. Our first Africans were qualified as State assistant nurses. We were established! The future looked settled. I went to bed that night, radiantly happy, flushed with success, heady with the first draught of popularity.

7

Further Vistas

Christians often seem to have the impression that 'be-coming a missionary' is some form of metamorphosis by which a radical change of nature is achieved. Someone, possibly deeply stirred at a missionary meeting and challenged by the need of some less-privileged people, feels constrained to offer for overseas service. Almost inevitably this 'offering' comes to be regarded as a 'holy call' to a sacrificial vocation. The whole idea becomes wrapped in a veil of romantic splendour, so that even the candidate may fail to observe the unreality of it. The tendency of congregation and friends well-nigh to hero-worship the missionary only increases the dilemma. Looking at the situation honestly and critically, many may know that, mentally, physically, or spiritually, the candidate is unsuitable for missionary service. Some would-be candidates do not even have a burden of prayer for the peoples they hope to serve, nor have they ever sought to bring their immediate friends and neighbours in their own country to a knowledge of their Friend and Saviour, Jesus Christ. Yet they vaguely hope that as soon as they board the steamer or plane to take them to a foreign land, something mystical will occur and transform them into their image of a 'missionary'.

Nothing can be further from the truth! I believe that, at its simplest, a missionary is one sent by God to live a Christian life, usually amongst people other than his own. It is living which counts. This may include formal preaching, but it will certainly include personal relationships, and these often have to be worked out under most trying conditions. For example, many missionaries discover that it is far from easy to adapt themselves to a completely different climate. The native foods may be hard, not only on the digestive system, but also on the aesthetic tastes. The language barrier may constitute a difficult problem, especially in early years. One cannot choose one's friends. Two missionaries of vastly differing backgrounds, likes and dislikes, may be thrown together for several years with no choice of other companionship. One is often expected to do jobs for which one is not trained, and which may be actually distasteful. Yet in all this, one is called upon to reveal Christ, to live a Christ-like life, to be a 'missionary'.

It is then that one realises it is not the journey in the steamer that changes one's nature. I did not escape from myself by going to Congo. Rather, I came to know myself better, perhaps more as others had already seen me. The ordinary trials and frustrations of life that meet us all were just as real in Congo, and, in some ways, were more pronounced, as there were fewer ways of avoiding or circumventing them. For myself, it was only as I allowed the Lord to show me my own pettiness, or wilfulness, or pride, in different circumstances and problems, that I became willing to let the Lord teach me of Himself. 'Take my yoke upon you, and learn of me', the Lord said, 'for I am meek and lowly in heart.' What happened in the two years following my first taste of success as a missionary doctor shows simply how very much I had to learn of Him, for surely no-one merited the description of Christ-likeness less than I, if it was to involve the phrase 'meek and lowly in heart'.

The day after I returned from taking my students to Pawa for their State nursing examination, Jack Scholes came over to the dispensary to see me at midday. He informed me that the Mission field committee, then in session at Ibambi for their quarterly meeting, felt that the time had come to implement the suggestion made the previous year at the field conference that the medical programme of the Mission should be run from Nebobongo. They would like me to make preparations to move there that week.

I felt as though I had been slapped in the face. Stunned by the sudden overwhelming realization of what this decision would involve, battle royal raged in my heart. Standing surrounded by my first achievements—nurses, buildings, outpatients—I envisaged the gruelling task ahead, and resented the apparent thoughtlessness and thanklessness of this demand, coming at this particular moment. Rebellion flared up within me, and I determined to withstand what I felt was a bigoted, even stupid, committee blunder, sure in my own soul that it was totally detrimental to the over-all vision of God's will and pattern for the Mission medical service.

Mr Scholes agreed to my impassioned demand that I might come over and see the committee that evening. All day the fire smouldered in my heart. My mind seethed with bitter criticism against the 'committee', unhappy in the certain knowledge that the decision was made, in part at least, because of personal antagonisms. I therefore felt quite justified in arguing that it was not in His will. With the clinics finished, hospital clean, school over, I washed and changed, going over and over what I intended to say. My arguments and proofs were all ready. I thought I knew what they would reply, and I had already planned how I would prove their arguments false. A fellow-missionary who was staying in my home at the time tried to calm me down, but I was in no mood to listen. I went across the compound, seething and unhappy.

I had to wait. Mrs Scholes suggested we pray together. Never! Pray? With my heart aflame and my tongue poised for battle? Impossible! Quietly, she herself knelt and prayed for me out loud. Slowly the fire died out, a hopeless helplessness flooded me, a feeling of 'very small littleness', and I began to see the pointlessness of battle. Then she talked with me, of Jesus, and His deep, deep love: 'He that toucheth you toucheth the apple of his eye' (Zech 2:8). It was not the committee, not a group of fellow-missionaries, but the Lord Himself—through them, it was true—who was sending me to Nebobongo. He had a great purpose, possibly a difficult, even dangerous, way; but He would go with me. At Ibambi He could not do for me what He wanted to do, to make me 'more like Jesus'. It was His hand, His nail-pierced hand, that held the hammer (even the committee!) to fulfil His purpose, to drive the nail fully home to take its place in the building of His church: 'All things work together for good to them that love God, to them who are the called according to his purpose' (Rom. 8:28). When called to the committee, I listened quietly to their proposals and was given the grace to agree. And looking back now, how glad I am that the Lord overruled and constrained me to obey.

On 30th October 1955, I left Ibambi in the Mission truck with all my possessions to go seven miles north to Nebobongo to take over the responsibility of station leadership and the development of a Mission medical service. Evangelist Agoya and his wife Taadi, with their six children, went with me. They had had to return to Ibambi from their work at Bomili after eighteen months' missionary service as Taadi was desperately ill with her sixth pregnancy, and we had grown very close to each other, as sisters in the Lord, during those anxious months.

So started a new life. Mr and Mrs Coleman and their young family had left for furlough the previous week after caring for Nebobongo for a couple of years. I joined Florence Stebbing, a capable nurse and midwife, who had already had some four or five years' service at Nebobongo. The work generally was in a discouraging state. In 1953, the Belgian Red Cross Hospital at Pawa had closed the large and flourishing leprosy colony that Mission nurses had supervised at Nebobongo since 1940, taking over a thousand of the camp family to their own new centre, some nine miles further north. The remaining two hundred patients had scattered to surrounding villages, refusing to be coerced to this Roman Catholic hospital, preferring to forgo treatment. The beautiful colony, with its rows of homes, neatly-laid-out gardens, and flourishing acres of food crops had reverted to jungle. There was almost nothing left to be seen of it. The station workmen, many of them previous camp patients, were drifting away, as Nebobongo was no longer considered a treatment centre. However, the small, neat, brick-built maternity unit, with its ten beds and well-equipped labour ward, continued, due to Florence's constant care and love, staffed by a group of pupil midwives whom she trained with endless patience.

There was also the orphanage, consisting of two long, low, brick buildings, filled with small wooden beds, each with a separate room at one end for the five Christian women who cared for the thirty-eight noisy, happy toddlers! What a sight to see them all in an open verandah, on forms by the low wooden tables, with folded hands and bowed heads singing 'Grace' before the steaming bowls of rice, plantains, and manioc leaf were handed round! They were all ages, from nought to ten, most of them dressed in bright-coloured cotton rompers. Each of the five women carried on her hip, slung from one shoulder, one of the newest arrivals, still bottle-fed.

The station layout was interesting. Our land lay all to the north of the Paulis-Ibambi road, half a mile of road-frontage on a sharp bend. Opposite us, to the south, was forest and dense undergrowth, sloping away down to a stream and marshland. Florence took me on a tour of inspection. We started at the Paulis (eastern) end of the roadway. All the land to our right was cleared, rising from us in a fairly steep embankment to a half-mile-long, flat plateau-top, parallel with the road, 120 yards back, and mostly only about 50 to 70 yards wide before falling away again, plunging downhill at both ends to streams and freshwater springs, and centrally leading away to the old colony for leprosy patients. We left the road by the first entrance, and climbed up to a very nice, almost square, brick-built home with grass thatch roof where Florence was living. It had four rooms, a kitchen and bathroom and, out behind, a cookhouse. Walking along the plateau-top, westwards, we looked down the steep hill to our right to the African workmen's village, some twelve homes, many of them urgently needing repairs or renewal. To our left there was a large mud-hut home where maternity patients waited for their babies, and this house, too, was obviously in very bad repair. Continuing to our right, we passed a lovely church building, low brick walls and pillars, and newly thatched, standing on the rough cement floor of the old home of the founder of the leprosy colony, Mrs Edith Moules, who had started the work at Nebobongo in 1940. The church could seat about eighty to ninety, and was also used for primary schooling for the orphans. A few were in there as we passed, being taught the rudiments of reading, writing, and arithmetic by one of the pupil midwives. But one had the impression that teacher did not know much more than those taught, and probably very little was getting across. So we came to the maternity compound, with brick-built, grass-thatched buildings for normal and infected cases, and houses for the midwives.

The station was divided into two by the road that ran north-south through the middle, from the main road back to the old leprosy colony. Crossing this, we came to the second large European home, where I was now to be installed—a house with some eight rooms and bathroom, and a verandah. There were no Africans living within hailing distance of either of our homes; our cooks and their families lived down in the village. Opposite my home, across the wide drive, there was a coffee plantation (where today the primary school stands). Further westwards was a large open courtyard, with two long, low dormitories for the orphans, their kitchen, and the open verandah for meals. On again, we came to a long narrow stretch of level wasteland.

We went to inspect the water supplies, scrambling down to the streams through rough undergrowth, along narrow muddy tracks. They were in bad shape, dirty, overgrown, full of insects, the sure source of sickness. We made our way towards the leprosy colony, but all was overgrown. Even the roads were hard to decipher in the new jungle, and we stumbled home not a little discouraged.

That evening, I met the whole family in church for a welcome meeting. We eyed each other speculatively. My mind was full of housing problems, water supplies, feeding, clothing, administration, sanitation, counting how many there were and trying to calculate what it was going to entail. They for their part were wondering if I would stay, whether they were going to have security again and jobs, if I would work in with them or shout at them and throw my weight about. But slowly, together, we thawed out towards one another, and it would seem that we all decided that first evening to trust Him to work it out for us, to unite us as one family and make a success of the new venture.

Next day, with Agoya and two of the senior station workmen, we got down to it. We walked all over the ground a hundred times, with paper and pencil and tape-measure. We drew up plans and discarded them, and started all over again. Eventually, it began to take shape and a new vision crystallised I sent a message to the church elders responsible for the work in our area, asking them to meet with us and discuss our plans. First, we wanted them to seek out relatives for as many of the orphans as possible, or else Christian friends who would adopt them into their homes, as we felt that to make a start with the hospital, we must take over their buildings and build more around them in that courtyard. Second, we wanted to build a completely new workmen's village in a healthier spot, on the long level stretch of wasteland at the western end of the station. Third, we wanted them to find us a teacher for our children, the orphans who would stay with us, the children of the evangelist and the workmen and the nurses. Fourth, we wanted them to find us a team of eight willing Christian workmen to make bricks down at the old brick-kiln, ready for new hospital buildings.

They agreed, and we all set to with a will clearing land, cleaning water-holes, digging new toilets, planting food gardens. It all took time, and it was a full year before we began to see results for all our labour. We made many mistakes, needless to say: sharpening the teeth of the long double-handed saw without setting them first, for instance; building the firing-holes in the kiln too widely spaced so that they fell in, so losing us 17,000 of our first 22,000 bricks; miscalculating the volume of hewn trees for kiln firewood on the Government return sheets involving us in tremendous expense; building a new dispensary as a roof on pillars only, with no walls, so that it was blown away in the first hurricane storm. But we learnt!

There were more serious mistakes, too. Out of twelve orphan children who were taken home to Christian relatives or adopted into various homes, eight came back to us, unhappy and underfed, and we had to re-think our programme for them. We realised that we could not sacrifice them to the cause of progress in another direction. We were unable to obtain a school teacher for them, so I taught them myself for three hours every morning. But I taught them as I knew how, and when they took exams to go to the central Mission primary school at Ibambi, to pass up from our grade 3 to their grade 4, they all failed. I had used English methods and these were unacceptable in a Belgian colony.

Letters came from other missionaries asking why I couldn't visit their stations, as I was the Mission's doctor, not just Nebobongo's. I regret to say I was annoyed and wrote indignant replies reminding them that they had sent me to Nebo, and pointing out that having, as I did, station responsibility, I was up to my eyes in work—administrative, building, and educational, as well as medical. I urgently needed a chauffeur-mechanic to relieve me of all the endless driving for weekly food-markets, and for emergency patients. One day a young man arrived with his wife and two little boys from the Wamba station, saying he had heard I needed a chauffeur and he wished to offer for the job. We were thrilled! We showed him a house in our new village, and everyone welcomed the family and helped them to settle in. Next day at morning prayers, there was a call for the ambulance. I called Daniel to me, passed him the car keys, named a student nurse to go with him, and gave him the scribbled note of appeal with the address. He just stood and looked at me. 'Well', I asked, 'what do you want?' I then discovered he had never even sat in a car before! He had come to be taught to be a chauffeur mechanic! He learnt, and I learnt a lot too, in order to teach him! But he became my most valued friend during the next three years and an extremely good chauffeur.

More serious still, I was working almost round the clock. My days began at 5.30 a.m. in the hospital wards, and rarely finished before 10.30 p.m. in the office. In addition, there were frequent night calls, emergencies that broke in upon an already tightly packed programme, operative responsibilities that sorely tried me and left me tired and worn out afterwards. As a direct consequence my quiet times alone with God in the morning, drawing fresh strength and inspiration and guidance, began to peter out. I still did regular Bible study as I taught for three-quarters of an hour every morning in church before the day's work began. But it was becoming automatic. The joy was slipping away. The desire for prayer fellowship with whites or Africans began to fade. One knows how closely physical tiredness and spiritual ill-health are linked, and this tiredness faces so many missionaries who have to cope with the problems of under-staffing and overworking.

Little things began to make me irritable. I remember one day, a Thursday, when I did an eye-clinic in the morning at 9 a.m. I had got the house ready, darkened rooms, instruments out, and two patients came. After they had gone, I waited a little while, had coffee, and then another came. After that, and a further wait, I cleared up everything and prepared to go to the hospital for ward-rounds. At midday an old lady was led to the verandah of my home. My houselad came to tell me that she wanted her eyes tested. I was annoyed and asked where she came from. It was from a nearby village, so I refused to see her, saying she could have been in time for the 9 a.m. clinic and must come back next week. I turned away and went in for my lunch.

Shortly afterwards, my senior dresser, John Mangadima, came to me. He was grieved, and rebuked me for turning the old lady away. 'Could you not see that she was blind? She has waited all morning at the roadside for someone to come to lead her to the Christian doctor who heals people. She is a soul for whom Christ died, and you have harshly turned her away. Would He have done so?' Since then, I have always lifted my heart in a quick, silent prayer as I go to answer the door, that I may receive every visitor, whatever the hour, in His name and for His sake, showing His love and gentle kindliness and courtesy.

Meanwhile the work grew on all sides. We urgently needed extensions in the maternity compound where some forty babies were being born each month and some twelve pupil midwives were in training with three qualified girls in charge. We urgently needed more room in the hospital compound. By this time we had two wards, one with eighteen beds in it for women and children, and one with eight beds for men, yet we often had as many as fifty patients at a time needing hospital care. The out-patients had to be seen on the verandah, sometimes as many as 150 at a time, with nowhere to sit for morning prayers, or for treatments, and no shelter when it rained. The other building, which acted as laboratory, pharmacy, theatre, and a place for sundry other 'odd jobs', leaked badly and also needed a damp-course built in.

We had no hospital village for the countless patients who came from far-distant places and needed daily clinic treatments. Our own new station village was growing apace; there were already two neat rows of eight houses each. But the number of student nurses and young workmen grew faster than the village. We had several acres of land under cultivation, with large crops of peanuts and rice, manioc and plantains, paw-paws and pineapples. But still we had to buy nearly one ton of food each week for our ever-growing family. Once again, we had over thirty orphans in our care, but at least two of the women who cared for them were now too old, and really too weak, to continue their work of drawing water, cutting firewood, and endless laundry and ironing, cooking and feeding, as well as mothering and spiritual care.

We now had over thirty children of primary school age in the four first grades, as well as twenty student nurses in the three years of their course; and all the teaching fell on me! The administrative work, involving government forms, accounts, reports, letters, grew at about the same pace, and yet all had to be done somehow, usually after 10 o'clock in the evening, often with many mistakes made through sheer weariness. But where could one call a halt? To which department could one say 'No'? Everyone had a claim. Needs abounded; our reputation had grown particularly for eye clinics and maternity work and tuberculosis, and patients came to us from as much as 400 miles away. Could we refuse them?

It is easy for Christians at the home base to say that a missionary should not do too much, and should take one day off in seven. In theory, we all agree. But when one is a doctor, single-handed, with no other medical help for 50 or even 150 miles in any direction, it is hard to put into practice. How urgently every missionary society needs new recruits to share the work-load. This would seem to be the only practical solution to this world-wide problem.

Others argue that missions should not tackle institutional work, such as schools and hospitals, but leave these to the government. In our area, and in many, many others, this would merely mean that thousands of children would have no schooling, and thousands of patients would die each year, as the government just has not enough skilled and trained servants, nor a sufficiently stable economy, to begin to shoulder the work of this vast responsibility, willing though they may be.

In January 1957, we had another triennial field conference, this time with a difference—our African church elders were to take part with us. The conference was to be bilingual. Bangala and Swahili were to be used for the joint meetings of Africans and Europeans; but other meetings would be held separately to discuss specifically church (African) or Mission (European) matters, bringing together the findings at the next joint meeting. Dr Harris and I both presented medical reports, and then the southern group of churches added an urgent plea concerning their need for a medical service in the south, particularly requesting a general surgical service. After much prayer and discussion it was suggested that Dr Harris should come south from Malingwia to join me at Nebobongo. There he would train me in surgery, and then I would leave him at Nebo, and go south myself to start again a similar work for the churches there.

After the conference had ended, Florence Stebbing went on furlough. John and Elsie Harris joined me at Nebobongo for a brief week, with Joy and Cyril Taylor and their two little boys. Then they all left for their different stations, and I was alone. It was a strange feeling, but I loved it! For one thing, it was a tremendous challenge. Could one cope with the multitudinous tasks alone, and keep all the services going smoothly? By the Lord's strength and enabling, yes! And with it all, I found full scope for such determination and vision and administrative ability as I might have. But I do not doubt that it made me selfish. I had no need to consult with others, nor to consider their desires or feelings. I had no time-table to keep except my own. I had no need to be careful not to over-drive others. I could work at the pace I preferred. My African team worked willingly with me, each in his own department pulling his weight and doing his job, so that the whole machine rolled smoothly on. I felt a great glow of pleasure and pride. But with it there was an uncomfortable pricking of conscience that this was to my glory and not necessarily His. I was proud of them, each one of the big family, and they were mine—my nurses, my workmen, my hospital, my vision. And He had to teach me that they were His.

Ruth Dyer, another woman missionary, joined me for two months to do language study as she was moving from the northern to the southern area of our field, and also to be my companion. We were very happy together, and she helped me tremendously in preparing for the arrival of Dr Harris and his family. There was sandpapering and revarnishing of furniture, doors, and windows, painting woodwork, supervising the workmen in distempering the big house. We did each room in a different pastel shade, using methylene blue, mercurochrome, malachite green, and flavine from the dispensary to stir into the baths of whitewash! They looked first-rate, the colours giving it a really professional touch. The Harrises were expected on Tuesday, 2nd May. We killed a chicken and prepared a feast. They didn't come. Ruth left me that week. I thought we must have got the week wrong, so next Tuesday we killed another chicken and prepared another feast. Still they didn't come. The next Tuesday I felt I couldn't go on killing precious chickens, so we did nothing—and they came!

On 16th May 1957, just as dusk was falling, they drove in. I was in the hospital with an emergency case—a man had been carried in with a horribly torn foot. As light was failing, and it was nearly supper-time, and I was tired (we can always make lots of excuses!) I hadn't lit the pressure lamps in the hospital, but was working in the half-light on the verandah outside, in most unhygienic conditions, and in a most unmedical manner. The first thing I knew of their arrival was when Dr Harris walked up behind me. I felt my pride fizzle out of me. I was caught doing everything just as one shouldn't do it!

8

SLIPPING BACK

Next day Dr Harris and I walked round the whole site together as I showed him all aspects of the work. At midday we went to his home for family dinner, and I saw that, except beneath the pictures, all our beautiful colours had completely disappeared, bleached out by the sun. And I had a slight premonition that this might be a picture of myself. After lunch we gathered together for prayer and discussion, and to seek for a happy division of labour. In the evening we had fellowship with the church elders and laid before them our suggestions. Thus I officially handed over the leadership of the hospital to Dr Harris.

How hard it came to me! Little had I realised how utterly Nebobongo made up my life, how each workman, each nurse, each child had curled themselves into my heart as part of my family. And now, officially, they were no longer mine. For the next year I fought out this fight, and through it found myself in depths of despair, seeing myself as a failure, useless, realizing that I had built the work around myself, and my personality, and my vision, instead of on Him. Mine was written on everything, instead of His. And how deeply it hurt, as, gently and lovingly, He had to prise my hands off His treasured possession.

There seemed to be endless frustrations. I had grown to love the liberty of leadership, the joy of working a thing out and seeing it through and making a go of it. But now I was once more just a junior missionary, and my ideas did not always make sense to those working with me. Through the past eighteen months I had learnt a good deal about administration—in my own way! But book-keeping and office work were certainly not my strong points. What the fourteen different books said should be in the fourteen different accounts corresponded to what could be found in the fourteen carefully labelled porridge-oats tins. But how I achieved this was not always so clear! Those who took over from me had somewhat more accurate views and more accurate methods, and doubtless suffered many headaches in sorting out and clarifying many mysterious entries. But it was not by any means easy to accept the very definite change in emphasis regarding financial affairs. I had felt so clearly led through the years in what I called a 'Muller' practice. As God gave a vision, I would seek from Him the tenth part of the needed finance to see the project through, and then launch out in faith, trusting Him for the rest to come in as it was needed. Now I had to toe the line, so to speak, to a very different method of working, though doubtless it was the more usually acceptable. Now we asked the Lord to provide all that was necessary for a project before commencing work on it.

No doubt I was something of a visionary, and all my hard work and labours were working to one end, the fulfilment of a very clear vision of what I felt was Congo's greatest need, particularly in our north-eastern Province. I wanted to see bush clinics every fifteen to twenty miles, looked after by well-trained African dressers, where preventive medicine, child welfare clinics, ante-natal clinics, and school-children clinics could form the prominent part of the work, along with the early diagnosis and prompt treatment of all the current endemic diseases, tuberculosis, malnutrition, leprosy, intestinal worms, etc. This could be followed by immediate transference to the centre for any not responding promptly to treatment. I longed to be freed from the central work, so that I could set up and organise, and then regularly visit, clinics such as these. I felt that they would need a fort-nightly oversight at the start. The people of an area would be told what day and time the doctor was expected and could gather at church centres where the local catechist or evangelist would buy up the opportunity with the ministry of the Word of God. I personally had little interest in the hospital routine work, feeling that there were several government and Red Cross hospitals in the area which these clinics could use, especially for surgery. So the nurses' training school at Nebobongo had developed with this special emphasis, the preparing of young men to carry the responsibilities of bush clinics, both as evangelists and as medical dressers.

Now, however, a change came, and I was not willing to recognise the vision of another if it did not happen to coincide with my own. And what a continual cause of friction in church and Mission this attitude can be! Many in the Mission, and this certainly included the majority on the committee, felt that an established central work with proper surgical facilities was of greater importance than a string of 'inefficient clinics'. If I must travel, they said, why not tour the Mission stations, and help the other European nurses who were struggling to keep small hospitals and maternities going throughout our area with very little outside medical help or encouragement? Under pressure, I agreed to do a six-monthly tour of the stations, involving a five hundred miles' circle to the south and a similar circle to the north, in a huge figure of eight. But our vehicle was old and not really road worthy; the roads were shocking, and the first tour coincided with the height of the wet season. When eventually I got home, I felt utterly exhausted and depressed and discouraged. We had had endless difficulties with the car; two nights had been spent on the roadside; the response had been poor with only very small clinics at each place; the financial outlay had been very considerable, and I felt it just was not worth it. But the real cause of my depression was simply that I could not put my heart into backing up the vision of others when I felt it ran contrary to my own. I had certainly not learnt the grace sufficient for every need, nor the joy of being spent for Him in just any way that He might direct.

Back at Nebobongo the hospital was being developed, particularly on the surgical side, and much attention was being paid to the efficient training of the nurses ('male ward orderlies' is probably a more accurate description of our lads!) in ward care and technique. I continued with the school teaching, but now I had to learn to work with others. I found I couldn't have the lads just when I wanted them; they might well be involved in a ward-round, or even in theatre. Nor could I keep them late in school as I often did in the past, for other folk had their timetables to arrange as well. In my heart, I fought against these changes. Dr Harris would invite me to carry my share of the work in the hospital and to join him in the theatre, as had been planned at the field conference, so that I could learn surgery with him before going south. God overruled and undertook for us, but there is no denying that it was a stormy year! So many times my spirit rebelled. I was quick and impulsive, where my colleague was slow and methodical. Our African fellow-workers were quick to spot the lack of cooperation and failure in agreement on many matters, and some would have played us off the one against the other.

The sense of frustration and of failure grew. The devil made accusations on every level. My free, happy, outgoing love to the Africans was turned against me in my heart as I began to feel that I loved them more than my own white fellow-workers. I loved to go and spend a weekend with Pastor Ndugu in the bush, sharing his home and meals just as though I was one of the family, and found that I enjoyed it more than being invited to another missionary's home. My heart accused me on the level of Christian living. I was so often irritable, and there were even occasions when temper flared up inside me as I felt that a faithful African fellow-worker had been misjudged or wrongly treated. My heart seemed so hard. I was so often critical and proud in my outlook. Along with this my communion with the Lord shrivelled, prayer became a formality, Bible reading a burden. I longed for liberation and peace and joy.

This sense of frustration need never have occurred had we been more willing to recognise each other's gifts. Life would have been easier if we had all realised that one approach may be needed for a pioneer work starting almost from scratch, but that other methods may be required as the work becomes established and less makeshift. Surely we all know that God has His pioneers; but He also has His consolidators. And it might have been easier for both of us if we had not tried to mix our differing gifts, but had each been given separate opportunities for their fulfilment.

Be that as it may, in my own eyes I felt again that I was a failure: empty, cold, unreal. It seemed I was putting on an act, with mixed motives, and deep in my heart, cold doubt began to rear its head. I faced again the old taunting of the devil. Are you really saved? Could you be so hard and critical, could you lose your temper, could you be so jealous of another, if the Lord Jesus was really dwelling in you? You preach it all, but you don't live it. It isn't real! With my white fellow-workers I felt keenly frustrated. The root cause was misunderstanding. I felt they were critical and had misjudged much of the work just on the reports of others without coming to see it first hand. Equally, I felt a growing barrier with my African friends, since I feared to share with them in the freedom of previous years, sensing that my somewhat unconventional approach only served to increase 'white' antagonism. And so I felt alienated almost from God Himself. There seemed to be no contact, just a sad yearning and loneliness.

One morning, I was taking morning prayers with our Nebobongo family, reading from Philippians 3:1-11. I chalked a large red cross on the blackboard, and listed on the left all the things man counted dear unto himself—public opinion, popularity, worldly wealth, security, etc. Above this I wrote the word 'dung'. To the right I placed the words, 'That I may know Him.' Suddenly the Holy Spirit came down on the congregation, and with much crying many made their way to the front and got right with God. The move started amongst the pupil midwives, but spread rapidly to the student nurses and workmen. My heart cried out to God. How could I be used in this manner to bring others to the foot of the cross, to repentance, to joy of salvation, and all the time my own heart was so cold and untouched? I turned to the African elders and blurted out the depths of my own needs. Then I rushed from the church. Back in my own home I threw myself on the ground in a desperate, frantic plea before God for His mercy and grace to be extended to myself also.

The work of God continued in the church for several hours, amidst strong tears and joyous singing. Pastor Ndugu was passing through Nebobongo on his bicycle on his way to Ibambi, and hearing the noise, went to the church to see what was happening. There the church elders told him what had occurred and described how I had left the church. He came to see me. Quietly he sat beside me and listened to my broken, somewhat incoherent outburst. Then he left and continued on his way to Ibambi. That afternoon he returned, went to see Dr Harris and then came across to see me. He had Mr Scholes's permission to take me away to his home village for a week or so. He just told me to pack a haversack and get my bicycle, and together we cycled the sixteen miles to his village. There he gave me a room in his house-and there followed seven days of prayer and fasting. At first the heavens seemed as brass, the Bible cold and meaningless. By Sunday evening, I felt I could bear no more of it. If the Lord did not meet with me I would accept that I was a castaway. I would continue my ministry to the African church as a teacher for the nurses, I would continue to teach the Word of God which I never for a moment doubted to be the absolute and certain truth, but I would not accept a missionary's allowance. I joined the Pastor and his wife round the fire, out in the verandah, as the others of the village scattered to their homes at about 10 p.m. We sat in silence, a silence you could feel, almost hear. As they earnestly prayed, slowly the Spirit of God reached through into my heart and broke down the barriers of pride, the frigid restraint, and revealed so much of self. He helped me to unburden my heart, to reveal all the rottenness and sense of failure, the fears and criticisms, the pride and selfishness. Then, so gently and quietly, Pastor Ndugu took up my words, point by point, and led me to look away from myself to the Christ of Calvary. He dealt with the need of restitution on certain points, the need of apologizing and asking forgiveness on certain others, and a great calm came.

Four amazing days followed, spent in the presence of the Lord. It is hard to describe or put on paper the preciousness of that week, spent alone, utterly given over to the influence of the Holy Spirit speaking through the pages of Holy Scripture. My mind seemed to be more crystal-clear than I had ever known. I felt no need of sleep; I had no consciousness of hunger, nor of any bodily pain or discomfort. There was a tremendous, overwhelming sense of His presence, a deep awe and wonder, I felt caught up, as it were. Even time seemed to pass with no reality. I met Him. There was little or no emotional involvement. But there was a great sense of eternal reality, of light, of truth.

I remember cycling back to Nebobongo early Monday morning to be in time for a new week in school and wondering how to share with my African friends what the Lord had done for me. When I arrived, there were three senior student nurses on the verandah. They came over to take my bicycle and haversack, and at once began praising the Lord and shaking my hand as they saw the light of happiness in my eyes! I didn't have to say anything. Then they told me that for four years, ever since 1953 when the Lord first started to pour out revival blessing on the church, they had been praying daily for me that I would let the Lord work in my heart as He had in theirs. What faithful, loving friends surrounded me.

This was not the end of the battle—by no means! It might almost be called preparation for the next round. During the next few months the devil sought every means of causing dissension and discouragement as he so often does when we seek to make a new beginning with God. On every side, I felt his attacks. I felt I was almost too tired to continue to accept the pressure of medical responsibility, and at times I felt that I would gladly have continued as a missionary if it could be without the title of doctor. I could never get away from myself or my responsibilities. Wherever I went, I was still the doctor and a crowd of patients would gather. A weekend off duty simply was not possible, and yet it was becoming very necessary after five years' steady work. I was tired of sharing my home with one and another, and the lack of privacy that this involved. And yet I felt deeply convicted by my attitude, knowing how readily others had shared their homes with me. I still felt misunderstood and criticised (possibly where nothing was intended) concerning my manner of living and eating, my friendship and unity with the Africans, my passionate desire for the setting up of the mobile village ministry, and other issues.

Added to all this, news from my dear mother and family was not happy at this time, and my heart ached to be back in England, possibly to give my mother a home, and to care for her and love her. No doubt sheer physical weariness at the end of five years of intensive work added to the struggle. I was also very hard at work trying to complete a textbook for the nurses' school in Swahili before going on furlough—typing out the manuscript, correcting proofs, preparing stencils, duplicating some hundred copies of each page, and then putting them together for our Mission press to bind.

I had eventually received permission to commence village clinics. Now that Dr Harris was also at Nebobongo to carry responsibility for the hospital and station work, I had opened forty clinics covering a four-hundred-mile circular tour. Alternate weeks I spent on the station, teaching nurses and primary school, and helping in hospital and maternity work. The weeks in between I spent out in the district visiting these forty clinics, seeing up to 2,500 patients a week, preaching the gospel, healing the sick, training catechists in the simple use of twelve medicines left in their care at each of these centres. Much though I loved this programme, as others had foreseen and warned, it was tremendously tiring and exacting and should never have been commenced at the end of one's term of service.

During the last months before furlough, Susan came into my life and home. She was a foster-child of Pastor Ndugu, a girl about sixteen years old. Owing to the fact that she had been expelled for persistently breaking school rules, she had only had about four years of primary school teaching. Following this she lived for several years with her foster-parents in the village, rebellious and hard. At last she had responded to the claims of the Lord on her life, and came to Nebobongo to train as a midwife. But within three months, she had been found to have the dreaded marks of leprosy. It nearly broke her heart and we had a hard battle to hold on to her for the Lord. At last He won, and she agreed to come and live with me and to help in the home, whilst attending classes with the other pupils, but sitting apart. We became very close friends and I shall never forget the wonderful early morning hours, spent round the fire with cups of coffee, studying the Word and praying together. We worked together through the first three books of the Bible, preparing notes in Swahili for a future commentary for the church. At this time also I was invited again to take morning prayers on the station, and it was a great joy to study and search out, and then present, the great truths of Scripture through the Letter to the Colossians, an hour a day for three months.

Then in June 1958, my brother and his wife and son prepared to visit me, as they were travelling home to England for a year's leave after nine years in South Africa. Great preparations were made to receive them! Susan and I travelled all one night to Stanleyville to meet them at the airfield. They were unfortunately delayed, and after waiting forty-eight hours for them, I set out on the return journey the following evening. Many advised me to wait till morning, but I was impatient. I drove all night and at 5 a.m. we left the road as I fell asleep at the wheel. By God's grace we were not killed, although the van was wrecked. After several hours of shock, I was helped by kind friends who took me back home and cared for me.

That Sunday, there were farewell services at Nebobongo as I was to leave for furlough within ten days. Pastor Ndugu preached amongst others and I shall not easily forget his gentle, gracious rebuke. He preached on Haggai 1:5-6:

'Consider your ways. Ye have sown much, and bring in little; ye eat, but ye have not enough; ye drink, but ye are not filled with drink; ye clothe you, but there is none warm; and he that earneth wages earneth wages to put it into a bag with holes.' I know that he was not preaching at me, but nevertheless I felt it nearly summed up my five years in Congo, especially my ministry at Nebobongo. There had been endless hours of sowing, yet what was there to show for it? I thought of all the love and advice and godly wisdom that had surrounded me, yet how had I benefited from it? Had it not run out as money through holes in the pocket?

My brother and family came the next Monday, and we had a marvellous three or four days together, using Philip Ndugu's car to show them all round our area. Everywhere we went they were given a tremendous welcome. They left on their way home to England on the Friday morning, and the following week I also left by air for my first furlough. I had a month at home with my mother before entering the Tropical Hospital for treatment for chronic amoebic dysentery, and later for an appendectomy. I was very ill during the initial treatment. Due to this illness, and the heavy sedation I was being given, plus the great weariness after five years of missionary service, I allowed myself again to become depressed. I still had not learnt how closely linked are physical and spiritual health. This all-too-simple ruse of Satan to call reaction "failure" seemed to catch me out each time in seasons of strain and weariness.

Whilst in hospital, I received a letter from my sister Diana. She was a nun in an Anglican enclosed order, a contemplative community. She had had special permission to write to me when they heard how ill I was, and sent, under constraint of the Holy Spirit, a few verses from Hosea 2:14-16: 'Therefore, behold, I will allure her and bring her into the wilderness, and speak comfortably unto her. And I will give her her vineyards from thence, and the valley of Achor for a door of hope: and she will sing there, as in the days of her youth, and as in the day when she came up out of the land of Egypt. And it shall be at that day, saith the Lord, that thou shalt call me Ishi; and shalt call me no more Baali.' These were not verses that would normally be chosen to send to someone sick in hospital, but without doubt, they were the verses the Lord had chosen for me, to wake me from a state of lethargy, and to deliver me from this frequent accusation of the devil about being a castaway. 'The valley of Achor for a door of hope.' It was a great promise looking forward to future triumph. In the valley of Achor, Joshua had dealt drastically with Achan's sin, the disobedience which had brought defeat on the children of Israel as they pressed forward into Canaan following the victory at Jericho. The cause of their defeat was put out of the camp and faith in God for future victory was restored. So God's judgments become the gateway through which we enter into His promises and go on to possess our own inheritance in Him.

Immediately following my five weeks in hospital, I embarked on a series of deputation meetings covering a large area of the British Isles. It lasted for twelve packed weeks, and I loved every moment of it! We were so busy I had not time for introspection! I was extremely nervous at every meeting, and felt a great burden to find the Lord's mind and message each day. But He blessed abundantly. I spoke mainly about the Revival, but often told also my own testimony, how hardness of heart and pride had held me back from entering into the full blessing for four long years, but how eventually, through the ministry of Africans, He broke my pride and dealt with me also. Many people were challenged during those weeks of meetings, and several testified that their lives had been completely changed as they met anew with the Lord. I was wonderfully happy; but once again, my personality being what it was, I found success and popularity going to my head. All the time I had to watch and pray that my rejoicing should be only in Him.

The following Christmas, at a Graduates' Fellowship Conference at Swanwick, through the prayerful interest of a doctor friend, I was put in touch with the Mildmay Mission Hospital in Bethnal Green, East London, and in February started there as a Houseman and Casualty Officer. It was strange being back in an English hospital, and not a little terrifying. Almost immediately, we were in the throes of an influenza epidemic. All hospital beds were taken over for the acute chest cases and many elderly people died. We seemed to be on duty almost twenty-four hours at a stretch, and I found I was working longer and more tiring hours even than in Congo! Time for quiet and prayer in the early morning was almost non-existent. I was often too tired, and fell asleep when I tried to pray. How common an experience amongst Christian Housemen! It is well for us to remember that God understands and that a quiet time of a particular length and pattern is not a kind of magic formula, the one essential mark of the keen Christian. Rather, it is the spiritual attitude of heart and mind that counts and sustains at such periods. I loved the work, and threw myself wholeheartedly into every part of it, including ward services and prayers for the out-patients down in Casualty. I made every effort to be absolutely conscientious in my work for each of the different consultants who visited the hospital and was pleased when they seemed satisfied. Once again, I was driven forward by the desire to be a success.

This was a time when I began to look back and to compare the work I was doing at Mildmay with that in the Congo. Also I began to receive a monthly cheque for the very first time in my life! This brought a sense of security. I could buy things for my mother and her home; I could plan for us to go on holiday together. I was also putting aside for my return to the Congo, and sending monthly gifts to help them at Nebobongo. But the work at Nebobongo and its importance began to change colour, so to speak. I recalled the things that had occurred out there, the criticisms that had been made, the failures in relationships, the many frustrations in the work. Previously, I had been willing for the Lord to show me that I was at fault. I wanted Him to deal with me, to empty me of myself in order that He might mould me into the likeness of Jesus and fill me with Himself. Now it no longer seemed like that. Why was I always in the wrong? Why did I always have to give in over everything that occurred? Why hadn't the Mission put money at my disposal for the medical work? Why hadn't the menfolk at other stations been more willing to help me at Nebobongo with buildings and repairs, with sanitation and feeding problems, with the upkeep of the car and the oversight of workmen? Why in fact had they put upon me, a woman doctor, jobs which ought to be done by men? And so the devil worked his subtle business and seeds of bitterness, jealousy, and envy were sown. And with it all came a growing sense of insecurity for the future and a realization of great loneliness.

Suddenly I saw the answer clearly, and apparently the way to claim the answer. With this new sense of urgency, I argued myself into believing that God owed it to me to work it all out my way. I too had the right to marry, to have a husband, someone I could lean on, someone to care for me, to protect me, to be always there as friend and counsellor, to take the responsibility, even to repair the broken furniture! Surely He could not ask me to go back again to Congo single. Perhaps for the first term of service it had been reasonable to expect this of me. There had been jobs to do that perhaps I should not have been so free for had I been married. But now, surely, it was different.

Temptation followed temptation. The devil put the thoughts and desires and growing hunger first. Then along came someone apparently eminently suited (so I thought!). Though he was a true Christian, I soon found out that he had no call to overseas missionary service. So I sought to be released from the Mission, feeling that he would never ask me to marry him whilst he knew I was committed to returning to the Congo. How subtle the adversary is! This new attack began as a desire to have someone by me in Congo. But if this was not possible, Congo would now have to be sacrificed, that I might have him for myself. We were thrown into each other's company for six long months, and I passionately desired that the Lord would give me the fulfilment of all I longed for. We had prayer and Bible reading together on an evening. We went out to services or to open-air testimony together on Sundays. He was always kindly and gracious. He never encouraged me; I only wished he would! I cut myself off from the Mission at this time, sensing that they would disapprove and knowing all the arguments they could use too well! I bought new clothes, and had my hair permed, and set myself to win him.

9

Fresh Vision and Triumph

My somewhat obvious un-spiritual state at this time led many to pray for me. Some of my friends persuaded me to go away for a long weekend to Herne Bay Court. Arriving on Friday evening, tired and depressed, I went to the final meeting of the previous house-party, with little heart or interest. As my eyes were already closing, heavy with sleep, from weeks of over-tension and mental unrest, the preacher announced as his text Hosea 2:14-16, '… the valley of Achor for a door of hope.'

I do not know what he said; I do not know who he was. I only know that every nerve felt raw and alive. These were the verses my sister had sent me nine months earlier when I had been ill in hospital. I went to my room that evening, fearful, afraid to meet God, knowing what He wanted to say to me, but no longer wanting to listen. I wanted things my way now. I didn't want to be made hungry again after God; I didn't want His promise of love and comfort. I felt I had been following a will-o'-the-wisp for long enough, and I was a failure. This kind of life wasn't for me, and I didn't want to be cajoled into trying again.

I could not silence His love. The Hounds of Heaven were bearing down on me. I longed for Him with one breath. I longed for husband and home and the comfort and security this would offer with the next. I struggled till tears—burning, gasping tears—ran down my face. I struggled till exhausted. I fell asleep—He was there! I forced myself awake; I even leapt out of bed and splashed my face with cold water. I threw the window open. A gentle May breeze in the still moonlight calmed me. I slept again, and again He was there, gentle, loving, stern, demanding, beautiful, worthy. The sense of His presence faded as I sank into deep, troubled sleep. Morning light only brought back a bitter sense of battle. Why should He ask me to relinquish this that I most wanted?

I went back to London on Monday, knowing He would win—indeed had won—but nevertheless not wanting to give in, not wanting His victory, yet terrified to lose Him or to drive Him away. What a mess! How clever the devil is! I did all I could to close my ears, to refuse to listen. At the same time, I longed for deliverance, for a deliverance which the next moment I didn't want! How contrary can we be?

One morning, several weeks later, I was struck in my morning reading by Galatians 1:15, 'When it pleased God…to reveal his Son in me….' I couldn't shake off the thought. 'Can't you see? Can't you see?' a voice seemed to whisper to me. 'Christ dwells in you. It is Him you are bent on destroying, not yourself. He is you. Christ in you, the hope of glory.' I felt baffled, uncertain, unable to bear the revelation, yet this was the truth I had searched for all these years. The simple naked fact of truth—His Son in me. Not just for me, but in me.

Next week I went to Keswick. Others had made this possible for me, arranged a locum and booked for me to stay in the IVF women's camp. The one from whom I so passionately desired human security and love and strength went too. I went to almost all the meetings. I had determined that the Lord should speak to me, that I would hear and that I would obey whatever the cost. And then I left Him to do it. I can remember the tormenting thought that perhaps I had gone too far. Yet however much I had rebelled and kicked, He knew that I loved Him, that I was bound to Him for ever and longed deep down to serve Him. In my extremity, I had no-one else to whom I could turn. O God, don't leave me; don't cast me off!

On Tuesday evening I attended the meeting in the large tent, physically exhausted after having climbed painfully to the top of Scafell Pike during the day. The address was based on 2 Kings 2:1-11. Elisha's journey with Elijah, and the speaker applied it to our life's journey in retrospect. They began at Gilgal, the place of original committal (do you remember meeting Me on that evening of New Year's Day, 1945?). They passed through Bethel, the place of Jacob's vision where he erected his altar of surrender (do you remember meeting Me in the hospital that day in March 1950?), and came to Jericho, the scene of Joshua's initial victory (do you remember that day in October 1955 when I took you from Ibambi to Nebobongo?). Then Elijah offers young Elisha again the opportunity of remaining with the school of the sons of the prophets: 'Tarry here; you do not need to go any further.' But he refuses to leave Elijah, 'And they two went on' down to Jordan, down into the place of death, the place of separation from self and self-interest.

I was wide awake now, urgently listening, desperate to go on with the Lord even though it meant death to self. 'Ask what I shall do for thee', Elijah tells Elisha. And the quiet voice of the Master seemed to echo the question in my own heart.

I stayed to the after-meeting, awed, fearful, yet knowing that I must answer that voice and receive again from Him the reply. A quiet, unobtrusive counsellor came and sat by me. At last, in tears, I asked the fearful question: Could He forgive deliberate, wilful sin? Could He restore and recommission one who had chosen her own way, and I a missionary on furlough? The whole rotten story of the last few months was at last out, and with joy I knew that He had forgiven me. I told the Lord I was willing for anything He would say to me, and to do anything He asked of me, unconditionally.

I think I knew at once that I was forgiven, but I could not feel that He could 'lightly' forget. I was not sure that He would re-commission, or that He would be willing to use me further in His service. I felt that I had entered a 'second-best' experience, but my fight was over. I felt very exhausted but deeply relieved to know that He was again in charge. The next evening, after an amazing address on temptation, my friend and I went out together and agreed to give up meeting one another. There was a deep wound in my heart, but it was the only way for any future peace. The following day, while I was still at Keswick, I received a telegram, calling me to Newport for an interview at the St Woolos Hospital in connection with a House-surgeon's job there for which I had applied. I had a deep inner conviction that God was definitely at the helm.

As the wound slowly began to heal I realised that a new calm had taken possession. The intenseness of life, the acute awareness of every situation, the passionate longings and yearnings all seemed to have been replaced by a quiet acceptance. There was a sense of resignation, perhaps; a consciousness that I had no rights—no right to quote terms, no right to expect grace, no right even to feel, to feel saved, or happy, or at peace. I accepted utterly that, by the immense immeasurable grace of God and according to His predetermined counsel, Christ was in me and that He should now live out His life and purpose as He saw fit.

I wrote at once to Mission Headquarters, thanking them for having granted me a year's leave of absence, thanking them for their sympathetic prayers during recent months, and asking them to consider my reapplication for full membership at the next quarterly staff meeting, and also to consider an application to return to the Congo in May 1960.

My six months at Mildmay having ended, I went at once to Newport and took up my duties as House-surgeon. There was no applicant for the post of Houseman to the obstetrical unit, so I helped out there as well, and had three weeks' invaluable experience, including doing my first Caesarian operation under supervision! Then the Lord arranged another opportunity for me. The boilers in the theatre sterilizing unit had to be repaired and the theatres were to be closed for three weeks. During this time, the surgical staff were going to take their annual holiday. This included the medical superintendent who was also in charge of the obstetrical unit. I was invited by the board to help out for that three weeks as an acting registrar. So I had the opportunity to learn something of the running and administration of a large British hospital, and of work in all the departments, which was to be directly related to the tasks that lay ahead, especially those of training African personnel in administration in the future Independent Congo.

The months at Newport were tremendously happy and busy ones. We worked closely as a team with ward and theatre sisters and nurses, and had plenty of night emergency calls. I had the joy of spending Christmas at hospital, and what a day it was! Dinner on the ward with staff and patients was almost a seven-course meal! We visited and chatted with everybody. The theatre staff, knowing my connection with Congo, had decorated the long corridor as a jungle track with palm fronds and elephants as a welcome to their jungle doctor! The ward service, for me the crowning joy of the day, seemed to be greatly appreciated by patients, relatives, and staff alike. At the end of the service, Sister presented me with a cheque for £50 from both patients and staff to buy a general anaesthetic machine for the Nebobongo hospital. I was deeply moved by this symbol of their deep love and affection.

After Christmas we put on our 'variety show'. Hardly, perhaps, the kind of task one would associate with a missionary on furlough, but strangely successful, and viewed as yet another avenue for showing the relevance of the Christian gospel to our everyday life. Each ward, each department, all the different groups of staff, including carpenters and electricians, took part, each saying thank you to the others for their part as a team in making the wheels of the hospital run smoothly. Even the Consultants joined in the grand finale which represented the crowning of the chief bard of the year at the Eisteddfod! It was a great (if amateurish) success to crown weeks of tireless preparation.

There followed three months of holiday and various meetings, including a happy week amongst the students at the Missionary Training College at Glasgow, and two weeks with friends in Northern Ireland. At the WEC quarterly staff meeting, my request to be re-admitted as a member was granted and immediately an application was made for reservations on the Castle Line ship sailing on 20th May from London to Mombasa. This was followed by the usual bustle of shopping, listing, packing, labelling, visits to shipping agents and photographers, visas and permits, and at last we were ready to go.

It was not so easy leaving mother and home this second time, especially as rumours were beginning to circulate of anticipated trouble at the declaration of Congo's Independence in just about six weeks' time. I remember my last Sunday evening at Christ Church, Bromley, when I gave a short testimony and asked their prayers for the coming term of service. 'Is anything too hard for the Lord?' Even the unrest, political upheaval, communist infiltration and influence? It might be that our days would be short; it could be that our work would be taken from us. Suffering and persecution possibly awaited us in the Congolese church.

But with their prayers we could steadfastly answer, 'There is nothing too hard for Thee.'

With me on the journey out was Elaine de Rusett, an Australian nurse coming to join me at Nebobongo, and young Bill McChesney, a 24-year-old American. I remembered so clearly my first voyage and the goodness of the senior missionaries to me in fellowship and in language study. I therefore felt a great responsibility not to fail the two new recruits who were with me. Each morning, after breakfast, we met together in our two-berth cabin for prayer and Bible study. We read together through the book of Nehemiah, and day by day I talked to them about one of the stations of the Congo field, introducing them to the workers and the background development, the present work and situation and needs, and as far as I could, the Africans at each place. During each day I encouraged them to give some time to language study and helped them all I could. One day on board, after I had apparently been 'mothering' them, a dear elderly lady came up to me and asked if Bill and Elaine were my two delightful children? That cured me, much to their delight! I myself benefited considerably, of course, from going steadily through the Swahili again and revising my knowledge of both grammar and vocabulary. In the afternoon, I had the joy of helping another group of friends on the boat with their Swahili language study. They were going to Kenya in Government service. There was plenty of time for quiet, for prayer and study, for meditation, for letter-writing, and reading books.

At Genoa we had three days in the port whilst cargo was being loaded. We wandered over the town together. I can still see clearly a great storage shed down by the docks with a huge notice in Italian forbidding trespassers. Bill sauntered up to the door with his usual charming, disarming smile, and wandered in to look round. I was horrified and pleaded with him to come out. The last thing I wanted was to run into trouble in a foreign land where we were not known and did not know the language. Bill looked at my troubled face and grinned impishly. 'What's up? "The world belongs to all of us, so make yourself at home."' 'Bill,' I said, 'Can't you read the notice?' 'No; me no read Italiano.' What a lad! Always full of fun, yet always so gracious and courteous. We walked the whole circle of the town, along the hilltops, following the ruined fortifications and walls, collecting wild flowers which he would send to his mother. She was not to see him again. Just over four years later, he was martyred at Wamba during the Simba rebellion.

On arrival at Mombasa we were forcibly reminded of the difficult days that lay ahead. The day previously, while still at sea, I had received a cablegram asking me to consider seriously the advisability of staying in Nairobi until after the Declaration of Independence in Congo, so that we could see how things would go. The sender, a relative of one of our missionaries, pleaded with me to think twice before taking these two new recruits into such obvious danger. At Mombasa the customs officials and immigration officers would not stamp our passports nor give us leave to get off the ship, until we had pledged our return fares to England. They told us that, with still a fortnight to go before the Declaration of Independence, white refugees were already pouring into Kenya and Uganda from Congo. They advised us strongly to continue the round journey and to go home! They pointed out forcibly that they could not accommodate all these refugees in their countries, and therefore could not take the deliberate responsibility of adding three more to their problems. We pledged our return fares and left the ship. As we went down the gangway, carrying suitcases and briefcases, an African porter came straight up to Bill, the only man in our group, and took his baggage, leaving us women to struggle with ours. Bill laughed, and felt he had at last reached a country that did things the right way round! Then he reached out and gave us a hand.

The shipping agent, Mrs Passmore, had us cleared through customs in no time, and everything was soon on to the train. So began our long journey up country through Kenya and Uganda. I was wise to some of the problems this time, especially in regard to the necessity of ordering a 'night-sack' with blankets from the guard. On my first journey no-one had told me how bitterly cold it could feel after sunset, as we climbed 5,000 feet up to Nairobi away from the stifling heat of sea-level, and I had frozen all night! At Kikuyu station, as the train shunted to a stop, there was my college friend, Sylvia, with a vast dog, come to meet us! It was quite exciting to meet up in the middle of Africa for just a ten-minute chat on a railway platform. She was teaching then at the Kikuyu Girls' High School.

On again, to Kampala, where we had to 'fill in time' for several hours, waiting for our connection to take us on to the head of the railroad. This final stretch of the journey took us through the most glorious mountainous country, up and up towards the Congo-Uganda border. I felt heavy with the responsibility of taking these two with me towards the dangers that everyone threatened, although of course both of them had made their own decisions before the Lord. But I was earnestly hoping that one of the senior missionaries would meet us at Kasese and, having read the cablegram I had received on the ship, make the actual final decision. What a joy as we piled out of the train, to see Frank Cripps waiting with the Mission truck! In no time we were loaded up, and piled in, Elaine and Bill travelling with Frank Bates, a young Australian missionary who had also come to meet us, and myself with Frank Cripps, whose special responsibility was the Mission press and the training of Congolese printers.

Soon we were over the border and through customs without the slightest difficulty. A little further on a halt was called at the roadside to sing the doxology and to thank God for having safely brought us thus far, into the promised land, surely 'for such a time as this' (Esther 4:14).

10

TREASURES OF DARKNESS

What a welcome home! Did one ever fear that perhaps one wasn't really wanted? All along the route in, as we passed each out-church and village clearing where I had worked and preached, we were greeted by crowds of school children, together with the evangelist, catechist, and their wives, all waving and cheering. Then at Ibambi, what joy it was to see again the Bible school students, printshop workers, school children, nurses, all singing and happy and shaking hands. Finally, we reached Nebobongo itself to be met with big hugs and kisses of welcome home, and their 'special' hymn, 'Stand up, stand up, for Jesus, ye soldiers of the cross', learnt for the occasion. It was a thrilling day indeed—walking all round the station with John and Elsie Harris and their two small children, David and Lois, to see all the improvements and new buildings and permanent roofs, and then down to the village to greet all our dear Africans and fellow-workers.

John and Elsie were very tired. They had been out seven years, hard years with many changes involving two different language areas, and they had both had spells of sickness. They were ready for furlough and glad to hand over the responsibility. So I was back into harness once more, and how good it felt! There was need to walk carefully, to 'feel' the new climate of opinion with Independence only two weeks away. I listened in to all I could: nurses, patients, village men from over the way, and also radio reports from Stanleyville and Leopoldville. There were rumours, stories, vague threats, unrest, and uncertainty.

One evening that week there was a meeting of our station elders and the male nurses in the dispensary. After a while they sent for us whites, all four of us. They were polite, but were obviously leading up to something. Eventually Joseph Bumukumu brought it out. 'We want to appoint an African leader', he said. 'Everywhere else has done it. At the Red Cross Hospital Dr Kadoner has handed over authority to a senior male orderly, Gwo-gwo, and he has become the new director. We want you to hand over to John Mangadima.' We waited, tense, a little uncertain, praying hard for wisdom. Then John Mangadima himself spoke, and saved a difficult situation. 'I don't mind being in charge of the nurses and the general administrative work. But I'm not a doctor and we can't do without our doctors, and I couldn't ever be over them.' All round there was a gentle 'letting-out' of held breath. They were content; we had not refused their request, but they themselves had made their choice that they wanted us to stay. We were quite clear that there was to be a new emphasis of authority, but we were equally sure that He would steer us through the initial rapids.

So 30th June came. For us it was a day of prayer and praise, with a football match in the afternoon, and a sense of waiting. Mayaribu, the headman of the nearest village, came to visit us, with six other senior village men from the immediate vicinity. They came wearing colourful, native straw hats and flowers, each carrying a little bouquet of flowers and some eggs. We went out on to the verandah to greet them, and Mayaribu made a little speech of welcome saying that they, the headmen of the region, invited us, their 'strangers', to stay with them in their new Independence. We were thus publicly 'accepted'. It was a moving moment, and we responded accordingly.

In the following days, all work continued as usual in the hospital and maternity compound, the only difference being the oft-heard cry 'Uhuru!'—Freedom! Liberty! Everyone seemed to be carrying a bouquet of flowers and wearing native hats and loin-cloths like their forefathers in place of the European clothing which was more usual in our area. Slowly the initial fear and tension relaxed, and somewhat amazedly, we accepted that Independence had come without demonstration or lawlessness.

Suddenly a different note was sounded. There was mutiny in the army at Leopoldville, which led to the rapid evacuation of Belgians and their families following wickedness and the raping of white women. Panic filled the air. Overnight, the whole picture changed. On Thursday, 15th July, two Mission cars passed our station going north. Later in the afternoon they returned with others, and called us all to go to a meeting that evening at Ibambi. Two of our senior missionaries had arrived that day at Nebobongo for medical care. Together the six of us, soberly and wondering, made our way to the centre. We began to gather in, until eventually there must have been over twenty of us. Everyone had different stories to tell, things seen, things heard, things feared. It was very hard to think levelly in such an atmosphere of anxiety. Truckloads of soldiers had gone through that very day, singing in local tribal languages of what they would do to us on their return. Within an hour, some fifteen of the missionaries had signed a list to say they wanted to go over the border, at least temporarily, to see whether things would settle down. Soon the great evacuation had begun. Throughout the night they packed and sorted and left, car after car. So it was that next day, tired and puzzled, I found myself back at Nebobongo alone. Alone, that is, so far as white companionship was concerned. It was a strange feeling. Even my car had gone to help carry those who felt they should leave. And yet there was a quiet peace, knowing that He had brought me to Congo for such a time as this. We tidied up the two missionaries' houses, packing away everything as neatly as possible, and then had a meeting in the church to discuss our immediate future. I found I was surrounded by a love and sense of security and protection that I had never known before. A deep new bond had been forged, and I knew that it was indeed He who had told me to stay with them at this moment of their great need.

Together we decided that the church elders should be formed into an executive committee responsible for all station affairs, spiritual and material. Agoya was appointed President, Mangadima as secretary, and Basuana was made responsible for the youth. The three together were to act as treasurer. I was unanimously asked to remain with them as advisor and friend in all matters. We had a wonderful time of prayer and praise.

That evening, a truck full of soldiers passed. During the night, alone in that large house, each time a rat scurried over the bamboo ceilings I started up in fear. At about 2 a.m. I got up, and knelt in prayer, and asked the Lord to liberate me from this dreadful fearfulness, and if He would, to send me someone to sleep in the house with me. I hadn't even got back into bed when there was a knock at the back door. I was terrified! This was it! They'd come for me. I could hardly force myself to ask who was there. 'We are', they answered, 'Mama Taadi and Mama Damaris.' I flung the door open, and burst into tears as I drew them into the house. 'The Lord woke us from sleep (in different houses, on opposite sides of the compound) and told us to come and sleep in your house so that you wouldn't be alone in these dangerous days.' I hugged them, made them up a couple of beds, made us each a cup of

Ovaltine; we read Daily Light together and then settled down again for the rest of the night.

Next day the Lord sent two other white ladies to join me, missionaries from another WEC station forty miles to the north. It was agreed that we should stay together for the first period of Independence until we saw how things would be. It was a joy to welcome them. I remember that first evening discussing at prayers together the recent puzzling events leading up to the evacuation of half the Mission and the fact that the final straw had been the threat of rape to white women by the mutineering army. Surely the Lord had died on Calvary for this as much as any other sin? It wasn't our sin or shame. We could remain pure before the Lord with His purity no matter what happened. Fifty years ago missionaries risked their lives from malaria or wild animals. Today it might be a different price they had to pay, a different danger to face; but surely He was still the same wonderful Lord who was worthy of any sacrifice made?

We had a month together, dividing up the work and responsibilities between us and doing everything alongside the Africans, helping them daily to carry more and more of the responsibilities. Many times they would say, 'What shall we do if you also have to leave us?' One weekend soldiers did visit us. I was away at Pastor Ndugu's village at the time. They made no trouble. We heard of troubles in other areas; rumours in fact abounded. But we saw little or nothing to trouble us. We often went up to Ibambi to discuss plans with the missionaries there. On one of these visits we heard of the decision which was eventually taken for two of our menfolk to go to the Ugandan border to collect those who had evacuated, those, that is, that now wanted to return. So on Friday, 20th August 1960, just four weeks from their departure, we prepared a huge meal for seventeen at Nebobongo, to welcome them home again. As they drove in we ran out to greet them looking especially for our nurse, whom we were so anxious to have come back to help us in the maternity compound, the hospital, and the leprosy camp. What a deep blow of disappointment it was to find there was no nurse in the party for Nebobongo! Yet here too, doubtless, the Lord was working, as it forced my hand to put more and more responsibility on the African nurses and midwives.

Elaine de Ruseti joined me for two happy weeks, to glean all she could of Congolese dispensary ways and tropical drugs and dosages before going 250 miles northwest to our furthermost station to help them. Then again I had four weeks alone, my two lady friends having returned to their own station. This was a very busy period indeed, a foretaste of what lay ahead. In our immediate area of 200 miles radius, where there had previously been seventeen doctors and surgeons, we were now reduced to three, one a leprologist, one a pathologist, and myself. We were faced with the difficulty of emergency surgery, none of us being trained or practised in such. Patients came to us from terrific distances, some having been carried through the forest for several days slung in a blanket on a pole between the shoulders of two carriers, and their condition on arrival was often too awful for description. Sometimes we worked round the clock. Weariness became habitual. To hear a truck drive up ceased to cause the fearful dread of soldiers but brought instead an equal horror as to what new emergency was being brought in. God enabled me through those weeks, even though a severe mental battle raged, to learn to trust Him for each needed victory.

Trouble was reported a hundred miles south. As a result three missionaries were brought north and came to live at Nebobongo, including Florence Stebbing, with whom I had worked for the previous five years! She took over at once the oversight of the maternity work and leprosarium, but there, too, she had many difficulties. Since Independence an African midwife, Naomi, had been placed in charge. She was apparently doing very well, and appeared to be teachable. But she did not like having to work alongside a European again, and created much unpleasantness for Miss Stebbing. They were certainly not easy days. We longed to help our African colleagues, and to trust them, and to give them the authority they coveted. Yet we had to see to the maintenance of medical discipline—hygiene, cleanliness, locking up and signing for dangerous drugs—all of which they were beginning to think were merely 'white obsessions'.

An urgent call came from the young Congolese Government that I would go to help them at the hospital at Wamba, sixty miles east across the Nepoko river. So I started to work two days a week at Wamba, doing ward-rounds and operations and clinics for Africans and Europeans. It involved leaving home at 5.30 a.m. to be at the hospital by 8 a.m. Sometimes we did not finish until after 8 o'clock at night which meant not getting home until 10.30 p.m. Weariness increased. The work was not satisfying at Wamba, as I had no authority over the nursing staff and knew full well that the treatment I ordered was frequently not given. Discipline was almost unknown amongst them, and certainly none had the slightest understanding of a professional conscience towards the patients and towards the accurate administration of drugs.

On Tuesday, 13th February 1961, I set off for Wamba as usual, accompanied by John Mangadima, who was going to assist me at the day's operative list. Six miles from Wamba we were flagged to a halt at one of the out churches, and warned to return. 'There is great trouble in Wamba. All the whites are being tied up. Go home.' We argued that, as medicals, this was not possible. We had a responsibility to our patients. Whilst we discussed the matter, the crowd of casual passengers that had been travelling to Wamba by my van disappeared with all their goods! Mangadima and I continued alone. I had urged him also to remain and wait for me at the church. 'Never', he exclaimed. 'If it is safe for you to go, I go with you.' Just before Wamba we were stopped by wild rough soldiers at a barrier. Menacingly they commanded me out of the car. John stopped their wicked intentions by saying, 'Do not touch her! She is "one of us", our doctor', using a word in the local tongue meaning 'blood of our blood'; and they desisted. They took us into town to the Government offices. Here, as their doctor, I was promptly promised free passage, despite the curfew imposed on all other Europeans. Even as they spoke, two Belgian planters were brought in and roughly thrown into an inner courtyard. Fearfully, we went on to the hospital, where we heard the reason for it all. That morning, the report of the murder of Patrice Lumumba had arrived. Not a single nurse had remained at the hospital and there was nothing we could do. We went to our Mission station a quarter of a mile from the Government post where there were four missionaries working, and discussed with them the present dangerous situation. Then we set out to return home. At the large junction of three roads six miles out there were barriers across all the roads and numerous soldiers were inspecting the cars and trucks lined up on all sides, searching for hidden Europeans. We pulled in, turned off the engine, and settled down for a long wait. Suddenly, we were waved forward. We drew out, and as we approached, the barriers were taken down; each soldier came to attention and smartly saluted us. We sailed through! God had gone before us and caused someone among the soldiers to recognise my car. Presumably they had received instructions from the Wamba Government to treat 'their doctor' with respect.

It was not always so easy. Two of our senior lady mission-aries working in the southern area of our Province were grievously ill-treated and humiliated by the women's group of the Lumumba party. These women were quite as wicked and ferocious as the most brutal of the soldiers. Miss Kingdon at Wamba was threatened many times. I was stopped one day in Wamba High Street, as I set out home after a day of operating, because one of my indicator lights had not worked. Forced from the car at gun-point and driven into the police courtroom, I was held there at attention for over two hours.

We never knew what they might do next. One night about this time, thieves broke into my house. Apparently they had drugged (or attempted to poison) me. But my dog had eaten most of my supper as I was not hungry, and she died next day. They stripped the house of curtains, cloths, jumpers, cutlery, foodstuffs, even my glasses and watch from the very room where I was asleep in bed. It left a horrid fear for weeks, making sleep very difficult.

Heart-break followed. One Sunday evening, Miss Stebbing and I were having prayers together. We heard a noise from the maternity compound and listened intently. Was this the noise of the outpoured Holy Spirit, of revival blessing? Yet something did not ring true in our hearts, and with a lantern we set out to investigate. We met Mama Taadi and Mama Damaris coming up from the village, also attracted by the noise and with the same thoughts in their hearts. Together we walked across. We found our four senior midwives and several pupils, dressed in their native clothes instead of hospital uniform, having a meeting in the compound, singing and beating an empty forty-gallon drum, and dancing. Before I had time to investigate further, Mama Taadi called me aside and asked the two of us to go back home. We did and prayed earnestly for wisdom and guidance.

Two hours later, the two Bible women joined us and told us the sad story. The crowd, with the midwives, had been singing in the native tongue songs of filth and mockery, to our hymn tunes, deliberately imitating many of the expressions of the times of the revival. They were joking about and jeering at God and all that is holy to us. In the wards, in the midwives' homes, in various parts of their compound, more than ten men from surrounding villages were surprised, and sent off. We spent the night in prayer, our hearts heavy with grief, a deep sense of failure and disappointment mingled with righteous indignation and horror at the wickedness that had been deliberately perpetrated by those whom we trusted, those in charge, those who had been preaching the gospel in the wards and clinics each day.

We spent the next day in prayer and fasting, and sent out into the area for the parents of all the midwives and pupils, and for the Church Council for the area. On Tuesday we all met together, and eventually it was unanimously decided that the maternity compound must be closed and all the girls dismissed. We must make a fresh start. The girls appeared to be amused, certainly in no wise subdued nor troubled. They went off, laughing and joking. Was it bravado? Was it a cloak, a bluff? How we longed that this might be so. Every girl was told clearly in the hearing of her parents, that if she was repentant and attended regularly at her local church, we would consider her readmission to the training school the following September term. They left; and within five months we heard that more than half of them were expecting babies. I thought my heart would break. How had I failed them? Where had we gone wrong? 'Independence' meant only this to so many, the removal of all restraints, throwing over all discipline, living as they liked, as unto themselves.

That same evening, as I drove to Wamba to take two pupils back to their parents, I arrived at the Mission station there just in time to assist at one of our missionaries' confinements, her first little one, a lovely girl! It certainly was a precious end to a tragic day, though it served to highlight the cunning of the devil in taking one of God's most precious gifts and debasing it into lust.

By this time, we were beginning to know many shortages. Village shops had none of the essentials that we wanted, powdered milk, salt, matches, sugar, flour. Even petrol and paraffin were very hard to get. Many Europeans had taken their cars off the road. For six weeks we had had no letters from home, which also meant no allowances. We did not know what it all meant, except that our Province was being boycotted by the rest of the Congo to make us toe the line. I was one of the very few still travelling to and fro, and therefore became the postman for our own local mail, calling in at all the plantations and shops and the Roman Catholic compounds on my way to and from Wamba. We had a good Administrator, and his assistant was also very friendly and kindly to us. One day I took all our Intermediate Campaigner Clan, boys and girls, about twenty-four of them, all in uniform and carrying flags, to greet the Administrator at the Wamba territorial headquarters. As we arrived, we found that it was an important public occasion, with a party political harangue from one of the Ministers up from Stanleyville. My young folk stood at ease, in ranks, by the central flagstaff, in full sunshine, for two hours, listening to an impassioned political speech in a language that hardly any of us could understand! Making our way forward afterwards, I was led up the steps to be introduced to the Minister as 'their doctor', and in turn I was able to introduce the youngsters. They sang to him, and saluted, and drilled. Then he gave a further twenty minutes' speech on their behalf! He spoke very highly of them, and stressed the need of putting God first if Congo was to advance, and the need for all young people to learn discipline and obedience and hard work if they wanted to help their country forward. It was a great day!

The first anniversary of Independence Day was approaching. Schools had to be closed beforehand, as many people feared an outbreak of trouble. The church planned a day of conference for prayer and praise at Ibambi. Our Campaigner Clans at Nebobongo set off at 5.30 a.m. to march the seven miles to Ibambi, before the sun got too hot. There were about ninety of us, all in uniform and with flags flying, singing every step of the way—for those who could keep enough breath going! The church was well packed with over 2,500 of our local Christians attending. During the day, I did not feel too well, and by evening, when it was time to set off on the march home, I was very glad indeed to be offered a lift in a car. On Saturday we had a sports day arranged by the Boy Campaigners to which they had invited young men from the local plantations and the fat factory, and also the regional chieftain. It was a very hot and tiring day, which I thought accounted for my headache and feeling of fever. By Sunday, I realised that I was not well, but managed to struggle through the day's services, including the wonderful Communion Service in the evening when four of the Europeans from Ibambi joined us. On Monday I stayed in bed, and that was the beginning of a long illness.

Through that first week I remained at Nebobongo. Suzanne and Elena, two African nurses, slept in the home with me and did all they could to look after me. I tried to help with seeing hospital charts daily and giving any advice I could but the fever stayed high, and interludes of delirium and great depression alternated. Treatment seemed to be ineffective. The following week I was moved to Ibambi, to relieve Elaine and Florence, who already had all they could manage. At Ibambi I was nursed by Miss Muriel Harman. I suffered another week of swinging temperatures and ever-increasing weakness, constant vomiting, and severe headaches, before eventually the illness began to respond to treatment, and at last, after five weeks, the fever ended. I was very thin and appallingly weak. Just as I began to get up and sit in a chair, I developed jaundice and seemed to be as ill again as the previous week. This dragged on for another ten days. I felt embarrassed at being a burden to everyone, and so on 13th August I asked to be allowed to go back to Nebobongo, and slowly to resume my work. The two missionaries there had had a heavy time during those six weeks. However, the weakness just dogged me and made me virtually unable to do anything. Ten days later, I felt I could go on no longer, I was just too weak to do anything. I vomited everything I tried to eat; the pain never let up. I felt the end was very near, and asked my two co-workers to call the church elders.

Even as I asked, they arrived at the back-door saying that the Lord had constrained them to come to anoint me in the name of the Lord. They prayed for me, anointing me and believing for His touch of healing. To me it was an act of obedience according to James 5:14, but I did not ask for healing. In a few hours the vomiting ceased, the pain eased, and I fell into a restful sleep. Next day, others had arranged for me to go away to Egbita, to the two lady friends who had stayed with me at Nebobongo the previous year, and a car came to collect me and take me to them. There was still an overwhelming weariness and weakness, but certainly less pain. And from that day, I slowly recovered. I spent six wonderful weeks at Egbita, being utterly spoilt and nursed back to health. Towards the end of my stay I spent hours each day preparing lecture notes in French for the coming school year for the nurses. It was very moving to realise how much the believing prayers of our Africans had played in my recovery, how they were growing towards maturity and making decisions for us, instead of our always making decisions for them.

When I got home for the next school year, early in October, my work at the Government hospital at Wamba had finished, for they now had regular visits from a UNO doctor. There were five doctors in the area, two of them excellent surgeons, and the terrible strains began to let up. But the shortages increased, and what goods there were we could purchase only at black-market prices. Blankets that I used to buy for the patients at 17s 6d were now over £3. Bowls and buckets could not be obtained. Penicillin was unheard of. We were down to our last thermometer. So in May 1952, I went the long 250-mile journey to Stanleyville with two Africans to see what we could do. We visited the Labour Exchange to discuss the possibility of getting permission for the local chiefs' men to build us new wards at the chiefs' expense. We visited the Treasury to discuss the possibility of the nurses receiving Government salaries. We visited the hospital and the Minister of Health to discuss our need of drugs and equipment. We visited UNO Headquarters and discussed everything and everyone! All this in an attempt to try and persuade someone to be interested in a little bush clearing called Nebobongo, and all on foot, dusty mile after dusty mile, as the car was being repaired in a garage. Most visits reached a satisfactory issue only after about five tries. Persistence and grace were essential! At last we had lots of promises, some letters, and a truck (borrowed from the Government!) full of blankets, bowls, buckets, thermometers, and drugs, and we were all set to go home. While filling up our van at a local pump, I had my briefcase seized from the front seat of my car, with passport, driving licence, identity card, and all my papers.

The British Consul, Mr McGurk, could not have done more for me. He knew all the right people to see, and the right things to do and say, and within ten days I had a new passport (flown up from Leopoldville, with cabled permission from England), new car papers and permits, new medical certificates all signed, and almost all at someone else's most generous expense. Truly people were deeply kind to me, not least the delightful BMS family I stayed with, Mr and Mrs Saunders and their young son, who gave up his bedroom to me for my prolonged four-week visit.

At last, very encouraged, we reached Nebobongo to receive a grand welcome home. The boys' examinations followed. Then came the Independence Day celebrations. Two days later, a little lad, Timothy, the son of one of our church evangelists, was taken desperately ill. I had him in my home so as to be able to give him the very best possible attention, including night nursing care, and the next day we realised he had smallpox. We had eight cases in all. Timothy died the following Saturday. The father and I buried the child at midnight, alone in drizzling rain, to avoid every possible chance of infection. All the contacts were isolated in my home. It was a deeply anxious ten days. We vaccinated, in all, some 80,000 people in the area. There were some fantastic reactions to vaccine, ulcers right down to the bone, awful sloughing, high fevers, and three more patients died. At last, it was over. There were no further cases. The whole station had been bound over in strict isolation and quarantine. They responded wonderfully. One letter had gone out, the first day, duly stoved and disinfected, to seek prayer from home. When she received it, my mother had rung the convent where my sister lived and the community bore us up all through that week, day and night, and God stayed the hand of the epidemic.

Very exhausted, never having properly recovered from the illness of the previous year, I was given permission to go away for six weeks for a complete break, out of the tropical steamy heat of Congo, out of the political unrest and constant threats and fear. I had a wonderful rest and returned very much refreshed. When I arrived back in Paulis by plane

I was met and driven home to Nebobongo. There I received such a welcome you would have thought I had been away for a year, not just six weeks!

Storm-clouds were now gathering in the church. Before Independence, all Europeans were invited to all church meetings and were on all committees. Now things were changing. There were tensions. There was a growing consciousness that the Africans did not wholly trust us whites, afraid that we were not really willing to give them absolute equality, absolute authority. They wanted to have their Independence in the church just as others had it in political matters. They wanted Africans to be in charge in every department, including the handling of the finances. The problems were very similar to those of adolescents all over the world. The desire to stand on one's own feet, and not be eternally tied to mother's apron-strings is only natural. So the missionaries were no longer invited to church meetings. Sometimes they were not represented on councils or committees. Decisions were made in the church with no reference to the Europeans or their opinions.

Affairs seemed to come to a head at Christmas 1962 over church finance. There was a good deal of heat in the church meetings and not a little bitterness. Above all, there was this tragic lack of confidence between Africans and Europeans. One day two of the pastors and two schoolmasters came in for coffee, obviously very full, as it were, of the recent troubles. I stood a book on the table between us and asked them if they from their side photographed the book, and at the same moment I took a picture from my side, and then the two films were processed, would they say that my camera lied because it saw the opposite side of the book with a row of black faces behind it, so different from their photograph of the front of the book with a white face behind it. They saw the point, and we had prayer together and yearned that He would help us all through this difficult period of growing-pains.

Then came an unfortunate occurrence. In the summer, we had a young man named Gabriel Mangeyi brought to the hospital with tuberculosis. We knew him well, as he had been a student nurse at Nebobongo years before, but had been dismissed for adultery. He was now married to a woman well known as a harlot. His mother came with him to nurse him, but I forbade the wife to come to the hospital, trying to protect the twenty or more student male nurses from her evil influence. However, she came, and after three nights, Gabriel's mother came to tell me that this woman had sinned with the son of my evangelist Agoya.

The case was taken to the church, amidst much heart anguish. Throughout it all Stephen, their son, repeatedly denied the accusation of Gabriel's mother. But the council decided that Agoya and Taadi would have to leave us to take over a small village church, so that their wayward son could go with them to be under their direct discipline. For various reasons, however, action on their decision had to be postponed. Taadi was ill, and also expecting another little one. Also the church had no evangelist whom they could send immediately to replace Agoya. So several months passed without the sentence being implemented.

Thus it was that Agoya and his family were still at Nebobongo when we heard that Gabriel had been brought to repentance at a church conference and had confessed that the whole story had been a lie, to 'get even' with Agoya who had been responsible for his dismissal years earlier. My heart lurched badly. I felt I never wanted to see Gabriel, his wife, or mother again after such evil.

On Boxing Day, this mother came to see me at Nebobongo to say that she wanted my forgiveness. 'What for?' I asked. 'I don't know', she replied, 'but the church says I cannot take my Christmas Communion while I have anything in my heart against you.' I felt anger well up in my heart. What deceit! To say she didn't know what she had done or for what she sought forgiveness. She went on her knees to me, and in a moment, I struck her, pulling her to her feet and demanding that she never kneel to me, but only to the Lord. Stunned she left me, and miserably I turned and entered the house. I had lost my temper, I had struck an African. After an hour's fighting with myself, I went out, got into the van, and set off for Ibambi to take the matter to the church council. On the way, I overtook the woman walking back to Ibambi and gave her a lift. It was not the easiest of journeys!

Arrived at Ibambi, I went straight to the house where the African church elders were meeting, told them exactly what had happened, and asked them to mediate between us. They were amazed. Apparently this was the first time that a European had taken a case to the Africans and not to the other missionaries. They heard the case, African fashion, and eventually we both sought forgiveness and shook hands. Next day, the two pastors came to see me at Nebobongo. Very humbly they confessed that it was jealousy that had caused them to insist that Agoya and Taadi should leave Nebobongo because I thought so much of them. Now they wanted our forgiveness and to assure them and myself that the church had agreed that they both should stay with me. And so that day yet deeper and closer links were forged between my heart and theirs as they acknowledged that I was indeed one of themselves. Humbly, I realised that God was blessing us through it all, and teaching us to walk together in close fellowship without the barriers of pride and race.

National events were moving fast. Thieving was rife. It was hard, if not impossible, to get justice. Jealousies and suspicions were on the increase. Every man was afraid of his neighbour lest he lose his job through false accusations, and no man lightly agreed to help a European lest he lose his job through being thought to fraternise or encourage neo-colonialism. John and Del Gunningham, fellow-missionaries from the north-west of our Province, joined us for her confinement, and he did a wonderful job putting a new permanent roof on the other missionaries' house on the station. Whilst they were with us we had a visit from the Inspector of Medical Schools from Leopoldville quite unexpectedly, and Del did wonders in catering for everyone! Then the local chiefs sent us men to build new wards, an out-patients' block, and a new primary school for the children. The station was a noisy hive of activity for many weeks. The building programme was not without incident, grumbling, and strikes, but we managed to steer through without too bad a break, and eventually everything was completed.

Christmas 1963 came and went without undue incident. But early in 1964 we began to hear rumours and odd scraps of news of troubles down in the south of Congo, including rioting, looting, and burning of villages. Unrest in our area increased. Shortages were more acute, prices were spiralling, and wages kept going up and up. Tensions between Africans and Europeans were no longer hidden.

As before, this was reflected in the church. The devil seemed to be fighting hard to destroy the work of years. Misunderstandings were rife; seeds of bitterness were sown in many hearts; feelings of distrust grew between different groups. Yet through it all God most graciously continued to bless the ministry of the gospel and many souls were added to the church. Through the four years since Independence we had taken a chapter a day from Scripture in our morning Bible School at Nebobongo, starting from Genesis, with a synopsis and analysis of each book as we commenced and finished it. The elders had followed right through the course, with detailed notes, forming each one his own commentary in Swahili. And now we were nearing the end. On Saturdays we had had classes for studying the doctrines of the Christian faith and always these were amazingly well attended. The choir was an active integral part of our church life, and the eighty members sang a Swahili translation of Handel's 'Unto us a Child is born' from *Messiah* at the Easter conference, with no orchestral accompaniment other than the birds. They had learnt it to a tuning fork, line by line, in tonic sol-fa!

During the year, various projects began to come to fruition after years of praying. A branch of the Evangelical Alliance had been formed, uniting all the six Protestant Missionary Societies working in the north-east Congo. This was the corner-stone of the foundation of an Inter-Mission educational programme for creating one united full-grade secondary school, to prepare our Mission-trained youngsters for University entrance so that we might have keen spiritual men in the future government of Congo. There was also an Inter-Mission Medical programme for creating one central hospital, sufficiently well built and equipped to be passed by the government as a training school for African paramedical and nursing personnel. These were thrilling days, and I was very privileged to represent our Mission at several of these Inter-Mission conferences discussing these programmes.

Then in July 1964, we had our triennial field conference, attended by all the missionaries and by two representatives from each African church council in the area. About twenty-four of us, and nearly sixty of them, met for a week of prayer and fellowship, and to discuss placing of personnel and projects for the coming three years. It was a blessed week, and many of us felt that God was very specially present in our midst, breaking down barriers, bringing us back to each other in a fuller unity and trust, and dispersing us afterwards with a renewed vision and purpose.

As we looked back during the months of travail that followed, we were always so grateful to God that He allowed us that week of united fellowship. We did not then know that it would be the last time that many of us would ever meet in that manner. Within six months, four of our missionaries were to be murdered, and all of us driven from the country. But our last memories were to be of the joy and happiness and unity of church and Mission together.

11

Nearly Exhausted

Throughout the years since Independence, there had been a strange spiritual battle in my own heart. Often an apparent darkness and loneliness hedged me in, yet always there was the complete certainty of being in the centre of His will; often I lacked any consciousness of His presence and knew no burden in prayer, yet always there was quiet confidence of being a 'vessel only'. I had a growing hunger after Him, and a deepening realization of the wonderful process of identification with Christ for the Africans I was trying to win. 'Christ in you, the hope of glory' was the phrase often in my mind. He was working out His love for them through me. Every act of service was a manifestation of His love.

The church of Jesus Christ in Congo seemed to be going through a process of adolescence, and there were many growing pains. For fifty years the missionaries had been working in the area, preaching the gospel and training the early church, much as a parent does a child, with a somewhat similar relationship, one of paternalism. Now the child, fully grown, becoming yearly more educated and sophisticated, learning of other lands through radio and travelling, was demanding her independence, unwilling for the close parental discipline any longer, fighting to break free, determined to show that she could stand by herself.

There were many tensions. Some missionaries felt that the church was ungrateful for the years of sacrificial love, and that they were no longer wanted. Yet they were sure that the church was not yet ready for them to leave. The Africans felt that the missionaries did not trust them, that they always wanted to 'boss', to be in charge, to tell them what to do and how to do it. The problem was particularly acute in the matter of church collections and other general administrative decisions. The Africans broke loose. They held their own meetings, dispersed their own finances, and asked advice of no-one. The 'parent' was hurt. Mistakes were made; finances were in a muddle; debts were incurred. The Africans were proud and would not concede that anything was wrong. They were afraid they might incur the 'told-you-so' attitude. The missionaries began to withhold their offerings, feeling that the funds to which they had been contributing were being mismanaged. The troubles increased and some difficult years ensued.

On top of all this, possibly due to the great strain through which all were passing, there were misunderstandings amongst the missionaries themselves. I myself was criticised for siding with Africans against the missionaries, whereas one's aim was to seek Him in each situation and to see Him glorified in each life. There was consequent loneliness, linked with overwork and weariness. At such times I recalled again all He had suffered for me on the cross of Calvary; now it was my privilege to share the suffering for those I was trying to reach. He was made sin for me; how closely was I willing to be identified with Him? With them? Was I prepared to face the cost?

Our Mission motto was deeply burnt into my heart: 'If Jesus Christ be God and died for me, then no sacrifice can be too great for me to make for Him.' This was my firm belief, and I prayed to God that I might be found worthy.

On 7th August 1964, came the outbreak of the rebellion in the north-east province. We were caught absolutely unawares, not having the slightest thought of all that might be involved. I was setting off in the Mission truck to Kampala in Uganda, a thousand miles east, to collect two tons of medical goods and supplies, food and petrol, when the news that Stanleyville had fallen to the hands of the rebels reached us. We waited to see what this would involve. No-one was very perturbed. We had had troubles and riots for the last four years.

Eight days later, on Saturday, 15th August, the soldiers reached us. A truck-load drove into the hospital compound bringing with them a wounded civilian. That was the start of five months of occupation. They were brutal and coarse, rough and domineering. Their language was threatening and obscene. All of us were cowed. We did exactly what they demanded, mostly without argument. We gave them what they asked for without debating the price. Africans carried flowers and shouted the slogans of the day as an act of obedience to the new powers. Rumours poured round us. We heard of murders, brutalities, beatings, stealings, looting, and burning. We did not wish to be involved, so we obeyed. We heard that the rebel army had taken first Wamba, and then Paulis, with very little resistance. Some said that the streets ran with blood, that they had to walk with care not to step on a corpse. All the previous leaders, all those who had been in government pay, were being systematically liquidated. They were searched out, evilly treated, and ultimately brutally murdered. Cars and trucks in the area were commandeered. To hear a vehicle on the road was synonymous with the approach of the army. Whenever they came to the village they brought a terrible sense of fear, a presence of evil and wickedness. And they were for ever passing, passing. Would they enter? What ought we to do?

Thus began the war of nerves. We had rebels amongst the patients, especially in the men's ward, and I felt they could well be spying on us. Care was necessary in every word we spoke. The soldiers came to visit friends day and night, but one never knew when they drove on to the compound for what they had come. Many times they told us in those first weeks that this war had nothing to do with us Europeans. It was a party-political, civil war. They had nothing against us as whites, and especially as Protestant missionaries. They wanted us to stay and continue with our task. When the New Order was established, they would recognise our good work officially and do all they could to obtain the supplies we needed. But in almost the same breath they would threaten us that, if we meddled with politics, if we interfered with their method of administering justice, if we helped any 'wanted' man to hide in the hospital, then we should be treated as traitors and shot. And the hospital would be burnt to the ground. It was not easy to keep calm in such an atmosphere.

Suffering? Yes; it began early on. The mental suffering of uncertainty, not knowing quite what they would do, nor when. At Nebobongo we were virtually cut off from the rest of the Mission since we were not allowed to travel. And we were completely cut off from the outside world, for there was no mail or radio communication with anyone outside the Province. There was no way of letting anyone know how we were. At first we all thought it would speedily be over, one way or the other, and that we should be allowed to continue our work under the former or latter government. Then things began to drag. We saw truckloads of young teenagers passing along the road and were told that they were conscripts going to the front to fight. We never saw any coming back. We saw a van go by full of European nuns and priests. Later it returned. Where had it been and why? We feared for them and what they were being made to suffer. We heard that the local chief had been caught, bound, and beaten; then he was taken to the people's tribunal at Wamba, found guilty, flayed alive, and eaten. No wonder we did not sleep well. No wonder we were not hungry.

Suffering? Yes; in fear for our own people. One of our girl nurses was assaulted. Two of the women were taken from the maternity compound rudely flung on to a truck and driven off. They threatened to take two of our little girls to 'serve' the soldiers. Primary school children were being rounded up in other areas as army conscripts. Would they come and do the same here? They inspected our homes, searching for transistor radios and tape-recorders, threatening death should they find any. I had none; but would they go and search the other home where both the missionaries had them? They demanded food, and clothing, and spectacles. I gave what I had. Then came the time when there was nothing to give, and they raised their rifles to strike me as a liar, and I feared for the physical pain. A male nurse, away on holiday, made his way back to us through the forest, telling of being hunted for ten days, his father having been murdered, his home burnt and looted, and his mother dying of heart failure. We were one with them, identified with them in their suffering, and our hearts bled with theirs.

Suffering? Yes; the day when they turned against us whites. News was seeping through that the National Army was employing white troops, mercenary soldiers from South Africa and other lands, and that the rebel army was being turned back. Rebel soldiers were being killed despite the witchcraft and the promises made at their initiation rights. It must be that the white man was using a more powerful witchcraft, possibly emanating from the white people in the area. Therefore we were to be bound and herded together, possibly shot. They were brutal and drunken. They cursed and swore, they struck and kicked, they used the butt-end of rifles and rubber truncheons. We were roughly taken, thrown in prisons, humiliated, threatened. We were driven forty miles north to be shot—but God intervened and we were driven home again! The whole church had been praying ceaselessly for our deliverance. We were four weeks under house-arrest, four weeks filled with petty interferences and pilferings, endless threatenings and uncertainties. The Christians rallied round wonderfully to help us and out of their poverty poured on us gifts of chickens and eggs, rice and peanuts. Each time a truck-load of soldiers arrived they were always there beside us, to protect us and encourage us.

Suffering? Yes; impossible though it seemed, the situation got worse. We were taken away from our dear Africans and placed under close guard, under prison conditions, in the Roman Catholic convent at Wamba. We saw the nuns wickedly treated, beaten and humiliated. We were completely at their mercy, and yet strangely God moved upon them to protect us, and also to feed us. Rumours fed our fears, and each long day led into a long night of waiting, hoping, expectant for deliverance the following dawn, but only to meet with disappointment—and to start again. We heard that our stations had been utterly ransacked and destroyed, and we longed for news of our Africans. Were they suffering for having befriended us? We felt we were always being watched and had to take extra care of all that was said and done.

Then came Christmas Day, and with it the next move. The soldiers began taking us group by group, in a small open van, a hundred miles east. The idea, apparently, was to keep us with the retreating army as front-line hostages. The group I was with was taken on the Sunday, but after travelling only seventy-five miles, we were put off at a house in the jungle— nineteen defenceless women and children surrounded by some seventy-five men, soldiers, and others, all filled with hatred and evil intentions towards us. Food was scarce; water almost unprocurable. Danger was imminent; fear was in the very air we breathed. Wickedness surrounded us on all sides; it seemed inevitable that we should be killed. And in my heart was an amazing peace, a realization that I was being highly privileged to be identified with Him in a new way, in the way of Calvary.

I witnessed the outpouring of hatred against the white man. I became very conscious of the extent to which we had earned this. If I was willing to be identified as a European with the sin of the white people against the African in the past fifty or more years—the injustices, the cruelties, the hardships, cheap labour with flogging, black women-folk and illegitimate children, bribery and corruption in courts and administration—then perhaps, in some small way, I was privileged to be part of the extirpation of that sin. We whites had to be identified with it, to bear its penalty, to suffer for it, that Africa might be rid of it, to start again freed of it. This was our hope; this was what made it worth while. Somehow He was working out His purposes for our Congo; somehow He would bring ultimate blessing out of the terror of all this suffering; for He alone could make even the wrath of man to praise Him.

Now the end seemed very near. We were expecting death at any moment. The guards were becoming more and more restive. A sense of oppression was closing in on us. Suddenly there was a distant noise. Was it friend or foe? Everyone stiffened and listened intently. We were bundled into an inner room, flung on the ground, kicked and beaten. Then the guards retired, locking the door. We heard the distant noise growing; it was machine-gun firing! Hope soared— could it be our deliverers? They mustn't pass us by; they must see a white face somehow; we must show them we were there. Would our guards fire on us through the window? Nothing seemed to matter any longer except the thought of deliverance.

I threw myself forward towards the window. There were jeeps, trucks, men, noise, shouting, firing. Someone was kicking at the door. Women were crying, children were sobbing. The door gave, and a white man burst through to us. The room seemed to fill with white soldiers.

'It's all over; don't cry, mother. Yes, yes, we'll take you all. No hurry; take your time. We can't take any luggage, I'm afraid, as we're a bit full up.'

So their chatter soothed through our tumultuous thoughts. We were safe! It was all over. We were still alive. The terrible nightmare was over.

12

GLORIOUSLY WORTH IT!

Home! It was less than three days from the moment of deliverance, but it was hard to believe it. The mercenary soldiers had been kindness itself. That Wednesday evening we were taken to their barracks in the Paulis brewery, all ten of us Protestant missionaries together, united at last with our two menfolk. They carried up jugs of hot water for us to have the first proper wash for many weeks. They served us a lovely hot meal which we could eat in peace, not fearfully glancing round in case of trouble. They brought us mattresses and blankets to sleep in comfort on the floor of their large sitting-room. Next day, they showed us all over the site, chatted with us, photographed us, and at last waved us farewell as we left in a great American transport plane along with 125 other refugees.

At Leopoldville we were given a tremendous and moving welcome by the missionaries there who had been anxiously praying for us and waiting for us over the months. On New Year's Day everyone helped us to get clothes, to arrange passports and papers, to book seats on a flight to Amsterdam. That evening we were again in the air, flying towards Europe—from 90° to snow! At each stop on the route friends known and unknown seemed to vie with each other in giving help and showing consideration, especially at Amsterdam where we changed planes for the final flight for London.

Through a battery of television and newspaper cameras, to the customs sheds, and straight to a telephone booth. Excitedly I put in a reverse charge call—I hadn't a penny in the world— and there was dear Mother's voice. What a moment!

That evening I was home. The long five months of nightmare were over. But it was not immediately easy to wake up and realise that we were still alive. We had lived facing and expecting death for too long to accept easily the fact of life again. Family, friends, newspaper reporters, church, letters, flowers—it was an overwhelming welcome, as to one back from the dead. At hospital, where we went for general medical check-ups as soon as an appointment could be made, we were all given every kindliness and consideration, and were each recommended to take a fairly long spell of quiet convalescence. For me, it was nearly ten weeks before I really snapped out of the stupor and daze, back to reality, and began to realise once more that life had present-tense claims and that there was still plenty to be done!

After a lovely four-week holiday with my mother and sister down in Cornwall, mainly sleeping, eating, reading, and resting, I felt reorientated, for He enabled me to look back on it all and to see it was a great privilege, offered to me from His nail-pierced hands, gloriously worthwhile in His perfect economy. There followed six months of deputation touring, which took me all over the British Isles and twice to the continent, speaking at some two hundred meetings, telling of the great and all-sufficient grace of Jesus Christ, and urging people to accept the burden of believing prayer for our Congolese church.

We knew nothing of their needs at that time. Had they suffered reprisals for our deliverance? We longed over them, travailing again that Christ might be formed in them. It was a glorious tour. My desire was to present a positive message of His redeeming love, of the greatness of Calvary, the privilege of suffering with Him, the realization in a new way of His pre-eminence. As I told the story of His dealings with me to His praise and glory, my heart became fully comforted and in tune to accept all the suffering as from Him. The wounds were healed. The mental shock was alleviated. Slowly He filled me again with a great joy and wonder at His precious goodness.

Then in August a thrilling day arrived, bringing our first letters from our Nebobongo family. The National Army had at last reached them and delivered them from the long ten months of rebel occupation. The first, dated 6th June, was filled with praise to God for His goodness to them and to us in keeping us all safe. They told of all the rumours they had heard of our fate, of their fears for our safety, and of their great joy for us when they received our letters from the hands of the delivering soldiers of the National Army as they arrived on 5th June. These had taken five months to travel forty-five miles!

A group of the faithfuls had stayed at each of our stations, guarding the property as best they could and watching and praying daily to see how the Lord would overrule. In April, however, the rebel soldiers had made Ibambi their headquarters, taking over all the houses and everything they could find, hoisting their flag, and ordering the remaining Africans to serve them as house-boys. Some managed to get away, with nothing but the clothes they wore and their Bibles in their hands. They lost everything just as we had. 'We are now as we were when you first came to Congo fifty years ago', they wrote. The rebels had declared that on 15th June they would kill all the evangelists. But on 5th June the delivering National Army walked in! Everyone had fled to the jungle for fear at the approach of the army and troops, but were soon persuaded to come back to the station. What a day of praise followed! The great church at Ibambi was filled to overflowing as crowd after crowd gave thanks to God for their deliverance. 'All the church monies have been taken; all the chairs, tables, etc., destroyed. But we have one piece of wealth left—our salvation. How we thank and praise God that He sent you to us to give us the only true wealth, that no man can take from us, that cannot be destroyed, the truth as it is in Scripture, our Lord and Saviour Jesus Christ. Hallelujah!'

Letters began getting through to us, week by week, and all were similarly full of praise and joy, and ended with a plea to us to return to help them and to have fellowship with them again as soon as it was safe and possible to do so. Our hearts were stirred. There were no grumbles, no bitterness, just praise. And the sense of their need was overwhelming. Two and a half million Congolese in the north-east province without one single doctor, black or white, with no secondary school teachers, their shops empty, no grain for planting, without clothes, food, or medicine. At once, we put in our applications to go back just as soon as it was considered reasonable by the powers that be. I continued deputation with renewed vigour and refreshed vision, telling of their need for our prayers, and for further personnel for the tremendous task of re-establishing all the church services they were so sorely in need of—I would add an em dash in herespiritual, medical, educational. Two months in a post-graduate course followed, preparing one's mind for the task ahead, and letters went to and fro. A new programme was slowly emerging in our hearts to meet the new day of opportunity as well as the urgent needs of the hour.

Our Africans, both the local Christians and those in local government, want us back to work alongside them, as brothers and fellow-labourers. But it will be, it must be, a new relationship, that of adults of maturity. No-one who has been through such sufferings can come out the same as before. I believe we have been welded into one as never before. The tensions and suspicions between African and European have been destroyed; and we must see to it that they are never restored.

At Christmas 1965 we had a wonderful family reunion, the first for seventeen years! My brother and his wife, my three sisters and their husbands, together with seven nieces and nephews were all gathered together, and it certainly was a great day. It was just one more climax to this amazing year, as each one could look back and praise God for His infinite goodness and preserving care in so many different ways. It was also the occasion for saying farewell, as I set my face to prepare for returning to the land of my adoption. Making lists, shopping, packing, labelling; visits to shipping agents, consular offices, and to doctor and dentist; arrangements with bank manager and with income tax offices. Then came the final meetings and farewells, the letters and reports. But above all, there was the joy of planning for, and purchase and construction of, a fully equipped mobile hospital. This is a long-wheelbase Land Rover, with its overweight springs and four-wheel drive to stand up to our impossible roads, fitted and equipped with a small laboratory, pharmacy, dispensary, and everything needed for major emergency surgery, and convertible into a caravan at night, with electric light and air-conditioning! A long-cherished dream is at last seeing the light of day, provided by the generosity of Christians, stirred to give to help the Congolese in their need, through the many deputation meetings. Surely He has seen fit to give it to us 'for such a day as this'.

11th of March 1966. What a day of joy; the day we sail for Congo, back to our beloved African fellow-workers, to take up the task again that He has committed to our hands. We go back at a time of unprecedented needs. In our northeastern

Province, with its two and a half million Congolese, there is a strong, virile, active church, with her own pastors and elders. But they ask us to join them to help in the vast task of education—primary, secondary, technical, medical, and theological—at a time when they have only a handful of Africans trained for teaching in senior primary schools, a hundred or so for junior primary, but none for the senior schools. There is the essential need of aid for their medical programme, for they have no doctors, less than a handful of fully qualified nurses, and only a hundred or so assistant nurses, scattered in badly damaged, poorly equipped, rural dispensaries, with no medicines, no supervision, and the constant threat of the outbreak of serious epidemics. They look to us also for help in organizing youth work and training the new generation to take its place in the world with respect and not shame, with courage and not constant fear, with honour in the place of bribery and corruption. They need men and women to help with the printing of good literature, with its writing, translation, and distribution; to help with the establishment of a theological college for the training of pastors to lead the young church, men who will take their place as teachers in the different area Bible schools for training their own evangelists. Possibilities abound on every side. The doors are wide open. The invitation has been issued to all who have seen the vision, and heard the call of the risen Lord, to those who know the joy of the mystery, 'Christ in you, the hope of glory.' Surely indeed in the coming years, we are going to see 'the valley of Achor' become 'a door of hope'.

Epilogue

I have used some of the three weeks which it takes from London to Mombasa to put the finishing touches to this story of God's dealings with me. As I have read the chapters again, it is clear that certain landmarks stand out very clearly. There are lessons which I had to learn and warnings which I still need to heed.

Firstly, I would put the realization that in myself I was a failure. I was unable to reach the standard I myself had set, let alone God's. Try as I would, I met only frustration in this longing to achieve, to be worthy. I'm sure that, for me, this first lesson had to be thoroughly learnt so that, when I did come to acknowledge God as my Lord and Master, I might not succumb again to the temptation to feel that I could succeed or achieve anything ultimately worthwhile in my own strength.

Secondly, I had to learn that, of myself, I could be ashamed of sin and hate its consequences, but that I could not actually hate the sin itself. On the contrary, I found pleasure in it. I despised myself for enjoying what I knew I ought to hate, but I continued to enjoy it nevertheless. Like Paul, who describes what seems to have been a similar experience in Romans 7, my position was, 'I do not do the good I want, but the evil I do not want is what I do.' Now hatred of sin is a gift of the Holy Spirit. After trying hard to make myself hate what

I knew I enjoyed, and nearly despairing in the effort, I came at last to the limit by asking God 'to make me willing to be made willing to hate what He hated', and He graciously did for me what I asked.

Then I had to learn that there are some glorious views en route, as well as many pleasant valleys, that do not necessarily help in the upward climb. Certain experiences came and entered my life. They could have grown big and all-important, but when measured against the course of the journey they were non-essential to the main progress. Again, other incidents were eventually found to be of passing interest only. But they might have seriously hampered the journey if carried along as an important item. I gladly accepted and entered into each experience as God graciously bestowed it, but I had to learn to cling to Him, my Guide, and not to the various feelings stirred by the passing views.

Then those wise words of Elizabeth at Mission Head-quarters in my training days have remained with me through the following years as a beacon on the path: 'If you're doing it for me (or for any man) you may as well go home…You're doing it for the Lord and He saw the first time you cleaned it…' The day all our midwives had to be dismissed and the maternity compound closed, I asked myself, how had I failed them? Where had we gone wrong? Recriminations, accusations crowded into my mind. What will the Mission say? Or the church? This was fear of man. 'You are doing this work for Me, and I have seen all you have poured in, of heart and soul; I know.' So He breathed peace into my striving heart—the same old message, but ever new.

Another deep truth I have learnt, and one we can all cling to, is that God is personally interested in us as individuals and that He will engineer our circumstances and daily lives so that He can thereby make us like Jesus. This takes the sting out of much that could otherwise hurt. He allows various accidents and happenings to occur, which will affect us deeply, perhaps, only so that, through them, we may be drawn closer to Himself.

There were the times of deep humiliation, coupled with a sense of insufficiency, both as a doctor and as a missionary. Here, too, these negative experiences were allowed to reveal positive truth. Only as I found my own insufficiency did I realise His sufficiency. Such ability as I had to lead, to organise to administer, all tended to strengthen my personal ego and pride. This was true also of my popularity with the Africans and the respect I received from the Government. My pride was big enough already! It was a stalwart prop on which I leant for self-encouragement to continue and to stick the job. God had to take the prop away, and I did not like it—until I found that He was there, willing to fill my every need and to give all the encouragement I desired! Even my inverted pride in my inabilities had to be dealt with. I said I could not operate. I had not been trained and I was scared stiff. I just wasn't willing to trust the Lord to work this out. I did not want Him to make me willing to operate; I wanted to go on not wanting to! But when during the first six months of Independence He allowed every surgeon in the area to leave, I just had to operate. Then He showed that He was able to undertake for this need also as I was willing to be made willing. My pride in my inability had been as great a prop in my self-preservation as my pride in my abilities was to my self-realization. Both had to be taken away that I might learn that Christ wanted the pre-eminence in every department of my life.

In the introduction, I mentioned the importance of distinguishing between the slight going down from a peak experience in order to set out across the valley to climb another higher peak, and the real going down of returning to base. The former may appear to be a stretch of the journey in shadows, but the latter would have been acknowledgement of defeat and failure. For many years, I did not discern this difference, and thereby suffered many long heartaches unnecessarily, listening to the devil's accusations instead of the Spirit's counsel.

Another clear truth that has come out so forcibly into the sunlight through the last few chapters is that God has no second-best. This is very often a contradiction of terms. If I am in God's will for me, it is His very best for me. God is eternal present tense. If I step out of His will, then I deliberately choose my own path and I have nothing of His best. When I confess my error, seek His loving forgiveness, and return to His will, then at once He restores me. It is always present to Him, so at the moment of restoration I am in His present will for me. Once repentance is real, and forgiveness sought, the past is past, and has no longer an interpretation in the present. The present may well be different from the 'might-have-been', it may well be affected by the consequences of previous disobedience and sin which can leave their mark on both character and circumstance, but nevertheless, it is the best in the immediate now. I have found this to be a most liberating and glorious truth. If it were not so, who among us would not live his life in an atmosphere of continual regret?

The night I was first taken captive by the rebel soldiers He worked that liberation for me in the midst of all the horror and anguish! I saw it in a verse in Peter's Epistle: 'For what glory is it, if, when ye be buffeted for your faults, ye shall take it patiently? but if, when ye do well, and suffer for it, ye take it patiently, this is acceptable with God' (1 Peter 2:20). In that moment, I knew utterly and unquestioningly, whatever the past might have held of failures, that I was in the second half of the verse. God allowed the circumstances to be such that even I, so often a veritable 'doubting Thomas', could not argue. Therefore He showed me, with a gentle smile, a smile of reproof perhaps, that I had taken so long to learn, a smile of deep love that I truly wanted to learn, that I was 'acceptable with God', and this could only mean that I was in the centre of His will. Certainly this could be no 'second-best'.

The last months of 1964 brought to a culmination so much of all He had been teaching me through the years. The suffering just seemed to highlight His love. I have summarised in my own heart the specific lessons of my months in captivity to help me not to lose anything of their wonder and their worth:

1. Participation in His suffering is necessary to each one if we are to fulfil His will in this world;
2. The pre-eminence of His Son is essential that we may know in very truth His all-sufficiency at all times;
3. Praise through His sacrifice is possible even in the midst of danger and horror, as we rejoice in His working out His purposes.

Above all, I have learnt a little of the tremendous privilege of walking with Him, of being identified with Him. Christ not only bore my sin; He was made sin for me. He identified Himself utterly with us sinners that He might redeem us. Now if He should seek a body, a vessel, in whom to live, that He might identify Himself with the deepest needs and hungers of Congolese hearts, was I willing to be this vessel? More than willing! I entered into the great privilege of sharing about the One who had paid the supreme cost.

'Brethren, I count not myself to have apprehended: but this one thing I do, forgetting those things which are behind, and reaching forth unto those things which are before, I press toward the mark for the prize of the high calling of God in Christ Jesus' (Phil. 3:13-14).

Afterword

Helen closes the first volume of her story with a new beginning. She was going back to the Congo, but it was a different country, and she was different. Fifteen months at home in England had refreshed her physically and spiritually, and writing *Give Me This Mountain* had helped her understand and give shape to memories of her first eleven years in Africa.

But she was not yet ready, in 1966, to write about the full extent of her suffering at the hands of Simba rebels on the night of October 29, 1964. In *He Gave Us a Valley*, she alludes to the brutality and coarseness of her captors, but it was only in *Living Sacrifice*, a book published in 1980, that she told the full story of what had happened on that night.[1]

Around 2:30 am, a group of soldiers forced their way into Helen's cottage at Nebobongo. Two male nurses had been sleeping in her front room as bodyguards, but they could not keep the soldiers out. The invaders ransacked her house and smashed whatever they didn't steal. Finally, when she thought they were leaving, the lieutenant, the leader of the pack, commanded her to go into the bedroom and get

---

1 Portions of this section are adapted from my chapter, 'Helen Roseveare: Faithful in Sacrifice,' *12 Faithful Women*, (The Gospel Coalition, 2020).

undressed. Instead, Helen ran outside and tried to hide in the bush. The soldiers found her and dragged her back in. One of the male nurses fought to protect her and was beaten until he lost consciousness. Then the lieutenant raped her.

In that moment, Helen said that she felt completely deserted by God. She cried out to him again and again, "Why, why, why?" And God answered her:

> In the darkness and loneliness, He met with me. He was right there, a great, wonderful, almighty God. His love enveloped me. Suddenly the "Why?" dropped away from me, and an unbelievable peace flowed in, even in the midst of the wickedness. And He breathed a word into my troubled mind: the word *privilege*.

> "These are not your sufferings: they are not beating you. These are My sufferings: all I ask of you is the loan of your body."[2]

It's important to me to use Helen's own words to describe the peace she found because I can't say I understand it. It was a peace that passes understanding. Helen didn't attribute her suffering to a God who was two-faced and angry or one who was unable to protect her. Instead, she saw that the same loving savior who had meticulously provided a hot water bottle and doll to two little orphans had allowed her to suffer for him, and she considered that a privilege.

In the miserable months that followed, Helen didn't always *feel* peace. She was held captive for a total of 5 months, and just before she was liberated by international mercenary troops, she was raped a second time.[3] She felt frightened and hopeless many times. But each time she kept walking by faith, returning to her hope that the Man of Sorrows, well-

---

2   *Living Sacrifice*, p. 22.

3   Alan Burgess, *Daylight Must Come: The Story of Dr. Helen Roseveare* (London: Michael Joseph, 1975), p. 195-196.

acquainted with grief, was her companion and would not let her suffer in vain.

During Helen's time in Africa, life at home had not stood still. Helen's parents separated in 1954 and divorced a couple of years later. Helen never directly discussed her parents' divorce in any of her books, but her father explained it this way in his own memoir:

> Here I must record that behind all the activities I have mentioned, home was not a happy home. The war had separated Edith and me in more ways than one, and in the ten years that followed, we never managed to revive a sense of companionship.... Early in 1954, I removed myself.[4]

After the divorce, her father moved to Malawi to become headmaster of a school. He remarried and lived there for the rest of his life. Helen's mother never remarried, and each time she went to Africa, Helen felt torn about leaving her alone. But her mother encouraged her to answer the Lord's call, and so she returned.

—BETSY CHILDS HOWARD

---

4 Martin Roseveare, *Joys, Jobs and Jaunts: Memoirs of Sir Martin Roseveare* (Malawi: Blantyre Printing & Publishing, 1984), p. 56.

He Gave Us A Valley

Contents

APOLOGIES

Very few names are used throughout this book. This is not because I think I achieved all this alone. It is not because I am unaware how deeply indebted I am to the many who made up the team throughout the years. I have not wanted to involve any in the responsibility for my mistakes, my thought processes, and sometimes faulty deductions. The blame is mine; the hard work was ours: the glory is God's alone.

1

Laying Foundations

We chugged steadily across Lake Albert in the small steamer. The mosquitoes were ferocious, and yet unable to imprison me within the butter-muslin walls that surrounded the low bunk in my insufferably hot cabin. I leant on the bulwarks, gazing across the dark ripples, piercing through the night to get my first glimpse of the mountains of what was then the Belgian Congo.

A deep excitement surged through me as the earliest grey of dawn touched the peaks. Was it really possible, after all the years of training and planning and expecting, that at last the true adventure was to begin? I was twenty-eight, with a university degree in general medicine and surgery, from a good, happy home background, stepping out into a new beginning. It was 14 March 1953.

Eight years before, in my first year at university, I had met some Christian students whose quality of life had so challenged me that I was forced to face up to the demands of Christianity. After three months of listening and questioning and watching, various circumstances led to my spending a week at a houseparty in London during the Christmas vacation. I turned up at Mount Hermon College to join a gathering of keen Christian girls and young women, training as officers for young people's camps and houseparties the following summer. I just didn't fit; I didn't talk their language. I couldn't understand their spiritual jargon—but I could understand their happiness and friendliness.

I soon found that I enjoyed the orderly Bible study sessions, and I started to read avidly through Paul's letter to the Christians at Rome. The truth began to penetrate my thick skull—it was true! It was no myth. It was no out-dated fairy-tale. This God was real, and true, and vital. He cared. He cared for me personally and wanted—fantastic realization!—my friendship. By the end of the week I had capitulated to the clear facts, the obvious reasonableness and the exciting challenge of the gospel. God loved me enough to die for me: would I say thank you? I would and I did. God loved me enough to have a job for me to do in His service: would I sign on? I would and I did. Perhaps it all seemed a bit of a gamble at the start. I knew so little, but I knew I wanted peace of heart and purpose for living—and no-one else had offered me both. No other religion or political group even hinted at a way of deliverance from sin, a fresh start with a clean slate, a new indwelling power to enable me to achieve the goal. A Christian leader at the houseparty wrote a verse in my newly-bought Bible: 'That I may know Christ, and the power of his resurrection, and the fellowship of his sufferings' (Phil. 3: 10). I went to read the verse in its setting that evening, and was tremendously challenged at Paul's dramatic way of stating what I was beginning to feel:

> But what things were gain to me, those I counted loss for Christ. Yea doubtless, and I count all things but loss for the excellency of the knowledge of Christ Jesus my Lord: for whom I have suffered the loss of all things, and do count them but dung, that I may win Christ, and be found in him, not having mine own righteousness, which is of the law, but that which is through the faith of Christ, the righteousness which is of God by faith: that I may know him, and the power

of his resurrection, and the fellowship of his sufferings, being made conformable unto his death; if by any means I might attain unto the resurrection of the dead.

Phil. 3: 7–11

A terrific gamble! What if it didn't pay off? What if it was all an illusion, unreal and untrue? Wasn't it almost too fantastic to believe anyway? Wouldn't one be dubbed a religious fanatic?

Despite the crowding in of such thoughts, I was amazed at myself. Within minutes of a great personal transaction between myself and God, whereby I simply thanked Him for dying for me, believed Him for His forgiveness, and accepted His invitation to serve Him, I had already an ability to laugh at these apparently-specious arguments to put me off. I knew with an unshakable assurance that God was real, that His salvation was true, that I was accepted by Him into His family and His service. God's orderly array of facts in the Bible, plus the consistent witness of the unhypocritical, outright good lives of my new friends, plus now the new ingredient of the persuasiveness of His Spirit in my heart, won the day for me. A great sense of thrill, mingled with a growing sense of privilege, took possession of me.

It took six and a half years to get my medical degree, six months in a missionary training centre, six months in Belgium studying French and tropical medicine—and at last, the five week boat and train journey to East Africa and across half of the great continent to the border of Congo.

Then started eleven extraordinary years of hard work and happiness, mingled with heart-breaks and disillusionments, heights of apparent success alternating with sloughs of despair; yet the net result of all this, judged by the world's standards, was not particularly impressive.

By August 1964 a small 14-acre plot of land in the great Ituri forest of the Congo basin had been turned into a 100-

bed hospital and maternity complex with all the necessary ancillary buildings and services. Many of the actual buildings were already there before ever I arrived; many of our team of workmen had been trained by previous missionaries. Subtracting the inherited start from the visible finish, it might seem that we had done very little in those eleven years.

I suppose one hundred patients underwent surgery each year, some of whom would otherwise have died; one hundred young men and women were trained as hospital orderlies and assistant midwives, all of whom would otherwise have remained in relative ignorance; many thousands of babies were born, who would have been born anyway, but with a 50% increase in the chance of survival; many tens of thousands of sick were treated, scores of whom would certainly have died without our help. But there were moments when I was tempted to ask if this was enough to warrant the enormous outlay of energy and strength.

Individually, and as a team, the medical group involved in the project had learnt a lot over the years. But would that accumulated knowledge justify the expenditure involved and make the whole thing worth while?

The first of many missionary-lessons were taught and learnt right at the beginning in 1953 at Ibambi. Starting with nothing but an upturned tea-chest, a camp table and a stool, a primus stove and a saucepan, I discovered what it was to be fenced in with difficulties. With no helper, black or white, so much that should have been done to maintain medical standards just proved impossible. Good training told me that a patient with a high fever and chills, painful eyes and profuse sweating was probably suffering from malaria. Treatment in those early days was quinine in a suitable dose according to the weight of the patient, but only after the diagnosis had been confirmed by the laboratory, by seeing the parasite in a blood-smear in the microscope. This microscopic procedure, even in an adequately equipped laboratory, would take a well trained technician at least five minutes. With fifty or more patients daily showing symptoms of malaria, this would have added over fours hours to the day's work. With no electricity, these four hours would have to be worked into the programme during daylight. And besides these fifty malarial patients, there were probably fifty others with chest complaints, fifty more with abdominal pain and diarrhoea, and countless more with ulcers and sores. Chest patients needed ten minutes each for history taking, examination, and diagnosis, even without laboratory examination of sputum or radiological examination of lungs. Yet they probably received a cursory glance. Each abdominal sufferer needed careful stool examination besides all other routines, possibly some fifteen minutes each...

The day simply wasn't long enough. And so malarial symptoms prompted treatment with quinine, with a quick estimate of weight and no laboratory confirmation. I actually asked God to give me a gift of discernment so that I could pick out the one or two really sick patients with pneumonia or tuberculosis from the line of people with coughs and colds. Similarly, one built up through experience an almost uncanny sense which sorted out the roundworm sufferers from the hookworms, and the amoebic dysentery sufferers from those with bacillary infection—and God overruled.

When I began to realise that over 200 patients were being treated daily, and record cards showed that probably 75% or more were responding immediately to the initial treatment given, I began to see that it was not necessarily a lowering of standards to treat malarial symptoms without laboratory confirmation, rather, it was a necessary adaptation to circumstances, with a change of method to achieve the same goal, and with somewhat more realistic hopes of success. These same 200 patients daily, having received something that aided their physical pain to subside, were then much more open to listen to the preaching of the gospel.

Then the first students came. What a motley crew they were! Yokana and Mangadima both from seventh or eighth standard (the equivalent of first or second year at an English secondary school); Mapuno and Bakiogomu and two other lads probably from fourth-grade primary schools, and non-achievers at that; and then Elizabeth Naganimi with no formal education at all, but a bright, keen spirit and a desire to learn and serve. So my second round of difficulties started. I was not a trained teacher, I had no course material; I was going to try to lecture in a mixture of two 'foreign' languages, French and Swahili, neither of which was the first language of student or teacher, and lastly, I was not myself a nurse, and therefore did not know the subject-matter that I hoped to teach.

Again God came to my rescue, and slowly we learnt to overcome this second hurdle. For the first eighteen months of our new training school, we wended our way day by day, with moment-by-moment improvisations to meet each immediate need. God taught me to teach as the need arose. There were huge and hideous ulcers every day in the clinic, so I taught how to cleanse them, curette them, treat them, and bandage them. A patient came in with burning fever, and so we launched into a lecture on how to use, read, and understand a thermometer. In the ward, a post-natal mother developed a high temperature, so we taught the dangers and causes of infection, and how we could prevent as well as treat them. A baby was brought in with broncho-pneumonia, and I demonstrated the use of the stethoscope and how to arrive at a diagnosis. An endless stream of patients, with a seemingly limitless supply of abdominal symptoms, provided us with material to discover the use of the microscope and to learn to recognise every possible species of intestinal parasite.

Students and lecturer learnt together and language very soon ceased to bother us. We created our own course material (aided eventually by the notes of a senior missionary health officer) and went at our own pace. The day of reckoning lay ahead, when we went together for the State final examinations. I for one was intensely nervous, and feared the ditch beyond the hurdle would be our undoing. But the students, in blissful ignorance of what was involved, confident that they knew what I had taught them, and assuming that this must be sufficient, went through with their heads high. By dint of interpreting French questions and Swahili answers, the examiners were eventually convinced that all but one of our group would do good rather than harm, if let loose in a rural dispensary; we went home rejoicing with six Government stamped and signed certificates, and six 'medical evangelists' were launched into our new medical service.

There were other difficulties too, on a more personal level, regarding my relationships with my fellow-missionaries. Early on these problems led to loneliness and a sense of insecurity, of not being wanted or welcomed or quite trusted by the fellowship. This, combined with the work-load and consequent inability to take a night off-duty, or to go away for a week-end, brought out in me an irritability and shortness of temper that often caused me considerable loss of sleep. I'd always had a hasty temper, but this had largely been under control for the previous eight years, since my conversion to Christ. Now the hot and angry word would burst out again, before I could control it, and to my shame. Patients who came to the dining-room window while we were at the midday meal would get a sharp word from me to 'go to the dispensary, and not bring your germs to our home'—and a sad look would come to the faces of senior missionaries, who treated every visitor to their home with kindliness and respect.

Evangelist Danga, in charge of the catechists' training course and the workmen's programme at Ibambi, took me to task for this un-Christlike behaviour. 'Don't excuse yourself. Call sin sin, and temper temper. Then face up to the fact that your white skin makes you no different to the rest of us. You need His cleansing and forgiveness, His infilling and indwelling, the same as we do. If you can only show us Doctor Helen, you might as well go home: the people need to see Jesus.'

During my eighteen months at Ibambi I was enormously helped by Danga and the student catechists, by Bakimani and the Bible School students, and by Pastor Ndugu and teams of church elders from various areas of the Ibambi church, to put up two large wards and outbuildings around our dispensary. They taught me to use an axe; to choose the right tree to resist termites and rotting; to select good clean grass and durable fibres for thatching. I learnt how to plan the layout of the building with regard for the prevailing wind, the slope of the roof with regard for the tropical rainfall. I knew how to dig out lime from the right forest streams, and to make whitewash for the walls, not only for its aesthetic look but for its disinfectant value. Together they taught me in the evenings, around the fires, to slice well-dried bamboo and to bind it correctly to make strong, resilient beds, and to weave palm-fronds for roofing and grasses for mats.

Then in 1955, following the graduation day of our first class of students, the medical team was asked to move from Ibambi to Nebobongo, seven miles north. We were asked to take over the care of the maternity and leprosy centres, with the associated orphanage, that Edith Moules had started fifteen years before. Here there were 14 acres of land, sloping down one way or another from a half-mile-long central strip of plateau. Available for immediate use were two brick-built, thatched bungalows for missionaries, similar buildings for maternity care and midwives to the north, and for orphans and widows to the south. A large, unfinished dispensary building half a mile to the west was almost all that was left of the previous thriving colony for the care of leprosy patients, nearly one thousand of whom had been transferred to a Government camp eight miles to the north, or else returned to their forest villages.

So we moved and restarted our medical centre, this time with the outpatients' clinic in the sitting-room, the pharmacy in the dining-room, and the night nurses' room in the guest-room of my new bungalow home. We became instantly aware of our urgent need of other arrangements! The smell and the noise by day, the disturbed hours and the ease of theft by night, made life almost intolerable. New buildings were a must. But how? There was no Bible School with its students, no catechists' school with its workmen, and we did not even have our own church pastor with his team of elders. So who would put up our needed buildings?

I often felt very frustrated by the church arrangements, by which Nebobongo was only an outpost from Ibambi and not a church in its own right. This greatly aggravated the difficulties with regard to buildings. For anything we needed, or for permission to do anything we planned, we had first to apply to Ibambi, which involved a cycle-ride of seven miles of switchback road in all weathers. This became a constant irritant. The danger of a hot, unguarded retort when asked to do a medical trip to some distant outlying place for one of the missionaries, when I felt (possibly unjustly) that they were unwilling to see our need of help at the medical centre, became more and more real.

We were such a small, insignificant team, yet we were asked to carry such a huge and important burden. At first there were only Florence Stebbing and myself as the missionaries involved, with Agoya our evangelist and his wife Taadi, a group of paramedical auxiliary students, pupil midwives, and a handful of men, discharged from treatment in the leprosy care centre during the previous years. None of us had talents or training as builders, plumbers, electricians, or mechanics. We learnt by trial and error to make bricks and to fire a kiln: I went to Ibambi to copy in diagram-form their beehive kiln, and then to a local rubber plantation where the Belgian agent had a large, six-firing-hole wet-brick kiln. We discussed the various possibilities, the amounts of firewood necessary for each type, the ease of construction, and, in addition, how to fill in the Government forms needed to authorise the construction as well as to pay the taxes for the firing.

Later again, between clinics and classes, we learnt painfully and slowly the difference between cement and concrete, and how to make each to a consistent quality; how to lay foundations and footings, do corners and bonding, set doors and windows; how to prepare roofing timber and to hoist the triangles and fix the trusses; how to square the corners of the asbestos sheeting and bore the holes for fastening it with nails; how to fix a ridge so that the building did not leak, and the guttering to take advantage of the rainfall.

But it all took time and money; it involved sore hands and blisters; it needed tact and wisdom in handling unskilled labour on nominal wages. And sometimes it was truly hard to see if it was really worth the effort. Through it all, the unskilled labour became at least semi-qualified, to the standard to which the teacher had been able to be taught! This did something for general self-respect and morale, but it also did something in regard to desire and demand for higher wages!

During these years there was the continual problem of responsibilities beyond my training. If the ease with which I responded to the missionary call to service overseas was due in part to my own inherent dread of professional criticism and competition, and the realization that in the heart of the Ituri forest this was unlikely to exist, now there was the horror of responsibility. True, in the medical missionary's life there is unlikely to be much pressure in the rat-race for promotion. On arrival at Nebobongo I became immediately, in the eyes of the national population and the missionary personnel, if not in my own estimation, the senior consultant surgeon, physician, paediatrician and obstetrician. But there was no comrade, no colleague, with whom to discuss cases or to share problems. Always I had to make the decisions of life and death by myself: and I knew only too well how inadequate was my training for this vast responsibility.

In particular, the burden of care for white colleagues weighed on me. Not that I ever wished to treat white any differently from black: far from it! But my African patients did not know enough to be critical. They trusted me unquestioningly and loved me unreservedly. They knew instinctively that by God's grace I would do for them the very best in my limited power, and that this was better for them than no care, or even than witch-doctor care. European patients, however, knew what they wanted, and what they expected: they had home standards with which to compare our frail and insignificant service.

Then these same Europeans stopped coming to me. Missionaries and tradesmen alike started to make the long, tiresome journey northeast to Dr Kleinsmidt, or the even longer journey south to Dr Becker. And I allowed jealousy to creep in and increase my frustration. How perverse can one be? I feared them when they came, and was hurt when they didn't come! I felt vaguely humiliated by my failure to provide the service that they wanted: and I felt even more wrapped up in a medical loneliness and weariness.

Then in all this whirlwind of activity—construction of new and repair of old buildings; teaching of students and preparing their course material; caring for patients, surgical, medical, and obstetric; leading the spiritual as well as the physical life of our family of workmen, students, pupils, and children; organizing and supervising some forty-eight rural clinics; ordering and preparing our drugs and medical stores; supervising the work in the small laboratory and down in the leprosy-care centre—in all this the Lord graciously visited our Nebobongo work with revival.

For four years the revival fires had been burning brightly in all the surrounding area, from some 700 or 800 miles south to 100 miles north, from 200 miles west to 100 miles east. Possibly about 100,000 forest villagers had been touched by the fervency of the Christian church in those days. Church services were alive and exciting: no longer slow, monotonous hymns and short, uninteresting sermons. Now everyone sang from their hearts with their faces alight with joy; everyone listened to the preaching of the Word with interest and expectancy. Lives were changed, and ordinary folk lived out what they believed in. Hypocrisy and insincerity were hardly known any longer, especially among the older members of the congregations.

In an ever-changing congregation like ours at Nebobongo, where patients came and went and the student body changed every two years, we needed continuous waves of revival to keep us alight. Joseph Adzanese from the Ibambi Bible School, with his wife Mary, and another couple came to spend ten days with us. Much prayer had been made before and during the convention, and the Lord graciously worked in our hearts. Pupil midwives were first touched: sins were confessed, hearts were cleansed and then filled with joy. Next the blessing spread to the workmen and their families; and finally to the paramedical auxiliary students.

Through the ministry of that convention, and a further ten-day visit to Pastor Ndugu's village, twenty miles away to the east, I also was deeply blessed by the fires of the Holy Spirit. In particular, the Lord revealed to me the sin of criticism of others, pride in my own achievements, failure to trust Him in my own inabilities, almost glorying in my frustrations. He showed me again the dangers of over-busyness, much doing, tireless activity, if it wasn't backed up by prayer. How easily it would all lead to spiritual bankruptcy, and work for work's sake, with no goal of spiritual fruit. In a prolonged period of time apart, alone with God, He filled me again with an intense joy and the deep peace of His abiding presence.

Shortly afterwards, I went home to England for furlough and much needed rest and refreshment, and a period of further medical and surgical practice, so as to be better able to cope with the tasks of the future.

Back to Nebobongo in June 1960, as the great day of Congo's Independence dawned. John Mangadima was appointed as Administrative Director of our medical centre, in accordance with the practice of the hour. John had been one of the first group of students who arrived for training in July 1953 and qualified in October 1955. Since then, he had followed two years of training at the Bible School at Ibambi, where he qualified at the close of 1957 as an evangelist and Bible teacher. He returned to Nebobongo at the beginning of 1958 and worked alongside Dr John Harris, another missionary doctor who was in charge at Nebobongo during my period of furlough. Mangadima was proving himself a very able medical auxiliary, a conscientious surgical assistant, a keen and willing administrator: but more important still, from my point of view, a real companion and friend.

Four troubled years of strains and tensions shook the new, young Republic, during which time we sought to consolidate the work of the medical service and to prepare national workers, such as John, for the task of leadership and responsibility. For this, above all else, we required Government recognition for our training programme, and legal certificates in the hands of our qualified workers.

Ever since the inception of the training school for paramedical workers at Nebobongo, we had been applying for this recognition. It was true that, before Independence, our applications had been made with no very great fervour. It had not seemed so essential then, and we had known that the all-Roman Catholic Government was hardly likely to favour a Protestant medical service with official recognition. Through the years of the colonial era, our students had been able to sit their final examinations alongside other students in the region, drawn from similar schools run by the Roman Catholics. The priests had not demurred, as my services as a lady doctor were available to help the nuns in the area as required.

But following Independence, our African colleagues started to put pressure on us to make the school 'official'. This was not just as a status symbol, but also because of a growing fear that only paramedical workers with authentic diplomas would ultimately be accepted into the nationalised medical service. Perhaps I was slow. My French was poor, and my efforts were spasmodic; my conviction of the rightness of the move was half-hearted. Whatever the reasoning, the recognition had not come. Then a letter came, implying that all unrecognised schools, paramedical as much as secondary, would be closed down. To be accredited was suddenly an urgent necessity.

Fresh letters were written, new forms filled out, different applications put in. Nothing happened! No response was received. John Mangadima pleaded with me to try again. I was fearful of annoying the authorities by my impatience:

I was fearful of grieving my team by my apparent indifference. Eventually I reapplied.

One day, as I was using ten spare minutes during the lunch break to clean out the carburettor of our van, a smart car drove up to my front door. There was Dr de Gott, the local government doctor from Paulis (now Isiro), and with him two strangers, whom he introduced to me as I hastily wiped my hands. They were Dr Trieste, a government inspector from Kinshasa, and Mr Jenkins, a male nurse with the World Health Organization, together responsible for the medical and paramedical teaching programmes throughout the country.

I was shattered. My always-scanty knowledge of the French language seemed to desert me altogether. I was tongue-tied at the awfulness of the situation. This was our legal inspection. On the next hour depended all we had worked for during the last ten years.

Tears stung my eyes. It all seemed so unfair. Why could they not have warned us, sent us word, allowed us time to present ourselves in the best light possible? The telegram to warn us of the date of their arrival arrived two days later, and presumably they never knew that we were completely unprepared.

Dr Trieste almost ignored me, talking rapidly to Dr de Gott about plans they had for developing the three Red Cross hospitals in our area, Pawa, Babondi, and Medje. They had just come from Pawa, with its superb ultra-modern buildings and equipment, and excellent laboratory facilities. They were going on from us to see the other two, and also Bafwabaka, the large Roman Catholic centre. They had merely stopped at Nebobongo on their way through, to save petrol. The very way they talked showed that they had never even considered recognizing us.

Their patronizing tone put me on my mettle. We put on the very best show possible. As they went round, I refused to be cowed or defensive, and staff and students responded wonderfully. They spoke up in answer to questions and challenges far better than I dared to hope. I launched out into French explanations, amazed at my own audacity.

True, we did not then get the recognition we so much coveted, but we were not just written off. We were given two to three years to improve our buildings and to increase our patient/student ratio. In fact the report was remarkably conciliatory, and even complimentary in parts but, as the inspectors were leaving on that traumatic afternoon, I sensed a complete lack of sympathy between the central government inspector and the local jungle situation.

We did not get recognition. We did not have legal diplomas. There seemed nothing more we could do at the time. What frustration to realise that John Mangadima, capable and mature enough to step into my position, had no official papers to legalise such a move. Legally, he was an 'assistant nurse', as his general education had reached only a certain level. Practically, he was an able houseman to me in surgical and medical services, and a capable assistant in administration and organization.

Not only was I frustrated in my own keen longing to see a national take the lead, but so also was John. He was frustrated in that he had not sufficient outlet for his keen ability, not sufficient stimulus for his acute mind, and particularly not sufficient general knowledge to appreciate that all this was due not to the white man's superiority and unwillingness to hand over, but rather to circumstances of place and timing of birth quite beyond our control. His natural nationalism made him often appear proud; his frustrated leadership ability made him often appear bossy and even offensive to others in the team.

Then suddenly in August 1964 we found ourselves plunged into the horrors of the Simba uprising. The brutality and coarseness of those evil men almost overwhelmed me. Through ten months at Nebobongo they wrought havoc, destroying property, stealing possessions, inflicting cruelties, instilling fear. Shops emptied of all stores. All work ceased and the economy crumbled. Good men were murdered, many others tortured and mutilated. All sense of order and discipline disappeared and anarchy took over. We foreigners were rounded up and taken off to prison, from where we were eventually rescued by the National Army and flown to our various homes. The nationals were hounded and threatened, their homes often burnt and all their possessions looted. Schools were all closed, and even small school children rounded up to serve as 'Simba reserves', with many being killed in battle. Hospitals and dispensaries tried to stagger on, till all supplies were exhausted: and then they too closed down and medical workers, like all others, slipped away into hiding in the great Ituri forest.

Many times in the first ten weeks John, like others, stood by me, and would gladly have given his life if he could have protected me. One day, a carload of apparently friendly rebel soldiers drove up to my house. John went with me as we crossed the courtyard to them from the school. They asked to be given berets, such as they had seen other rebels wearing. These others had declared that they received them at Nebobongo, but in fact they had stolen them a few days previously from the store of Youth Club uniforms in my home. There were none left, and I said so. Immediately one of them accused me of lying and of refusing to give them what they wanted. He raised his rifle to strike me with the butt-end—and John threw himself between us and took the blow. Eventually we calmed them down with a quip of humour, offering them each a bowl of loganberries and condensed milk and saying that, in English, these were also called 'berries'—and the situation passed.

Another night seventeen wild youths, armed with spears, clubs and crowbars, swarmed into school, demanding our vehicle, the keys and the driver. After much haggling, I was eventually forced to drive them to Wamba, seventy miles east, in darkness and rain with no lights or windscreen wipers. Two miles up the road we pulled in at a plantation factory, to ask for petrol and motor-oil. When a local mechanic brought these, he was then asked to repair the lights and self-starter. I meanwhile stood alone in the dark, conscious that death was very near. I had earlier deliberately disconnected lights, starter, and wipers, an act that, when discovered, would be considered blatant sabotage and worthy of instant death. At that moment I became conscious that I was not alone. Turning my head, I found John once again standing beside me, and Joel, a first year student, with him.

The lights shone out. Shortly afterwards the engine revved up. In a moment of startled silence as the engine cut out, the rebel lieutenant asked if it had been an act of sabotage. 'Assuredly', the mechanic replied: and seventeen enraged youths turned on the three of us, now clearly visible in the full glare of the headlights. The three of us tensed to take the assault, expecting to be instantly in the Lord's presence, when, suddenly, all seventeen were checked, poised in full charge, unable to move a muscle. God had stepped in. It was as though we were surrounded by an invisible barrier of heavenly glory, which blinded our assailants as the midday sun might have done.

'Go on! Kill us—it doesn't matter. We shall go to be with Jesus which is far better. But one day, God will demand our blood at your hands.'

Suddenly, inexplicably, as though they had forgotten our existence, they swung round, loosed from the grip of the paralyzing power. Laughing and jeering they piled into the van, forcing the mechanic to drive them away into the night.

And the three of us were left there in the dark and the rain, alone and cold, but alive. As we walked home in awestruck silence, my heart was deeply moved that these two had stood by me, ready to die if need be, rather than let me face the ordeal alone.

The same happened on the day I finally left Nebobongo. I had been captured several days previously, taken away at night with only the clothes I stood up in. We had been driven to Isiro to be shot, and then had been reprieved, brought back and since held under house-arrest. A senior officer of the rebel troops had visited us and agreed that it was best for the three women missionaries from Nebobongo to stay with those at Ibambi. Then someone had casually remarked that I had not been given time the previous week to 'pack my suitcase'—in the midst of assault and wickedness!

So the rebels had arranged to escort me to Nebobongo to collect whatever I needed to return and live at Ibambi. On arrival, they gave me an hour …

The Nebobongo church council gathered at once in my home, and we read from the Bible and had prayer together. Then I handed to one the keys of the office and showed him the books and all the money in hand. Together we agreed to divide it all at once, and to give it out to each member of the 'family', rather than leave it to be stolen by the rebels. I had listed all my 'property'—portable typewriter, ancient bicycle, pressure lamp—and written a letter transferring ownership of each item to one and another member of the team. I talked to Mangadima about drugs and equipment, medical and surgical procedures, and handed him the whole responsibility for the medical service, as acting director in my absence.

Their total silence, tear-filled eyes, pathetic nodding acquiescence in everything I did and said, told its own story. Hearts were being torn open. Each was reeling under the sense of impossible and unwanted burdens of responsibility, and the realization that the one they loved and respected and relied on was actually leaving.

The rebels came back and ordered me to the lorry—plus the hurriedly-stuffed suitcase. And my little adopted daughter Fibi, just ten years old, clung to me, sobbing pathetically.

'Mummy! Mummy! Take me with you! Don't leave me behind again! Please, please, Mummy, take me too!'

My heart ached with a great twisting pain. I hardly dared to look at the child as she clung to my skirt and I pressed her to me. I kissed her tight curls, as my eyes were blinded with tears—and heard a quiet voice beside me:

'Doctor, when Jesus was on the cross, He turned to John and asked him to look after His mother. I'll take your little girl in the same way,' and he gathered Fibi up in his arms and carried her away to his own home. In the moment of my urgent emotional crisis, John had been able to swallow his own grief and the poignancy of his own loneliness and need, and rising above it, to think only of my need.

Then, after we had been driven away, John quietly took over the direction of the medical centre, showing great wisdom as well as courage. Rebel soldiers were everywhere: some were in the wards as patients, one young man with compound fractures of thigh and leg in the surgical ward, and another with severe schistosomiasis in the medical ward. Everything the nurses did was watched and reported. Entering the pharmacy stock-room daily became hazardous, as rebel gangsters always followed, and it needed endless tact and skill to steer them out without their looting the shelves. There seemed little possibility of obtaining any further supplies, and John realised the urgency of preserving all that remained and using it sparingly and without waste: most certainly, they could not afford loss by looting.

Late one night, silently, alone, alert, and watchful, John slipped over to the store and set to work. He divided everything into ten piles—penicillin, aspirins, anti-malarial drugs, vermifuges, sulphonamides and vitamins, syringes and needles, thermometers and bandages, powders and creams. He parcelled up each pile into cartons and plastic bags, listing each article as he did so. Then, glancing cautiously round the deserted courtyard and listening intently for the sound of anyone else awake and prowling, he slipped out with one load, one tenth of all he had.

In the early hours of the morning, he woke a village workman and handed him the precious packages. 'Go out now, from the back, in the dark, and bury these somewhere. Tell no-one; don't look inside. Then if rebels demand to know anything, you can honestly say you know nothing. One day I shall ask you for them, but till then, forget about them!'

John quietly repeated this procedure, going every twenty minutes to nine other different workmen. By 4.30 a.m. he had delivered all ten precious burdens, and no-one knew that another had also received a similar task. By daylight, everything was buried and all traces covered—and John took a quick hour's sleep before the new day's activities burst upon him.

Through the fifteen ensuing months, roughly every six weeks or so, he visited those ten homes again, one by one, under cover of darkness, and recovered his precious stores: and the hospital continued caring for the sick, rebel and civilian alike. Many must have marvelled, and possibly questioned, the apparent ability to continue treatment all that year, with never more than a week's supply of drugs visible! But John kept his secret locked in his heart till after the deliverance by the National Army, and our return with new stocks and supplies.

Other problems faced John and the evangelist Agoya. One was the presence in the nurses' training school of several students from distant parts, who did not know the local tribal languages. Every time rebels raided the hospital and nurses' homes there was danger of a beat-up, as all strangers were suspected of hostile activity. So they arranged for these students to leave and go to stay, two by two, in church homes in nearby villages, away from the main road. But there, another problem arose. Now, instead of the rebels suspecting them, it was the local population who rose against them, treating them as spies as they could not talk their language.

So they were all brought back to Nebobongo, and Agoya and John arranged to care for them themselves, in a hurriedly constructed dormitory not far from the medical centre, hidden in the local forest land—and there they remained in safety through six months of rebel activity.

At last the National Army arrived and drove out the rebel forces. Nebobongo became an official refugee camp, and troubles even worse than those of the rebel occupation broke upon them. Everyone hiding in the forest was commanded to come out to one of these official camps, so that the National Army could move into the forest to flush out and kill all the rebels. Our small village with facilities for about five hundred under normal conditions was suddenly overrun with several thousand starving refugees—and who was to control the mob?

John and Agoya, with other Nebobongo workmen, did all they could. Every refugee was allocated a 'spot' for sleeping. Church and classrooms were used, as well as every home and cook-house, and even some of the hospital wards. People were packed in like sardines. Workmen patrolled the food gardens and the avenue of fruit trees, and gave out stores as they could, but nevertheless wholesale destruction and looting commenced on a scale far beyond that of the rebels.

Suddenly the leaders found that the students they had so carefully guarded throughout the rebellion had become the chief of the looters. My lovely home had become a battle-field: 'first come, first served' was the order of the day. The students stole drawers from the sideboard to make suitcases and took the very books from the shelves to make mattresses! Too late the leaders moved in to protect property—there was virtually nothing left to protect!

Then the day came when these same students packed up 'their' belongings to set off on the long trek of 300 miles or more to their homes. National soldiers heard they were setting off, and moved in rapidly. According to the new laws, none could 'walk', that is, travel from one region to another, without the Colonel's permission. The students were therefore taken to the Colonel. One was actually his nephew! Before signing road-passes for them, he demanded that each one should open his suitcase (the drawers of my cupboard closed with padlocks stolen from the pharmacy!).

There was a pause. Soldiers stiffened, alert to the students' hesitation. A menacing silence filled the air.

'Open up,' the Colonel commanded in a cold, quiet voice.

The suitcases were full of stolen property—my clothes and my cutlery, pharmacy drugs and hospital equipment. The punishment for stealing at that time was death.

At that precise moment, John cycled up, driven by some inner sense of urgency, and took in at a glance the whole affair. The six students would be shot, including Samuel Yossa, the Colonel's nephew. There was no favouritism, no tribal link now, which could save those who used rebel tactics: they would be wiped out.

John stepped straight through the group and stood before Colonel Yossa.

'Sir,' he spoke with quiet respect, and yet with fearless authority. 'I am responsible for these young men. Let me die in their place.'

A stunned silence. All eyes seemed riveted on John, and then slowly moved to Colonel Yossa. The latter hardly knew John, nor all that was represented in the drama before his eyes, and he turned to his local adjutant for advice.

'This man is our doctor, sir. He is utterly trustworthy, amazingly capable, the medical director of the local hospital. These are students from their training school ...' His voice trailed away. The situation was beyond him. What could he advise? He'd never heard of anyone offering his life for others. He and most others were maddened by the criminal act of the students, especially after the way John had cared for them through the previous months. So far as he was concerned, they deserved death. But John...? It was impossible to comprehend.

The Colonel gazed steadily at John and marvelled. Yossa was a godly man, and he deeply admired the quiet courage and devotion of this young man before him.

'Take them away', he said to John, 'and deal with them as you see fit. Don't let them come near us again.' And he dismissed them all.

John told the students to close their cases and go back to Nebobongo. He was tired and emotionally exhausted. He watched them go, with eyes full of sadness, unable to understand why they hadn't responded to all they had heard of the gospel. The Colonel touched him gently and John turned. The older man held out his hand and they shook hands, one gentleman with another, and the Colonel quietly said: 'God bless you, sir. And thank you.'

As John turned to leave, a soldier gave him six road-passes for the errant students, at a signal from the Colonel, and two days later, the students left Nebobongo to trudge homewards—sobered perhaps, yet rebellious and angry at heart, as their suitcases had been emptied and each filled with two days' food rations only.

From then on, from July 1965 until our arrival in April 1966, John and evangelist Agoya did all they could to reorganise life. There was much to discourage, and at times they were tempted to despair. Chaos and disorder were on all sides. Shattered buildings, roofs riddled with bullet-holes; not a glass window intact; doors and windows and their frames ripped out for firewood. My home was stinking with filth, as the 300 refugees housed there had feared to leave the building during the twelve hours from sunset to sunrise. The refugees had completed the destruction of the primary-school buildings started by the rebels, smashing forms, desks, and blackboards for beds and firewood. Nothing was safe from them.

The committee, organised by John and Agoya, counted up all their resources, everything they had been able to salvage. They brought the books up to date and prepared for a six month 'period of delay', knowing that they could make no contact with the outside world till far more had been achieved in the way of 'mopping-up' operations. The leaders found they had sufficient funds to allocate a very small token salary to each workman, with which they tried to encourage them to pull themselves together and start work again. Buildings were the prime concern. They checked up on each, evaluating the degree of damage and what would need to be done to make them, at least temporarily, usable. They balanced one against another, and so decided to rip down one to repair the next.

The work proved to be positive therapy against the depression caused by the senseless destruction of the rebellion, and against the disillusionment setting in from the apparent inability of the delivering National Army to do anything for their succour. As the people pulled together to do something of worth, their minds started to tick over and they were slowly persuaded that it was really possible to start all over again. The more they chatted and discussed the pros and cons, the more they came back again and again (so they told us later) to the phrase: 'If only they [i.e. the missionaries] come back', and they realised how much we had meant to each other, black and white, just in the even tenor of our everyday lives.

They tackled my home first. The whole long south wall had to be pulled down, the roof shored up, and then all rebuilt, using bricks gathered from the other missionary dwelling which had been destroyed. New window and door frames had to be invented—and the local carpenter Bebesi mysteriously produced a saw, plane, and other necessities, suspiciously encrusted with red earth! Up in the roof, a smashed packing case provided shutters for one window. And so on. Greek merchants had returned to Isiro, forty miles north, and Aunzo, my cook, was authorised by the group to go and bargain for a roll of cloth, using the tithe of all their meagre monthly allocations—and from this, sheets were made for my bed, curtains put up at my bedroom window, and a cloth laid on the bamboo table that the leprosy patients had laboriously plaited for me.

Taadi, our evangelist's wife, gathered the women together and organised a veritable battery of activities: from a baby crèche to four classes for the primary school children; from digging, weeding, and planting food-gardens to gathering in large quantities of firewood for hospital and homes. Somehow she scrounged one precious chicken from somewhere, and daily they watched it fattening for my welcome feast, for, they reasoned, 'She must come back to us soon!'

After the initial flooding with some 3,000 local refugees, these were allowed back to their own villages to start life again: then came the second wave of several hundreds of refugees from 60 to 100 miles in every direction, mostly from the south, desperately seeking food and clothing, housing and security. They were grouped according to tribes, the healthiest in each group being appointed leaders. Each group was assigned a small area down in the largely disused leprosy camp, where they were told to build a new row of dwellings, with cook-houses and toilets, and to cultivate a stretch of land behind each dwelling. Slowly, a degree of self-respect and disciplined order was inculcated. There was ever-growing optimism and, I was later told, the frequently-expressed confidence: 'Surely our doctor will come soon!' For me, it was not quite as simple as that.

2

AM I WILLING TO RETURN?

We had been rescued from captivity on the last day of 1964 and flown home to England. The ordeal over, we had time to rest and recover. By January 1966 the civil war in the republic of Congo/Zaire was virtually at an end. National Army leaders and the major in charge of the mercenary troops were prepared to invite missionaries and traders back to the northeastern region to assist in the work of rehabilitation, so we were each faced with the question, 'Am I willing to return?'

That there was need for rehabilitation workers was undeniable; the task to be performed was reported as Herculean. Utter destruction and devastation had swept through the vast territory, leaving hundreds of burnt-out villages, derelict schools, plundered hospitals, destroyed shops, and thousands of pathetic refugees, homeless and hungry.

Each of us had to weigh up the situation: the need was glaringly obvious, but so also was the almost total lack of material aid to meet that need. The lull in rebel activities was clearly reported, but so also was the sheer impossibility of flushing out every rebel soldier from the thousands of square miles of dense forest. The declared wish of the majority of the population for the return of their 'foreign' friends to help them start life again rang clearly in private letters and public broadcasts, but so also did the definite opposition of a minority group, who felt that the very presence of the foreign missionaries and traders had actually caused some of the worst atrocities of the rebellion.

I looked back as well as forward, as I tried to make the all important decision. So many memories kept interrupting any orderly line of reasoning, making it almost impossible to reach a sane conclusion. It certainly seemed a crazy thing to do, to go back and start again from the beginning, with nothing except the knowledge that a similar uprising, with similar incidents, could easily happen all over again.

As I tried to review the past thirteen years, the kaleidoscope of experiences that had led up to that final devastating experience became blurred. I could not think beyond the five months' captivity in the hands of the Simba rebels, with their savage brutality and the wanton destruction of all that had seemed so real and worth while, the bestial, heartbreaking, ultimate cruelty of humiliation and rape, of fear and fierce physical pain. The vividness of this final frightful nightmare tended to blind me to all the joy and achievement of the previous years.

I could not just cancel out, as though it had never been, the memory of that awful night of 29 October 1964. I had to learn to live with memory in an understood perspective: I had to learn to accept it as part of the whole before I could possibly face going back to the same place, the same work, the same companions. So I deliberately relived it...

...the shattering hammering at the double doors of my bungalow home at Nebobongo in the early hours of the morning; the rough, hoarse voice demanding entry in the name of the rebel army; the fear, oh that dreadful physical torture of fear, with the throat dried and almost closed, the heart strangled and almost stopped, unable to breathe, unable to think. The near panic of senseless unreality. All of 'me' twisted in an agony of terror—and then the calm quiet that seemed to take over like an outside force.

As I nervously clutched a flimsy housecoat over my night-dress, pulling back the bolts of the door, God had seemed very far away and I had felt very, very small and alone. They had swarmed in: rough, uncouth, jeering men in various oddly assorted garments, smelling of dirt and drink, demanding the man of the house. One separated himself from the rest, in army uniform, leather-belted with holster and cartridges, dark angry eyes, a sense of smouldering hate: clean-shaven, I remember with surprise, with a hard mouth and discoloured teeth. They searched the house; their greedy hands stole what they saw, and their greedy eyes sought me in the glare of their torches. One touched me, and I winced and drew myself inwards. They started to go, stumbling and drunken, laughing and wicked.

The lieutenant had called me back, down the short corridor to my bedroom. 'Go in and ...' Perhaps I didn't hear; perhaps the hammering in my ears of surging blood and fear made me think he said 'undress': he denied it later. I fled out into the dark night, stumbling in the mud, fighting down wild panic as I fell.

'My God, where are You now? Where is Your peace now? Where victory?'

The soldiers came. Naked beams of light stabbed the night, and I was alone. They found me, dragged me to my feet, struck me over head and shoulders, flung me on the ground, kicked me, dragged me to my feet only to strike me again— the sickening, searing pain of a broken tooth, a mouth full of sticky blood, my glasses gone. Beyond sense, numb with horror and unknown fear, driven, dragged, pushed back to my own house, yelled at, insulted, cursed.

'My God, my God, why have You forgotten me, forsaken me?' the wild cry of a tortured heart—alone, oh, how alone!

Suddenly Christ had been there. No vision, no voice, but His very real presence. A phrase came into my mind, 'led as a lamb to the slaughter', and I saw as it were the events in the garden of Gethsemane, the trial scene, the scourging of Christ, the long march out to Calvary bearing the cross, to the crucifixion. One outstanding fact seemed to dominate the whole: He made no resistance. For my sake, He went as a willing sacrifice. Then, as swiftly, He spoke into my heart: 'They're not fighting you: these blows, all this wickedness, is against Me. All I ask of you is the loan of your body. Will you share with Me one hour in My sufferings for these who need My love through you?'

Two such contradictory reactions possessed my heart in that instance. How could He ask me to love these wicked, evil brutes? And yet, how could He, almighty Creator God as He was, condescend to ask me to do Him a favour? Always I was on the asking end, telling Him my needs and expecting Him to give me all I needed: and here He was, presenting me with His need and offering me the inestimable privilege of satisfying that need—the loan of my body.

Even as these thoughts chased each other through my dulled mind, the horror of the night continued. I screamed in pain, humiliation, fear—above all, fear mingled with pain. Yet, at the same moment, an intense sensation of peace, a strange, deep joy, as He, God, took over from me. Such a mixture of emotions, perhaps it can make no sense to others, yet He was real—vital, vibrant, real.

My mind tumbled forward to that day six weeks later, in the convent prison in Wamba, when I had tried to comfort a beautiful young Italian nun, to restore her sanity after repeated raping. She too had given up home and loved ones to come out to Africa to serve God. Maybe I didn't often feel much sympathy for the Roman Catholic cause; maybe we'd had wordy battles on various occasions as we had struggled against each other and yet, in our suffering, we were one.

This young nun had suffered till her mind was torn apart with distress. Her whole reason for living was gone: she had failed to keep her vow of chastity (so she reasoned, unreasonably) and so was eternally damned.

Now we groped towards each other, despite religious and language barriers, to seek the face of the God who is love, who is peace and power and truth, in the very midst of all that was hate and turmoil, our weakness and their falseness.

'Have you ever stopped to think that the Virgin Mary was called an adulteress by her own friends?'

She recoiled from me as though I'd struck her. Her eyes, dulled before with numb misery, sparked with anger in defence of the holy name that I had degraded.

'Stop!' I pleaded, before she could form a reply. 'Think! Be realistic! It's true. She was pregnant, yet not married. Joseph would say nothing. She just said that it was not his child. What could they all think? Of course they accused her, cold-shouldered her, left her alone and thought the worst of her.'

I paused to let the apparent shock sink into her fuddled mind. Her eyes pleaded for mercy. I was adding misery to misery. Was I just mocking her, trying to torture her, cashing in on her private suffering?

'Child' (she seemed so young, so vulnerable, so pathetic). 'Mary accepted all that with joy for you and me, that the Saviour might be born, the pure, holy Son of God, born of her, Mary, yet conceived by the Holy Ghost. She took the libellous taunts, she bore the stigma, in dignified silence, triumphing over it, because God was in her'—again a long pause, and she slowly let out her breath—'for you and me.'

Slowly light began to enter the dark eyes. Could this be true?

'Can you take this sin of cruel man against your flesh for His sake, as Mary took the world's condemnation? You haven't sinned: God forbid! It isn't our sin. They've sinned against us, yes, but we are only bodies for the Saviour to indwell. You haven't lost your purity—rubbish! We never had any anyway: all our self-righteousness is as dirty rags in God's holy sight. But if we have Him who is all pure indwelling us, their wickedness can't touch Him or sully His purity.'

She began to talk, to unwind, to tell me of that awful night and the whole nightmare of humiliation. After suffering bitterly at the hands of the coarse soldiers, she had been singled out and taken to the Bishop's Palace. 'But surely he was brutally murdered? Why am I being brought here?' her tired mind had questioned.

The cruel, mocking face of the Colonel of the rebel forces would never leave her. In her Bishop's home, to add insult to injury, the Colonel had claimed her as his wife. All she had, all she held dear, all she understood, was destroyed, shattered, trodden underfoot.

'Why me? Why twice? Why couldn't it have been another?'

Dare one offer her the obvious solace? 'You protected another. Perhaps because you were taken twice, another was not taken once.' Even in offering this obvious 'comfort', my own heart shrank in horror at the implication, and yet peace and strength came with the wording of the comfort. The God of peace had breathed those words, and they held peace for our hearts. We eyed each other: it was a solemn moment in the very presence of God and slowly both of us felt a great inflowing of immeasurable peace. We touched God, and healing poured into our hearts. That was the first week of December 1964.

I was brought face to face with my own reasoning, my proffered comfort, during the last three days of our captivity, after that bizarre Christmas of 1964, still imprisoned in the convent at Wamba. We had celebrated Christ's birthday despite our prison conditions, with praise and prayer, carols and a crib for our nine children, even with an enormous turkey for lunch! Then the rude interruption of our midday meal: 'Pack. You're being moved.' Curt, to the point.

As always, the fear—the unknown always seemed more evil than the known. Was it just a trap? The first load of nine nuns and four others…the second trip with eleven priests and our two protestant men…a third trip…the waiting, the fierce hoping despite hope, the anxious uncertainty. Then our turn came, at 8.30 p.m. on Sunday night. Rough, crowded, cold, dangerous. That frightful moment when our apparent friend, the Commander of the rebel military police, who had protected us during our five weeks' imprisonment in the Wamba convent, left us, and we lurched on into the night, with only an evil lieutenant in charge.

The stop—nowhere, but a house looming out of the darkness. The harsh order to get out…and the truck took off into the night, back towards our prison in Wamba. My eyes followed the disappearing roar, while my stomach knotted in a cold sense of despair, a certainty of unutterable evil.

We were ushered into the first room: a settee, a few chairs with no cushions, a table at the other end. Windows seemed to be all round and rough guards seemed to be everywhere. We sat crouched on the cement floor, our backs to the wall, watching warily like trapped animals. Three or four younger guards, slightly better dressed, swaggered towards us and we shrank back. The first grabbed at a young woman missionary and Jessie Scholes, wife of our team leader, moved quickly to intercept him. There was an ugly moment as he raised his gun to strike her angrily for interference…and the younger woman leapt up, almost offering to go with him, rather than see Jessie struck or hurt.

'She's suffered before', my coward heart encouraged me.

They dragged another to her feet and took her away. I shrank wretchedly behind the settee and watched her go, with misery and fear in my heart.

'What did you counsel that young nun? OK for another, eh, but not for you?' So some voice seemed to taunt me. Still I shrank and prayed to remain hidden from their wicked seeking eyes.

'They're looking round for more prey. Don't forget, everyone left in here, but for you, is so far untouched,' and there seemed to be only one young guard at that moment.

He took me, out into the dark.

Half an hour later I stumbled back into the front room, without looking at anyone, stumbling over dozing forms in the darkness, till I found the settee and threw myself down, wrapped in my own misery. My mind was agonizingly tired. I seemed to be only just holding on to sanity. We were waiting for death, almost all hope of deliverance gone. There didn't seem any point in resistance. Why couldn't they just kill us and be done with it? Why the suffering first? Who would be benefited by all this?

The others weren't back: my heart winced for them and I found solace in praying for them, for their minds, for an ability to accept. Perhaps because I was a doctor, or because my life hadn't been all white in the past, or just because I was me, I had been able to adjust mentally to some extent to this new method of attack against the missionary.

One of the other girls stumbled in…minutes ticked by on leaden feet. Another came back. My heart went out to her and my arms drew her down beside me. She sobbed helplessly. We didn't talk. I just held her close to me and loved her, till she quietened and dozed in utter exhaustion. How much her love to protect another had cost her. Oh, those brutes, those brutes, how dared they touch her?

I shook myself from reminiscing and tried to think soberly and constructively. Those five awful months of captivity in 1964 were only a passing episode. I needed to remember honestly the work from 1953 to 1964, and all that God had enabled us to achieve in His service; and then to discover if my part in this work in Congo/Zaire was finished, or if in fact He wanted me back there to help in the mammoth task of reconstruction.

Just what the task might involve was practically impossible to imagine from the comfortable affluence of an English home. How extensive had the destruction of the rebellion been? Greek traders, brought to prison in Wamba in December 1964, one month after we had been captured, had reported everything destroyed—buildings, equipment, school and hospital supplies—but we had hoped that they exaggerated. Then the first letters to come out of the war-torn region in August 1965 told us of the loss of all things, and we began to sense a little of what might be the truth.

Doubts gnawed in my heart. Did it really make any sense, starting all over again? The devastating destruction, the enormity of the task of reconstruction, the infinitesimal offering we would have to share: and then what? What had happened once could flare up all over again. What guarantee had we of any lasting peace? What assurance that we wouldn't be wasting our time, that newly-erected buildings wouldn't be pulled down, that newly-stocked hospital pharmacies wouldn't be ransacked?

Were we really wanted? How could one begin to assess this in realistic terms? I didn't want to force my services on the Africans if, in truth, they didn't want me, or would rather be without me. During the years since Independence was declared in June 1960, foreigners had frequently been shown that they were not welcome. Doubtless we deserved much of the treatment we got. For fifty years Africans waited, stood, were ignored and by-passed while Europeans were served immediately with courtesy and given a comfortable chair in pleasant surroundings if a slight delay was unavoidable. It wasn't really surprising that there was a backlog of African hurts to be worked off, by reversing the roles: 'I waited, so now you wait.' Unfortunately, the white man had little of the patient forbearance and amazing long-suffering of his African partner, and would often retort or flare up, thereby giving the tormentor great satisfaction at realizing that the needle-prick had found its mark, and so perpetuating the process indefinitely: 'as white, so black.'

True, it was no use being over-influenced by the memory of the coarse shouting of one drunken soldier at a road-block—'Go back, you dirty white colonialist! Aren't you the cause of all our trouble?'—however unnerving it had been, that wild stormy night. Nor must I dwell too much on the treatment I had received at the immigration offices in 1961. A well-dressed, correctly-spoken officer had ignored me all day, leaving me standing outside on the veranda from 9 a.m. till 4 p.m. My passport lay on his table. He chose to see some twenty or so nationals, all but two of whom had arrived after me, and then told me to 'come back tomorrow'!

Yet these were straws in an anti-colonial wind.

There were of course other straws which blew differently. John Mangadima, as my surgical assistant and close friend, had gone with me, on 13 February 1961, the two-hour weekly journey to Wamba by car, for a day's work at the government hospital. Just before reaching Wamba, we had been flagged down and warned to go home.

'All is chaos. People are fleeing. All the foreigners are being held in prison.'

Puzzled, uncertain, fearful, yet knowing that we must go on to fulfil our medical responsibilities to the patients, over a hundred in number, who were waiting for us, we drove on towards the town. Halted and challenged (and mentally almost demoralised by fear) by a gang of rough soldiers at a makeshift road-block in the suburbs, we were eventually escorted to the authorities. Suddenly everything changed. Smiles, hand-shakes, pleasantness on all sides, and a piece of paper giving me freedom of movement as 'their doctor'. Probably no higher honour could have been offered me at that moment, but the conditions were hardly auspicious for recognizing honour. However, that day I was accepted, and wanted, as a doctor to serve them; that day the soldiers stood to attention and saluted as we drove past.

Unfortunately, I had different treatment only four weeks later, from the same soldiers, the same authorities, in the same buildings. I was then held prisoner for four fearful hours, because my indicator lights had failed to show I was turning right off a roundabout. The car was brought to a halt by violent gesticulations and wild shoutings. I was ordered out in no uncertain manner and hounded into the police station, accused of no-one-quite-knew-what, pushed around unceremoniously and threatened continuously. I was ultimately fined £20, which I did not have on me. Asking permission for a policeman to escort me to the home of our missionaries for assistance, I was shouted at and ordered not to prevaricate, told to 'pay up or else…'. Deciding that silence was the better part of valour, I just stood. Struck and jeered at for not knowing how to answer, becoming muddled with fear and uncertain in my comprehension of the local French, I just stood.

By then I had been as convinced that I was not wanted as, four weeks before, I had vaguely dared to hope that I was wanted. So government officials, soldiers, and police had made it pretty clear that, by and large, they no longer wanted the interfering presence of the foreigners.

But what about our own students and medical workers? Was there possibly a different attitude there? I longed to believe that, after the eleven years during which we had lived and worked together, some might be able to overcome the national distrust of the foreigner. Couldn't they believe that we honestly only wanted to help, with no ulterior motive, no paternalism, none of the 'neo-colonial imperialism' about which they were indoctrinated daily from eastern broadcasting stations?

I recalled a particular episode at our Nebobongo medical centre in 1962. John Mangadima, besides being my assistant and friend, was also a strong nationalist, for which I respected him. Sometimes this came over as an 'anti-white' spirit, as on the occasion when the wife of the national regional administrator spent three months in my home, due to difficulties during her first pregnancy. On one of her husband's rare visits to her, John approached him for his advice concerning the scale of wages that the missionaries paid to nurses and workmen. The administrator called a select meeting of local leaders of our medical centre in my sitting-room, and then asked me to attend. I was frankly nervous, as I had never known if we were wholly within the present law or not, nor whether our interpretation of the law would be acceptable to whomever was in power at any given moment. If the administrator had said that my scale was not acceptable, it could have landed me in enormous difficulties, such as back-paying all hospital employees for two years to government professional salary-scales, involving as much as £5,000, or a prison sentence to equivalent value, which in Congo at that time might have been for the duration of my life!

We met in strained silence, each avoiding looking at the other. I was scared, but I didn't want to show it. John was half-ashamed, half-belligerent. He loved me and respected me, and he didn't want to hurt me, but nevertheless he wanted to know the truth. He reasoned: 'Everyone knows that the white foreigners are not always straight: they can play with words to forward their own ends.' Not that he blamed us. He really believed that I meant well, but I was white. It wasn't my fault, he knew, but he couldn't ignore it. He felt responsible for the other members of the team who were more easily swayed by my words.

Damaris, the head midwife, was obviously grieved. She wished this confrontation had not occurred. She believed that I'd be hurt and would have done anything to protect me.

Taadi, the evangelist's wife, sat beside me, obviously horrified that anyone could dare to question my word. She believed in me implicitly, and yet she feared some sinister, unknown force.

Each one waited for the other to start. The only one at ease was the administrator. He signalled to John to 'state his case'. John was afraid now, the eyes wary, weighing his words carefully.

'Basically, is it right, under the excuse of a private contract, to pay salaries far below the government minimum?'

Put like that, it sounded mean, and God knows that I never wanted to be mean. But it was this or nothing, and wasn't this better than nothing? There could be no hospital, no church medical service, if we had to pay government minimum professional wages. We simply didn't possess the money.

'Show me your pay-book', the administrator ordered John. Grudgingly he passed it over. He and I were both afraid of being proved wrong, yet neither wanted to hurt the other. The air was tense.

'Really, you are fools', commented the administrator to the world at large. 'In the world there are two groups of people: those who work for a salary in this life with no preparation for the future, and those who give no thought to the present but are well prepared for the future.' I almost gasped; who would have thought that a government official could talk like this?

'You have the immense privilege of belonging to the second group; I have the stupidity to belong to the first. And you want to change over?'

John looked decidedly uncomfortable; Taadi was beaming; Damaris smiled her gentle, sad, understanding smile; I breathed a little more easily. The administrator never did answer the actual question. I was to remain for ever in doubt as to whether I was legally right or wrong; but he changed the whole atmosphere and authorised us to continue to find our own solutions.

Had I been able to look into the future and see the tremendous problems of the same kind that lay ahead I might well have decided against returning to start again in 1966. Even without that foreknowledge, there were lurking doubts in my mind as to whether our students would really want us back or not. I knew full well that they desperately wanted classes, teaching, anything we could give them to get life going again. But they were students, educated men and women, not children, and they would be bound to weigh up the cost. Was the apparent price too much to pay? It would mean deliberately subjecting themselves again to what they could only call white domination and paternalism—once again having to say the eternal 'thank you' and to kow-tow to those who seemed always able to give.

I tried to look at the situation dispassionately, to see it with their eyes. I was asking them to trust and believe me, often contrary to their common sense; to believe in my poverty and therefore inability to pay Government wages, when they could see what to them was my blatant affluence. I owned and ran a car; they couldn't. I had curtains at my windows and mats on my floors; they didn't. If I fell sick, I went for medical aid, even if this involved a 500-mile journey by air; all they could afford was a second-hand bicycle. This was all undoubtedly true, however poor I might be in comparison to my counterpart in England, or, more to the point, my African counterpart in Zaire itself. It was true, even if I could comment that I chose carefully and prayerfully how to deploy what little money was at my disposal. My so-called self-sacrifice and generosity were of my own choosing and should not therefore be thought to merit a favourable acceptance and understanding on the students' part. Could I honestly envisage a situation in which I could so get alongside the student body, so listen to their viewpoint and their suggestions, that they would be equally willing to listen to mine, and in mutual trust we could beat out solutions to the many problems that lay ahead? If I wanted to be sure that they trusted me, was I really sure in my own mind, firstly that I was wholly trustworthy, and secondly that I was willing to trust them equally?

As I tried to weigh it all up, it certainly seemed questionable whether we would receive a welcome on returning to serve in the Zaire of 1966, from government officials, soldiers and police, qualified medical colleagues and co-workers, or from the student body. And yet...

The letters came...

Mangadima, now acting director of the church medical service in our area, wrote and told me of the well-nigh emptied shelves in the pharmacy, and of the endless queues of pathetic refugees and patients seeking medical care that the team were no longer able to supply. He told me that five of the team were working at Nebobongo and four others back at their outlying rural hospitals, so far as he knew, doing what they could with practically nothing. He mentioned that all were working for love of their own people, as no funds were available for salaries. He told me that eleven of the forty-eight students who had been in training when the rebellion disrupted classes had made their way back to Nebobongo, asking if he, John, could not teach them 'till our Doctor comes back'. He ended: 'We don't really expect you to come back after all you suffered from our people, but if God should persuade you to, we will never cease to thank Him, and to love you and care for you as never before.'

Damaris, head midwife at Nebobongo and now in charge of the maternity unit there and the small team of pupil-midwives, also wrote. She told how wonderfully, even miraculously, God had helped her during the months in the forest, both in caring for the orphan babies committed to her charge, protecting them from sickness and starvation, and also in helping women during their confinements in the forest and in the maternity-unit, with little equipment and no help but God's. She told also of the bullet-ridden roof and walls of the maternity-unit, of the smashed windows, of the looted beds and mattresses, of the stolen instruments and equipment. She ended: 'When you come back to us, Doctor, we shall have nothing to offer you but our love, but of that you shall have an unlimited supply!'

Colonel Yossa of the National Army, the uncle of one of our students, wrote to tell of the appalling needs of the people, thousands of refugees needing medical care, thousands of young people needing training: 'If you will come, I personally will do all in my power to ensure your safety, and to assist you in procuring the necessary supplies with which to tackle the task to be done.'

Pastor Ndugu, the spiritual leader of our local church through the eleven years I had served at Ibambi and Nebobongo, a man I had learnt to love and respect, wrote: 'Can you consider returning to us? We need your love and understanding and fellowship; we need your courage and vision and determination; we need your knowledge and wisdom. We have little to give you in exchange, except our love and care, and the peace of God, in the knowledge that you are doing His will.'

Mike Hoare, the commander of the mercenary troops who delivered us from the rebels one year earlier, wrote to others: 'The needs of the people are so overwhelming, that we are prepared to accept responsibility for the safety of the missionaries if they wish to return to start the work of rehabilitation.'

A former student, Cornelius Balani, wrote: 'Don't blame us, Doctor, for all that has happened, but pity us for all we suffer. Come back, please! We are waiting for you expectantly. As God enables us, we will see it never happens again. Please don't remember as important the occasions of student unrest and disobedience: but remember rather the joy and gratitude of those whom you helped to succeed, and know that we others today need you to train us also to serve our people in the medical service.'

Bebesi, carpenter and mason, one of the senior workmen employed by the Nebobongo hospital, wrote briefly but succinctly: 'One wall of your home has been blown out and all the roof riddled with machine gun fire. The other missionaries' home is far worse. So we are stripping it to repair yours. It will be ready for you in two months. I will make shutters for all the windows, as the glass has all gone. I will make you a new bed. You can pay us something when you come, if you want to: but we are happy to work for you without wages, as we love you and want you back.'

3

Back In Harness

During the three-weeks' journey by boat to Mombasa in March 1966 there was ample time to evaluate my decision to return.

During the year at home, as we had spoken of our African brethren in their suffering, we had built up for ourselves an image of what we passionately wanted to believe. This image had become more real to us than the fading reality of our own sufferings. We accepted the biblical truth that 'in everything God works for good with those who love him', and then we allowed our imagination full play. We pictured the blessing our African co-workers were entering into, in direct proportion to the magnitude of their sufferings.

When their first letters had come, this imagery took even more definite shape and our hearts were thrilled. We glimpsed a preconceived vision and set about preparing for its fulfilment.

Why didn't someone shout at me: 'Pie in the sky!'?

It would have been a good thing if someone had taken me firmly to task, and forced me to listen to sense. Human nature just doesn't work like that. Intense sufferings and emotions do not always produce a total change of personalities.

I had to get down into the valley and look at things a little more realistically: to wake up to life's hard blows and not live in a little world of my own. God did get me to the place, during that sea-voyage to Africa, where I was willing to go back without expecting any dramatic change, willing to accept the difficulties and frustrations that are everyday occurrences in Africa. I should have to learn to see it all with their eyes and understand with their hearts. At home, some had thought we were rather wonderful or courageous, or some such adjective, to be going back to Africa again. But our Zairian co-workers weren't likely to think like that: doubtless they were expecting us to return. They had also suffered. Had we not been together? I had had a year's holiday, and hundreds of Christians had given generously to replace all I had lost. Our African friends had just plodded on.

'Why didn't you come sooner?' Would that be their question? Would I be hurt by their reasoning?

Then, too, for a year they had carried on alone: they had managed the finances, repaired the buildings, cared for the sick, been responsible in the pharmacy.

'Will she take it all back from us again?' Would I feel they were obstructing the fulfilment of my vision by their pride, or their obstinacy, or their unreasonableness?

They needed me to raise money for their wages; they needed me to provide the drugs and the equipment, the training and the transport; they needed me as a buffer between themselves and the Government, giving authority to their work.

'Will she do what we want her to do?'—with no question about my vision or my preference, my training or my conception of what I ought to be doing as a missionary. Was I going to resent their reasoning?

During the sea-voyage I became conscious of the old fears again. Why on earth was I going back? Large areas of our region were still in the hands of the rebels. Half a million Africans in the Isiro area had not seen a doctor for eighteen months. Communications were almost at a standstill, and shops were empty of all supplies.

My active imagination painted the scene of long hours and heavy responsibility, not enough drugs and poor co-operation from the government, uncertainty and insecurity, and I began to think I was a bigger fool than even I had previously reckoned!

Five days in the intense, still heat of Mombasa hardly helped to encourage us! Everyone fights for themselves in a bustling African port or railway station, and noise is an integral part of getting the job done. No good 'thinking white' here. Gathering all our luggage together, re-labelling it for the 1,000-mile journey to the Zaire border, weighing in, clearing customs, loading on to delivery trolleys for port to rail-head, re-checking, paying—all with the rapid calculations needed from one currency to another, and from pound weights to kilograms—in the never-ending roar and rush, heat and haze—all this was a mammoth task, or so it seemed to me!

We faced what seemed like endless delay in unloading the vehicles, endless red-tape in clearing the ton of medical supplies in our van, endless bureaucracy involved in getting permission to drive the 1,000 miles across two African independent states to a third with all the customs formalities, and bearing British licence plates...and then on the fifth day I found that the van's battery was missing. My heart sank.

'Possibly the battery has been stowed in the rear of the van, back in England, along with the cab seats, spare wheel, windscreen wipers and other movable parts, to prevent stealing,' I murmured hopefully.

All right, I was allowed to open the vehicle and unload, in the presence of the bonding officer—and also in the presence of the blazing overhead tropical sun! Slowly and laboriously, I shifted half a ton of equipment out of the van to the ground, sorted out the needed parts for the journey north-west, and then painstakingly reloaded. There was no battery. There was very nearly complete exhaustion.

The van was sealed and bonded. Four o'clock struck, and all the officials melted into the sticky air except for one agent, who set about to tow me and mine into a bond garage for the night. I climbed into the cab, behind the fast-shut windows, to join the eight hours of captured sunshine in a veritable oven, and I had to struggle to hold back the tears.

Eventually, Jessie Scholes and I did escape from the stifling heat of Mombasa and started out on the long climb to the cool of Nairobi, 5,500 ft above sea level. Up again, to 8,000 ft; through the rift valley with its magnificent views; yet again up, to 9,000 ft, and then across undulating hills and down the long slope to Lake Victoria and Kampala in Uganda. More immigration and customs formalities, opening a bank account and doing essential shopping, servicing the van and registering with the British High Commission; and then we said goodbye to Ugandan civilization and set off on the last lap to Zaire.

It was hot and dry. The murram roads threw up clouds of red dust. All along the route smiling villagers and happy school children waved to us. Herds of wild elephants and wildebeest, wart-hogs and antelope grazed in the surrounding grasslands. So we reached Pakwach, 1,000 miles up-country from Mombasa. This was then the railway terminus, at the source of the Nile.

There to our joy were all our thirty-nine pieces of luggage, but we had no papers with which to claim them—that is, not the right pieces of paper! Three hours of typically African haggling and bargaining, spread over a two-hour midday siesta break, eventually secured their release from a highly-amused station-master, by an almost-demented lady-missionary doctor! Hiring a lorry from a local Indian trader was child's play in comparison, and thus everything was transported to the Zaire border, still fifty miles ahead of us, up a tremendous escarpment of narrow, twisting rocky road with glorious views.

It was hard driving. At one place we ground to a halt, and I had to search for the book of instructions to discover how to get into low-ratio gears! At another awkward and narrow hairpin bend we encountered the local bus descending the mountainous route, loudly demanding that I reverse to the previous 'passing-point'—which I equally loudly refused to do, demanding my right of way as the ascending vehicle.

'No,' yelled the bus driver, 'I'm the biggest vehicle.'

'Doesn't matter,' I retorted, 'I've a trailer and can't reverse here.'

'I've forty passengers. You must let me through!'

'I'm a doctor: you must concede my right of way!'

Eventually, through sheer inability to reverse down that hill with the trailer, and with dogged pigheadedness, I won! So we continued on through billowing dust to the Ugandan border. Customs formalities were quickly and efficiently completed, and we set off on the eight-mile journey through no-man's land to the Zaire border.

Here we hit reality head-on. A young American was waiting for us. In fact, he had been patiently waiting for five days! He had the necessary documents to clear all our drugs and equipment, and the van itself, through customs, duty free—but there were no officers when we arrived! After a two-hour wait they rolled up, smell and gait revealing only too clearly where they had been. National Army soldiers accompanied them, carrying rifles, and we quickly realised that we were under a military regime.

It was a strange feeling, this long-anticipated home-coming, so unlike the carefully-rehearsed imagery. It was rough and raw, with coarse language and barely-concealed dislike, drunken and disorderly. It was terribly akin to the rebel occupation—and a tight knot constricted my stomach, and fear welled up in my heart.

'Why have I come back? I must be mad...'

That first night, at the Christian village of Rethy, we were graciously welcomed by missionaries to their bare home, stripped by the rebel occupation. I slept badly and, in nightmare, re-lived the whole horror of those five months of captivity, waking in a sweating panic with one idea only, to get out as soon as I could. I was sure I had made a mistake in coming back. I had thought I'd truly forgotten the suffering. I had thought the fear had died. It hadn't.

I thought I would be wanted, welcomed. I'd built up my own image of what I expected the new relationship to be between national and foreigner, as a result of the suffering—and it just didn't fit.

As we drove from the mountains of Rethy down to the foothills, to Nyankunde, I tried to fix my thoughts on the task ahead of us. Here, at this small Christian village nestling among encircling hills, was the possibility of developing a medical centre and training school for national paramedical workers, and I had been invited to join the team. Dr Becker, a seventy-year-old veteran American surgeon, was already here with two or three European nurses, working in the small thirty-bed hospital that had escaped the ravages of the rebellion.

Dr Becker had worked for over thirty years in Congo, mostly 100 miles to the south at Oicha. Except for his far-superior talent and knowledge, his work there had been much as mine at Nebobongo, with surprisingly similar results, both as regards the painfully unsympathetic inspection by Dr Trieste in 1963, and the traumatic cruelty and disruption caused by the rebellion in 1964. He and his wife had not gone home for furlough, but merely across the border to continue their work in a similar hospital in the south-western region of Uganda. The moment that it was considered 'reasonably safe', they had returned to their labours in war-torn Congo.

I spent one evening with them at Nyankunde, on our way through to our own region. The church was willing to offer us, as a medical team, forty acres of land in the valley next to their own. Already available were two small wards, and two homes for doctors and nurses. In their own valley there was also a fairly small building that had been the outpatients' department, with laboratory, pharmacy, and dressing-rooms, before the rebellion. The immediate suggestion was to develop the second valley with a 250-bed hospital and maternity complex, a large block for outpatient clinics and chapel, a building for doctors' consultation-rooms and special ancillary needs, a central laboratory, pharmacy, and operative block. The old outpatients' clinic building could perhaps be used as the paramedical training school until new premises could be built.

We talked far into the night. The need was obvious: the means were non-existent. It would have to be team work. Would I ever fit in after years of 'running my own show'? On Saturday we drove on down from the mountain grasslands into the dense forest jungle and through to Isiro. During that long drive over some 300 miles of rough murram roads, mostly through thick, tropical rain forest, the packed-earth surface cut and criss-crossed with deep gullies from the torrential rains, there were long stretches without a sign of habitation. Then the scattered villages, poor and derelict, seemed to contain only the old, and small children. The many barriers with National Army patrols to control any rebel movements were the only sign of young men. At each of these barriers, we were made very conscious that we were not welcome. The rough drunken soldiers seemed to feel the whole rebellion was, in some mysterious way, our fault.

We approached Isiro, our district town, at 10.00 p.m., tired out. The busy, bustling high street with its gay and noisy shops was deserted and silent, roughly shuttered and desolate.

By now, almost in tears and twisted with fear, I was certain I had made a terrible mistake. Emotionally, I just couldn't take it. I told my companions that I'd have to leave.

'O.K., fair enough. But you are our driver for the moment. Take us on the last fifty-mile stretch tomorrow, and we'll make arrangements to get you on the first army plane to fly out next week.' I'd rather face the shame of failure in the relative peace of England, than bask in England's acclaim for courage in the blatant revolution of Zaire. We were not wanted. No-one was calling us brave, or weaving haloes round our heads, or hoisting us up on pedestals. Far from it. We were unwanted, in the way, a nuisance. Hadn't they told us clearly enough to get out and go home, and leave them to cope for themselves without our endless interference?

Next day was Easter Sunday, 1966. We drove into our village of Nebobongo, 1,500 miles from the east coast of Africa, at about 8.30 a.m.—and we were mobbed! It was just overwhelming. They were all in church, as we drove up the hill into the village, and they just poured out: Taadi, Damaris, Riotina…I couldn't name them all; they came so fast. Then there was John Mangadima, and my twelve-year-old Fibi. We cried a little, among all the hugs and laughter. Nurses, midwives, workmen, house lads, wives, children—all hugs, kisses, handshakes, tears, laughter, hand-clapping, singing, praying, rejoicing.

The news had flown down to the leprosy camp, and the patients came up the hill on their stumps, singing and laughing, with bunches of hibiscus and frangipani gripped by their fingerless wrists. Tears ran freely at their abundant love.

On to Ibambi, at about 9.30 a.m., just as the 3,000 local Christians were coming out of morning service. It was quite indescribable. Pastor Ndugu and his wife Tamoma just hugged and kissed me till I felt I would break down altogether. We were nearly torn limb from limb. We shook hands and laughed and wept for a full hour, before being swept back into church for a service of praise and thanksgiving. One has to hear a choir of 3,000 singing from their hearts to believe it possible.

Three thousand faces were radiant, alight with an inner joy and peace.

However, I remember beginning to notice the marks of suffering, the scars on wrists and bodies...then the poverty. The men were in beaten-bark loin-cloths, the women in grass skirts, as they had been fifty years ago when the first missionaries arrived, but as I had never seen them before. There were practically no Bibles or hymn-books: everything had been stolen or destroyed. Some were unbelievably thin, all their ribs sticking out, from months of hunger and near starvation. The lovely church building was pock-marked in the roof, and walls, and floor, from the strafing of machinegun fire. There was a look of tired strain in many eyes.

Then again, all was swallowed up in the tide of joy, in just being reunited, in knowing the two years of rebellion-suffering were over. The tears did much to wash away the ache and the fear, and eventually blotted out the nightmare and restored peace of heart and mind. Here we were wanted. There was no doubt of that!

They said they had not dared to believe we would ever come back: 'not after all you suffered', they said—and yet their suffering had been so much greater than ours, so long-drawn-out and hopeless. We had gone home from our sufferings and, surrounded by the love and generosity of Christian friends in the homelands, we had been re-equipped and refreshed. They had nowhere to go: this was home. They too lost all, but there were none to replace their loss and re-establish their way of life. Yet they were not morbid, or jealous, or filled with self-pity, just amazed that we were back.

To me, the sense of being wanted was almost stifling in its intensity. They loved us so greatly, I was almost ashamed at how little I deserved it. When we had left them during the captivity, we had distributed all our possessions among them, rather than see the rebels claim everything. We had hardly dared to expect ever to return. Now several Africans brought back to us these gifts to help us settle in again—table and chairs, crockery and cutlery, curtains and blankets—everything they had been able to hide from the devouring hate of the rebels.

In the week that followed, I visited several of the primary schools in the area and talked to children and teachers, and to our educational director. It was truly remarkable how they had carried on. Some groups were gathered in the open air under palm trees, the children doing their writing and sums in the dust of the ground with their fingers. Other groups had put up palm-frond shelters, and children were using bark slabs as slates, with scrub-thorns as pencils. Masters were teaching all the subjects, including elementary geography, agriculture, and hygiene, with no textbooks. 'All I can remember, I tell them, and they repeat it till they've got it by heart,' one young teacher told me.

Hardly anywhere did I see a blackboard or any chalk, desks or forms, exercise books or pencils. There was just no equipment. Yet as I entered a school-compound, the children would leap to their feet, give their little bow of courtesy with their arms crossed on their naked chests, and then beam at me with happiness. Everywhere they sang, often in four-part harmony. Everywhere they were thrilled to see and welcome a visitor. Nowhere did I hear grumbles or complaints at their poverty—yet the needs were so overwhelming, the task seemed completely impossible.

Sometimes the teachers would unburden their hearts to me. They felt their own government had forgotten them, passed them by. Who would remind them? They had heard that all those teaching with the old pre-independence diploma would be required to give up teaching in a year or so, as only the newer, senior diplomas would be recognised Who would upgrade them? Or who would replace them? The school buildings everywhere were in terrible disrepair, equipment largely stolen or destroyed, yet there were more children than ever before demanding teaching. Who would rebuild and re-equip the schools?

The educational director of all our primary schools was obviously at his wits' end, dejected and frustrated. Government demands seemed so unrealistic and unsympathetic. The new demands for senior diplomas would cause the inevitable closure of most of our schools. The law binding us to pay the minimum salaries would cause many to be redundant, at a moment when we needed everyone! He had hardly any money available, few qualified staff, no equipment, and the buildings all in disrepair, yet the population had gone up by 50% in the previous six years and there were thousands and thousands of children clamouring for teaching. Where should he start? Which way should he turn? Which task should he tackle first?

'Couldn't you please help us?'

They urgently needed someone to train more schoolmasters, taking evening classes, organizing correspondence and vacation courses; to open a secondary school for the crowds of teenagers; to supervise the primary schools; to help sort out all the correspondence relating to government-subsidised salaries—and I could help them. I even longed to help them. Yet …

The medical needs were as great. There were hundreds of sick and no dispensaries, no nurses, no equipment. There were no drugs. The immense difficulties of transport and obtaining import licences were practically insurmountable. Yet I was there among them as their doctor, and they clamoured for help.

The first day after our return we drove our van, the Mobile Hospital Unit, plus trailer, up to Nebobongo, amid enormous enthusiasm. Road-barriers went down before us, happy, smiling guards saluted us, and the Nebo family turned out in force to greet us. How thrilled they were! It was exciting to show them everything—the folded-up stretcher support and the rolled canvas stretcher on wheels; the basin for scrubbing up; the six cans for our stock medicine; cupboards with fitted microscope, laboratory equipment, balance, pharmacy equipment with all the surgical equipment with autoclave and drums; and the forty fitted tins of drugs. The fan, the electric light, the tent extension, the window and fitted mosquito-netting—they looked at and studied and exclaimed over everything. We unpacked and sorted out, put on shelves and filled long-empty bottles from dispensary, maternity, wards, and leprosarium, to a continual chorus of excited amazement.

Yet as I went across to do a ward-round, I knew only too well that it was as a drop in a bucket compared to realistic needs. The only thing not in short supply was the patients— thin as rakes, with bloated bellies and spindle legs with great weeping raw areas; tuberculous coughs seemed everywhere, glassy eyes staring out of emaciated sockets. Skin diseases, eye diseases, intestinal diseases. One little three-year-old with cerebral malaria; another with Kwashiokor, weighing only nine pounds. One little boy had an acute cancer of a knee with secondary chest complications. I wrote up treatments from the new stock of medicines just being unloaded from the van to the pharmacy, and knew that, when they ran out, there were no more—nothing but poverty everywhere. No-one had money to pay for treatment; no-one had money to pay a nurse's salary; no-one had money to repair or refurnish the wards. Nothing but poverty: nothing but poverty. The words beat a tattoo in my brain, even in my dreams—mixed with the endless bullet-holes.

I had been down to see the leprosarium, where another welcome party awaited me with flowers and banners. A tremendous effort had been made to repair the large dispensary, but every wall was 'pockmarked' from the machinegun firing.

I went on a tour of inspection in the maternity block. Everywhere needed paint, but there was none available. Doors were splintered with bullets, and the walls even more pock-marked than in the leprosarium. A great effort had been made to make the roof rainproof, plugging each of the hundreds of bullet-holes. Walls were newly whitewashed, cement floor freshly scrubbed—but this only seemed to accentuate the innumerable bullet-holes. All the ten beds had been destroyed, and the mothers were lying on the floor on raffia mats. The delivery-room had been scrubbed spotless, and a vase of gaudy yellow-orange daisies nodded at me from the delivery table. Two soap boxes on crude legs, covered with butter muslin, housed two minute premature babies and even here, the mosquito-netting was torn with bullet-holes.

The midwives' homes were clean and tidy, yet leaking badly, roofs strafed by machineguns. There were no lines of clothes as in the old days, no books, no private possessions— they had lost everything and were bravely starting again.

Back in the hospital, we were called to the operating-room to see a woman who had been struck by a falling tree. I found everything scrubbed and ready for an emergency, a drum freshly sterilised that day with all they had left. There were no scissors, one packet of razor blades: only round-bodied needles and some out-dated cat-gut of rather large dimensions. Looking up as I was scrubbing my hands (in a new basin I had brought that day) I saw one panel of the ceiling had been blown to bits, and two others were pock-marked. Glancing round, every wall showed bullet-wounds, kindly covered with fresh whitewash, but glaring reminders of recent suffering.

The radiographic unit had apparently been totally destroyed; there was no sign of it. The anaesthetic machine had been badly damaged. And everywhere bullet-holes. Poverty and bullet-holes.

They were to be my diet for weeks to come as we fought to overcome both.

Then there were the refugees. They came in droves, endlessly. Mostly they came from the south, shuffling over 50 miles of rough mountainsides, up from the Ituri river basin, over the gold-mine range, and down into the Nepoko river valley. They were destitute and starved. Their pinched faces, bloated bellies, yellowing hair, and raw, bleeding feet haunted me for weeks. They told us of hundreds more who never reached us, lying down and dying by the roadside as the final weakness and inability to go on overwhelmed them. And the others just moved on, driven by desperation, unable to mourn, unable even to care.

Day after day, week after week, they came. Who passed the word down the line, that Nebobongo had something to offer? No-one ever knows where hope is born, but their stubborn determination to live, to survive, fanned the flickering hope into a steady beacon of light—and the hundreds became thousands, who trudged relentlessly on. Desolate, hungry, naked, sick. Out of hiding, out of suffering, with nothing— no clothes, no food, no tools, no homes.

One month from our arrival back in Zaire, having soaked in a little of the appalling needs everywhere—for schools and teachers, for hospitals and nurses, for refugee centres and supplies—I made my way to Kinshasa, over 1,000 miles away, across the vast jungle basin of central Zaire to the western border of the continent. There, amongst other projects, the Protestant Relief Association managed to get 14 tons of supplies together for me: 60 bales of blankets and clothing, 150 cartons and sacks of dried milk, over 100 sacks of bulgur corn, half a ton of medicines including precious antibiotics, and umpteen sacks of bandages! I managed to buy some £400-worth of blackboard paint and chalk, exercise books and pencils, basic textbooks and maps for one hundred primary-school teachers. Besides which, some hoes, axes, knives, and scythes were bought to tackle the great need of rehabilitation.

These were all loaded aboard barges and began the slow journey up-country to Kisangani, where the barges would be unloaded and the supplies transferred to lorries. Then there would be the long, 300-mile journey over fantastically difficult roads. They might conceivably reach Nebobongo in two or three months' time, if all went according to plan!

I flew home to Nebo to continue organizing the distribution of clothing and food that we had been allocated by the local relief organization, encouraged to know that these other 14 tons of supplies were on their way. Agoya and John Mangadima, along with other helpers, were tireless in their care for the hundreds of sick and the thousands of destitute. Immense patience was needed in keeping order along the vast crowds as twice a day they mobbed the 'distribution centre', the small courtyard outside Agoya's home. There, each received a measure of rice or bulgur, a measure of palm oil and one of salt, a bundle of greens and, once a day, some protein addition—dried fish, sardines, corned beef, peanuts, or beans.

In the middle of our multitudinous tasks came a sudden, urgent request to go to Isiro to see Colonel Yossa, of the National Army. The week before, I had met some Greek traders who had told me they were going to Wamba, where 6,000 refugees had just been liberated by the army. The Greeks had mentioned the destitute state of the refugees through malnutrition and sickness, and also the desolation of the small town, with roofless and windowless homes and broken-down, empty stores.

Now Colonel Yossa wanted to discuss with me the medical needs of these people. He told me that two young Belgian doctors had been in, with a team of national nurses and a supply of medicines, but they were frustrated by the enormity of the task and the paucity of their means, and also by the bribery and corruption, the stealing and selling of supplies, even within the team.

The Colonel appealed to me to do something—anything to help. 'You missionaries have your own way, and you can succeed where we have failed.'

I wavered and wondered. Could we tackle it?

'There are probably some twelve thousand—they all need you.' My heart lurched. It was sheer lunacy to touch anything so huge. 'Please think about it. We're not ready yet, as we must flush out the rebels from the surrounding jungle and make it safe for you first. But I'll send for you when we're ready!'

Meanwhile, a hundred jobs clamoured for attention. We worked all one morning moving the pharmacy across from the badly-damaged hospital building with its leaking roof, to a room in my house. Every bottle and tin was scrubbed and relabelled, every drug was counted and listed, a long and messy job, but well worth while when finished. Another missionary spent hours sorting and checking three cartons of second-hand spectacles, labelling each lens and packing them in order. Some workmen were busily putting up four classrooms for the primary school; another group were cutting poles in the forest for a new home for our evangelist Agoya and his family.

In between other occupations, I squeezed two hours each day to give revision classes to nurses and schoolmasters in Mathematics, French, General Sciences, Geography, and Scripture. The aim was to prepare them for the entrance exams to special government two-year courses, so that they could be upgraded to the new minimal standards.

Ward-rounds were of course a priority. We did all we could with what we had to help some of the tragedy that faced us. Every day, each ward seemed full of pathos: deeply-lined faces, emaciated bodies, skin strung taut across sharp bones, racking coughs, listless eyes. Some particular cases stand out clearly in memory, such as a thin, eight-year old girl eaten up with a tropical ulcerative disease with great open, weeping sores; a ten-year-old boy with sarcoma of the knee; a four-year-old with cancrumoris, the whole upper gum and lip eaten away back to the nose with a black necrotic ulcer. Always there were pneumonias and cardiac failures, gross anaemias and tuberculosis, every stage of ascites and avitaminosis. The eye diseases had to be seen to be believed. And in the first two months, we finished our precious initial supply of anti-malarial and antibiotic drugs. Where and how to get more was still unanswerable.

Our leprosy patients demanded their share of love and care. During the first few weeks I managed to see them all, old and new, and do fairly thorough examinations and make out new report cards. We had nearly 400 new cases of leprosy in the four years from Independence to the Rebellion: but now, following the deliverance, we were flooded with almost another 400 new cases among the refugees.

I was given an overwhelming reception. Everywhere was spotlessly clean—pharmacy, treatment centre, examination room, waiting hall, hospital ward—tables and cloths, report cards and medicine bottles. Outside, the courtyard was swept clean, and even flower-beds weeded and tended. The half-mile long road through their village was bordered with pineapples, and neat, well-cared-for food-gardens with peanuts, rice, manioc, and plantains behind each small home. These people might be sick, with fingers and toes mutilated, their feet and hands often ulcerated and stumped, but they were happy and hardworking.

Throughout this period of two or three weeks, we kept hearing reports that the people at Wamba were in great need, with many, many dying of starvation and illness—and I wrote a note to Colonel Yossa to say that I would go for a week in mid July, if medicines could be procured. I suggested he should get an American army transport plane loaded with relief supplies from Kinshasa to Isiro, and we would see to fair distribution at Wamba.

I had to go to Kisangani on another urgent errand, but I talked there also of the urgent need at Wamba for relief work. Suddenly things started to happen. Bill Gilvear of Relief Agency talked it over with 'Big Bill', an American in charge of a private air service, put at Zaire's disposal during that difficult period. I was bull-dozed into preparing a report of what I thought I could handle (clothing and blankets and food for 10,000, and medical supplies for treating at least one quarter of them). These were made out in six copies, in French and Swahili, stamped and signed, and flown to the American Embassy. I thereupon became terrified at what I had offered to do and, not for the first time, wondered why on earth I had become so involved.

Radio messages started snapping over the thousand miles from Kisangani to Kinshasa. Our request was reiterated and confirmed. Eventually it reached the President's ears. Everything seemed to be whirring into top-gear activity.

Then a message came that Kinshasa would provide drugs, but we must collect our own relief goods. So I set out on a crazy walk round Kisangani, from store to store, from Greek trader to Indian trader, from Protestant Relief warehouse to Catholic Relief warehouse: and slowly, by sheer stubborn determination, I coerced them into supplying me with over 10 tons of corn, oats, bulgur, wheat, milk, soya bean oil, plus clothing and blankets.

Then the 15-ton transport plane flew in from Kinshasa, and I hurried out on to the tarmac to check the bulk supply of drugs, only to find the plane was empty. 'The General of the National Army is sorry, but your order is too big.'

Another almost frenzied rush around town. The pilot gave me only two hours to collect what I could before he must take off, if he was to make Isiro in daylight. The Spanish doctor at the government hospital gave me all he dared; the newly opening medical faculty of the university shared all they had with us; Dr Barlovitz, a private doctor in town, supplied a huge crate from his own clinic; both pharmacies in the high street fell to my impassioned pleas; and what with twelve more bales of clothes and blankets, two more tons of milk and soya bean oil, we filled that plane in those precious two hours!

I tried to get my breath back on the one-hour flight to Isiro, and started to plan for the task ahead. Lists of urgent needs flashed through my mind: camping equipment—beds, blankets, kitchenware, food, tableware, chairs, tables. Lists of people I could ask to help me—Colin and Ina Buckley from Isiro, Agnes Chansler from Ibambi, a junior nurse from Nebobongo, my cook and the Wamba pastor would all need to go.

When we reached Isiro, life really began to move fast. We faced deluging rain and miles of slippery mud. At one point on a steep, narrow hill, with deep water-gullies each side, two lorries were already stuck! I ploughed out in wellington boots, measured the gap, and weighed up the possibility of getting through, when the Egyptian driver of the second lorry offered to drive mine through in exchange for a lift into town—an offer I accepted gratefully!

Packed up, with trailer behind, we set off on the hundred miles to Wamba on the Saturday afternoon. As we crossed over an almost non-existent bridge into the Wamba territory, we were struck with the desolation—broken-down houses, unkempt gardens, deserted villages submerged in a wilderness of weeds.

Perhaps notes from my diary of the next seven days will give the best impression of that fantastic week.

Saturday 16 July. Arrived at the post at dusk, we went to report to the officer in charge. The first shops we passed, the transport house, the government offices, the post office were all completely roofless and destroyed. The prison still stood in its sordid square. Along the one main road, all the gardens had been cleared and tidied, buildings were mostly inhabited by army, and in fair condition: till we reached the shops. One, two, three, four—the main shopping centre— utterly destroyed. What pathetic waste! We found the two white mercenary officers sitting with our Greek friends, Mr Mitsingas and Mr Dimitriou. We chatted amiably, and told them we wished to stay at the Mission for a week.

Up at the Mission, we went straight to Daisy Kingdon's home—in fairly good condition. It had been the 'Simba' headquarters and office, and was now being used as National Army government office. Various families in possession, but they moved out for us. We swept and cleaned, and slowly moved in. Certainly rough living! None of the original furniture. Few odd tables and rickety chairs, and doorless, shelfless, cupboards, and dirt! Windows and doors largely without hinges or fixtures—but we soon had a pot of tea boiling and felt ready for anything.

Back again to see the Greek merchants and 'borrow' buckets, bowls, mugs, etc. for the work of distribution, and then to the Catholic Mission to invite them to take part with us in the distribution.

Sunday 17 July. Three church services and fellowship with some 500 church members. Prepared for tomorrow. A team of 50 helpers are all ready, each knowing their part. Chairs, tables, cards, date-stamps and ink-pads, bowls, buckets, mugs, spoons—all have been checked and distributed to the helpers. Bamboo 'fences' have been erected to guide the crowd where we want them. 200 vials of penicillin have been prepared, and 16 syringes and 144 needles sterilised. Between us nearly 5,000 report cards have been serially numbered.

Monday 18 July. A grand day! We heard them coming at 5.30 a.m.—and in no time some 400 were queuing up. All the helpers were soon in place, each with their necessary equipment. Primus stove burning, with saucepans of syringes and needles; bowls of Quaker oats with mugs for giving out; bottles of iron tablets; and so on. At eight o'clock we 'opened the doors', and in half an hour we had near anarchy! About a thousand people scrambled to get in first! At that moment, the mercenary lieutenant and three Congolese soldiers drove up in a jeep—and in ten minutes, perfect order!

By midday, we were through for today. 2,600 people had passed through, of whom 400 received medical cards, 70 of these being for severe malnutrition (almost 3% of those we saw). Ten of these malnutrition cases were deeply pathetic to see. One woman with six children—all emaciated, with swollen feet, sores, yellowing skin and hair. We gave what treatment we could, of supplementary protein and vitamins and also penicillin injections.

It is interesting that only 16 per cent of the people were in acute need of medical aid: probably 50 per cent were suffering from diarrhoea, mainly due to malnutrition, but doubtless also due to intestinal worms and dysentery. Ninety-four people had severe eye infections. We expect to see much more sickness tomorrow, now that the news will have spread around.

During the afternoon, a note came up from the African head-nurse at the Government hospital—a woman obviously needing a Caesarian section operation. I went down at 4.00 p.m. And we did it together with the one and only blunt scalpel, four artery forceps, no spongeholders, no gauze, no general anaesthetic—but all went well. We had no masks or gowns, just gloves: and no nail brushes. What poverty! But we had lots of faith and goodwill, and God helped us.

Tuesday 19 July. A thick, damp mist as light slowly broke through this morning, and the queue had started. By 9.00 a.m. there were about 2,000 to the left of the church porch, all with tickets from yesterday; and about the same number to the right, stretching as far as the eye could see, across the compound, all along the football field, out and across the main road, and down through the gardens opposite. And still they came! Everything was very orderly, with two soldiers to help us outside and fifty-six church elders helping with the distribution inside.

In all today, 5,176 people went through, representing 2,032 families. Of these, 1,015 received medical help, about 20 per cent. The malnutrition cases were truly pathetic. Skin and bones, oedema and ulcers, thrush in their mouths and glazed eyes. We gave each of them milk, every two to three hours—they just grabbed it, and cried for more. They were starved and desperate.

At midday, two more truck-loads of supplies arrived— milk, oil, corn and clothing. In the afternoon, some essential shopping, plus pulling a molar tooth for the Greek trader! In the evening, we erected more barriers to direct the crowd for tomorrow's task of distributing clothes—trousers and a shirt for each man, a piece of cloth and a blanket for the children, and a dress for each woman.

Wednesday 20 July. What a day! We're all almost worn out! By 6.00 a.m. the battle was on, in a cold damp mist, a queue stretching away to the far boundary of the compound. When the doors were opened, the flood released! In seven hours, 4,630 had been through, including 650 sick, receiving penicillin, worm treatment, eye ointment, iron tablets and milk. Then we prepared for the 'first-timers': a vast and ever-increasing crowd. In four hours, we had let 2,238 people through, and treated a further 328 sick, bringing today's total to 6,868 people served with oats, corn, iron tablets and each receiving a garment, and 978 sick helped medically.

From 5.00 to 6.00 p.m. it poured with rain and I was soaked, walking up and down the line, keeping order, enforcing discipline, acting as a barrier against gate-crashers. Many 'Simbas' joined the lines, but I'm afraid I hauled them out. I just couldn't agree to giving them food and clothing after all the suffering they have inflicted on others. The last two hours, we had the car headlights on the queue: the extension light on the exit: and two pressure lamps and five storm lanterns in the hall.

On Thursday, all the population is expected to clean and weed the town and surrounding area. I've been to see the Congolese lieutenant this evening, to ask permission for our sixty assistants to have a day's holiday, and also for the 1,400 people on penicillin treatment to be allowed to come up for their injections. He agreed amicably.

Thursday 21 July. I suppose this amazing week will end one day! This morning we did some 600 injections, treated over 100 Kwashiokor children, tried to keep order among the thousands who hoped for food and clothing distribution, encouraged the soldiers with a good deal of humour to keep calm and not to throw their weight about!

This evening, we have given out full food rations to the 116 'helpers' and their wives and families—about 550 altogether: and clothes! What a tremendous job, fitting every little boy and girl, woman and man, with a suitable garment. It has taken a long time, but we had to do it after dark, to avoid attracting another vast crowd. Giving out clothes attracts more than even penicillin, and far more than food!

Friday 23 July. By 6.00 a.m. there were vast queues in every direction, and a great wave of unbelieving disappointment when I broke the news that we could serve no newcomers, only those with tickets in their hands. Once again at the door a green date-stamp on their medical cards, a purple date-stamp on their food cards: divided into four files, to receive a mug of Quaker oats and a mug of soya bean oil: passing by the medical workers for penicillin injections, eye ointment or bandages: handing in their tickets at the exit, where I collected all food cards, and any medical cards with five consecutive dates, and returned other medical cards dated for a final injection tomorrow.

Everything moved fast. Keeping the count was quite exhausting work. At 9.30 a.m. Ina Buckley brought me a mug of coffee and two sandwiches. As I took a bite, a passing child grabbed the sandwich from my hand and absolutely shovelled it into his own mouth, and then looked at me pleadingly for the other. I have never seen such desperate hunger—I could do nothing but hand the child the second, and watch it disappear in a few wild, famished gulps. Oh, if only folk could see the pathetic need!

We were finished by 11.00 a.m.—every flake of oats had gone: every drop of milk was finished. 4,885 people had passed through and each received some help at least. Tidying up, sorting out, writing reports—and an early lunch.

The continual noise and crowds, pathos and needs, have been very wearying and we are all feeling that a week is all we can manage at a stretch.

Saturday 23 July. Our time at Wamba has ended.

In some ways, a success story: over ten thousand refugees helped with food and clothing and medical care. Yet this was one small group, perhaps one per cent of all that needed doing. Already the government was talking of plans to repeat this week in some fifty other needy areas, but they have not the personnel or the supplies to implement their plans. And we realised that we had hardly scratched the surface of the tremendous and appalling needs.

4

How Could I Be So Foolhardy?

In the welter of need, each of the returned missionaries and the church elders sought to find his own priorities. It wasn't easy, in the middle of everything, to see the wood for the trees. Why were we in Zaire? And what were we meant to be doing, individually and as a group?

After three weeks at Nebobongo and in the area, soaking in the needs of schoolchildren, patients, and refugees, I went back to Nyankunde to discuss and pray with Dr Becker, as to what we should tackle first.

Dr Becker had already made his own decision: that all interested missionary societies and church congregations should create a new medical team, and that together we should build one good, central hospital for the vast region, where Africans could be cared for in body, soul, and spirit, to the highest possible standards. Would I join him?

For a week, Dr Becker had to be away from Nyankunde, working at the mountain hospital of Rethy. So I went with him and we worked together, doing ward-rounds, general surgery, outpatient clinics, and special eye clinics day after day. All the time we discussed the various possibilities of this tentative plan. At one moment it seemed possible that we might approach the government and offer to take over one of their hospitals, as at Bunia, and run it for them. But as we discussed it, all the impracticalities became so clear that we dismissed the idea. We became more and more certain that a Christian centre was needed, where Christlike behaviour as well as teaching formed the essential basis of all the activities. We needed the right to appoint, discipline, and dismiss staff, in order to maintain spiritual and medical standards. We needed the right to select students for our training college from our respective church secondary schools.

As we discussed and worked together, a definite over-all plan began to form itself in our hearts and minds. Our vast region was some 500 miles square, a great basin of tropical rain forest, bordered to the east by the mountain range on the foothills of which Nyankunde was situated. If we could develop a 250-bed hospital at the centre with facilities for 1,000 outpatients daily, and first-class medical and surgical, obstetric and paediatric care, all this could support a training school for twenty-four students annually in a three-year course. Young men would be trained as medical auxiliaries to run rural hospitals and dispensaries, and young women as auxiliary midwives to run the accompanying maternity units. We envisaged a network of a possible dozen regional hospitals, in the care of European nurses at first, helped by Nyankunde school graduates, until these could be upgraded and able to take over the leadership: and each of these regional hospitals to be surrounded by some ten or a dozen rural dispensaries.

Our imagination ran on, and saw every one of these medical health centres served by radio-contact to the centre at Nyankunde, so that any nurse or auxiliary, national or foreigner, could discuss difficult cases directly with a doctor and receive all possible aid from the centre. Then we realised the essential need of a small plane and pilot, to link up every outpost with the centre, with half-mile long airstrips to be cut out of the forest at each dispensary and hospital.

Quickly our minds moved on to the problem of medicines and equipment. We would need a central pharmacy at Nyankunde to undertake all the problems of import licences, customs duties, transport, reception, checking, stocking, sorting. From here each outlying hospital and dispensary could order its monthly needs.

The next step in our thinking was easy: one doctor from the centre should be freed from other responsibilities each week to fly to one of the regional hospitals to do a week of medical oversight and surgical care, to help the nurse in charge with administrative problems, and to distribute the needed drugs and equipment. Thus the benefit of our work at the medical centre at Nyankunde would be spread over the largest possible area, and give the maximum help to as many as possible of the five million inhabitants.

Throughout our discussions, my mind kept flicking back to the need of a training school, to train Africans to the highest standards of nursing and medical care for their patients, as well as in diagnostic principles and practice; to train them for the job that most needed doing, in the outlying regional hospitals and dispensaries. I was mentally listing the subjects to be taught, how many hours of each to each class, methods for combining practical with theoretical training, report sheets to record the progress of each student. I was picturing classrooms and laboratory, nursing arts' demonstration room and assembly-hall, offices and record filing. I could visualise dining-hall and dormitories, uniforms and entrance exams. Each evening after prayers, as I went to bed, I scribbled my thoughts down, covering reams of paper. I drew up lists of suggestions, lists of possible students, lists of proposed courses practical and theoretical.

My heart and mind were caught! Already I was visualizing the future years, seeing graduates from our training centre serving all over the region, not merely as skilled medical workers, but above all as medical evangelists. With my whole being I believed in the rightness and necessity of teaching and training others to do my job. To me, this was virtually an obligation laid upon me, in exchange for permission to live in Africa. My principal desire was to train medical auxiliaries whose prime objective was to show Christ to their patients, not only in preaching, but through the standard of their medical practice and the loving care given to each individual.

Back at Nyankunde the following week, we paced over the 40 acres (20 hectares) of land that we were being offered for the medical centre. Dr Becker had already commenced building, and had already in his heart and mind a vision of the whole. We were situated in the bowl of two hills. Around the hills, as we looked up the valley, were to be the homes of the medical staff. The school and playing-field, dormitories and dining-hall, would be in the centre. Then spreading out down the slope below, away to the north, the hospital, with laboratory and pharmacy, X-ray and maternity, operating theatre and intensive care unit. Twin wards were to be built on either side of a central corridor: and finally the administrative block and offices, outpatient hall, clinics, and chapel.

There was room already assigned for a 'self-help' village; for distant patients who did not require hospitalization, and also for a small tuberculosis village, leprosy-care centre, and psychiatric wards; for laundry, garages and workshops.

So I returned to Nebobongo again, churning over all the exciting new possibilities, and wondering how I could 'sell' my vision to the Ibambi church elders. I needed the local church to be with me in this project, or I felt sure it would fail. I wanted them to release me from my immediate task at Nebobongo, of helping children, patients, and refugees in our own church area, to go far away—350 miles of rough roads, two days' driving to start a school. It all sounded a little lame, put like that. Would it sound like running away from overwhelming, obvious, pressing need, to hide myself in a small, comfortable spot doing a small, enjoyable job? How could I convince them that it was for their own good? If I can train some of their sons and daughters, I told myself, to obtain the new government medical auxiliary diploma, they would then have workers for several hospitals and dispensaries, instead of just me alone at Nebobongo.

I knew this was true, but I also knew it didn't sound convincing. A bird in the hand is worth two in the bush. A doctor now seeing to their multitudinous needs at Nebo seemed more worthwhile than the vague possibility that in a few years' time they might have some half-qualified help. 'They are never going to be doctors, are they?' I could hear them asking.

Throughout the long, tiring fight against mud and ruts, during nineteen hours of journeying, including being pushed and tugged out of two giant-sized mud-holes, my mind ploughed on at the problem. Was it right? Could it work? Would the others agree? Could I 'sell' it to my WEC colleagues, nationals, and missionaries, by promising to visit them twice a year, to supervise our medical services? The awfulness of those 350 miles appalled me, and then I would have to add a possible further 1,000 miles' circuit to visit our three northern, central, and southern hospitals and their many dependent dispensaries. The road surfaces were deteriorating rapidly; some bridges were dangerously near to collapse; many of the hills were practically impassable after rain. My heart failed at the prospect of regular trips.

Back at Nebobongo, I met the church elders and nurses to tell them of all our deliberations at Nyankunde, and the proposals for the new school. They were stunned. I had only just got back to them. They had no other doctor: how could I ask them to agree? Even the suggested twice-yearly visits raised little enthusiasm. The prospect of a monthly visit by a doctor/surgeon by plane certainly fired them to set to and cut an airstrip out of the surrounding forest, to make this dream a reality. The fantastically high fees proposed for students at Nyankunde Nurses' School were terribly discouraging to them in their abject poverty, and I vowed in my heart to procure scholarships from somewhere.

For two days I prayed over this with them, and we sought God's mind. Then together we went to Ibambi to meet the church council, and again I rehearsed carefully all our proposals. Their discouragement was hard to accept. They just couldn't bear to think of my going away again, and no-one to replace me. I dared not even encourage them over much by promising visits from the 'Flying Doctor Service'. Our small hospital at Nebobongo suddenly seemed so utterly primitive, after I had visited medical centres of the other missions, with their electricity generators, running water, permanent buildings, and crowds of outpatients. I had become ashamed of our little medical centre. Had I been so immersed in my own inadequacy that I had fatalistically accepted poverty and inadequate buildings and supplies? I seemed to have done so little for them—and yet I reminded myself that many hundreds had been healed in body and spirit through the work at Nebobongo during the previous twelve years.

Another two days of prayer, and we discussed the problem from all aspects. On the second day, they received a letter from a missionary who had been the director of our secondary school. We all knew that, during the year of the Rebellion, he had gone to work for another church area. Now they were anxiously awaiting his return to re-open the school. He was their one hope for the thousands of children needing secondary education, and also for the training of national teachers for the hundreds of primary schools. But his letter came to tell of the overwhelming needs down south, with over 1,000 boys finishing sixth-form primary school that summer, and only one teacher available to accept them into secondary school. Therefore he was asking the church to allow him to stay down in the south for a further two-year period. Our church council was stunned. Their own overwhelming need was so appallingly apparent that they simply couldn't believe that their one secondary-school director was not returning. They felt deserted.

And there was I, doing virtually the same thing. How desperately we needed reinforcements in the way of school teachers, doctors, nurses, and secretaries, as well as mechanics, builders, electricians, radio technicians, air pilots, and general administrators. Where were the workers to fill all the gaps?

Eventually, by the end of the week, albeit grudgingly, the council agreed to wish me God-speed, and allowed me to go ahead with the new vision that had started to burn in my bones. I left immediately on the long journey to Kinshasa, the capital of Zaire, to lay the plans before the central government and to secure their rubber-stamp on our blueprints.

The country was, of course, still emerging from the torture of the two years of internal strife and bloodshed, so ordinary methods of communications and transport were almost nonexistent. I hitch-hiked the 1,500 miles in an army transport plane, noisy, cold, uncomfortable, but free! Then started three weeks of foot-slogging and dogged perseverance, to seek the right people for our cause, and to persuade them to be sufficiently interested for a sufficiently long time to grant us some sort of pledge of their co-operation and assistance.

At the same time as I was presenting our plans for developing a Medical Service centred at Nyankunde, I was also endeavouring to procure residence visas in the passports of the five WEC missionaries. What a thankless task! We had applied for these over seven months previously, and had not heard a word since then. The Christian travel agency that handled these affairs for us was non-committal and discouraging. I was not the only one seeking a visa; it appeared! And no-one really knew how to tackle the task, or hurry officialdom.

A taxi-ride two miles up the main boulevard; a vast flight of steps, a wide corridor with many doors; folks hurrying here and there, doing nothing apparently but carrying huge portmanteaux; others holding up the walls as they discussed at length, in high-sounding French, why they should not do what their superior had ordered, and why he had no right to order them to do it anyway. Down a narrow flight of stone steps, to Chancery. It was truly Dickensian, even in the elaborate, outdated vocabulary. A large, elderly African came forward and I explained my need.

I was nervous and anxious not to offend or to appear in any way critical of their right to make me wait seven months. Yet I was eager to state the case clearly, even if apologetically, trusting they would then serve me. He retired to his desk and began searching in the only file in it, among some twelve sets of application papers and photographs. Eventually he sorted out our five and came back with them. Again I went through all our reasons for applying for permanent visas. At last he motioned me to leave that room, pass through a door in the corridor, and re-enter the same room by the next door, to the same counter but farther along.

Here I explained to the same man all that I had already told him twice. After a short delay, he led me into another, larger room, almost empty except for four large desks around the edge and Congolese officials perched on high stools behind them, through an opening to the second half of this hall, with a further four desks, only here the officials sat on chairs!

I was led to one senior official and introduced to him. I repeated my story, clutching the five sets of application papers with their photos. He took our passports and examined our expired visitor-permits. As he had not fully understood me, I repeated the circumstances of our arrival in Zaire during January and March. He went and discussed the matter at length with another official. They returned together, and I recited again the tale of my distress! Conferring together, they decided to send me to 'Immigration'—'just over there, by the monument'. He gave me a note of introduction to 'Immigration', asking that I be treated with courtesy and alacrity as I had already waited seven months.

I set off to walk 'just over there, by the monument' and took a quarter of an hour to reach the monument, and a further five minutes to discover the office. I waited in a queue, and showed my letter of introduction. I moved to another queue at a window and repeated the performance. From there I moved up two rooms and joined another queue. They passed me on to an office at the 'back', but the official there was obviously not pleased to be found, just twenty minutes before closing time. The argument grew fairly heated, but all he assured me was that I was 'unofficial' and must become 'official'.

A Belgian technical adviser offered to drive me back to the Ministry of Foreign Affairs, guided me back to Chancery, introduced me to the same large African to whom I had already told my story three times, who escorted me back to the high official who had sent me 'unofficially' to Immigration. He accepted all my precious sets of applications and photos, promised to 'process' them the same afternoon, and told me to go to Immigration the next morning, by which time I would find that I was truly 'official'—but by then I had no letter of introduction! I felt I had moved a distinct step forward, but subsequent conversation with others who had shuttled for months between Chancery and Immigration brought me a large measure of doubt as to whether I would ever see our forms again, officially or unofficially.

So, next day, to Immigration—no news, but forcefully told not to go again! Back to Chancery, where I drew a blank: just 'Come again at 2.00 p.m.'.

Back again that afternoon, and that time I actually saw our five names on a list that had been sent to Immigration for indexing. When (and if!) that list returned, I could collect our visas. Chancery said hopefully that they might be ready in three days: everyone else prophesied they might be ready next year!

Three days later, in the torturing heat, I presented myself once again at the Ministry for Foreign Affairs, looking for our visas. From there I was once more directed the mile to the Immigration Office. But no luck! The applications had passed through the first office, to another—but who would stir them out of there, no-one seemed to know!

A week later the search was still on, but by then I had an able assistant, Jessi Nkoma, a very accomplished, educated African. Under his pressures the application papers were eventually found and transferred to the right office, and the man in charge promised them for the next day.

So Jessi went back for me the next morning, but was told to return in the afternoon!

That evening, he burst into the home where I was staying, waving my passport triumphantly in the air, duly stamped with the required resident visa! But…not the other four! 'Tomorrow…'

Meanwhile our main business was to gain recognition for the Nyankunde project for a medical centre and training school. During my first week in the great city I had made my way to the Ministry of Public Health to see the Secretary General, Mr Nandu. While I was waiting for him in the ante-room, Dr Trieste, the inspector of all medical and paramedical education in Congo/Zaire, came in. Recognizing me from that traumatic inspection at Nebobongo three years previously, he was gracious and even courteous, and arranged to see me in his office at the end of the following week, when I could present him with our proposed school programme.

Mr Nandu arrived and received me in audience most enthusiastically. He listened patiently and keenly to all my explanations and to our three main requests, namely:

a. recognition for the new school, immediately;

b. a five-year period for the war-stricken north-eastern region, during which candidates might be accepted for paramedical education with less general secondary education than demanded elsewhere;

c. upgrading and recognition for our older paramedical assistant nurses, trained between 1950 and 1964.

It seemed obvious that I was not the first doctor to approach him about these burning questions. He felt that if I presented all this to Dr Trieste immediately, before the meeting of ministers the coming week, there was a good chance of the first two points being granted at once. This would then allow us to bring in the older assistant nurses, who showed capabilities of being upgraded, during the five-year extension programme.

I was really amazed at how quickly he had assimilated all that I had presented, especially as I myself was becoming increasingly tired, with the strain of talking and thinking in and listening to French all day, and keeping exactly to the appropriate points with each different official to whom I was presented.

When I eventually reached Dr Trieste's office, I was even more tired, from ten days' foot-slogging to get the necessary documents signed for presentation to the Ministry, and not a little discouraged by it all. Dr Trieste walked in ten minutes late for our appointment, nailed me with two sharp, piercing eyes, and demanded brusquely: 'What do you want?' There were no preliminaries, no introductions, none of the courtesy of our earlier encounter, and a hint of. 'I've no time for you; two minutes at the most. I'm a busy man...'

'All I want is...'—a moment's hesitation—'sympathy' I added quickly, remembering that inspection at Nebobongo three years ago, when he had declared our training school unsuited for government recognition, despite our ten years of sweated labour.

I think he was taken aback momentarily by my reply. There was a pause; then he actually smiled!

I leapt in and outlined hurriedly the whole desperate situation in the war-torn north-east; and, refusing to be daunted by my obvious inability to get the subjunctive tense or right concords into my utterly ungrammatical French, I rushed on into the plan forming in our minds to meet those needs.

He listened, at first idly, doodling on his blotting-paper, then more intently, eventually becoming caught up by my enthusiasm into jotting down notes. Then things started happening.

'OK. How concrete are your plans? Have you a time-table for how you can achieve all this? Building plans? Curricula?'

I gulped—gazed—and pledged anything he wanted!

'Give me the use of a typewriter, paper, carbons, and a pen, and I'll produce all you want.'

'Go ahead then—use my desk. I've a meeting with the Minister in ten minutes. I'll tell him that I want to see him again tomorrow with your proposals.'

He left, and I started to work, from 10.00 a.m. through to almost midnight. I drew plans and drawings of proposed buildings; I worked out time-tables for a four-year course both for students and for staff; I made out a decidedly optimistic budget with no suggestion of where the funds would come from. Then I worked on proposed record cards and diplomas, methods of organization and suggestions for how to bend the present law to allow for the recovery of the north-eastern region over a five year period. It all seemed a wild gamble of imagination! I nearly got cold feet as I realised I had no authority from our team at Nyankunde to commit them so completely.

At midday I managed to contact Dr Becker through the Missionary Aviation Fellowship radio network, and got his permission to go ahead. I'd no idea how much he then understood of what I was promising to do in his name! But he was wholly in the project and prepared to back me all the way.

By midnight, I had left the completed file on Dr Trieste's desk, drawn up as an eight-year project to establish the training school, with buildings up to the required government standards, curricula following the suggested government scheme, and all the staff necessary to implement it. And I fell into bed in a daze of doubt. How could I be so foolhardy as to think I could ever achieve it? But God...!

For two weeks I had to wait for a word from Dr Trieste, but at last the word came. He then took me on a wild tour of various departments, from one end of the city to the other, seeing secretaries, functionaries, administrators, and eventually the Under Secretary to the Minister. As we went, we gathered up papers, documents, forms, course material, models, books for our non-existent library (though most of this material was for a course either junior or senior to our proposed one: there just wasn't any available material for what we wished to teach), and an enormous quantity of enthusiasm, goodwill, and encouragement.

'Go ahead with your plan. We'll send inspectors up as soon as we can.' With this I had to be content. No written word, no signature, not even a firm promise, but I inferred that recognition would follow inspection if we could complete our side of the bargain in the stipulated time.

And so back to Bunia to give a full report to all the team at Nyankunde, to start work on preparing entrance examinations, and building plans for the first phase of the new training college.

A week later I set out for Nebobongo, despite many transport problems. I managed to hitchhike a lift on a cargo flight to Kisangani with two and a half tons of pork! I had been waiting two days at Bunia for a regular flight that never came, when I saw a DC3 come in and begin unloading cargo. I went quickly through the waiting-hall and out on to the tarmac, to see if I could possibly get a ride. A Greek was loading pig carcasses. A Belgian gentleman also wanted a place. Two passengers would be allowed by the pilot if two carcases were unloaded. Much heat ensued, and argument in many languages. 'Impossible', the Greek roared, working out his financial loss through such an arrangement.

I just stood quietly by, with my suitcase, in the shadow of the wing of the plane, and waited.

Fiercer arguments—greater heat—still he shouted: 'Impossible!' They all went off to the office and I heard the altercation continuing. Someone came out to the plane; two carcases were taken off, carried back to the hall, and weighed, and my heart rose.

More shouting, gesticulating, fury; the Greek returned, and the two carcases were thrown back on. Still I waited.

Then it all occurred again... And the pilot and co-pilot arrived, obviously furious. 'Get in quickly. Go up to the cockpit and sit in the co-pilot's seat—make yourself conspicuous!' Totally baffled by the last part, I did as I was told. The pilot revved the engines up, we taxied out, and climbed up into the air—when I was told to make my way back to a seat amongst the pigs! I gathered the pilot was mad with the trader for thinking a miserable pig's carcase more important than a lady doctor! He then made it clear that he took me in his seat at his expense, and the old trader could care for his own conscience!

Our students who had been in training before the rebellion sat their entrance exams for Nyankunde. Papers came in from eleven other centres and schools, and I spent a day marking and sorting, finally selecting four classes of twelve students each for the first year at Nyankunde.

The fantastic activities of the week among the refugees at Wamba came as a surprising interlude in all our other activities, including steady preparation to leave Nebobongo to start a new life at Nyankunde. As the date to move grew nearer, all sorts of alarming rumours also grew. Kinshasa radio reported violent uprisings between Katangese troops with mercenaries and the National Army, involving the death of Colonel Chache. Colonel Yossa went from Isiro to Kisangani to verify reports, and found himself landed in prison. General Mulamba was expected in Kisangani from Kinshasa, and the air was full of speculations.

I met with the Greek traders in Isiro and discussed how all this might involve us. It seemed probable that there had been a planned 'coup', as the Katangese troops had all left our region some weeks before and there seemed no obvious reason for their return. Some were frankly optimistic; others, hopelessly pessimistic. When the evening news stated that the 500 whites in Kisangani were 'safe', it sent a shudder through me, to hear again the sort of language we had heard all through the Rebellion. In Isiro, there were two or three days when officers were having difficulty in maintaining calm and order among the excitable troops. The major had even wanted to blow up the bridges on the Kisangani road and cut down trees as roadblocks. As excitement and rumour mounted, all the soldiers were made to lay down their arms.

We missionaries were requested to stay at Ibambi, despite the rising tensions, as the sub-lieutenant said that our presence would give assurance and exert calm in the explosive atmosphere; he promised to send an armed escort should we need to be evacuated in a hurry.

But when 26 July, the day for leaving, dawned, we all felt that it was right for me to go ahead with our programme and to start the journey to Nyankunde. Our Land Rover and trailer were loaded to capacity. Pastor Danga of Wamba and my friend, Jacqueline van Bever, were in the cab with me, and behind, like sardines: were John Mangadima; his elder brother, Naundimi; Benjamin, my house lad; and Cornelius Balani, a senior nurse from Poko with his wife and two little boys. Over half a ton of goods were packed in tight around them!

We spent a night at Isiro, and set off at six o'clock on the Wednesday morning, 27 July. Within fifty miles our troubles began. There followed 150 miles of the worst roads I had ever travelled. We struggled through deep ruts, thick mud, and potholes into which the whole front of the van would sink. Water channels careered crazily down every hill, cutting the road into uneven halves. We travelled, one wheel each side, weaving to and fro with the crevasses, and holding on for dear life to avoid slipping and slithering into them. The road was an endless switchback, and every hill a nightmare, every valley worse.

We travelled mainly in low gear, often in four-wheel drive, several times in low-ratio gears. We stuck twice, at a crazy 60° angle. We pushed and prayed, and ploughed through. My hands were nearly blistered, my shoulders ached. Time and again, I waded through in wellington boots to measure the depth of a hole, or test the firmness of a narrow ridge.

We arrived at another mission village, Lolwa, at 9.30 p.m., utterly exhausted, having been the first truck to make it after a terrible storm the previous night. We were held up at barriers and chatted our way through, with smiles and sweet meats, till the soldiers laughingly waved us on.

The next morning, Thursday, on the last 50-mile lap of the long journey, we burst a tyre on the trailer! Not carrying a spare, we had to repair it somehow, despite a four inch slit right through the outer cover! We crept the last ten miles at five miles an hour, until we arrived at the large cement signpost by the roadside, Nyankunde Mission and Hope Hospital. The words spurred us on with renewed courage. We swept up the side road for three miles' climb towards our future home, the engine roaring out our conviction of hope for the new adventure starting on the morrow.

5

You Build, I Teach!

Two days later I stood on the terrace outside the home where I was staying on the mountainside, and gazed out, as dawn slowly broke across the valley. The opposite hills were wrapped in low-lying mists and just the peaks reflected the pink glory of the new day. Bird-song chorused on all sides. I watched as the distant hills drew nearer, their contours rising from the dissipating mist, through the foothills to the rounded summits. The air was tangible with the fragrance of the frangipani and the stillness following heavy rain. Here and there I could see clumps of gum trees and golden acacias. Suddenly there was a vivid flash of startling blue as a weaver bird swooped by, drawing my eyes nearer across the valley. Fields of pasture land, scattered farmsteads, rounded hummock hills, the lush green following the winding riverbed, and so my eyes came to the hospital buildings below me, part hidden by bright yellow acacias and rose-pink flowering shrubs. Four wards, theatre, and pharmacy to my left, laboratory, X-ray, and maternity to the right; beyond were the foundations of administrative and outpatient departments. Nearer, there were the pupil midwives' temporary quarters and then just below me, and stretching up the mountainside, a wilderness of long grass and brambles, a field of some four to five acres: this was our school!

For a week I looked, and planned, and measured, and thought, and tried to envisage, in the place of wild elephant grass and rough brambles, a training school for national medical auxiliaries to serve the church of the northeastern region of Zaire. I dreamt of dispensaries opening up all over the quarter million square miles, staffed by Zairian graduates of this school—able, responsible, spiritual—and I saw the streams of refugees, of hungry, naked, and sick, adequately cared for by well-trained, conscientious health officers, nurses, and midwives, trained at the Medical Centre.

I walked and stumbled in this field, measuring its slope and realizing the difficulty of levelling and building: slithering in its mud—thick, black, heavy alluvial soil, washed down from the mountains, covering an impervious red-clay subsoil holding the water, damp and unsatisfactory for drainage or hygiene. I carried the mud back home, up the hill, in inch-thick clods on my sandals. As I gazed across the valley, imagining the immediate needs of temporary homes and classrooms, and the future replacements of dormitories and dining-hall, laboratories and library, trying to see into the future, I could see only mud! Acres of mud, and difficulties, and frustrations.

I had come to Nyankunde full of faith and vision and enthusiasm...and now, was a little bit of mud going to discourage me? No! I was sure that God had said: 'Go forward' and so 'go forward' we would. During the coming week I expected students to arrive. Just how they would come was hard to say, but we had sent out messages by modern radio and ancient bush telegraph to invite any young men or women, with a minimum of one year's secondary education and a desire to serve as medical auxiliaries, to come during the first week in August. Some who had done entrance exams probably wouldn't turn up; others who hadn't done the exams might well turn up. So I waited expectantly.

Meanwhile, the news grew steadily more unsettled. Fighting had broken out only 50 miles from us, between two frontier tribes, and several were injured. One hundred miles south, a 'gang' of about one hundred armed rebels (Simbas) came down from the mountains and attacked the population. The local National Army lieutenant rose to the occasion and practically wiped them out with machine-gun fire and mortars, but there was an uneasy tension around as a result. Two wounded National soldiers were flown to Nyankunde for surgery.

Then we heard that, to the north, another missionary and his wife had had their new six-ton diesel lorry commandeered. Katangese and mercenary troops appeared to be pouring into Kisangani from all sides, and whites were said to have been evacuated. Some even added that all 'Simbas' in prison had been liberated and given arms. Greeks added to the gloom by telling us that Isiro had been stripped bare and all vehicles commandeered by the mercenaries. They said that all whites had fled the area, several over the border into the Central African Republic.

Added to this sort of news, we had our own 'extras' in the way of fairly violent earth-tremors, almost daily. Nyankunde had been considerably shaken in March 1966 by the earthquake that hit the Ruwenzori mountain range, and these rumblings now shook our hills fairly constantly. Despite the happenings around us, the medical team went ahead and held their first official meeting of the 'Board of Directors'. It lasted from 11 a.m. to 9.00 p.m.! We drew up statutes for the new intermission medical project, got everything decently translated into correct French and typed up in five copies. Now we really felt officially 'launched'!

I filled in time while awaiting the arrival of students by visiting the local chieftain to pay my respects, and to ask permission to cut poles in his afforestation area, at 3p for a 10 foot pole. We needed some 1,500 such poles for the plan I had made out for our initial building programme. I also managed a trip to our local township of Bunia, some 30 miles to the north-east, to lay in stores for the school kitchen. It was quite exciting thinking and ordering in large quantities, such as half a ton of rice, ten sacks of flour and ten of sugar, ten cartons of soap at a hundred pieces each, forty-gallon drums of petrol, paraffin and palm oil, besides looking at bales of cloth and blankets, dozens of buckets, bowls, lanterns, mugs and plates, huge cartons of matches—there seemed no end to the list.

And then they came! There were twenty-two students in the first batch. I can still picture them as they arrived. Manasse: tall, debonair, light-skinned, wearing sunglasses and looking down from some lofty height of self-importance—he managed to make me feel very small! Jack, short and thick-set, very dark-skinned, not bright judging by his entrance paper, but with an air of knowing all the answers which I found a little intimidating—accompanied by a quiet, inoffensive little wife and four rowdy children. Peter: oh, dear me! From the first, Peter and I clashed. I remember one day in class: two of us staff were struggling to keep three classes going, and we were teaching in shifts, from 6.30 a.m. till 8.30 p.m. every day. It was necessary to make some slight adjustment in their time tables to allow Miss Fuchsloch to fit in the necessary hours of practical supervision in the wards. The change was written up on the blackboard, and Peter stood and drawled, in his near perfect French, with a superb disdain for the usual student/staff relationship: 'Has the government approved this change?' The class held their breath, never quite sure whose side to take. I held my breath and counted ten—and then quietly replied that the Government had suggested the change. A gasp, then the class clapped, and the bubble was pricked for that round—but there were many such rounds in the ensuing two years.

I remember most clearly those who gave most challenge, but there were others: quiet, gracious Joel, who had been with me at Nebobongo before the Rebellion and stood by me fearlessly when I was nearly killed—back now to finish his courses, with his unobtrusive young wife; Joseph and Ganisius: Ruandese refugees, taller than the Zairians, a little aloof perhaps, or else only shy and reserved, good-looking young men, hard workers, always courteous and helpful; Job, dull and heavy—he had not passed the entrance exam and we never quite knew how he got in, except that he came with the crowd from the south with a 'good story'—but he never quite rang true to me; Seth: small and wiry, like a house sparrow, bright as a button in appearance and speech, but completely the reverse where academic achievement was concerned! How he ever passed the entrance exam remains a mystery, unless he had been helped by Jack. He became known to everyone by his invariable response to each and every request throughout his three years with us: 'No problem, no problem'—and then, equally invariably, a howler would follow.

They had arrived in groups of four and five, each group from different directions. Some were chatting nonchalantly, self-possessed; they felt they knew the ropes and were just coming to continue their ordinary way of life, but in our setup. They knew the medical director, Dr Becker, and were prepared to show other newcomers what to do. Others were shy, withdrawn, very fearful of this new start in their lives. Yet others, like Peter, were proud and rather disdainful—they had already completed three years of secondary school and considered themselves a cut above the rest, a little unsure whether we were worthy of the honour of their presence.

Nevertheless all were tired, dirty, and hungry. The fortunate few had been brought the hundred miles down the escarpment by car, Manasse among them; the less fortunate had spent five days hitchhiking in transport lorries over 300 miles of wild jungle country, often helping to push the heavily-laden vehicles through seas of mud, or even to unload and later re-load their transport truck in deluging rain, for a spring to be repaired. A few local students, such as Joel, had cycled or walked across the valley, carrying their precious bundles of all they possessed tied up in bright-coloured cloths, or packed in rough soap boxes. All were expectant, wondering, and a little dazed after two years of suffering to be given this chance to continue their schooling.

Two years ago, some of these were in our Nebobongo nursing aids' school; others were in different primary and secondary schools throughout the region. They were ordinary, teenage students, happy, free...they didn't have much in the way of clothes, or housing, or personal possessions, but that didn't count much. They studied when they felt like it, and played when they didn't! Football was more important than textbooks. Yet at the end of each year, like students all the world over, they suddenly became stuck to their books, the football field deserted: and then, all smiling, they passed their final exams with flying colours and looking as though they thought they deserved it!

And then the holocaust of the civil war, the Simba Rebellion, had swept across their horizon, absorbing everything before it. They were the lucky ones, still alive—many, many of their classmates were gone, killed, murdered, liquidated. They had seen whole classrooms of fourteen-year-olds rounded up, herded into waiting lorries, driven off to the 'front'—singing, shouting slogans, their morale boosted by liquor and drugs, and the pledge of the power of witchcraft to bring them back victorious. Hardly any had returned. And these others, after two years of hide-and-seek in the dense forest, avoiding involvement in the tragedy of war, had survived and were seeking to pick up the threads again.

Slowly they gathered in the driveway behind Dr Becker's house. I took their names and welcomed them, sitting at a camp table on a wooden chair in the open yard. In front of us was our field, five acres of steeply-sloping land in the bowl of the hills, shoulder-high with rough grass and thorn bush, and huge clumps of elephant-grass towering above. Their eyes strayed across the valley, wondering where the school was, where the dormitories were, as I and John Mangadima, once again my assistant director, gave out blankets, plates, mugs and spoons, lamps and bowls, matches and soap.

Manasse strolled forward from the group. 'Where is the school, Doctor?'

With as cool a wave of the arm as I could manage, indicating the field and rising mountain-slopes, 'Over there', I replied.

Their eyes slowly turned and followed my pointing hand.

'And the dormitories?' Manasse continued, refusing to show any reaction. 'Also there', I replied, my eyes now challenging his for further comments. It began to sink in—there was no school, no dormitories. Yet...hadn't I invited them to come? For the moment I left the subject, and turned to the immediate needs of sleeping accommodation for that first night.

The local headmaster was lending us two primary-school classrooms during the summer holidays; several church elders had offered to house one or two students; some of the missionaries managed to squeeze in one or two in their already overflowing homes. As we called each name and assigned them to a home or room or dormitory, we were conscious of mutterings and murmurings, and I seriously wondered if we were going to be able to win them round. These young men, mostly seventeen to twenty years old, all secondary-schoolboys, representing nine different tribes, from six different church areas and backgrounds, presented us with a tremendous challenge. Could we win their confidence? And would they trust us to direct them during the coming crucial years? Not only were they young men at the cross-roads of their individual lives, but they were young citizens at the cross-roads of emerging African nationalism. The problems seemed to loom higher than the elephant grass. These proud young men, full of their own importance at having secondary-school education, with all the determination to assert their independence, would they agree to weed, and clear, and cut, and build?

Later that afternoon they drifted back, and we surveyed the valley together. We pushed our way through the tangled undergrowth, measuring out ten-yard plots. Then we scrambled up another steep rise through a forest of elephant-grass and came out on a small level platform, and, laughing and breathless, looked back down the valley. 'That is our school,' I said, with a sweep of the hand across the waving green maze. Students eyed me quizzically, some almost hostilely. Could I be serious? Again they looked at the waste below us, and ourselves heavy with thick black mud, and our clothes full of thorns and burrs. And I appealed to them openly.

'You build, I teach. Are you willing to get your shirts off, take up the tools, and turn that valley into a school village by sheer, dogged, hard labour? Will you clear and dig and weed the ground? Will you go out into the afforestation areas, 6 to 10 miles away, and fell trees, hauling them back on your bare shoulders? Will you build and roof and thatch? Will you stick at it till we have a school village to house us all and all the families of our married students? Then I will teach you—my word, I may not know much French, I may know even less about politics and economics, but I can teach, and those of you who want to learn to be dressers, orderlies, nurses, health officers, medical auxiliaries, I'll teach you all I've got!'

A stunned silence met me, as the reality of the proposition sank into their minds. So I really was serious. This was no joke, no white man's sense of humour. I actually meant it: 'You build, I teach.' It was fantastic. It just couldn't be real. Some closed their eyes and shook their heads, as though to shake off an unpleasant nightmare.

'We'll meet tomorrow at 6.30 a.m. in the courtyard for your decision', I said jovially, inwardly quaking with doubts lest they would not respond. So we made our several ways down the hillside to our homes in search of an evening meal.

There was a special welcome service arranged in the church that evening, led by church elders and medical staff, Zairians and foreigners. The students all came, possibly as they had nowhere else to go. The theme was 'workers together with God'. Slowly, as different ones spoke and through the singing of the hymns, I felt some of the students begin to thaw towards us, accepting the challenge. Others, however, remained withdrawn, their eyes wary and suspicious, if not actually hostile.

Next morning dawned misty with drizzling rain. I went out to the courtyard and rigged up a couple of planks on some broken cement blocks that I rolled into position. I put out my chair and camp table, and sat down to wait for the students. I began reading my Bible, a short morning portion. They did not come, and my reading continued to the end of the chapter. Still they didn't come, and I continued to the end of the book. I was wet and chilled, and very nearly discouraged. So much lay in the balance.

During the previous week, many of the legal representatives and senior men, African and European, of the six participating mission/churches had met to form an administrative council. During the meetings I had proposed that the students themselves should build their own temporary homes in the school village. If we started at once, building through August and September, I reckoned we could start classes in October 1966.

My proposal had been met with incredulity and open laughter!

All the available finance at the centre was already allocated for wards, outpatient departments, homes for the missionary staff, drug supplies, medical and surgical equipment. The school would have ended the list. We should have to wait till the fall of 1967 to get started. But I was impatient. My own particular 'bee in the bonnet' had always been that 'no white man is justified in working in Black Africa unless he/she is teaching'. I could see no ultimate justification for the medical centre, except for the college. There had to be a centre as the college could not function without the hospital and all its ancillary departments; but equally, there must be the college to give the centre credence.

But could I build the school with nothing? The other council members were justifiably sceptical. It must have sounded a wild-cat scheme. Strangely enough, no-one actually asked me how much money I had available or how I would feed the students during the three months of building or how I would procure the necessary supplies for the first term. No, the one burning question had been: 'Do you honestly believe that you, a foreigner, and a woman into the bargain, can persuade secondary-schoolboys, nineteen/twenty-year-old youths, with a consciousness of their own dignity as the "white collar" workers of the future, to build?' No-one asked me what I knew of building, nor who would measure out the land, plan the development, collect the materials, construct the homes. No, they had just asked: 'Can you make students do it, willingly?'

And I had staked my reputation on it.

At 8.45 a.m. that first morning they arrived, and I had won!

I tried to pretend that I hadn't noticed they were over two hours late. I tried to ignore the fact that I was wet through with waiting in the drizzle. I tried to appear as though there was no question hanging in the air. We sang a hymn; I gave my prepared Bible study; then I started assigning work. The students let out their breath. I don't know where they had met, who was their leader, what led them in the end to agree with my proposal, but it was obvious that they had agreed, even though they said nothing.

In a businesslike way, we divided ourselves into three groups. Each group had a set of tools and appointed a group leader. One group of nine had axes to go to the nearest afforestation area and fell trees; the next had hoes to clear a dormitory site. The third had knife-like scythes to mow down the jungle of tall grass to the south of the dormitories, where we would start a football field and, beyond, food-gardens. Granted there was not much enthusiasm, and it was soon apparent that some had never handled an axe before. They certainly were an ignorant bunch where building was concerned. But suddenly someone said: 'OK. You win—we build and you teach!' and everyone started laughing at the sheer impossibility of the suggestion.

The ice was thawed, the tension gone, and I began teaching in earnest how to handle tools. We drew up the plans together, we paced out the land together, we marked off the plots, and I offered a bonus prize to the first group to complete their assignment. Two groups of nine youths each, to the two dormitories, each with a 6-yard deep toiletpit: and ultimately five groups of three married men each, to do three small homes, each with cookhouse and toilet. They even managed to become excited. But in no time their unaccustomed hands were raw and sore, and it wasn't always easy to keep them at it from 6.30 a.m. through to 5.30 p.m. each day.

I went out with the first crew of tree-fellers, walking the three miles across the rough hillside to the nearest afforestation area. We worked all day in twos, an axe between each pair, felling blue gums (eucalyptus) anything from 6 to 18 inches in diameter, and some 25 feet high. As they fell crashing to the ground, the second of each pair lopped off all side branches, clearing these of leaves and smaller branches, and stacking them for roofing framework. The first day, in our enthusiasm and ignorance, we overdid it, and as dusk quickly fell we were suddenly all of us just too dog-tired to make the journey home. We lay out there on the mountainside between the poles we had cut, and slept soundly. By next morning, I was so stiff and sore that it was hard to believe we would ever achieve our target. We struggled home in the early morning dawn for breakfast— and were inwardly furious to find that no-one had missed us, let alone considered sending out a search party for us!

We made the most of every encouragement: the first poles erected called for 20 gallons of sweetened tea! The first roof on (it was Jack's house—they feted him, but there was a gnawing corner of suspicion in my heart that he hadn't really acted honourably. The other homes in his group were far behind, and he was obviously working as a lone wolf and not as a member of a team, often a danger sign) demanded an afternoon off for a football match!

We pulled together, and slowly the students began to realise that we could do it. Neat rows of houses began to appear; each day toiletpits went down a few more hard-earned inches, and we felt ourselves approaching our target-date for completion. It was the driest wet-season on record, or we could never have got that far. Others willingly helped us, hauling in lumber at all hours, or preparing meals for us. This involved more problems, as students from the north had never eaten the local manioc porridge and southerners could not stomach the palm oil; several said they could not digest corn flour, or beans, or other items of staple diet. But again, we learnt together.

The political news those days, or rather, the lack of news, was disturbing and distressing. The mercenary and Katangese units in the National Army were in mutinous revolt against Colonel Mobutu, the Head of State. Kisangani was cut off from us, and four prospective students from that area still had not arrived. Isiro was likewise cut off, and the eleven prospective students from the old Nebobongo school, coming directly into their third year of studies, still had not come. Mail arrived only intermittently, and told us of the evacuation of missionaries and Europeans from both these towns. A general sense of tension underlay everything, and one felt that at any moment a spark could ignite a new conflagration.

Then sickness attacked us, to add to our difficulties. Several students went down with severe bouts of malaria; then bacillary dysentery put nine boys on their beds for several days; then two developed typhoid fever. We were well into September, and really only half-way through our project. I wanted to provide decent eating and sleeping accommodation before starting classes. But it was clear to me that we would need three months to create a habitable village, especially as work now slowed down considerably for ten days. Small problems began to loom large. Grumbling started over the food rations, the housing conditions, the long hours I drove the students to keep them at the building. We had to evacuate the primary school buildings at the start of their new term, before our own first dormitory was ready. Tribal differences reared their head and became focused on the missing group from Nebobongo. The former students were all WaBudus by tribe, as was John Mangadima, my assistant director.

When it was obvious that classes would not start on 1 October and I proposed to postpone the official opening till 31 October, feeling was running dangerously high. Someone muttered: 'She's holding out for her WaBudu students to arrive.'

So I temporised 'OK, let's aim at 15 October—see if we can finish in ten weeks from starting.'

Then we had a fortnight of torrential rains. Our fields became a quagmire. Roads were impassable for hauling poles. Grass, urgently needed for thatching, was beaten down and damaged. Morning after morning we woke to drenching mists shrouding the hills and soaking the valley, only to be displaced by banks of dark, scudding clouds with more rain and yet more rain. It needed so much courage to believe we would ever finish!

Meanwhile, in between measuring and checking, weighing and building, and a multitude of other jobs to help the project forward, there was also a mountain of office-work to be done. Each student needed a personal file prepared, with past and present details of educational attainments, plus family history, medical records, and a word on his spiritual state. Accounts had to be kept, for all the building materials, transport costs, kitchen utensils, food, soap, paraffin and firewood, and all the essential equipment for starting a new secondary school. Lectures had to be prepared, time-tables arranged, and a hundred and one other responsibilities seen to, often between eight and eleven o'clock at night.

As the work neared the end, the problems seemed to intensify and multiply. Manasse walked off one day, over his strong-willed refusal to eat beans. The group of students working on the southern dormitory became sullen, as their building had to be taken down and re-done due to carelessness. Their determination to finish first had allowed slackness in accuracy, and poles were not properly measured, so that the roof-supporting poles were not absolutely horizontal. Had we allowed this building to continue, the roof-thatching would not have stood up to the heavy tropical storms for the length of time we planned, so those responsible were told to pull it down, and they didn't like it. Within a few days, the Mission's five-ton lorry and the Medical Centre's tractor, both heavily laden with roof-truss poles, twine, and grass, were bogged down four miles away in thick mud.

By the end of that week, however, Manasse returned—with a letter from an elderly lady missionary who had brought him up in a church orphanage, to say that he honestly could not eat beans, and we agreed to supplement his diet with animal protein. The southern dormitory group rallied and made a tremendous effort, working late into the evenings, to catch up with their northerly neighbours—and we helped them all Saturday afternoon (while the others played football) to fasten the roof-timbers in place. Our Land Rover went out and succeeded in towing the tractor up the hill, and eventually helped to deliver all the lumber we needed to complete the frameworks to our village buildings.

At the same time as all this, other activities were pushing forward. We cleared paths up the mountainside and staked out twenty-eight plots for food-gardens. We completed clearing a full-sized football field and attempted to level it a bit. We employed a local village tailor to get going on making shirts and shorts and aprons for the nursing students. Considerable hours were spent three times a week at local markets bargaining for our food needs. With no difficulty at all I found sixteen hours a day full of activity and sufficiently hard work to ensure eight hours' solid sleep by night—and no time left for preparing lectures.

After almost continuous rain for seventeen days, the sun returned, and work went forward again at a pace. The students were finding it easier now to do ten hours' hard work, without blisters or grumbles. But the opening date had been put back once more to 30 October and I could sense annoyance and frustration in many of them. So I wasn't altogether taken by surprise at their next move, even if hurt by their lack of trust and seeming unreasonableness.

A representation of each of the three proposed classes for the coming year, with John Mangadima as spokesman, went to see Dr Becker, the medical director of the Centre, with four main questions, which he sought to answer both fairly and clearly.

'Who is finally in charge of the school?' And one sensed the underlying question: 'Can Dr Roseveare expel a student, or have we a higher court of appeal?'

Dr Becker replied: 'Dr Roseveare has been appointed school director by the unanimous vote of the Administrative Council, African and foreign leaders of the participating churches and missions', and we stored away the knowledge that a disciplinary committee would have to be created as a satisfactory court of appeal.

'Why has the date of commencement of lectures been several times put off?' If the first question had raised an optimistic hope of intelligence, the second reversed this, as the answer seemed so obvious: 'The change of the date of commencement is due to the unsettled condition of your own country and through no fault of the missionary', not even mentioning that we had been quite unprepared earlier, with no homes, no books, no lectures.

'Why can we not start school till the northern students arrive?' They were speaking of those from the Nebobongo area, delayed by the mutiny in the army causing transport chaos in their area. These students were mainly for second and third-year classes, having begun their studies before the Rebellion. All were from the Nebobongo church area and mostly of the WaBudu tribe; and the question really meant,

'Is favouritism going to be shown to the WaBudu students, at the expense of the others?'

Amongst those expected from Nebobongo was the church elder appointed to be bursar/chaplain to our new school, Basuana, who had been with me during the previous twelve years. Dr Becker replied calmly: 'Obviously Dr Roseveare needs the school administrator to relieve her of many of her multitudinous duties if she is to be free to teach you in the classroom.'

Finally, 'Who has arranged the programme?' they asked, almost belligerently. In other words, was the whole plan merely a whim of mine, a fantasy, a hair-brained scheme, or could they be assured of receiving government recognition at the end?

Now I myself longed for real satisfaction on this point! But the government, who had given many verbal promises, had sent no letter, no statement, no signature. They just were not prepared to commit themselves. It was all a gigantic gamble yet I felt a spiritual assurance that God was saying 'Go ahead'. But could one build a school on that? Could one ask intelligent youths to risk their future on that? To put in four years of studies, paying school fees, for a mythical diploma and therefore a precarious salary at the end?

'Dr Roseveare spent three weeks, at her own expense, on your behalf in Kinshasa searching out and obtaining the official government programme, and pledges of full recognition.'

They were partly satisfied, though still suspicious. One could not blame their suspicions. I sensed the struggle of the newly independent against the feared 'neo-colonialist', and yet their hunger for the education I could give them. It wasn't going to be easy for them or for me.

At last, however, the initial building programme was practically completed. Water-piping brought fresh drinking-water to the village from the mountains. A 48-foot flagpole was cut, cleaned, and erected in the centre of the compound. Rubbish was cleared away; final touches put to finished buildings; 'hair-cuts', as we called it, given to the thatches; shirts and shorts were issued to the thirty-two male students, and blue-and-white striped dresses to the three girls; household equipment was provided for each of the eighteen married students. Some of their wives and children began to arrive.

Yet there was still no sign of the northern students, or of Basuana who would carry all the administrative load of the village, and so release me for the duties of the classroom. Could I go forward without him? Yet rising tensions among a few of the strong-minded students made us feel it was imperative to get going on 'Phase two'.

6

So We Were Launched

On Saturday 29 October, three months after we had started building the school village, we dedicated the college with a moving flag-raising ceremony, and launched out into the job of teaching.

Thirty-six students had arrived by then, and some two-thirds of the initial temporary-building programme had been completed. During the last week of October there was a sudden rush of final tidying—weeding, digging, sweeping, planting bright red canna lilies—to have the central courtyard cleared and each house standing in its own neat area. Fifteen missionaries and many Zairian colleagues had gathered on the newly cut road to the north of the village for the simple ceremony. The thirty-six young men in smart air-force-blue shirts with school pocket-badges, and olive-green shorts, and our first three girl students in blue-and-white pin-striped dresses, marched into the compound forming a large semicircle around the flagpole.

We sang; Dr Becker and others prayed; John Mangadima unfurled our new flag; Jack Sibaminya blew heartily on an ancient trumpet. All came smartly to attention for the National Anthem as the flag rose slowly to the top of the mast, uncurled and waved out bravely against a clear blue sky.

Suddenly the moment passed, solemnity disappeared, and dignified students turned into ardent footballers. Blue shirts and hymn books were speedily exchanged for white T-shirts and a ball, and 'marrieds' played 'singles'.

'Well, how do you feel now?' one senior missionary jocularly quizzed me over a cup of tea. 'Not bad, eh? You made it, despite all we prophesied!'

I hesitated, and sensed a sudden wave of fear: I was scared. There had been difficult, even tense, moments during the past three months as one might expect amongst any group of thirty-six senior teenagers. Yet I felt suddenly sick with apprehension. Could we carry out what we had set our hands to? The whole scheme seemed so futile, really, when looked at worldly-wise. Here was I, intensely proud of my developing new village, but in the cool light of reason I knew that it resembled a corner of the slums, over-crowded, extremely poor, muddy, and inevitably underfed. Why had I done it? My whole being had always longed to give the Africans as good as the Europeans had. We called our Village 'temporary', but it had cost a cool £1,000 already, and finance was running out.

Could I really run the school and the administration? What if Basuana did not come? Was my own knowledge any longer up to today's required standard of teaching? The difference between American and British medical methods appeared to be considerable. Was I sufficiently adaptable to be willing to teach in theory as the Americans would be doing in practice? I suddenly felt very small and very weary. Was I young enough to carry the load any longer, and the long strenuous hours which would undoubtedly be involved?

'Helen,' chided a colleague, 'a penny for your thoughts!'

'Not worth it!' I exclaimed with a grin, and came back to earth and the job of pouring out cups of tea.

So we were launched.

I remember that first Sunday, marching three abreast the half mile from school to church, all dressed alike with maroon trousers or skirts and white shirts—startling, to put it mildly! Certainly eye-catching, and I dared not turn my head to catch the varying expressions as we passed an admiring crowd. Some were curious, some sceptical, some amused no doubt: and yet probably all were hopeful that this hailed a new start. Dr Becker preached that morning, and John Mangadima gave a short word of personal testimony. It was a good service, and the student body seemed attentive and interested.

Liliane Fuchsloch had arrived back from furlough in Switzerland, in time for the opening ceremony. She was to become deeply involved in the teaching programme of the college, practical and theoretical. We had walked all over the new school compound, discussing all the plans and proposals. We had visited the new hospital and dispensary sites, and the old dispensary buildings. These, we felt, could be converted without too much difficulty into classrooms, to serve until our own new buildings were ready. We spent hours discussing courses and timetables.

Liliane had already completed two terms of service at Nyankunde and in the immediate vicinity. She had served the local community as nurse and midwife, and had helped on the staff of the nursing aids' school which had previously been at Nyankunde, from 1955 to 1960. She knew something of the pressures of time-tables involving theory and practical classes, lectures and supervision, with insufficient staff. She was French-speaking by birth, and knew something of the pain of listening to British and Americans hashing up her language in the wards. Could she stand it also in the classrooms? The radical changes that I and others were so glibly suggesting were to a work dear to her heart, that she had helped to build up and establish. How would she take it all?

'I think it is magnificent!' she exclaimed enthusiastically, as we finally got back to my room and a cup of coffee. From then on we worked closely together, and found we were on each other's wavelength!

We prayed over each decision and sought God's mind together on each problem facing us. We were both conscious that the coming year might prove decisive in the history of Zaire. No-one knew how long we had in which to offer any help in re-establishing educational and medical services. Would the whole economic structure crumble? Would the malcontents start a counter-revolution? Would the ultra-nationalists insist on the withdrawal of all foreigners before we could hand over properly?

It was no good theorizing. I could be neither philosophical nor political. There was a job to be done and we set about doing it. After that first Sunday of dedication, we had two days for final preparations before classes were to start on the Wednesday. We cleared an old storeroom that the church was lending us as a classroom. We arranged shelves, desks and forms, made by a local carpenter. We found two tables and chairs. We 'blacked' some boards, sorted exercise and textbooks, pencils and blackboard chalk, all brought out from England nine months before. The carpenter mended two broken window frames and made fixtures for our charts and models. Two missionaries installed electricity for us, with a line from the generator which served the local printing press. Lilian and I completed what preparation we could give to the time-tables, drew up a simple set of rules for the school, created a committee from local national church members and medical staff, and planned staff meetings for routine school direction.

So the stage was set and our training college launched. On the Wednesday at 6.30 a.m. the students assembled, all in their new nurses' uniforms, all expectant and curious, some probably a little fearful. After an opening hymn of praise, I spoke briefly on our college motto: 'Unto Him, without limits' taken from the Campaigner youth movement, of which most of our senior students were keen members. We tried to set out clearly and deliberately (albeit in hesitant French) the aims and ideals of the college. It was being formed as part of the local church to train them, not only as medical auxiliaries, but also as Christian evangelists. Our standards and rules were unashamedly based on the Bible. In our opinion, as staff, wholehearted commitment by each individual to the keeping of God's first and great commandment: 'The Lord our God, the Lord is one; and you shall love the Lord your God with all your heart, and with all your soul, and with all your mind, and with all your strength,' would knit us together as a family, and create from the outset the right sort of atmosphere that the college hoped for.

As I was writing my diary at the end of that first week, jotting down a few of the manifold happenings and listing the jobs that must have priority in the coming week, there was a great longing in my heart for the arrival of our eleven students from the north with Basuana Bernard, our college bursar. These senior students needed to get into classes at once with no further loss of time if they were to complete their courses in the year. Basuana was urgently needed to take over the oversight of the kitchens, the tailors, the new building programme and a hundred and one other jobs that I was still having to do between and after classes.

Suddenly my thoughts and day-dreaming were shattered. 'They've come!'

The courtyard was full of crazy noise—laughing, singing, and crying. We helped them down from the lorry, thick with mud, weary from sixty hours on the road, many painfully thin from two years of under-nourishment, several sick and feverish. Many of the younger children were fretful, sore from the bruising treatment of the truck over the atrocious roads, through days of deluging rain. Basuana, eleven students, plus the six wives, twelve children, and all their goods were eventually disgorged into the drive, to a tumultuous welcome.

There was Basuana, solid and tough at forty, utterly reliable and loyal, my right-hand man through our ten years together at Nebobongo, up to and during the Rebellion. He had been school chaplain and administrator, as well as maintenance man and my own close friend. His wife Andugui and five of their nine children were with him. He just stepped straight into my shoes, and carried all the burdens of building, feeding, and direction with a quiet, unruffled efficiency.

On the second morning after their arrival, at breakfast-time, he came to me with a list in his hand.

'Doctor, I've just checked the tool-shed. Three axes, five hoes, and two machetes are missing. May I have permission to put a padlock on the door and keep an inventory?'

I swallowed my desire to apologise for my inefficiency and told him to go ahead, fine by me!

At the end of that week he came again with another list.

'Doctor, we really need to employ a second cook for the school kitchens, and a couple of gardeners for the school food gardens. I've interviewed several people, and suggest we take on the following for a month's trial.'

Again, I gulped and grinned. It was good to have him back, and this sounded like old times!

'Go ahead, boss. Fine by me.'

All I was asked to do was to sign their contract in their workbooks and to pay them at the end of the month!

On the following Thursday, three students arrived from the 'big city', as we called Kisangani, the capital of our northeastern region. They came into class at 8:15 p.m., just as we were about to start evening prayers. They were given a tremendous welcome by everyone, escorted back to the village where they were taken to the dormitories, given a bed each with mattress and blankets, and then served a hot meal. How different from our arrival three months earlier, when not a single building was yet erected, and no hot meal available!

But the next morning, two of the three were waiting for me when I returned from school at eleven o'clock. They were full of complaints. 'Don't you realise that we have already done two years' secondary school? Why should we start again in first-year studies?' grumbled the lads, revealing their ignorance by their inability to comprehend that any new course of studies must start at its own first year.

'Don't you understand that we are secondary school boys, and therefore should not be asked to build? And anyway, if we should build, you would certainly be obliged to pay us full wages.'

I was just weighing up how to tackle their attitude when they continued belligerently: 'and the food! We have been accustomed to...', but I found that I had switched off, so to speak. This was what we had been given to expect from any coming from the 'big city', in sharp contrast to the gratitude of the forest-born students.

I allowed them to continue in their own strain, asking a question here and there, or expressing a doubt in the midst of their reasoning, for about an hour, and then felt I had had enough.

'Are you, or are you not, called by God to be medical auxiliaries? We are at present the only college in this vast region accepting students for any of the three possible option courses. If you are called to this service, you'd be well to accept what we offer and settle down. If not, it is well that you leave before I enter your names on the register.'

I suggested that they should leave me then, and come back at 2.30 p.m. when my assistant director would be with me.

John and I sent for them at three o'clock only to learn that they had already left.

On Sunday 6 November, I went the 30 miles to our nearest town of Bunia, after morning service, to meet the midday plane. We were expecting Jill Thompstone, an English nurse/midwife with teaching qualifications, who was coming to work at the medical centre on the college staff. However, there was no-one on the plane that I knew, not an uncommon experience where plane services were concerned!

Most days my waking hours, from 5.00 a.m. with coffee till nearly midnight, were packed tight with activity. School hours were from 6.30 a.m. morning prayers to 9.00 p.m. evening prayers just before the generators were turned off for the night. We managed twelve lecture periods between the three different classes, with meal breaks and school staff meetings sandwiched in between. Then home to light pressure lanterns, and to start marking books and preparing tomorrow's lectures. Through the first four years this daily preparation continued, always for tomorrow's lectures. We never seemed to be able to get ahead of ourselves. The subjects had to be decided on, read up, thought over, simplified, written out, translated into French, typed on stencils and run through the duplicator, the latter process sometimes being at about one o'clock in the morning.

At first the French was a tremendous strain for me. Until the Rebellion I had used French only sparingly, talking mainly in Swahili, the trade language. Now French was obligatory for all secondary school and higher education. I was never quite sure how much of what I said the students followed, nor how extensive was their limited vocabulary. Each Saturday we gave simple test papers, often on the multiple-choice question system, in each subject, on the one week's work, just to encourage them to study regularly throughout the year. These began to reveal how much (or how little) they understood. One of the best howlers during the first month was an answer to a geography question in the general knowledge paper, 'Describe the structure of the earth.' One student wrote: 'A nucleus of molten metals, surrounded by a sort of cement-paste to hold people on, so they won't fall off.' An attempt, perhaps, to explain magnetic force?

At last, on Saturday 19 November, Jill Thompstone arrived! We were thrilled to welcome her. Once the students heard her near-perfect French, they gave her an even warmer welcome than the staff had done! When Liliane and I prepared the year's time-tables, we had prepared one for Jill along with ours. Jill had been preparing for her life's work as a sister-tutor in Zaire for a considerable time, as she had been delayed two years by the events of the Rebellion. Now that she had arrived, she was as excited as we were to get launched.

Then, ten days after her arrival, one Monday morning, Dr Becker sent for us. He reminded us of the urgent, almost desperate need of the hospital for trained nursing help. In other words: 'Couldn't you and Liliane carry the teaching programme for this first term, or even the whole first year, without Jill's help, Helen?'

Dr Becker's eyes seemed to bore into me, and yet held an urgent sense of appeal. Just for a brief moment, I reeled as under a physical blow. We had so counted on Jill's aid to cut the heavy hours of teaching and preparation; but I could see clearly the force of all the arguments he began to assemble. Without an efficiently-run hospital, our students could not receive the necessary training. Jill herself would obviously benefit by working, for a time at least, in the hospital under our local tropical conditions, before trying to teach the students techniques suitable for African nursing practice.

I glanced quickly at Jill, and sensed the fight in her heart. She was longing to get into the teaching for which she was specially trained, and to which she had been looking forward for so long. Yet she was willing to fit in where she was most needed. I caught her eye, and we smiled as we understood so exactly what was going through each other's mind. Together we agreed to Dr Becker's proposal. That very afternoon Jill went to take over responsibility as theatre sister, continuing to give her mornings to language study and evenings to helping prepare lectures.

Another job Jill offered to take on immediately was to sort out the college accounts! I had tried almost in vain to balance these, between all the other activities. I never had been much good at this, back in my Nebobongo days, and obviously I had not improved at the exercise over the years. The vastness of the figures now involved, compared to those old days, staggered me. In the first four months we had gone through over £1,000 in freewill offerings and personal gifts from friends at home.

'Phew! If it has taken that much just to launch us, whatever is it going to take to keep us afloat?'

Somewhat daunted, I had fought on at the books, to get them ready to hand over to Jill in the New Year. Looking back and reviewing the achievement of those first four months, I was not only thinking of the £1,000 finance, but also of all the nervous effort, as well as physical, that had gone into each aspect of the initial building programme and launching. Could we really achieve what we were aiming at, in the eight years that I had specified at Kinshasa in May? The mountain of difficulties seemed almost insurmountable—physical, material, financial, medical, and spiritual.

The next day a letter came out of the blue, to encourage us. It was from the American consul in Kinshasa, proposing to give the college some financial help from their American A.I.D. (self-help) programme, on certain conditions. We, the college authorities, must guarantee the balance of the finance needed to complete the building programme; it must be completed in 'reasonable time'; and we must employ local voluntary labour, including the students. It was an encouragement, certainly, but also a challenge. Could we accept the conditions?

In Friday school, during the daily hour given to general science and applied mathematics, I took the students into our confidence and explained what might be involved by the proposed conditions. Together we drew up scale-plans of the proposed new college complex, classrooms, offices and laboratory block, dining-hall, kitchen and stores block, dormitories and living quarters, and finally sports facilities and grounds. We prepared a budget, including the hiring of a contractor, ordering materials, paying workmen and transport. I explained the need to submit progress reports to all those financing the project. The students easily became more excited than I was, as they conveniently could not see all the thousands of snags and difficulties that might crop up.

As they worked on their plans, I was busily calculating how many tons of cement we would need, how many thousands of bricks, sheets of asbestos roofing, cubic metres of timber, panes of glass. I was reckoning out the cost of masons and assistants at the present scale of salaries, how many weeks of labour would be involved, and how many miles of transport. Multiplying, adding, subtracting. I decided not to contract out to anyone but to 'do-it-yourself'. Eventually I came up with a tentative figure of costs per square metre of surface area. Then reckoning on inevitable rises in costs of materials and wages, the figure began to look astronomical, in the realm of £25,000 for the total project. Over a five-year period, that would be £5,000 annually, and this to be divided between the five main mission/churches participating in the centre. I began to get excited too, as I realised that it could be done.

I tried to explain to the students that the 20,000 hours of free labour that they had already contributed while building the temporary village could be counted in balance to this new permanent project, even though this would have to be done by skilled paid labour. That they found harder to understand, but decided to take my word for it, when they discovered that this meant they were not being asked to contribute more hours of labour!

Had I known then that costs of materials would quadruple and salaries treble before the project was through; that months would pass with no cement or other vital commodity available; weeks possibly with no-one available for a particular job needing specialist skills; that Zaire currency, and later both the dollar and sterling, would lose their value, I might not have been quite so sanguine in signing my name to the American A.I.D. proposal. Perhaps it is just as well in this life that we do not know too much about tomorrow while we still have today with us. Suffice it to say that six years after signing that contract and accepting an initial gift of £2,000, the programme was almost completed. But we faced formidable and unforeseen problems along the way.

7

Extra-Curricular Activities

Sundays began to take on a particular pattern. The students had been going out preaching each week with a local church elder in another missionary's vehicle. One Sunday I was woken at 6.20 a.m. to be told that the chauffeur who drove the students to the surrounding villages was ill: could I please drive them? Momentarily displeased at being woken so early on a Sunday, after working till after midnight every day the previous week, I checked a hasty comment and got dressed. After a quick cup of coffee, I drove down the hill in the Land Rover to collect some eight or ten students, and then thought of Jill. I ran across to her room and tapped on the window.

'Jill, we're going out preaching in the villages up the Irma road. Would you like to come with us?'—and in five minutes she was there! It was a perfectly lovely day, clear, with a low heat-haze over the hills and a cloudless pale blue sky. Jill and I chatted in English as we went, mainly of the students and their problems. One particularly was worrying us. He was a third-year student from the Oicha pre-rebellion school, clever and capable. He worked hard and was obviously determined to do well. There were periodic 'troubles' in school, as there will be in any large group of senior teenagers—student pranks that go too far, minor disobediences that nearly end in disaster, strikes over the time-tables or the food, or some such current problem— but Hezekiah kept apart from each episode, determined not to be involved in any insurrection. We were conscious, however, that he was not really pulling with us. I almost felt he despised me, for working with the students on the buildings, for talking colloquial Swahili more fluently than the official French, and for being a foreigner and a woman at that!

About eight miles out from Nyankunde, we drew to a stop at the roadside, under a large mango tree. Two students scrambled down, clutching Bibles and hymn books, and a pile of tracts and Gospels. The rest of us moved on towards Irma, as the two pushed their way up the narrow track leading through the waving maize to a hidden group of round huts, to gather children and adults together for a service. Just before Irma, two more students got off, at a long lane of thatched houses winding down into the valley, full of laughing children, goats and chickens, and various wary adult spectators. On again to the Irma prison, with its twenty or thirty inmates. They were mostly ex-Simbas, largely in their late teens or early twenties, all bored and disillusioned, and glad of the interruption to prison routine, even at the price of singing a few hymns.

Two more students stopped at the hospital: two at the further outskirts of Irma, near the army camp. We continued into the country, over the river, up a steep, winding hill, to a group of houses in a wide plateau of maize fields. Here we called a halt at what we came to know as 'our village'.

Honking the horn as we approached, we watched the children come running from all sides. A youth started to beat an old iron wheel-hub suspended from the beams of the palaver hut. The village elder came smilingly across from his home carrying two dilapidated chairs (the very best he had) for his 'honoured guests'. Handshakes and greetings all round, chatter and laughter, as slowly some sixty—or even eighty—folk gathered, it would seem miraculously, from nowhere. All were largely naked or clothed in torn tatters; they sat on branches or on the dusty ground, and they listened intently.

Hezekiah led the worship and he was excellent. He seemed to enter right into the lives and thoughts of the people, and talked as one of them. Jill gave her testimony that first week, in Swahili, and I remember how thrilled we were that we had gone. We went regularly after that first Sunday, and began to get to know the villagers.

Twin boys came regularly, sometimes in shining white T-shirts and little red pants, sometimes just tied around with a scruffy piece of cloth. An intelligent little eight-year-old girl always sat on the front row, with her small sister, and drank in all that went on—the hymns, the reading, the message and prayer. In two weeks she was singing the hymns by heart, her whole face lit up by an inner happiness.

One week, as the assistant student was preaching, her little sister, uncomfortable on her bit of the tree trunk, punched the little girl next to her, pushed her off and took her place. The second little mite, dirty as they come, with a filthy cloth round her, lifted up her head and howled dismally. Hezekiah quietly slipped across, picked her up in his arms, slipped back to his seat and sat and soothed her. She sat through the rest of the service in his arms, her head nestling against his chest trustfully and silently. That little act of loving sympathy, where another would have slapped the child, or told her firmly to be quiet or to get out, spoke more to the congregation of the reality of the gospel of love that we preached, than even the words we used. We thanked Hezekiah on the way home, and found that we were pulling together, after all!

Then there was our first Christmas. We had only two months to prepare an 'item' for college participation in the festival services. By then we had fifty young men but only three girls in the student body. What could we sing, and whom could we inveigle into helping us as sopranos? We wanted something definite, to mark the first Christmas of our training college, to involve us all and to glorify God. It should be sufficiently difficult to demand hard work and some sacrifice regarding time, if it was to be of any value as part of the curriculum, yet simple enough to be well executed, if it was to be truly part of the worship of the congregation. We chose the Hallelujah Chorus of Handel's *Messiah*.

We had sung this before, at Nebobongo, at Christmas in 1961, and I still had our tonic sol-fa rendering and Swahili version. Practices began in November. Qualified and pupil midwives agreed to join us, as did also three of the European nurses. A time had to be chosen to suit both groups from the college and from the maternity unit, and these had to be during daylight hours, as the church lighting system had not been restored since the Rebellion. So we fixed rehearsals each Wednesday afternoon at 1.30 p.m. The first week I turned up, armed with tuning fork and blackboard already covered with sol-fa hieroglyphics for the first page. I waited. By 1.45 p.m. A few had wandered in. By two o'clock there were about fifteen, and my patience was wearing thin. At last we started, and did fairly well for an introduction.

Next week, despite all our urging, the start was equally delayed. They appeared to remember very little of what we had previously studied, until I realised that they had all swapped places, basses deciding to sing alto, and tenors preferring bass. We started all over again, dividing them into four voices and taking their names to prevent too much changing in future. While I was teaching a section to the sopranos, the altos and tenors started chattering. Silencing them, we started again, and then several latecomers arrived and had to be sorted out into their places. I asked the altos to sing their part alone and a somewhat unmusical 'cat's chorus' resulted: the sopranos all roared with laughter. The male students were deeply offended and almost refused to try again. The basses, bored by the proceedings, were doing homework, and failed to respond at all when their turn came.

The practice finished in grim silence, and I left in glum frustration. During the following week, I painstakingly typed out stencils and duplicated one hundred copies of the Chorus with the tonic sol-fa. Next week, most arrived on time, waited in uneasy silence, sang as demanded and it needed half an hour to win their co-operation again and persuade them to enjoy the exercise instead of only suffering the agony. Slowly it took shape. I pressed for more practices— after evening studies, after lunch, each voice separately, in various groups. Time was running out. We were far from perfect. Could we really do it? Was it just a publicity stunt on my part?

Christmas Day dawned bright and clear. The students marched across to the church in their well-pressed Sunday uniforms, singing hymns, to the accompaniment of trumpets and drums. Slowly the church filled with a capacity crowd of 1,500, and many more outside the doors and windows. There was community carol singing, special items from different groups of primary school children, two good messages on the wonder of the coming of the Christ to redeem us from our sins, and then, as a glorious finale, the college was invited to sing the Chorus. It was beautiful and very moving, especially knowing all that had gone before in the preparation. A great hush of wonder settled over the whole congregation, who had never heard such music before, and one sensed that all hearts were lifted and filled with praise to God. As they finished, there was a long, silent pause that eased into a shuddering sigh of satisfaction. For us, it had made our Christmas complete and memorable.

At the end of that first term, in mid January 1967, Jill and I filled the ten-day school holiday with a rapid and exciting trip back to my old hospital at Nebobongo. The seventeen hours' driving to cover the 350 miles, mostly in sunshine, were accomplished with practically no difficulty. At one road-barrier, where a soldier was checking my driving licence and stamping all our road-passes, a discontented chicken started loudly protesting. The soldier then demanded road-passes for all our livestock. We just managed to suppress our laughter, and assured him that we had only one chicken which was to be tomorrow's dinner. Eventually, we persuaded him to accept our plausible explanation.

Florence Stebbing, my colleague through the eleven years' work at Nebobongo, had arrived back that same week, on her return after the Rebellion, and she had hardly had time to settle in before we turned up. Daisy Kingdon, one of our veteran missionaries, was staying with Florence, as it was considered unwise for any foreigner, especially a woman, to be on her own at that time. Colin and Ina Buckley, missionaries from Isiro, were also there, with two tons of supplies to help the hundreds of destitute refugees still pouring out of hiding in the forest to the south.

When Jill and I drove in, unexpected despite letters and telegrams (which eventually arrived after our departure), at 9.30 p.m. in the dark, the house which had previously been my home for many years seemed almost uncomfortably full. Camp-beds were everywhere, and bales of blankets, cartons of drugs and sacks of foodstuffs were stacked along all the walls. If our quarters were cramped, however, our welcome certainly was not! The unbounded joy of our Nebobongo team that I was back among them, even if only for a week, was very moving.

The week sped by. A visit to Ibambi to deliver stores that we had brought from Bunia turned into a busman's holiday, with a crowd of a hundred really ill patients to be seen. Then we went to see their new maternity-unit. Senior midwife, Martha Anakesi, had been responsible for its construction by the husbands and friends of her clientele. It was spotless in its fresh whitewash, and filled to capacity with contented mothers and babies. This visit was one of the highlights of our week. It was a great encouragement to me to see something of what the African staff could achieve on their own, and to know that we had had the privilege of some little part in their training.

Two days were given up to journeys to Isiro, the local township 40 miles north, to do essential shopping for food and stores; and to Egbita, another church centre some 40 miles north-east, to do a clinic for the sick and to examine eyes for reading glasses.

Our two Sundays were filled with 'missionary activity', preaching to a packed church, Bible study with the nurses, fellowship meetings with the church elders. As always, the abandoned happiness of the singing of the Christian family caught at my heart, and I realised afresh how much I was part of them.

Then five packed days of doctoring. Everything had to be included. One day included four hours in the leprosy-care centre examining fifty-two new patients and checking over one hundred others, writing up their report cards, checking on drugs and dosage schedules, and generally encouraging them. Another day we arranged a clinic for the eighty primary school children, checking teeth, eyes, skin, blood, and stools, looking for anaemias, due to intestinal worms or chronic malaria, leprosy, or tuberculosis. Yet another day we spent many hours in the pharmacy, cleaning, re-arranging, listing, making up quantities of stock drug mixtures and injection solutions, and a list of urgently required replacements.

When we had arrived, everywhere had seemed a little dilapidated and rather dirty. Thieves had broken in the previous week and taken all the operating-room linen, quantities of penicillin and vitally needed drugs, syringes and instruments, and the African staff were somewhat discouraged and depressed. The stores and enthusiasm that we brought with us did much to restore courage and replenish shelves. Everyone set to, with scrubbing-brushes and disinfectant, sewing machine and rolls of cloth, firewood and sterilizers, and the operating-theatre was soon transformed into its usual dignity. Seven drums were packed with new cloths, gowns, and gloves; three small autoclaves were all hard at work; floor, tables, and trolleys were spotless; rows of instruments, trays, and catgut had all been sorted into four general sets—and we were ready to start!

We managed five major surgical cases each morning, mostly hernias and fibromes, with a couple of emergency Caesarian sections. Afternoons were given to clinics—tuberculosis cases, leprosy patients, school children, eye diseases and those needing glasses, as well as regular outpatients' clinics with chronic malaria, undernourishment, intestinal worms, all complicated with severe anaemia. Each evening, a ward round to see some fifty very sick patients. Only the most seriously ill came to hospital, as their abject poverty made even our heavily-subsidised fees seem exorbitant. How we longed to do more for them, but how? And with what?

An incident occurred during our visit to Isiro, which somehow illustrates the problems of black/white relationships of that period. I had ordered a 40-gallon drum of petrol, and entered the shop to pay for it. While I was there, Jill hurried in to tell me that the drum had fallen on to the toe of one of the helpers and that 'the toe is half severed off!'

I'm afraid Jill was surprised that I did not go at once to see the man, but instincts, developed during eleven years in Congo, restrained me. I turned to the shopkeeper and reported the matter to him in Swahili. He at once went to see, and I delayed a little longer in the shop. Then we went out and saw the shop keeper standing on the kerb, arms crossed behind his back, four assistants working hard in sweating silence to load the drum on the trailer, and then to fill the four jerry cans and tank. Glancing round I saw the 'bystander' two or three yards away, squatting, holding on to his bleeding toe, and scowling at the shopkeeper. Jill urged me (fortunately in English) to go and see him. I gently pushed her away towards the van. Gathering our shopping-lists and handbags, and locking the van doors, I guided her away from the scene to do our other errands.

'Why?' she asked. 'Aren't you a doctor? How could you possibly leave him? And he was actually helping you when it happened!'

I tried to explain what might occur if we became involved, thus revealing that we felt responsible, which would be interpreted as guilty—a court case, two or three days' delay, insurance claims, lots of unpleasantness. I assured her that I was willing to give the man all he needed to be taken to the local hospital, but that I was not responsible, and that in 'these days' it would be very unwise for a white person to be involved in an accident in which an African was injured. Jill remained sceptical and was not too pleased with me, and I wasn't too sure in my own heart just how plausible it all sounded.

Ten minutes later, I went back to the van with a load of groceries, to be met by two policemen with open notebooks, and we were quickly surrounded by an interested crowd. Fortunately I remained outwardly calm, though the fear, born in the Rebellion, was nearly stifling me. Asked for an explanation of the 'broken toe case', I said the least possible, stressing the financial element in the knowledge that in African law this would absolve me from direct responsibility.

'I had bought this drum of petrol, which was being loaded on to my van by the shopkeeper's workmen, when this bystander apparently came too near and was hurt. Actually, I wasn't present at the moment of the accident as I was in the shop paying for the petrol and labour.'

Fortunately, the police (and crowd!) were satisfied, and turned to the shopkeeper.

'I'll willingly examine the man's toe, if you wish it,' I offered to the policemen, 'and drive him to the hospital should this be necessary.'

They assured me that this was not necessary; that they would see to it directly themselves—and they thanked me for my 'generous offer and obvious concern'. We left, and I couldn't blame Jill for the look of scorn that I had so easily accepted such undeserved praise, yet we were deeply relieved that what might have led to considerable unpleasantness had ended so peacefully.

Jill and I wanted our home at Nyankunde to be African in style, a home where Africans could always feel at home. We wanted it to be like our school buildings, so that there would be as little difference as possible between us. We wanted it to be made almost entirely of local material, by village workmen, so that Africans might be encouraged to build equally good homes in their own villages. It had to be within our income, and yet pass the fairly strict standards set by our local building committee.

The European family had asked Jill and me to consider building a duplex (two-in-one semi-detached bungalow), and by January 1967 the housing situation was sufficiently urgent to ensure that when we presented our plans to the building committee, they were passed with very little opposition. We were delighted!

We tramped over the hills to the south of the hospital and college, to choose our site. Higher up the views were glorious, but the land very exposed to the strong easterly gales; lower down, it would be much easier to reach the site with building materials, much closer to the college for supervision, but we would sacrifice some of the views. We timed ourselves clambering up and down from college to various sites: we cleared small patches, spent an afternoon at each, studying and reading, and eventually we picked a site to the west of the main valley, 'half-way up', really 'neither up nor down'!

Once again, in mid-January, when we presented our plans in greater detail, including the site and direction and drainage, we were thrilled that they were passed at once. On Monday 6 February four workmen started clearing the site: eight went to local afforestation areas to cut poles; others went farther afield for grass for thatching before the annual burning of the fields in early March. Yet another group went daily to dig out sand and gravel from various pits in the vicinity, and we began to watch the materials arriving.

Every day we would go up to the site to see how things were progressing, but it seemed such slow work. The ground was rock hard, and digging out a site from the mountainside really demanded great effort, especially with our very primitive tools.

At last the site was levelled to take our 40 foot by 26 foot bungalow. Then to drive 2 foot deep holes in the rock surface to take the poles, four main supports of 1 foot diameter, sixteen other supports of 10 inch diameter, and then almost 300 for all the framework poles of 8 inch diameter: what a task! Hands were blistered, one crowbar was broken, several pickaxes made useless before the job was completed.

Meanwhile others had cut poles to the right length, prepared the top end in a forked notch to carry the ridge-poles, and cleaned and prepared ridge-poles for the five main support-lines.

The first week in April was a school holiday for Easter, and so, early on Tuesday morning at 6.30 a.m., Jill and I joined the work force and watched as the wall-frames suddenly went up. Then the sixteen subsidiary supports; then the four main central supports—eucalyptus trees, straight and strong, almost 24 ft high—hoisting them slowly upwards, slipping their bases into the prepared pits, fixing them upright with forest-twine pulleys on all four sides. Quickly, the workmen roped scaffolding branches 2 yds high to hold the whole framework in position; standing on these, another circle of scaffolding 3 1/2 yds high completed the preparation.

On Wednesday we hoisted the ridge-poles. The outside wall ridges first; then scaffolding across the house at ceiling level; then the formation of a 'human scaffold', five workmen to each side of each of the four main support-poles, each standing on another's shoulders. It was an amazing and somewhat frightening sight to watch as we hoisted the main central ridge, a 40-ft long eucalyptus trunk, up the human chain of scaffolding, from ground to outstretched hand, up to shoulder-level, up again with outstretched arm to the down-reaching hand of the man above. Students stood around and a great silence fell as the huge pole slowly rose, and rose, and rose into the blue sky. All necks stretched back, eyes glued to the pole. The slightest slip by any man would have been disastrous. The final pushing upwards by the fifth team of eight men; the straining of every muscle …

'It's up!'—a cheer went up, as bated breath was released.

The roofing timbers went up quickly in the following week. Then the whole roof was closely covered with line upon line of strong stalks of elephant-grass, bound on with forest vines.

Others were preparing grass. Twenty-four tons had been carried in. It all had to be cleaned from bracken and foliage:

gathered in lengths, tied in 2-yd-long bundles 6 ins. thick, and then cut in half. Bundles were neatly stacked all round the house. Coiled lengths of split vines were soaking in waterbutts.

Amazingly, the dry season held. Rains were two weeks overdue. Each morning the sky was filled with dark, lowering clouds, but they blew away by midday and the building progressed.

The slope of the roof, at almost 45 degrees, scared the local workmen. Basuana, from the northern forest region, was accustomed to it, but they were unwilling to believe him that it was really safe. So I took a day off school, and scrambled up and sat astride the top ridge to encourage them when they started the thatching! This seemed to go very slowly: methodically setting the first line along the lowest edge with the cut end towards the ground and the long, loose leaves up to heaven, and binding each bundle to the framework; then line after line, binding on to alternate rows of elephant-stalks, patiently, accurately, knotting the soaking vine; twisting and knotting, twisting and knotting, slowly moving around the house, line upon line. At last it was complete, except for the final ridge.

Then bundles of longer, uncut grass were thrown like javelins from ground to ridge, and bound on strongly astride the ridge. The next night it poured with rain for five long hours!

This firmly beat the thatch into place. After three such storms, another row of grass bundles was attached astride the ridge. After yet further storms, a final third row was fixed into position and the roof was secure. Probably 18 tons of grass were up there, held by a few forest trees, tied down with thin twists of split vines. It seemed incredible that this could hold up against the fantastic tropical storms, gale-force winds and thundering rains. The thatch was 15 ins. thick when completed, and planned to last a probable ten to twelve years, before needing replacement.

Sheltered from the rains now, as the seasons changed, and working under the roof, a framework of thin branches or bamboo stems was attached horizontally outside and inside the pole structure, to all the outside and inside walls. We were into May when 'mudding' started and the wall-framework was stuffed with mud, smeared with mud, plastered with mud. Then it was left for two weeks to dry out before a final plastering inside and out with mud mixed with cow-dung, which set hard like cement.

Window-frames and door-frames, prepared by a local carpenter, were set in. Water was brought to the home by pipes from the hospital water-supply system, and Richard Dix, a missionary construction engineer in charge of the overall building programme at Nyankunde, gave us a bathroom and kitchen taps and a toilet. Cement floors were laid, doors were hung, walls were whitewashed, windows were put in. The outside was swept and cleared, and flowers planted—and by 30 June, Independence Day 1967, we moved in!

It really was exciting to be in our own little home. A local carpenter had made us some lovely bedroom, dining-room and office furniture, all in grained redwood. Curtains had been measured, cushions prepared, rush mats for the sitting-room acquired—and we were in, five months after starting to clear the ground. True, another month was needed to complete the small garage and cookhouse behind the bungalow, levelling the drive, clearing up the garden, but the job was completed in and around all the regular duties of lecturing and administration and hospital practice.

As our first school year drew to a close and Jill and I had a moment to assess the situation, various pointers prompted us to make a trip to East Africa. First, we urgently needed equipment for the new college laboratory, both for the first-year orientation classes in elementary physics and chemistry, and also for the third- and fourth-year students in medical procedures, requiring microscopes and chemicals. Secondly, my father was planning to visit us for a week and hoped we could meet him in Kampala and drive him back to Nyankunde. Thirdly, there was growing unrest amongst the troops in the National Army, with disturbing rumours of the possibility of an attempted coup to restore Moise Tshombe to power.

We packed up a minimum of supplies for the journey and set off early one morning, at the start of the long summer holidays. We travelled in the Land Rover with trailer, and took with us two Africans who had not previously travelled outside their own province, Basuana Bernard and Gandisi Benjamin. As we crossed over the great central mountain range at 8,000 ft, from Zaire to Uganda, and dropped down the escarpment to the east to the source of the Nile, our two African colleagues were tremendously thrilled. The motor-driven ferry across the Nile; the hundreds of enormous elephants calmly munching at the water's edge, eyeing us disinterestedly like ruminating cows at home; the thundering water at the Karima bridge near the Murchison Falls, with spray thrown up to form a fantastic rainbow arched across the valley: these impressive sights drew exclamations of wonder.

Walking up the streets of Kampala, a pleasant tropical town to us Europeans but an overwhelming city to our African colleagues, completed their amazement. The shops, the traffic, houses of several storeys, Indian temples, the lights at night, the airport and the arrival and departure of great planes with over a hundred passengers each…the days were not long enough to satiate their curiosity.

We acquired the laboratory and other school and household equipment we had come for, and packed the van and trailer to capacity. We met my father and started the long journey back to Nyankunde, going through the national park to see the Murchison Falls in all their glory.

Then followed a lovely week, in our new home which had been finished only two weeks before, but all the time we were nervously listening to radio broadcasts indicating the worsening situation and danger in our area. I must confess that I was glad when the week was up, and we set off for the border again before trouble broke. Once out of the country, into East Africa, I could relax and enjoy the long trip to Nairobi from where my father flew on to Malawi.

Jill and I spent a week camping near Nairobi before going to the Kenya Keswick Convention, where I had been invited to speak about our experiences in the Simba uprising.

Then the long trek back to Kampala, as the first lap of the journey back to Zaire, only to be checked by a request to visit the British High Commissioner. He asked us not to proceed to Zaire at that time, as the situation was so uncertain and they feared a fresh outbreak of hostilities.

Frankly, I was pleased to be stopped by authority. I feared to go back in. I had had enough in 1964, but I didn't want the responsibility of making the decision. Jill was champing at the bit to get back to the job at Nyankunde, and must have found my easy acquiescence most irritating, especially as I was the driver and she was entirely dependent on me for transport.

We were not the only ones 'shut out' at that time, and we soon met other missionaries. Some had just got out with great difficulty from farther south, due to the mutiny of the mercenary troops serving under General Mobutu. Others were on their way to Zaire for the first time and were understandably hesitant. We all waited for a green light from the British High Commissioner.

Meanwhile, to fill in time profitably and to try to prepare for the new school year ahead of us, we visited the University library for several days. We then travelled to the eastern border of Uganda to Mbali to visit the medical auxiliary training school there, to study their programme and course material. After a week there as welcome guests with the headmistress of the local girls' school, we journeyed back to Kenya and spent a wonderful month on a farm of friends of my father, whom we had visited a few weeks earlier. The holiday was a real refreshment, with plenty of time for reading, writing, and preparation for the new school year.

At last, impatient from receiving no news, no letters, no word from the embassy, we set out on the journey home and made an uneventful entry! There were no difficulties at the border, no customs duties to pay on our few purchases, no accident to the van, in fact nothing worthy of report at all. We drove into Nyankunde late on Saturday evening, hoping to start school on the Monday, and what a welcome awaited us! One would have thought we had been gone a year, instead of a month or so. Apparently that Sunday had been pin-pointed as D-day. If we were not back, all senior students were to be sent home, as the remaining staff felt they simply could not cope with all three classes, as well as all their own hospital and dispensary responsibilities.

Students poured out of the village and we were mobbed. Laughter and singing, crying and clapping. Missionaries seemed to arrive from every direction, and our hands felt limp from shaking, before we eventually reached home and settled back into routine for a new school year.

8

Seeking Recognition

After my visit to Kinshasa in May 1966, it was obvious that one of the very basic requirements, if we were to gain government recognition for our college, was that we should have permanent buildings to 'specified standards'. It was almost impossible to discover what these standards were: some said one thing, some another. I gathered that a certain cubic meterage of air per student per classroom was demanded, which was an interesting requirement in the wide-open spaces of our mountain site! Internal flush-toilets had to be included, even though the students would have to be trained in their use, never having met such things in their village life. Obviously, the building would have to be constructed in permanent materials, and this posed plenty of problems, compared to the simplicity of putting up our own small home.

We decided to tackle first a classroom block with auditorium, laboratory, library, and administrative offices; and later, to construct a separate dining-hall with kitchens and foodstores. Many and varied plans were prepared and studied and turned down for one reason or another. Eventually, a very simple plan of a 130-ft-long building, 40-ft-wide, with a long central corridor and rooms along both sides, was found to be the most economical as well as the most useful plan. The completed building would be four times as large as our home and would probably cost eight times as much. Richard Dix, the builder attached to the hospital, was basically in charge, but he had an enormous building programme in hand for the hospital and staff homes. So he agreed to allow Basuana and myself to tackle the job of school construction under his supervision. Eventually the necessary permission was granted by the local building committee and we started to prepare the site in June 1968.

Fifty thousand bricks were available, from a newly-built kiln that Richard had completed. Six tons of cement and 500 sheets of corrugated asbestos roofing were purchased. Louvre window-frames and glass were ordered.

Twenty-four workmen were employed in four groups of six, each group with a semi-qualified mason in charge, assisted by a villager who showed enough intelligence and initiative to be trained as a mason, and four locals for digging trenches, carrying bricks, making mud, and generally helping to complete each team. Basuana had the immediate oversight and direction.

The land was cleared and levelled, then Richard came, complete with instruments, to lay out the foundations. Basuana was fascinated! He and I had always squared our corners with the old three-four-five measurements and pegs, checking with equal diagonals, and making sure that all was level with a spirit level laid on our strings. This was quite different, efficient and accurate, and Basuana drank in every detail.

Then the digging of trenches, while others quarried huge stones from the mountainside near the local river. The trenches were filled with stones, carefully laid and levelled in concrete. Next, the four groups separated to the four corners, and the walls started to creep up. Between classes I used to rush over the half mile from our temporary school quarters to the new building, to check on corners and levels, bonding and mudding. Students used to rush over in break, and stand around in the dinner-hour, to watch. Everyone became excited as the gaps for windows began to appear. Then window-frames and door frames were bolted in. Then reinforcing irons and concrete slabs were laid all round the structure, and a further five lines of bricks brought the huge building to ceiling height.

Students would wander round inside in the evenings, trying to decide which room would be what, and getting a real thrill as they were allowed to help on Saturdays to speed the work along.

The dry season came and we were ready to put the roof on. But here we paused. Basuana and I had never tackled so large a building before, and we felt that we just could not manage a roof of such dimensions. Richard's workmen, under his supervision, had prepared the triangle trusses for us, and all was ready; but Richard had several other urgent tasks on hand and simply could not spare the time to put the roof on yet. So we started praying that the Lord would send us a 'roofer'.

Meanwhile, we did every conceivable other job that we could find. Richard sent a plumber over to help us prepare for putting in the water system. The masons got ahead with pointing the whole building. The carpenter hung doors and fixed window-frames. The workmen carried gravel for preparing the floors for cement. Still no 'roofer'.

We squared the corners of the roofing; we stacked the triangle trusses in place around the building; we carried sand for plastering the inside walls; we prepared timbers for surrounds under the eaves. We even cleared away all debris, smoothed the paths, planted grass and flowers, and cut a giant eucalyptus for a flag pole. Still no 'roofer'.

One Thursday evening in January 1969 Basuana came to me.

'Shall I dismiss the workmen and tell them not to come tomorrow? There just isn't another job to be done, and there's no point paying them for doing nothing.'

We eyed each other. We had worked together for fifteen years and just about knew the thoughts going through each other's mind.

'No', I said, grinning suddenly. 'No. Let's trust for the roof tomorrow.'

'OK by me', and we let the matter rest.

That night I was woken by a car coming up the hill, and peeped through the curtains to see if I was needed. No—the car drew up next door, at Dr Ruth Dix's house. Lights went on and I could hear voices. Shortly I saw Ruth leave and drive down the hill to the hospital. I prayed for her that all would be well, rolled over and went back to sleep.

Next morning, going down the hill at 6.20 a.m. to prayers with our workmen, before starting school, I passed a young American going up the hill. I greeted him and he nodded, but looked too weary to bother to speak. Suddenly Basuana came running up towards me.

'Do you know who that is, that you passed on the hill?' he panted excitedly. I didn't.

'He's a roofer!'—and as I realised the import of these words, the two of us turned and hurried back up the hill.

'Sir', I called out breathlessly.

He turned politely, if with a puzzled look.

'Please do excuse me, I don't even know your name, but is it true that you're a roofer?'

'I beg your pardon?' he said in a confused way. 'I'm Ruscoe Lee, but I don't quite understand what you asked me.'

Hardly surprising! We explained our situation, and he explained his. He had driven in during the night to be with his wife Rachel, who had been flown to Nyankunde the previous day for urgent hospital care under Dr Ruth Dix's supervision. And he was a roofer! During Rachel's two weeks of care and convalescence, Ruscoe worked hard with the African team and achieved our goal—the roof on!

There still seemed so much to do, though. Ceilings, electrical wiring, plumbing, flooring, plastering, painting—the jobs seemed endless. Then furniture began to arrive: forty desks and forms, fifteen tables, 180 chairs, cupboards, and shelves. All had to be sandpapered and varnished. Blackboards had to be plugged to the walls. Laboratory equipment, pharmaceutical scales and drugs, nursing arts' teaching models, charts and library books: all had to be listed and put in place.

Then in May 1969, at the annual meeting of the Board of Directors, we had the college officially opened, singing the National Anthem, raising the flag, cutting the red tape, and we were truly launched. The service, the speeches, the choir, the thanksgiving feast all soon became items of college history, but the sheer joy of teaching in good and adequate premises is a permanent present-tense reality.

Before the college building was finished, the inspectors had arrived! Since classes had started in 1966 we had kept Kinshasa in touch with us. We regularly sent them progress reports of every part of the Nyankunde programme. We continually put together what we considered necessary for a 'dossier', despite great ignorance as to what was really needed. Local educational authorities were loath to help us, as we were under the direction of the Ministry of Health rather than of Education. Now and again I'd catch a hint of a better way of presenting our material and at once we would re-compile the whole dossier, typing out several copies and sending them off to all the authorities that we felt might be even remotely interested in us.

For over a year we heard nothing from Kinshasa. Then someone passed us a verbal message that applications for recognition must go first through regional channels, then provincial, before approaching central. With unflagging willingness we started all over again, and actually achieved regional 'consent', for what it was worth. I rushed off to Kisangani, the provincial centre, clutching the regional letter of recommendation and all the carefully-prepared copies of our dossier.

A week of dogged perseverance followed. I went back to the same office twice a day, till eventually the provincial medical director was persuaded to give me an audience. Most graciously, he added his signature to that of the regional authorities, and suggested that I go next to the Governor of the Province (as he was then styled).

Another week of equally dogged perseverance, only at the last to be told that I had broken etiquette by going to the medical director before the governor.

'The governor will not look at a document already signed by a subordinate. His signature authorises medical and educational authorities to continue with their investigations into the suitability of the application.'

Back to square one. Another set of documents was rapidly prepared and taken to the Governor, who graciously signed them. Back to the medical director, only to find that he had just left on a six-weeks' tour of the interior. Over to the director of education, and roughly the same procedure through another week till I found him in and willing to listen, but it took several more visits to persuade him to take action. Even then, he would not sign our documents till he had had time to send an inspector up to see our standards.

I flew back east to Nyankunde and got back into school routine, teaching some twenty-four periods a week with all the preparations involved, as well as office administrative procedures. Everything was made ready for the promised inspector; no-one came.

At the start of a new school year, in September 1967, we actually received a specimen document from Kinshasa as to how to apply for recognition. We speedily re-prepared our ever-fattening dossier according to this newest formula, and sent off three copies to the address specified.

We waited in vain for an acknowledgment from Kinshasa.

We waited in vain for an inspector from Kisangani.

We sent letters of request to both. Eventually Kinshasa replied that they had never received our dossier. We did it again and sent it off by registered mail. Two months later, it was returned to us with a cryptic message that we deciphered to mean that we must submit our papers through the right channel.

What was the right channel? We sent to the local regional authority, to be told that their jurisdiction did not extend to paramedical schools. We went to provincial authority, to be told that they could do nothing till our previous papers of application were duly completed and signed. We reminded them that we were waiting for an inspector, only to be sharply told that this was now quite unnecessary. I promptly produced my earlier forms, carrying the Governor's signature, photostat copies of the medical director's signature, and the space waiting for the educational authority's signature.

He actually signed—and I sent them all off the same day by registered mail to Kinshasa, accompanied by our precious dossier.

Three months passed by.

In May 1968 the papers all came back, without the dossier, saying these forms were now obsolete, and would I please procure and fill in the new forms for requesting school recognition?

Where did one procure such forms?

Teaching and preparation continued.

In September, we received a new application form. Somewhat automatically we filled it all in, re-did the dossier, affixed all the end-of-the-last-year reports, and all the beginning-of-the-new-year reports, and sent everything off.

Teaching and preparation continued, in our cramped temporary buildings, while every effort was being made to speed the construction of the new permanent building.

Rumour reached us that inspectors were on their way. We tried to school ourselves to ignore such rumours: they only built up to frustration and disappointment. Yet one day they would prove true, so we did all we could to prepare. All student dossiers were checked and brought up-to-date. All didactic material was listed and catalogued. Our Swiss staff put in overtime to check and correct the French of our course material.

The inspectors arrived! In November 1968, one Tuesday afternoon, the Government doctor from our neighbouring town of Bunia drove out to us, with two European ladies (a Yugoslav and a Britisher) accompanying a Zairian from the Ministry of Health at Kisangani. This was it!

That first afternoon, in a continual drizzle, pushing our way through mud and rubble, we set off to inspect the new school building, then up to ceiling height (and awaiting its roof!). It was the biggest building I had ever been involved in and I sometimes felt guilty at its size, in those days of economic uncertainty. Would we be able to complete it, and would we really have enough students to fill it?

The national inspector asked endless questions about the size of each room, the lighting, ventilation, electricity, water supplies, and sanitation arrangements.

'My one criticism is that it is all too small. The minimum size of a classroom of a secondary school has been set up by my government as 48 square yards, or at least 5 cubic yards per student.'

I did some rapid calculations, quickly making a mental note of each room and its proposed usage. I then led him down the central corridor to the first- and second-year classrooms, where only the foundation was in for the dividing-wall.

'Will not this satisfy the requirements?' I queried, motioning to the one large, undivided room, 11 yards long by 5 yards wide. He paced it out, and no more was said. We never built the dividing-wall. Honour was satisfied on both sides, with no loss of face.

Up to our temporary mud-and-thatch village, through the two dormitories, the dining-room and cookhouse, the home of a married student with his cookhouse and toilet facilities. The students hadn't been warned: would they rise to the occasion? And anyway, could anyone really think our village satisfactory? Even in my own heart, proud though I was of the students for having achieved this village and being willing to wait for better accommodation, I knew that this was little better than the proverbial 'shanty town'.

'I think this is wonderful', one inspector commented. 'All local materials to meet local needs, within the local economy. Very commendable!'

Was I really hearing aright?

'And the rooms are so clean and tidy: a real credit to the college.' Boys, thank you!

We moved away, through the hospital compound towards our temporary school buildings. By now darkness descended, and the students were in the classrooms studying. We went first to our tiny office, where I tried to interest the inspectors in the filing system and the students' private dossiers, but they were obviously tired and not interested.

Next door, the five senior students were studying. All of these had been in our Nebobongo school before the Rebellion. They were older men, most of them married, and some with very rudimentary French. Before the Rebellion much of their teaching had been in Swahili, and I had not worried over much about this aspect when they came to complete their schooling at Nyankunde. The two ladies were watching them and making towards them. I tried to edge them away and into the large first-year classroom, where we had a crowd of keen teenagers with good French and an ability to express themselves. Unsuccessfully!

Moving into the fourth-year classroom, the inspectors started to ask the students questions about public health, the care of the tuberculosis patient according to the latest proposals of the World Health Organization, and I licked my lips in apprehension. Joel looked across at me, in hopeless bewilderment; Lawi was turning the pages of a book, at least knowing where to find the answers; when suddenly Gaston saved the situation, sailing into an excellent extempore dissertation on the care of the tuberculosis patient. There may have been some wild guesses; there was certainly some very original thinking. Grammatical howlers filled every phrase; but sheer enthusiasm for the subject of preventive medicine could not have been more abundantly portrayed if they had been schooled to it.

We did eventually enter the first-year classroom, where students were painstakingly copying down a very elaborate diagram of the interaction of hormones in the control of the health of the body. Their notebooks were beautiful. The blackboard diagram was the pride of my heart.

'This is absurd—quite outside the scope of the curriculum and of no possible real value to the work they are going to do.'

I felt like a deflated balloon. The national inspector had to leave us to return to Kisangani, and I was left to the mercy of those two highly-qualified, high-powered, W.H.O. lady inspectors.

The next two days were agony. They grilled me. Nothing seemed to please them. Mostly we sat in our sitting-room going through course materials and programmes, while other staff kept the school time-table going as best they could. The subjects that the inspectors were keen on were those that I knew practically nothing about, such as the growing importance attached to the teaching of preventive medicine and public health. The subjects I knew best, and loved teaching, and had spent patient years developing, were to them of minimal importance, such as basic anatomy and physiology, the science of diagnostic medicine, the principles behind the surgical procedures we employed. We just didn't seem to have any common ground. The more they talked and reasoned and explained and instructed, the more I felt that I was on a different wavelength, and had been altogether wrong in my whole approach to the establishment of the college and its standards.

Was the whole college, as I had envisaged it, only an outworking of my vision and individuality? Had I really felt I knew just how it should be done and, if they would let me, I'd prove to the government that I was right, until they would actually turn and thank me, even would eventually adopt my plan and method? Had I allowed some basic inborn feeling of white superiority to drive me along, irrespective of what the local government was demanding? Was I really training a new generation to be discontented and maladjusted, because their courses would not fit them to take their place in their developing country? Would they really feel underpaid according to government salary structure, because I had taught them too much for a junior diploma?

Could I really be all that these inspectors implied?

It certainly was a terrible blow to my pride. I simply couldn't face the enormity of the consequence of these allegations: all I could do was to pack and go home. What a fool I'd been, what a proud, stubborn fool—and I really had dreamt I'd be thanked for all my effort or, at least, I'd be satisfied by the worthwhileness of all that was to have been achieved.

By Friday midday I could take no more. I broke down and cried, and asked them please to stop. 'Better you talk to the other staff. They'll be more able to adapt. I've just made a mess, a proud stupid mess. I'll leave. The others will know how to benefit from all you're saying.'

My house-help, Benjamin, unable to understand as we talked English, and hardly better able to understand when we used French, could easily understand atmosphere and now tears. He was furious that these two strangers had so upset 'his' doctor, and tore off down the hill to the school to collect Jill and Liliane.

Meanwhile the two inspectors were equally horrified. Whatever had they said to upset me? 'But of course, the college is wonderful. It is one of the very best that we have seen in the country so far.'

But why on earth hadn't they said so before?

'But our job is to show you the one or two areas where it could be improved.' Liliane and Jill arrived at this point, followed by an almost savage-looking Benjamin, who was quickly dispatched to prepare coffee and biscuits all round. And we started again.

By that evening, the two inspectors had had a meeting with the students to encourage them, and to promise them that everything possible was being done to acquire the coveted recognition, and that, meanwhile, they had a college to be proud of. They had also a meeting with all the staff together, to present their final findings and to promise us that they would recommend us for immediate recognition and, following that, for upgrading to the status of a senior technical college. Furthermore, they had a meeting with all the missionary personnel of the medical centre, and explained again the great importance of close co-operation between hospital and college, the need to increase our bed capacity to 250 as soon as possible, and our qualified nursing personnel to a minimum of one to every fourteen beds, more than double what we had at that time.

On Saturday, Jill and I went out with the two ladies for a picnic, to the escarpment overlooking Lake Albert. It was a lovely, still, hazy day, and we enjoyed chatting about one thing and another, nothing to do with the college, until it was time to take them to catch their plane back to Kinshasa.

Arriving back at the college, we were immediately surrounded by students.

'Did it succeed?'

Did what succeed? We looked puzzled. Everyone talked at once. At last we made out that the student body presumed our 'outing' for the day was in order to bribe the ladies to give us what we so dearly longed for. We were tempted to roar with laughter—the whole concept was so completely foreign to our very English way of doing things—till we realised how utterly serious they were. This is what we should have done, as our students saw it; if we failed to become recognised now, it was indeed our own direct wilful fault.

And it was to be two and half years before we heard any more. That 'fault' was going to cost us dearly.

The first real indication of growing irritation among the students came during the final week of the 1969-70 school year, eighteen months after that inspection. Nothing had apparently come of it, and so, in frustration, the students staged a revolt against the staff—minor, perhaps, but no less traumatic.

They were impatient with their government for not providing legal diplomas. These had been virtually promised for June 1970—or so I had said. They hadn't materialised Had their government failed them, or was it possible that I, school director but foreigner, had lied? Had there perhaps never been an agreement, and was it all my bluff, to—to what? To satisfy my 'neo-colonialist' instincts to make them do what

I wanted? Or to satisfy my 'imperialist west' plan to achieve cheap labour for the hospital that we foreigners were running? Such were the thoughts fed to the students daily over eastern radio broadcasts. Perhaps they were true after all?

Anyway, it was easier to strike out against local known leadership than the far-distant unknown government, so we had to take the brunt of their frustrated dissatisfaction.

We were within a week of the final oral examinations. Petty irritations began to occur in all classes. Students came in late with no apology; others deliberately sat when answering questions, where the custom was to stand. Some refused to make any attempt to take part in discussion groups; all of them seemed suspicious and sullen. We had a meeting in the assembly-hall to try to heal the breach before the fuse blew, but we got no co-operation. Eventually one asked to see the diplomas that they were going to receive at the end of term, and with an almost audible sigh of relief we felt that we had discovered the root of the trouble.

Knowing that they would be disappointed that the official documents still had not come (weren't we all?), we had had new diplomas printed locally. They were as near to the coveted government ones as we dared to approach, using the same format, but keeping our college name and crest in evidence, and our motto clearly printed at the base: 'The Son of man came not to be served but to serve, and to give his life as a ransom for many.'

I went along to the office and collected one of each of our college documents—diploma, certificate, report card, annual bulletin—as well as road-passes and student passes for reduced rates on public transport. Back in the hall, staff and students awaited my return in strained silence. I showed each document in turn, beginning from the last, and briefly explained both its value and also its format. When I held up the diploma I was booed. Everyone started talking at once, and in the general hubbub I caught phrases:

'Why on earth is there a Scripture verse on a diploma?'

'What value has that piece of paper, with no government signature?'

'Who's going to sign it, anyway?'

'How dare you imitate a government document?' 'Who do you think you are, anyway?'

At last the noise exhausted itself, and I briefly answered some of the criticisms I had managed to distinguish from the torrent of angry comments.

'We have written permission from the government to produce our own diplomas again this year ...' angry booing interrupting me as I spoke, '... so long as we show clearly that it is not in fact legal', and the angry shouts drowned anything else I could say.

'Listen, fellows, give it a chance. The exams are on Tuesday. If the examiner comes as promised, if the exams are fair and you pass, if he stamps these diplomas with a government recognised seal and duly signs them as the government appointed official, won't that content you?'

Obviously not, as the torrent of noise increased again and ugly looks were being exchanged.

'I promise you that I have done all that I can to get the official documents here, and I won't cease to go on badgering the government till they come'—but my words were silenced in mocking jeers of 'wretched impostor', 'imperialist white', and 'it's all been a hoax'.

On Saturday morning I received an anonymous, badly written, poorly-worded, scruffy letter on a sheet torn from an exercise book. We called their bluff and sent it back for signature. Triumphantly, they returned it with all but four of the senior students' signatures.

On Sunday I carefully answered the letter, point by point, in polite, accurate French on college notepaper, explaining again all they already knew.

On Monday both sides watched each other warily, and no one moved.

Tuesday was our big day. Staff had worked hard all Monday to prepare the library for the visiting examiner, to prepare the questions for the oral examinations, to prepare diplomas and certificates to be duly filled in as each student completed his quarter-of-an-hour oral, so that all would be ready for signature and stamping at the end of the four hour session. On Tuesday morning, fresh flowers were placed on the table, trays for mid-morning coffee prepared, students alerted as to their order and practical details for the smooth running of the day: and we waited.

Promptly at 8.00 a.m. the Belgian doctor from Bunia drove in, alone. We had expected a Zairian doctor too, but we accepted the change philosophically. He worked hard and efficiently. The exams were quick and fair. Every student of second- and third-year classes successfully passed the required 60% mark. Diplomas and certificates were filled in, checked, signed, and stamped according to recognised international custom. And the doctor left us shortly after midday.

Normally all the students would have been in the assembly hall to greet the examining doctor and hear the results. Then speeches would be made by both sides, and considerable freedom of expression allowed to let off steam. That day the hall was empty: no-one came to hear the results. No-one thanked anyone. With some embarrassment, the staff saw Dr Marchland off and sincerely thanked him for his services and time.

Turning back into the school, we sensed the gathering storm, but met no-one. We cleared up and went home for lunch.

Then they came, a fairly small group at first, climbing the hill in silence. A last, fleeting hope that they might be coming to thank us for their schooling was quickly squashed as they lined up outside our small verandah and angrily shouted abuse at me. Two held batons menacingly. All looked hard and disagreeable. It was inconceivable that these were our own students, our friends, for whom we had cared, whom we had clothed and taught for the past four years. Their threats were sinister, using gestures and vocabulary learnt from the Simba rebels, and therefore even more frightening to my ears.

Through various stages, up and down the hill, they besieged our little home for the next twelve hours, and we were, quite honestly, scared. They sang lewd songs, they threatened us and shouted abuse at us, they threw stones at the doors and windows…but that was all.

Next morning, no students reported to the hospital for work. There should have been twenty-six of them, in the six wards, outpatients' department, laboratory, and operating theatre. There were none. Graduate staff, foreign and national, worked round the clock and saw that the patients did not suffer. Letters went to and fro; conciliatory offers were made; veiled threats were returned. Eventually at 4.00 p.m. they agreed to meet with Dr Becker as arbitrator, on condition that he went alone. Normally one would never question 'going alone', but even the tone of voice in which they demanded this was calculated to strike fear in my heart.

Then it all fizzled out. By the end of the week, all the ringleaders of each class had left for summer vacations. Those who were prepared to sign a statement of compromise stayed on to work in the hospital. Diploma day and festivities were all cancelled, but not before the staff and the four senior students who had refused to sign the original protest had all had their fill of insults and threats. The students suffered worst: their property was seized and fouled, buckets of water poured over their beds, everything they owned rendered useless.

It was perhaps only a petty show of frustration, as some tried to persuade me, but it left a dark stain in my heart. When I drove the first group to Bunia to put them on public transport for their various destinations, all at our expense, they had spat at me—and that burnt deep. Oh, granted that they were only students, and did not really represent the general feelings of the population; nevertheless they were our students and it mattered to me tremendously what our relationship was going to be in the future.

The very next week, at the end of the first half of our projected eight-year programme, I left for England for a quick three-month holiday. I needed a breathing-space to look at things from a distance so as to assess the real situation. Also I wanted a short time with my mother, who had been ill during the previous two years. She had spent many months in hospital, having operations on both her knees, and was then limited to two crutches and a wheelchair. While on holiday with her in Cornwall, I weighed up carefully whether I honestly wanted to face the students again.

What was being achieved? Were our results worth the price that was being paid? As I looked back over the twelve years of my medical career at Nebobongo, where I had been a full-time doctor—surgeon, physician, obstetrician, and paediatrician all rolled into one—I asked myself again: 'Is it worth giving up all that for this?' That is: giving up being in charge of a medical service for the problems of running a training college to staff such a service.

Many of my close friends were quite sure it was not worth such a price. Yet I remembered times at Nebobongo, too, when I had seriously questioned if being in charge of a medical service was worth while. At first, when I found myself so involved in building, and buying food stores in the market, and caring for orphan children, and developing the student nurses' school, that there was no time for being a doctor, I had grumbled. Eventually I had been persuaded to see that all these activities had brought me nearer the people. When my hands were raw with throwing newly-burnt bricks down from a kiln, the workmen understood and accepted me as one of themselves, whereas when I was drawing on sterile surgical gloves to operate on a seriously ill child, I was a thousand miles away from them, on a pedestal of respect and awe. When I fumbled around in the Kibudu language down at the markets, the village-folk roared with laughter and loved me, whereas when I was teaching in school in French, even the students held me apart as an object of discipline.

Later on, when I found myself so overwhelmed with medical responsibilities, endless surgical emergencies day and night, hours needed in the pharmacy for making up accurate solutions of drugs, time spent in the laboratory coping with tests and analyses beyond the ability of our students, so that there was no time for being a missionary, I had grumbled. Eventually, our evangelist Agoya had persuaded me to look at things differently.

'Listen, there are 300 people coming to our hospital daily. Why are they there?'

I wasn't going to be drawn.

'Because you are here! If you, the doctor, weren't here, they wouldn't come. And what do you think we are doing?' Agoya and his wife Taadi were both Bible School-trained evangelists, and Basuana and his wife Andugui were catechists, appointed by the church to full-time ministry in-the hospital.

'All day and every day the four of us are fully occupied talking to patients in the clinics, the wards, the health centres. Do you realise that five, ten, sometimes twenty people are finding Christ as their Saviour every week through this ministry?' He paused, and then added quietly: 'You know, Doctor, we can't all be the last link in the chain!'

My thoughts moved on to the recent four years at Nyankunde. I never did surgery now; I hardly ever entered the wards and only rarely helped in outpatients. The students did not respect me as a doctor, but merely tolerated me as a teacher. Even my teaching ability was now in question and was to become more and more so in the three years ahead. I was becoming an office-boy rather than a teacher, let alone a doctor. Was this reasonable or worth while? Did this really make sense under the title of a 'medical missionary'?

Someone else was to take over first-year teaching, including anatomy and physiology; another, the youth club and sports activities; another had been nominated to represent the school on the executive medical committee of the centre which handled school disciplinary problems. More and more, I was to sit and type out seemingly hundreds of government forms, adding up seemingly endless columns of figures and statistics, filling in seemingly useless reports and documents.

Why? Was something really wrong? Had I made a mistake, and somewhere got out of the line of the Lord's will? Basuana, on our school committee, had tried to talk sense back into me during the previous year.

'Listen, Doctor; think for a moment of Cornelius, and Isaac, and Bernard, and Mordecai; cast your mind to Poko, Aba, Nala, Oicha, ...' and he named a whole list of college graduates, and the places where they were then working.

'How many graduates from our college are now in full-time church employment, do you think? And how many patients are they reaching daily, not only with medicines but also with the gospel?'

I knew what he was heading towards without doing the calculation; however, he wanted an answer.

'Well, I suppose some forty graduates so far, and they're working in twenty-two of our hospitals and dispensaries, and so I suppose they are seeing at least 3,000 patients daily, and might be even more—and that is not counting the thousand patients daily here at Nyankunde.'

'OK. And how do we come to have these graduates?'

I thought back quickly over all the trials and tribulations of those first four years at Nyankunde, all the staff and workers involved, all the preparations, teaching, demonstrations, as well as office work that had achieved even our present position.

'You know, Doctor, the government demands a doctor's signature on all the forms and letters to authorise the very existence of this college. And really ...' and he used the same Swahili idiom as I had heard years before at Nebobongo from Agoya: 'we can't all be the last link in the chain.'

As I remembered all this and reviewed things from the perspective of the cliffs of Cornwall, in the quiet peace of a summer day, I let the impatience in my heart simmer down, and I made arrangements to go back to Zaire at the end of the month and to carry on.

9

Recognition At Last!

Without doubt, the government was grateful for all the funds channelled into its medical services from overseas by private agencies, including the enormous contribution made by the missionary societies, but they could hardly be expected to take this into account when planning a new national health service. We also had to realise that a country's self-respect cannot accept endless voluntary contributions, especially if these are in danger of dictating policy by their very largeness in comparison to the national effort.

So we were not altogether surprised when a move was made to change the pattern. Almost out of the blue, we heard that our application for government recognition of our college had apparently been (or was about to be) granted, and so the country's treasury had been authorised to pay a subsidy towards the salaries of the four registered, qualified teaching staff. With this short notification came four pay-sheets, and the assurance that the money mentioned could be withdrawn immediately from the local bank.

It was rather exciting, even if the cheques were small compared to homeland equivalents: about £60 a month for our nurses, £80 for the sister-tutor, and just over £100 for myself as medical director. I wrote at once to all those who by their sacrificial giving had kept our college going during the five years since the Rebellion, to let them know that the government intended to carry one-third of the responsibility in future. This would be increased by increments until they could economically afford to accept the whole budget on the national grid.

Accordingly, a certain degree of overseas support ceased. Simultaneously the government-promised aid failed to materialise. Hadn't God known the latter when He agreed to the former? There were a few 'light' months with hardly enough to pay the workmen. Then came the long summer vacation, when college feeding-bills and running costs reached their annual minimum and we maintained par. However, these same months usually included stocking for the coming school year.

Tons of rice, beans, groundnuts, dried fish, flour, sugar, and palm oil; thirty local-made beds with mattress covers and blankets for the new first-year students; uniforms, stationery, and classroom supplies all needed replenishing.

I had been ill in February of that year with a mild attack of tick-borne typhus fever, and the rather severe depression that followed this made it advisable that I should go home to England for two months to regain strength. At home, on holiday, I made out lists of all our college needs, I prepared lectures and time-tables, and I tried to rest and relax, rather than chewing my nails over the enormous, unresolved problem of turning my paperwork into practical realities.

I arrived back at Nyankunde on the first day of September with four days before the college was due to re-open. On my desk, amid a mountain of mail, was a statement from our regional educational authorities of a gift of almost £1,500! It was unsolicited, entirely unexpected, and probably unprecedented. Doubtless God had already arranged this provision when He allowed other sources to dry up temporarily. Even after twenty years of experiencing His unfailing faithfulness in such matters, and His amazing accuracy in timing, I still had not managed to accept the period of uncertainty with equanimity.

Now, with this generous gift in hand, we went the next day to Bunia and turned all the prepared lists into acquired realities, and then found we still had sufficient funds in hand for the first quarter of the new year.

Despite repeated efforts to correct our government paysheets, my own remained obstinately at just over £20 a month for several months, and then stopped altogether. The following April, along with others, I attended a teach-in at the regional educational offices in Kisangani, some 400 miles to the west. It proved to be an excellent and valuable, if intensive, three days, dealing mainly with various financial aspects of our service. This included how to fill in forms to apply for subsidies for salaries, equipment, and didactic material, and then how to fill in more forms when the response to the first set was not satisfactory.

During one session, the national lecturer told us of the dubious excitement being enjoyed at that moment due to the installation of a vast new computer to handle all national grid salaries for the armed forces and police, the telecommunication service personnel, educational, medical, and general transport personnel. He explained a little of the vast programming involved for each service, to include basics, educational bonuses, family allowances, transport and lodging expenses, all deductions for pensions, national tax, health services, and others. He explained how the punch cards were prepared from statistics provided, and the checking system employed before the final feed-in ticker-tape was actually ready. With all this, he indicated some of the thousands of possible hold-ups or pitfalls. Finally, various listings would reach regional, and then sectional, sorting offices, post offices and banks, for distributing to groups of services, through to area representatives, and so ultimately to the individual.

Pinpointing some of the hazards of the system, and how easily mistakes could get in but how hardly they could then be removed, he told us a story.

'We have a medical doctor as a director of one of our secondary school extension programmes, training medical auxiliaries. The punchcard code is DD, but when the computer met this for the first time, it queried it as a mistake, and so substituted D6. When this came through, the computer realised the error, as D6 would mean a secondary school director with only six years of secondary school education, an impossibility in our revised educational system. So the code was duly changed to d6—temporary director with six years of post-primary education—and the salary came through at about £20 a month. After a few months the computer caught up with its error, that a qualified medical doctor was earning only £20 a month, so it cancelled the pay-sheet and fed it back into the machine for correction, including back-pay. By now this totalled over £600. The computer had been taught that any monthly pay sheet over £500 must be an error, so again the result was cancelled and fed back in.'

Amid growing amusement as the story unfolded, the lecturer further explained that this school director had thus received nothing at all for several months. He looked across at me then and grinned, concluding: 'I confess I'm glad she's white, or she would doubtless have been on strike these months, living on my office doorstep, till we could sort out the computer!'

The school year 1971-72 went remarkably smoothly until the last month. As usual, an application had been made to the central government in February for a jury to be formed in June for our finalist students. Hearing nothing, we wrote again in April. As there was still no acknowledgment or response, we telegraphed Kinshasa in May. In the first week of June we received a telegram asking if we wanted a jury that year or no, and if so, when. Frantically we sent an answering telegram, and also an unofficial verbal message by radio. The examinations were due Tuesday, 12 June. We had one week left for arrangements.

We had a radio message on Thursday, 7 June that the central government had authorised the regional authorities to make all necessary arrangements, and they were glad to delegate their authority to sectional level. Would I therefore contact Dr Biki, the national government doctor at our local hospital in Bunia, and also the inspector of secondary schools at the local offices of the Ministry of Education, to arrange details?

We set off, on what proved to be a long trail. Dr Biki was not in. The Educational Office said that it would agree to whatever Dr Biki suggested for Tuesday the 12th. Dr Biki was not found in at all on Thursday the 7th nor on Friday the 8th. On Saturday, I managed to waylay him as he left his home in the early morning.

'No,' he said emphatically. 'I certainly cannot accept delegated authority by word of mouth. There must be written confirmation.'

Back to the post office to send a telegram to Kisangani, and to sit there four hours waiting for a reply. They were about to close at midday and I was growing frantic. Eventually our local post office relented and allowed me to use their radio telegram line myself, and I contacted the head postmaster at Kisangani. Understanding the urgency of the situation, he agreed to send a runner round to the Ministry of Education and to radio me back in half an hour.

I sat on by myself in a now-closed post office, not even sure if I knew how to let myself out, let alone how to handle the radio, telegram, and telex machinery.

Two hours ticked relentlessly by, and I felt it was a wasted job. I might as well give in, and return on Monday morning. I put my things together, turned off the machines, went to turn off the lights—when a sudden hunch made me try once again. Switching on the machine, I called in Kisangani post office, and they replied!

'We're doing all we can for you. A telex has been sent to Kinshasa, as the Provincial Medical Director who nominated Dr Biki as his delegate is away, giving examinations at Isiro, and we cannot contact him. We may hear by 5.00 p.m. And we'll radio you.'

I had to be content. I went back to tell Dr Biki this news, and he nonchalantly started talking about the examinations. Had we set the questions yet? Yes? Good, he'd like to see a set. Oh, you've got them with you? Excellent. Thank you very much.

He started flicking through the patiently prepared lists of thirty questions in each of twelve subjects.

'Have the students seen these?'

'Of course not,' I exclaimed.

'Why not? You must show them to the students at once. That is only fair.' You couldn't win with this man.

I went back to the post office and waited till six o'clock and tried unsuccessfully to call Kisangani several times. At last I gave up and went home. Monday found me back at the post office as soon as it opened. There was no telex, nor telegram, nor letter. Nothing. Eventually we established radio contact with Kisangani.

We're doing all we can. We have no contact today with Kinshasa. We have sent copies of all telex of the weekend down on this morning's plane. We'll radio you as soon as we hear anything.'

Time was running out. The date set for the examinations was tomorrow. I managed to contact the missionaries in

Kisangani by radio and asked them to get anyone possible from either the Ministry of Education or the Ministry of Health to their radio by 11.30 a.m. to rendezvous Dr Biki, and so give him the needed authority to act. I rushed off to persuade Dr Biki to come to the radio; but he refused. Back by myself, I spoke with the Kisangani authority and explained my difficulty to them.

'But we have sent Dr Biki a telegram nominating him for tomorrow's jury.'

'Please, can you send another, now, and I'll stand by for its delivery and take it out to him?'

'Certainly.' I stood by till the office closed at 4.30 p.m. No telegram. What could I do next? I went back to the Ministry of Education. The inspector was ready for the following morning and obviously irritated by the unnecessary fuss. I retired. Eventually I decided to spend the night in Bunia. Early Tuesday morning, I contacted Dr Biki at his home.

No, he had heard nothing.

No, he was not willing to act without proper authority.

I went back to the Ministry of Education, where the inspector shrugged his shoulders.

All day, I hovered from one to the other. Eventually at 4.30 p.m. there was a telegram for Dr Biki. No, the post office would not give it to me to deliver. No, they had no runner available to take it: it must wait till tomorrow. No, it would be no use my going for Dr Biki, as they were closing.

I felt frantic, when suddenly Dr Biki himself appeared! He took the telegram, read it, and brusquely said: 'All right, we'll have the examinations on Thursday, 8.00 a.m. Be ready!' and swinging round, he left. I rushed off to the Ministry of Education, but everywhere was closed; all the personnel had left for home. I'd no idea where they lived.

Once more I drove home and told everyone the news. On Wednesday I drove again to Bunia to be sure the Inspector of

Education would be available for 8.00 a.m. Thursday, and to arrange for his transport.

'I'm sorry, Miss. The inspector leaves today on the plane. He has other examinations booked elsewhere tomorrow. No, he hasn't left any instructions. No, nor has he left his rubber stamp.'

How could this happen? I stopped short as I realised that I was running round in ever-narrowing circles. I took a grip on myself and had a short time of quiet prayer.

Then I set out again. By lunch-time I had persuaded the Ministry of Education to send a primary school inspector to us. They had discovered the needed rubber stamp, and contacted their senior authority for permission to use it. I had the address of the junior inspector and knew where to find his home.

After lunch I went back to Dr Biki to ask if his chauffeur could go to pick up the inspector at 7.00 a.m. and bring them both to Nyankunde by 8.00 a.m. for the jury. I gave the address, and started on the explanation as to how to find the place.

'Over in the suburbs? Good gracious, no! My chauffeur is not going over there. Why hasn't he got a car of his own? If he must come with me, he can walk into the city.'

I was furious. The sheer snobbery, that 'we of the city' were a superior class to 'them of the suburbs', left me dazed. I knew this sort of thing back home among Europeans but I'd never met it among Africans.

'Please don't worry. I'll come in for him myself tomorrow morning.'

I turned to leave, when Dr Biki called me back. Picking up the copies of the examination questions lying beside him, he leisurely tore them across and delicately dropped them into his waste-paper-basket.

'Those are useless. No good at all. We need clear, simple questions on each subject, such as...' and for ten minutes he rattled off suggestions. I grabbed a pencil, dipped into the waste-paper-basket for a torn remnant, and scribbled as fast as I could.

'Oh, and my chauffeur will collect your inspector tomorrow', he threw at me as he finished.

I left him, seething inwardly at my own impotence. I was sure this had just been an idle show of power to put me in my place, but it all seemed so unjust, so unnecessary. I raced the thirty miles home, tore round to collect all the staff up to my home and explained the situation to them. Then we all worked half the night preparing new questions, typing sheets and rearranging things to fit in with the last-minute suggestions that Dr Biki had given.

At 8.30 a.m. they arrived and a grim day started. Nothing pleased him; nothing was right. Why ever didn't I know how to organise things better? At Kimpese they had done it this way—or that way—but never my way! Contrary to custom, he asked questions in the main, instead of the staff, and many students could not even follow his rapid French. They were all so nervous. Many questions were far too hard and simply not geared to our syllabus. He argued with the staff over almost every answer even. We felt the day would never end, yet as each student stumbled out of the room in a daze, Dr Biki wrote down a mark on his report card, invariably higher than any member of staff would have given. No student failed.

At last it was over. All certificates and diplomas were filled in. Augusta Johannessen, an elderly Norwegian lady who had been living with me all the year and tirelessly serving the school as our secretary, had everything ready for Dr Biki to sign within a few minutes of the last student leaving the library. Then the next row started.

He certainly wasn't going to sign anything. He had only been asked to witness the examinations. If Education wanted to sign, that was fine by him. No, he was adamant: he would make his report to his superiors, as to just how unsuitable the examinations had been, how poorly organised how 'altogether wrong'. He then strode into the hall to face the rows of dazed students, waiting in bewildered silence, to hear the end of the strange day. He faced them all belligerently, and swung round to me. 'Where's the list?'

All was ready, Sir. Here at once, Sir.

And he read out, to the dumb-founded college, the amazing list of 100% unqualified success. After an unbelieving pause, the whole student body burst into cheers. The senior student made a good quick speech of thanks, to which Dr Biki replied with extraordinary graciousness.

The following school year, 1972-73, started off quite normally. The previous year had been a good one. Mordecai Kasereka had been an excellent head student and diploma day had been a happy occasion for us all.

There was a large new first-year intake, including six girls. We were under pressure on all sides to take girls, to give them two years' general nursing training, and then a third year concentrating on midwifery. The whole north-eastern region, with a population of some five million, was urgently needing qualified midwives, women who could not only undertake responsibility in rural maternities for the care of normal deliveries, but also the care of complicated cases. Since the Rebellion it had been hard to recruit girls: there were not many in our secondary schools, and all who reached a sufficient level in general education seemed to want to go on to university, to prove their equality with the boys.

For the first time we had four girls who had finished the two years' general nursing training and were admitted to the third year to train as midwives. The staff spent considerable time and care planning their course and time-table, to make it not only efficient and practical, but also attractive. There were not really enough of us on the teaching staff to carry a four-year programme, and so considerable doubling of classes had to be manoeuvred. Third-year women midwives and third-year male medical assistants could follow almost half their programmes together with very little difficulty, and each would benefit from the extra material given to the other.

We had four weeks' training school with the new first-year students, while second- and third-year students had their annual vacation, and during this period the main preparation was done for the school year for all four classes.

In October we started full classes, with all third-year students, men and women, in class, and second-year students working on the wards. We were excited and expected a good year, with enthusiasm for the new courses. Application had been duly made to the government to recognise our midwifery section, as our nursing and medical auxiliary sections were already accredited.

From the start we found it heavy going, to say the least of it. By the end of four weeks, all the staff were tired of encouraging, persuading, cajoling the third year to work and study and co-operate. They simply wouldn't. A sort of don't-care attitude pervaded their classroom. Slowly, it became clear that the girls were the ringleaders. We invited them home to coffee and cakes, to share with them more informally our hopes for the success of the year's programme, and their prospects as the first qualified midwives under the new government plans. But no response. No enthusiasm.

Another staff member invited them out. Every effort was made to 'get through' to them, and eventually someone tipped me the clue we needed. I sent for them again.

'Someone tells me that there is an absurd rumour going round that you will not get diplomas of equivalent value to the men's.'

Silence. 'You know of course that this is rubbish. They are identical in value.'

Silence. 'Are you worried about the salary-scale at the end of your training?'

No answer.

I produced copies of both finalist diplomas for third-year studies. I produced the government wage-scale for paramedical workers, male and female. I produced the law-book, controlling paramedical training colleges, course materials and programmes.

No response.

I nearly lost patience, and told them to stop wasting their time and mine, to start working and putting their backs into their studies, to pull with the rest of the class, and to help us all to make it a good year.

They left, unimpressed—and school continued under strain. Another hint reached us, so we tried again. All the staff got together and invited Dr Ruth Dix, the obstetrician in charge of the maternity unit, to join us. We discussed together, prayed together, and then invited the four girls to join us for coffee and cakes, in a relaxed atmosphere.

'Have you any questions you'd like to ask me, about the syllabus this year, or the opportunities for service next year?' Ruth asked them. Vague indifference; monosyllabic answers.

'You know how much we are looking forward to having qualified help in our maternity units. I'm prepared to do all I can to help you to get all the skill and knowledge possible, to rise to the top of your profession.'

Polite agreement; nothing more.

Studies dragged on interminably, with none of the usual joy and fun. Quite honestly, we all became a bit bored with the effort of winning their confidence or trying to help them. Petty disobediences, frequent late arrivals, unwillingness to do any public service such as cleaning the school and grounds on Saturday mornings, refusal to attend church or weekly fellowship meetings, uncooperativeness at choir practice: all this harassed and aggravated us.

Then, during the ten-day Christmas vacation, the storm began to burst. A letter was written to Dr Becker demanding student representation at executive level. A meeting was called, and the students produced a list of some twenty demands, mostly involving pay for practical service in hospital during their training, redistribution of hours of service giving more to theory and less to practical, the right to know what staff did with their government salaries and a continuing angry demand to know why we were not yet a legally-recognised college with government diplomas.

Each demand was answered as reasonably as possible. All the staff managed to remain calm and polite, even in the face of outrageous demands touching their own salaries. Students were allowed to examine the books, to see the government pay-roll and the government schedule of distribution of hours for theoretical and practical teaching—all of which they had seen before, but every effort was made to satisfy them.

They tried to threaten that they would not work in hospital unless they were paid. The whole executive committee balked at this. Every student was being heavily subsidised already for schooling, housing, and clothing. Their practical work was part of their training. We all gave our hours voluntarily to teach and train them. Anyway, there simply was no money available to pay them.

'OK then, we won't work', was the student ultimatum.

'OK then, we don't teach', was the staff rejoinder.

Stalemate. I left the room. Why continue? We, the staff, did not need them, the students. We owed them nothing, but were willing to give them everything, as I saw it. Until qualified, they did need us, however unpalatable the truth might be. I was almost-tired of serving them as a slave, with just no response at all on their side.

The students went back to work. The staff returned to teach.

But the tensions in the classroom increased rather than eased. Classes were to divide after Christmas, girls having their own programme, practical and theoretical, until Easter, and the men theirs. That was when we finally found the underlying cause of friction. No girls turned up to their practicals; they all came to the boys' instead, and they came in a militantly aggressive way as Mrs Pankhurst of the English suffragettes might have done!

'We will not be treated as inferior to the fellows. We are equal. Give us our rights. We intend taking the same courses, the same exams, the same diplomas. We are equal.'

To suggest that to attend their own courses showed their superiority, as the men were not invited to be midwives, was to court disaster. The four militant female students were in no mood for reasoning. They had made up their minds—or rather, their minds had been subtly made up for them—that the only way to show their equality with the male students was to force this particular issue. We soon discovered that they had been systematically brainwashed during the first three months of the school year, over the radio. Broadcasts in French from Kinshasa, broadcasts in Swahili from farther east, had been repeating day after day that the women of Zaire must insist on their rights, demand absolute equality, refuse to be made out less than their male counterparts.

At Christmas, the final thrust had been made over the Voice of Zaire radio network.

'Girls in Medical Auxiliary Training Schools! Don't let your staff tell you that you can only be midwives! Don't listen to their specious reasoning why it is better for you to be a midwife than a health officer! Demand your rights! Fight for equality!'

And our four were going to fight!

We didn't give in easily. As we assured them, it was for their own good that we did all we could to persuade them to do midwifery. They were needed as midwives by the population.

'Isn't the first object of our political leaders that we should serve the people?'

As midwives, they would have jobs assured, but no-one would employ them as health officers, as we couldn't send a woman to a rural village on her own.

'Are you threatening us? We'll report you to the Party!'

And they meant it. And we didn't like it—and they knew it!

So they joined the men's classes. We closed the midwives' class for the year. We sent a report to the local government doctor and the educational authorities. The year crept on much as it had started, with a veiled campaign of passive resistance, no co-operation and less-veiled glances of contemptuous superiority.

However, the truth remained that we urgently needed qualified midwives, and that African culture made it strongly preferable for our girl students to train as midwives rather than as health officers. Ultimately we, the staff, felt sure that these same girls would regret the action they had taken. So we made plans to ensure that this would not occur again. At the end of term, when reports were to be given out, each second-year student was asked to sign a request form to be admitted to third-year studies subject to their exam results; and the men's form, all made out in the masculine, requested entrance to 'the health officers' course of studies, while the girls' form, written with feminine concords, requested entrance to 'the midwives' course of studies.

We sent for the six second-year girl students, explained the whole situation to them again, and gave them their request forms to sign. Forms were in duplicate, so that they could send a copy to their parents or to their local party member, should they so wish. No pressure was put on them. They could sign and do midwifery, or not sign and go home. As simple as that. There was no option open to the girls to sign for the health officers' course. We merely stated that the latter course was already full with sixteen male students.

We waited. One girl went home without signing, to 'discuss it with my father'. Three girls came up to see us to 'talk it over more fully'. Staff were nervous; students were edgy. The local government doctor, who had initially backed us and given us his authority to take this course of action, withdrew his support, and warned us that we might be heading for trouble with the party.

At four o'clock one Tuesday afternoon there was a knock at my front door.

'Good afternoon, Doctor. This is my father and brother', spoke a second-year girl student, indicating the two visitors she had brought up the hill.

'Good afternoon', I responded, and we all shook hands.

I suggested to the girl student that she go back to the girls' quarters, while I talked to her parent. I turned to go in and make them tea.

'No', the father snapped. 'She stays.'

I paused, took a deep breath, and turned to face them. The very air felt menacing. Then a mud-slinging contest started, voices were raised, tempers became heated, and I knew fear. I had no witness, no-one to quote me accurately, no-one to defend me against the outlandish accusations that this man was making against me. I knew fear of direct physical violence, that he would strike me, and I knew I dared not defend myself. I knew fear for the college, that, after all we had done to establish it, one foul slander from this man could lose us our government recognition. It was all so weird, so unreasonable. It was useless to reason with him: he had already decided on his course of action before ever he approached me. He was almost demented, beside himself with rage.

At last, others came and took him away, talked with him, and appeared to reach a conclusion. They went, and I breathed a little more easily.

Two days later a letter came, a copy of a letter of bitter accusation that this man had sent to the judiciary powers in Bunia, to the special powers that controlled the movements of foreigners and held our dossiers, to the party and to the National Army. He claimed that, as a foreigner, I was acting for a foreign power, against the best interests of Zaire, that I had ridiculed the party and the flag, and that I had stood in the way of his daughter receiving the best possible education provided by the government, showing sex discrimination and anti-party colonialism.

The case dragged on for nearly three months. Several times I had to appear in court in Bunia, costing not only £5 each trip, but also several hours of precious time. Reports were written and submitted, explanations were prepared and given, advice and consultation on all levels was sought and received. Lumbabo Eugene of our educational office was a tower of strength. He knew the right people to give us the legal help we needed, particularly with regard to court-room custom and language. He gave me his friendship and time without measure. He represented me several times, when he felt that an African could cope better than a foreigner. His report to the court officer on my reputation and relationship with local Africans was generous to an extreme.

Eventually the affair 'blew over', or was allowed to settle. I was acquitted, I presume, although no-one quite said so. Someone would have lost face had that been done. Those three months of court appearances and uncertainties were almost like the proverbial straw that breaks the camel's back. Not one word of appreciation from this parent for all we had taught his daughter; not one word of apology for his cruel lies and absurd accusations; not one word about reimbursement for all that the court case had cost me. No, but next term he was to come to Dr Becker and ask the medical staff of the centre to employ his daughter in the hospital, as though nothing had ever occurred!

Despite government salaries for the staff and a government doctor for our final examinations, we still had no paper to say we were truly recognised and accredited as a government college. We needed a legal identity number to put on all our government communications. We needed a formal statement with a clear signature to say that the government had agreed to our request for recognition. We still had not received any government diplomas for our graduating students with which they could obtain official posts with recognised salaries in the government health service. All we had was the salary for four foreign teachers. In the eyes of the government this was our personal money and we were not expected to account for its use, only to sign for its reception. If in fact we each ploughed it all back into the running expenses of the college, this was our own private affair and of no account to the government, however grateful they might be for what, to them, must be obvious generosity.

The students heard that we had received government subsidies, and so they concluded that the college was recognised This should have meant that the college was also receiving direct subsidy money for the use of the students, but this was not yet so. The facts were explained to the students, but they chose not to believe us. The only alternative was therefore to believe that we were lying, hiding from them the truth, presumably (in the thinking of the students) because we were stealing the college subsidy for our own private use.

They were shown the books and the government-salary pay-sheets. Members of the district educational office explained the situation to them patiently and in considerable detail. Still they could not, or would not, believe what we said, and a growing spirit of criticism and suspicion crept in between staff and students.

We applied repeatedly to the government to have some Africans on our pay-roll. True, we had no national with full teaching qualification available for our school staff, but we had some fine young men, graduates of our college, who stayed on at the centre to help train first-year students. Their main responsibilities were in the realm of the art of nursing (bed care and ward routine) and to control discipline in classrooms and dormitories. We felt that, if even one of them were on the payroll, students would be more likely to believe them than at present they were to believe us, when only foreigners were paid.

In October 1972, to our delight, three Africans were added to the pay-roll. All seven of us, black and white, went each month to the local educational offices to receive our 'salaries' and sign for them. Everything was open; each one could see what the other received, and we hopefully expected the underground mutterings and discontent and suspicion to subside.

What a vain hope! By Christmas, while women students fought for their rights, men students clamoured for cash. Their conviction appeared to be that the government money we were accepting as our salaries was meant to be their pocket-money! At their request (as I have mentioned) I showed them my monthly pay-slip, totalling about 32 Zaires (£30), on official computer form. They were dumbfounded, and yet still not convinced. True, they did not know that my salary-subsidy was so low due to a mistake in the computerization, but even they must have sensed something a little bizarre, when a qualified doctor with over twenty years' experience, director of a training college, was receiving the same as one of the college graduates with only two years' experience.

For six months the undercurrent of grumbles and suspicions rumbled on, periodically flashing into the open. I was ill for five weeks during February and March, and to make up to the students for all the lectures they had missed in that period, we offered to rearrange their time-tables. It would mean very heavy hours for the staff, perhaps especially for myself, but very little ultimate change for the students. However, the third year representative student came to see me to refuse categorically all the changes we had suggested, unless we paid them 'for the inconvenience'.

It was almost incomprehensible to us as a staff. Our African colleagues tried in vain to reason with the students, to show them that only they would be the losers: the staff were not sitting their final exams! To the students, apparently, it was equally incomprehensible that we were willing to put ourselves out for them with no ulterior motive. They refused to believe it possible, convinced that we were putting something over on them. They sent us their suggestions for the final three months of the school year, with an apparent ultimatum stating what they were willing to do if we did not pay them for their services.

We accepted their suggestions, just as they stood. It meant far fewer teaching hours for us. We determined among ourselves to carry the extra hours of practical service in the hospital, rather than make any further appeal to the students.

Then suddenly we heard that the scholarship grants were on their way!

We heard a vague, unofficial report that these grants were to be paid to individual students, and not to the college as previously indicated. Then we heard from a school in Kinshasa similar to our own, that they had received their grants. The next week we heard that violent trouble had broken out in that school due to a misunderstanding of the use intended by the government of this scholarship money. A visit to us in the Easter vacation by a staff member of another similar school helped us to understand a little better the problems involved, but gave us little guidance as to how to avoid the same violence in our own college.

Letters were sent to government officials at our local township and regional capital. Visits were made to two senior educational establishments in the area where scholarships had already been received. Gleaning all the information we could ahead of time, we prepared a document as to how we felt we should disburse the money when it came. Copies of this document were sent to the central government in Kinshasa and also to church leaders, regional educational directors, and local directors of other subsidised schools, to elicit their comments, corrections, or criticisms. We received no response. No-one was willing to commit himself.

A government conference in Kisangani on medical education enabled two of our staff to ask again for clear direction as to what we were expected to do when the cash arrived. Once again, there was no answer. Basically they would only say, rather cryptically: 'Wait until you have the cash: it may never come!'

Two members of this regional conference then flew up to inspect our college at Nyankunde. I shall tell more of this inspection in a moment, but during it they had an unpremeditated meeting with the student body, when they were faced with the same question direct from the students. On being asked what I proposed to do, I produced the document that we had prepared, not without considerable trepidation, as it was not a government document and we never quite knew how far we could go on our own initiative.

The inspectors read out the document, line by line, painstakingly explaining each phrase, as to how the monthly 10 Zaires (£8) for each second- and third-year student would be allocated, to housing, schooling, clothing, feeding, and finally 20% as pocket-money. After checking various figures against our annual accounts, the inspectors eventually said that they considered it an extremely good document, the allocation fair and reasonable: if they had any criticism, it was only that 20% was too high for pocket-money. The government reckoned that this was the money needed for existence, and pocket-money should be provided by the students' families.

I let out my breath with relief; the students almost hissed.

The atmosphere was electric, and I felt embarrassed before our distinguished visitors. Later on, over coffee, I asked if we had permission to allocate the 20% as pocket-money, and they assured me that, as director, it was entirely left to my discretion what I did, particularly as it meant that I was still subsidizing their fees to that amount out of my personal money.

We went ahead on this authority, albeit verbal only, and prepared documents in detail for every month of the current year, for each student, in duplicate, ready for the day the cash arrived. We trusted that, when it actually arrived, the students would be so thrilled to get their 20% that they would drop their mutterings, particularly now that they had heard their own authorities say that we were being more generous than others!

At the beginning of May 1973 a radio call informed us of an important conference in Kisangani for all those involved in paramedical teaching, particularly arranged for national and foreign nurses. I had been ill earlier in the year and missed many lectures. It therefore felt wisest that I should not go. I was also leaving the country soon, and it was obviously more sensible for those who would be carrying on to hear all the advice given. So Vera Thiessen, an American sister tutor in charge of the classroom teaching of nursing arts, and Camille Djailo, the national supervisor of students on ward practice, were nominated to represent our college at the conference. We prepared our 'file' of school dossier, information, statistics, and questions, briefed the two of them on all we wanted to know, and sent them off.

Then an urgent radio message three days later from Vera. 'They want to meet you, and are coming to Bunia tomorrow.' 'Who? Can you repeat that message, Vera?'

Nothing but crackles and static interference answered us; we could make out no more, but were left to guess at the inference. In fact, we were prepared. We had lived six years in a state of preparedness for this moment. All our files were up to date, our teaching material in order, our time-tables carefully balanced. School accounts and statistics were all ready for instant inspection. Nevertheless, there was a wild rush of activity, to polish and tidy and lay out everything available; to prepare beds and meals; to clean dormitories and iron uniforms. A sense of expectant excitement filled the air.

The next day, I went to Bunia with one of our African staff members and met the inspectors, a lady sister tutor from Kinshasa and a man from the Ministry of Education in Kisangani. We chatted happily and freely on the journey back to Nyankunde, where we arrived in time for the midday meal, generously provided and graciously prepared by Dr Ruth Dix. Then the afternoon was given up to the inspection. We did not spend long on the buildings: they were obviously pleased and satisfied. We spent longer in the classrooms and offices, in the laboratory and nursing arts' demonstration room. They asked many searching questions and listened carefully to our replies and explanations.

The blackboard layout of all time-table programming for each staff member and each student for the whole year, in a fairly complex double-entry eight-colour system that we had devised, drew the longest discussion, and they were obviously impressed. Accounts and bookkeeping, lists and statistics, honestly did not interest them, and only with difficulty did I persuade them to sign these for me as being satisfactory. We discussed in detail the balance of practical experience with classroom theory; different pedagogic methods and approaches; student-staff relationships; the place of party political involvement, especially where the Saturday active participation in manual labour was concerned, for medical workers. In everything they were clearly satisfied.

The next morning they met informally with the students for an hour and invited us, the foreign staff, to be present as well. There was an obvious element of suspicion. The students felt that the inspectors had probably sold them to the white staff and that we, the white staff, had talked the inspectors into accepting our point of view, as though we had something ulterior to gain through this inspection. Both inspectors did all they could to dispel this attitude. They openly praised the school, staff, and students, for the obvious achievements: buildings, curriculum, uniforms, esprit-de-corps, examination results. All spoke of success, which in turn revealed hard united effort.

'Are there any questions you would like to ask us?' I drew in my breath and waited.

'Is it essential that we girls should be midwives?'

A moment's stunned silence. I had not prepared the lady inspector for this particular problem of women's lib in our midst.

'Essential?' she parried. 'But no. If you wish to remain with your second-year training diploma in general nursing, and work in the hospital, of course you may. We offer you the privilege of continuing a third year in midwifery.'

'Why can't we study with the boys, as health officers?'

This went on relentlessly for twenty minutes, just as the staff had had it all year. The lady inspector refused to lose patience, nor did she use sarcasm, but she clearly stated exactly what we had so often repeated. It was a privilege for a girl to train as a midwife, but a girl health officer was not wanted by the population, and service to our people must be our guide.

Eventually, the educational inspector swung the question, and so a male student brought up next the vexed question of money.

'We hear there are to be scholarships, back-dated to January. How is the money to be handled, and by whom?'

Again the inspector replied with care and courtesy, examined in detail our prepared document, and agreed that what we had planned was exactly in line with government policy except that we were being too generous to offer them 20% as pocket-money! The students were furious, certain that I had previously primed the inspectors, or bribed them into saying what I wanted said.

Despite the hour of rather unpleasant questioning, as it seemed to me, both inspectors were very impressed by everything, including our student/staff relationship! They were quite amazed that we were able to encourage some 60% of our graduates to go back to the rural areas when they finished their studies at the centre, as most other schools found that only 10% were willing to leave the city life.

I remember, as I gave them mid-morning coffee before driving them back to Bunia for the midday plane, asking them hesitantly if we could know the final 'mark' that would be attached to our inspection report. We needed seven out of the available ten to become officially recognised It was so important to us, I hardly dared to breathe as I awaited some response.

The man shrugged and spread his hands. 'What can we say, really?' This left me still quite uncertain and on tenterhooks of anxiety. Had he any idea of the importance of that moment to me as the climax of twenty years' hard work?

'Listen,' said the sister tutor. 'You are the last of the forty-three schools in our vast country of this standard of paramedical education that we have inspected. We have already given two schools nine, so what can we give you except ten? There is just no comparison.'

I nearly fainted.

'Thank you,' I whispered. 'Thank you.' I was addressing them both, yet I was also addressing in my mind and heart all the staff and all the students, all the helpers and workers, all who had been involved. 'Thank You, God.'

10

Apparent Rejection

It seemed that our immediate goal, government recognition for the college, resulting in legal diplomas for the graduates, was almost achieved. I confess I was thrilled. For seven years I had been working for this. In fact, quite honestly, for twenty years we had been working towards recognition, even if not always at Nyankunde. We had asked the government in 1966 to give us eight years to achieve the standards required in permanent buildings, course material, and qualified personnel. Now, in only seven years, one year ahead of our proposed schedule, we were in sight of completion.

When government-subsidised salaries arrived for the teaching staff in 1971, we really knew that our request for recognition would be granted, as it was inconceivable that they would pay us unless they were content with our methods.

When government doctors were sent for the final oral examinations and were authorised to use the legal rubber stamp on our diplomas, we were even more certain of our ultimate acceptance.

When the inspectors had arrived and spoken so favourably, and shown us the copy of their report recommending 'immediate recognition, and speedy upgrading', it was obvious that it was only a matter of time before the coveted official document would arrive, recognizing us as a government school for training national paramedical workers. Add to this the fact that the inspectors had brought with them the blank legal diplomas for us to fill in for each finalist student of that year, and our joy was full.

Monday, 26 June, only four weeks since the inspection and eleven days after the final oral examinations, dawned like any other day of our tropical year, at 5.30 a.m., bright and clear, with a mild haze over the distant hills. I went down the hill early to college as we had a lot of work to get through. The other staff soon joined me in the library, where we prepared for the day's activities.

Each student had a six-week summer holiday to visit his own people and to collect his fees for the coming school year. Half of each class would go on holiday from 27 June till 11 August, while the other half worked in the wards and outpatients' clinics of the hospital. A week of overlap from 11 to 18 August made allowance for transport difficulties, and also enabled us to arrange our 'Big Day' with the whole college together.

We were inviting the 1968 graduating class to come for an 'oldboys' reunion on 14 August. The 15th would be a welcome meeting for two new doctors, Philip and Nancy Wood, who were expected to arrive early in August to take over the direction of the college. In the afternoon there would be the presentation of the diplomas to the new graduating class. The 16th was to be a farewell meeting and evening party for me, as I felt that the time had come to leave Nyankunde and to hand over to younger workers.

Arrangements were well in hand. Transport had been arranged for all those hoping to come. Local government officials had been invited to be with us and to share in the programme. The choir had been practising for five months. I hoped to have cassette recorders running throughout the three days and had acquired films for my camera, in order to have a permanent record of the final achievement of my twenty years' work in Africa. After the three days of festivities, at the end of the week, the second half of the student body, including all those finally leaving us at the end of their three years of study, would go for their holidays till the end of September. Those back from their homes would take over the hospital duties.

Before leaving for holiday, each student of the first group needed to receive his annual report card and class bulletin, a certificate in lieu of diploma, a road-pass and student identity card for claiming reduction of fares on public transport, and various other items, differing for each area and student. Usually we gave them their tickets if we had managed to secure these ahead of time, and some pocket-money to enable them to reach their homes without hardship. Added to this, each student needed to check the wording and spelling on his diploma which had to be sent to the government for ratification and signature.

Besides all this, this year each senior student was to receive a bonus gift, as we thought of it, from the newly-arrived government scholarship money. We had worked hard to decide how to allocate this money justly. The government had sent almost £10 for each second and third-year student for each month from January to July. When we completed the annual school accounts for 1 July 1972 to 30 June 1973, it was obvious that this £10 a month per student would barely cover the cost of feeding, clothing, and schooling the students, let alone housing and administration. However, we wanted them to have at least some of the money, as pocket-money, while we accepted the responsibility to continue a certain amount of subsidy.

Eventually we decided to give them 20% of the money for the six months January to June, and all the July allocation if they were on vacation. The 80% that we retained (for 35 students this came to about £1,500 at that moment) would enable us to prepare adequately for the coming school year, as the regional educational authority's gift had done the previous year. In future, the regular monthly income would help the college to run smoothly without being so dependent on foreign subsidies; doubtless this was the object of the government's scholarship scheme. We had already prepared carefully-worded explanatory forms for each senior student for each of the seven months involved. Each student would be asked to sign in duplicate for each month's allocation.

At 7.00 a.m. the first three students came in together; all third-year students who were being invited to return after their vacation to join the staff for a year as hospital supervisors. They would be largely responsible for the training of first-year students in the art of nursing. Albert Amuli was one of these, and he showed every promise of being an excellent and capable leader in the future.

Basuana, Vera Thiessen and I had sorted out all the 'piles' of certificates, road-passes, and money for each student. We explained things again carefully to these first three, getting them to check each document for signature, the correct date, the spelling of names; to check the road-passes and tickets for the correct destination. They knew the routine well from previous years. We then gave them a certain allocation of gift money, approximately the price of their journey home plus 50p for every night spent on the journey. Amuli lived six days' journey away to the south-west, almost 1,000 miles by road, and he received approximately £12 for this.

Then we explained again all that had been discussed four weeks previously when the inspectors had been with us, concerning the scholarship money. We showed them the duplicated receipt-forms and how the money was being used. We then offered them £22 each as pocket money to take home, and asked them to sign for it.

Probably my own subconscious fear didn't help the situation. I knew it might not be smooth sailing, though I tried to carry it off with an easy optimism. I knew that there had been mutterings among the students ever since they had heard that scholarship money was coming. And even before that, they had believed that, since the staff received government salaries, there must have been money sent for them which I was not handing over. They simply couldn't believe that their government would pay us, foreign staff, a salary without sending anything for them, the students. It mattered so much to me that all should go smoothly and without trouble. It mattered to me that they should trust me and not suspect that I was trying to cheat them or do them down. Instinctively we, the staff, knew that if these three senior students signed, the rest would follow suit. I tried to will them to accept our word and sign their names.

They pulled the piles towards them. Painstakingly and slowly, they went through each document, checking spellings, dates, signatures. They counted the money. They studied the receipt-forms. They made their own calculations. No-one spoke.

I tried to chatter nonchalantly, about their holidays, their families, our next year together on the staff and how much we were looking forward to having them back. I reminded them of our 'Big Day' and urged them to make every effort to start their return journey in time to be with us. All the time I was praying for them to sign.

We could feel the tension. They didn't look at each other. They didn't speak to each other. They listened to my patter and I almost believed that they were going to sign.

'Please, please sign', my heart was urging them. I feared whatever would happen if they refused. As always, I was uncertain of my ground. I knew that what we were doing was in accordance with government guide-lines. I knew that it was absolutely honest, and that the students were getting more, not less, than others would have given them. Yet if there was a show-down with government officials called in, in the present climate of an African country, with feelings running high against white foreigners, the whole situation could very easily be turned against us.

They wouldn't sign.

Each had been meditatively chewing the tip of his ball-point pen, checking and re-checking each form. I felt that each one was waiting to see if one of the others would give in and sign. Slowly each one put down the pen and pushed the money back towards us. As I remember it, they said nothing. Their very silence was a bit uncanny and unnerving.

Carefully and patiently, I went through all our reasoning again. I had the account books there and all the relevant government correspondence. I offered to show them anything they wanted to convince them that not only were we acting in accordance with their own government's wishes, but actually being generous over and above. Perhaps that was the mistake. The fact that we indicated that we could be generous to a certain degree made them question our ultimate honesty in saying that we couldn't give them all the money.

Still they refused to sign.

I know I was beginning to feel desperate. These were our best students, both academically and also spiritually. If they could be convinced that it was right that they sign, that they were making a mistake to refuse, the rest of the student body would probably accept their lead without too much difficulty.

They offered no explanation, no reasoning. However, we knew instinctively that they had made up their minds to accept nothing less than 100% of the back-pay scholarship money to January, and that probably they would consent to pay school fees the next year out of what followed. These first three were all graduating, so there would be no 'future payment'. I guessed that as soon as they had heard, via the African grape-vine, that the money was coming, £10 each month for the past six months, they had already decided what they would buy—a new suit, a transistor radio or a bicycle. What we were offering, 20% of it, simply made these purchases impossible and they felt cheated.

Perhaps they tried to reason about the rightness of their attitude and the wrongness of mine, though they said nothing.

'You've already fed us for these six months, so why take the money now? It's the same with clothes and housing and schooling. Why are you asking us to pay you back what you've already given? If you wanted it back, why didn't you say so last January, that it was only a loan?'

But they maintained a rigid, stony silence.

We sent the three away and called in other students, one by one.

With each one we had exactly the same situation. A careful perusal of everything, a silent reading and studying of the explanatory notes, an acceptance of all their papers and roadpasses—but a complete refusal to sign for and accept the money.

After about three or four more students, we called a halt for breakfast. During the break we gathered the other members of staff together and told them what was happening. Together we prayed that God would break the deadlock. We were almost certain that this was some kind of likilimba, an agreement between them all, like a trade union strike, plus threats of brutality for anyone who 'gave into the whites' and signed for and accepted their partial monies. It was a determined, concerted action by all of them to stand out for 'their rights', and to have the 100% of that back-pay scholarship money.

We decided to start again, and to call each of the three seniors separately and give them a chance to yield to our request without the direct hindrance of losing face in front of another. We promised that no-one should know who signed and who didn't. Apparently, this was another wrong move and only hardened their resolve to resist our efforts. We were not exactly skilled in the art of strike-breaking, nor of conciliation between management and floor!

When Albert came in, he very nearly gave in to our earnest pleading and exhortation. He had been mission- and church-trained all his life, and all his school and college fees had been paid by his local church and missionaries. Deep in his heart, he knew he was throwing away something of lasting value by refusing to trust us. He took the pen from me and drew the form towards him. He read it all again and bent over it, poised to sign. Then suddenly, abruptly, he pushed it from him and said. 'No, no, I can't.' Looking up at me, he continued in a self-defensive, almost pathetic whisper: 'What's the good of one signing, anyway?' and with this cryptic remark he rushed from the room.

We sensed, rather than understood, that fear had ruled him, a fear which perhaps we staff could barely appreciate. He knew what awaited him outside if he broke the oath that they had taken together to refuse to accept our terms, and he just couldn't face the consequences. It was no good my telling him that no-one need know. He knew that they would know at once when he joined them; he just couldn't bluff them all. And he was deeply afraid.

Throughout that Monday we saw, individually, each of the students due for the first holiday shift. We treated each one similarly, patiently, prayerfully. We refused to accept the situation. We prayed earnestly for a crack, that perhaps just one would have the courage of his convictions and stand out against the crowd. We had no real idea of what might be involved in the 'oath of allegiance' or of the threats employed by the ringleaders.

Girl students were also being asked to sign a request-form to return to do midwifery studies in their third year, instead of public health studies as the male students did. In asking this, we had known that we were throwing down a gauntlet. Only one second-year girl student out of the four, though five first year students out of the six, signed willingly, and then she pleaded with us not to let the others know that she had signed. This gave us even greater certainty that strong threats were being employed by the directors of the revolt.

On Tuesday, we started all over again. We asked Dr Becker to come and speak to the assembled college, to explain that what we were doing was absolutely in accord with the directions from their own leaders in government authority; and that either they signed and accepted the money they were being offered, or else they could go home without the money, which would be returned to the government. We were not free to choose what we would do with it: it belonged to the government. Obviously we could not hold the money, even though it was sent for college funds, unless the students signed for it, as the government receipt-forms were all made out in each individual's name.

We spent another seemingly long day, re-interviewing each student. We refused to give in half-way: we felt each one must be given the opportunity in private to change his mind following Dr Becker's words. No-one changed his mind. No-one signed his receipt-form.

I went to bed at midnight on Tuesday with a very heavy heart. I had discussed the situation carefully with our African members of staff, and with Africans in the local education offices. They all advised us to stick to what we had said, though they were obviously becoming nervous. If the students went to report the situation to local party headquarters, nobody was quite sure how the situation would look to an outsider. My heaviness of heart was not only caused by the impasse we were in, but also because these were our students. I loved them. I cared for them. For three years I had taught the seniors, preparing them for their future life-service, as medical evangelists in the service of the church and their fellow countrymen. They were like sons to me. Now I felt that they had turned on me, at the last moment—the moment of our apparent triumph with government recognition. Later, when I heard them arraign me publicly, I really felt that they had rejected me, but already I sensed their almost-callous spurning. They appeared to have put up with me, my leadership, my administration, and all the work we had slaved to do on their behalf to get the recognition; but now that it had come, they didn't want us any more. They wanted to show their independence of us. Even worse, I sensed that they didn't really trust us. All our reasoning was just words to them, easy words from the white foreigner to show once more how good and generous we were. It was as though all the daily radio brain-washing to beware of the deceit of the 'hated imperialist westerner' was suddenly bursting into fruit. They believed it, and so they did not believe us.

On Wednesday morning, Dr Becker rang me and asked me to go down the hill to see him. By now the whole college was involved, not just the half going on vacation. All but ten of the first-year students were on strike. There was hardly a student nurse in the whole 250-bed hospital nor any to help with the thousand outpatients. Everybody at the centre knew of the deadlock, and they were all watching closely.

'All right,' Dr Becker said to me as I entered his little office. 'We'll have the committee at six this evening.'

Uncertainly, I looked at him for some explanation. 'I beg your pardon, Sir?' I queried.

'The committee can meet this evening', he repeated, looking at me with obvious sorrow in his eyes.

'I don't quite understand, Sir. Which committee?'

He now looked puzzled and pushed a letter towards me.

'But you have asked for the executive committee to take over and sort out the problem in the college.' He spoke quietly, but there was a mild reproachfulness in his tone, at what must have seemed to him my deliberate obtuseness.

I picked up the letter, a piece of college note-paper, and read the short line of request for the executive committee to take over 'as we are unable to reach an acceptable solution', and then I read the several signatures. Dr Becker had not noticed that mine was not among them.

A lump rose in my throat. So my own staff felt I couldn't cope. I suppose I was unreasonable in my sheer weariness with the affair, but I felt that not only the students, but now also the staff had rejected my leadership. Doubtless this wasn't true in the slightest, but I was touchy. I guess that I was proud of being a good and fair and competent leader. I had led a paramedical training school all my twenty years in Congo/Zaire, and felt I really knew how to cope and handle affairs on all levels. And this was my last term, my last chance in a sense to show my colours. I didn't stop to think, or to ask the staff why they had taken this step. I had been ill only four months previously and this was probably a considerate action in order to save me too much involvement in sorting out the strike: but it just didn't register like that to me at that moment.

'OK. Sir. I'll see everything is ready', I answered Dr Becker politely, as I stumbled almost blindly from his office, wrapped in my own wounded feelings.

The day was spent preparing. There was a lot to do. All members of an extended executive committee had to be notified, including members of the local education office as they were closely involved with the college, particularly where finance was concerned. Certain local church elders were also invited, as the affair might well develop into a disciplinary one.

The annual financial statement was rushed through, simplified, duplicated, and made available in French and in Swahili for each committee member to examine and to compare with the statistical reasoning involved in the employment of the scholarship money. All this was also carefully laid out and explained on the large blackboards in diagrammatic form. A brief concise history of the application for the scholarship money was compiled, and copies made available of all the correspondence of the previous six months as it related to the affair in hand.

At six o'clock everyone assembled, but they immediately rearranged the room from usual committee procedure, to resemble a lawcourt. Dr Becker took the chair and I was asked to sit on his right. Then three representative students were allowed to enter, to present their case against me.

It was unbelievable, really. To me it was the climax of twenty years of service. If I hadn't been leaving Africa in three months' time, I might have been able to look at things a little less passionately, a little more objectively. But, nevertheless, the shock of hearing my own students give a carefully-prepared, reasoned attack on me would have been humiliating at any time. I was basically accused of stealing college funds. They reasoned that, since the staff were subsidised this proved that the college was recognised and that therefore we had been receiving student subsidies from the same date. That I had continued to demand £50 per annum per student, despite receiving Government grants, was plainly stealing. I was accused of lying, in denying these facts, of duplicity in being able to argue my way out of the situation every time it had been approached. They also stated that I had falsified the accounts and report-sheets sent to the Government so that they would not know that I was systematically misappropriating college funds.

The whole, long, twenty-minute tirade was recorded on cassette. It sounded even worse when I listened to it again the next day. The final cruelty was that the chosen spokesman for the students was Albert Amuli, our senior student, a man brought up in our own church schools and whose school fees had been consistently paid by church and missionaries.

By midnight we had achieved nothing. Much abuse had flowed. Mud was flung at many others besides myself, particularly anyone who tried to reason with them or show them how stupid they were being. We all separated and went to our various homes wearied, dispirited, discouraged. I couldn't sleep. I just felt utterly dejected, with a growing sense of personal failure.

I picked up my Bible and sought God's guidance. It didn't come easily. I prayed, but felt as though I was talking to myself, or, at best, to the ceiling. I wept, mostly out of self-pity. I tried the Bible again, rereading the passage for my next day's regular reading, straight through the four chapters of the book of Jonah. I seemed to get nothing from it at all: no consolation, no strength, no guidance. I cried out in desperation to God to give me something to meet my need. I read Jonah for the third time that night, and began to see some sense.

The storm that shook Jonah awake, that upset a vast crowd of people, the sailors, passengers, those who sent cargo, those who were waiting to receive the cargo, other ships with their crews and passengers, and cargo in the immediate vicinity, was all because God wanted to speak to one man, Jonah. When he jumped overboard the storm stopped, the ship reached its destination, and there is no particular indication that anyone was permanently affected. The sailors made a passing act of acknowledgment of the power of this God of Jonah by the offering of a sacrifice of appeasement: that was all.

'OK, Lord, you want to speak to me, and my deaf ears have caused this storm in which everyone—all the students and staff of the college and medical centre, all the 250-bed patients and over one thousand outpatients—is becoming involved. OK, I'll jump overboard, then what?'

So I wrote a letter of resignation as college director and sent it down to Dr Becker for the executive committee early the next morning. Probably, deep down in my heart, I didn't expect such a letter to be accepted, even though I had specifically asked that no-one question it. Wasn't I indispensable to them? How could they run and handle the college without me? So my heart reasoned, hoping against hope that they would refuse to accept my resignation.

They accepted my letter, presumably gratefully. I chewed my heart out in private chagrin and allowed my self-pity to make an enormous mountain out of the rapidly growing ant hill. Not only students and staff, but now fellow committee members, were glad to get on without me.

My home help, Benjamin, kept me in touch with events. All the second- and third-year students were sent home, having received 80% of their scholarship money, the college retaining 20%, all receipts having been duly signed. They were not to be invited to return unless they apologised for their behaviour and language, accepted a period of discipline from their local churches for having involved patients in their strike action, and signed a statement with regard to the allocation of future scholarship money.

They left on Saturday. Not one came to say good-bye or to shake hands. There were no photos of this qualifying class, my last group of students. There was to be no diploma day. All August festivities were to be cancelled—including the choir, despite five months of hard practising, and no recordings to take home. I went into Bunia, to give a report to the government education office, as we were directly responsible to them. I had to tell them and Dr Biki that there would be no graduation day celebrations as previously planned, to which they had already been invited. I felt very small. I wrote to the regional inspector of education at Kisangani, who had become a personal friend over the last two or three years and who had also been invited to our diploma day, both to represent the party and also to present the diplomas. I told him briefly of the recent events and the reason for the cancellation of our graduation celebrations. By then, my pride was truly laid in the dust and trampled upon.

'Is it really worth while?'

The niggling question that I wouldn't look at, that I didn't want to hear, kept pressing up into the level of conscious thought.

'OK Right now, after all your philosophizing and encouraging others, just answer: has it all been worth it?'

11

Was It All Worth While?

The question had to be answered, I knew, and it really
must be answered in Africa before I left, but for a few
weeks I couldn't bring myself to face it squarely.

I knew of course that the staff and committee had not
really rejected me. As I have said, I had been in hospital
only four months earlier with complete nervous exhaustion
after six months of intense activity. During that time I had
had to make three trips from Nyankunde to Ibambi and
Nebobongo, two by lorry, involving twenty or more hours
of hard driving in each direction. Each trip had involved
emotional, medical, and spiritual commitments. The first
had been for the triumphant funeral of our field leader, Jack
Scholes, whom I had loved as a father through eighteen years
of co-operation; the second had been for the Christmas
and New Year conferences of church and mission, probably
my last in Africa; and the third had been with regard to
establishing our church medical services within the new
government framework of a national service, with the
tremendous amount of documentation needed.

Apart from these journeys there was all the routine
work of the college, with more than twenty hours a week
in the classroom, preparation for classes, marking of test
papers, keeping of student report-files and general college

administration. Again, special extra work was being put in preparatory to handing over the leadership of the college to the two new doctors. Add to all this the growing tensions of a changing political climate, with increasing uncertainty as to the popularity of the white foreigner on African soil, and the scene had been well set for some sort of physical reaction. There was a limit, I suppose, beyond which I had just no right to push my body to keep up with my more ambitious mind and spirit—but I hadn't heeded the warning light. So a week in hospital had been essential, followed by four weeks of slow convalescence in the home of one of our kindly American nurses at the centre.

With this in their minds, it was hardly surprising that the team felt that they ought not to allow me to try to carry the load alone when the strike started. In fact, it would have been extremely surprising if they had sat back and left me to cope! It wasn't as if the college was mine (even though the way I spoke and acted might indicate that I thought it was), it was part of the whole medical centre, and we were all involved.

The staff knew my peculiarly stubborn streak, and that my pride would not let me give in to student pressure to lower the standard, as I saw it. Yet they could also see that there was another side to the problem. Looked at through African eyes, things were often not as clear-cut as they seemed to us foreigners. True, the scholarship money was given for the running of the college, but then the college had run for the past six months. The students had been fed from January to June and the food paid for, so why take the money for that now? They were clothed, and the tailors' salaries had all been paid, so why take money for that?

I was allowing myself to think that they, the staff and committee, had compromised by giving in to the students' blackmail: 'We'll report you to party headquarters if you don't...' And yet, deep down, I knew this couldn't be so.

They had clearly felt that a difference could and should be made between back-pay and future scholarship moneys. An agreement had been reached between management and workers, financially acceptable to both. To us, as college administrators, this was obviously unsatisfactory, as we had to plan ahead: get in stocks of food, books, cloth; prepare a budget for the coming year and government subsidies were notoriously unreliable. Yet through the previous seven years here at Nyankunde, God had never failed to provide all our needs. Couldn't He continue to do so? Did the coming of government subsidies change our reliance on God as sole provider for our daily needs? If so, we would need to look closely as to the underlying motive in the seven-year struggle to obtain recognition.

Then I had to realise that the students were not mine. How they would have resented my thinking of them in this way! Student involvement should only have been a small part of my total involvement in the local church situation. These particular students were only a very few out of the two hundred and more who had passed through the college.

Living went on. The routine responsibility of the end of another college year, with all the government forms to be completed and sent off by a certain prescribed date, kept me busy and occupied. The continued preparation for the arrival of Philip and Nancy Wood, both in the home and also in the school, filled most of my spare moments so that I hadn't too much time for morbid introspection. I had the opportunity to spend two weeks away from Nyankunde, at a neighbouring Christian village in the mountains with missionary friends, being much spoilt, and this did a lot to restore balance and perspective.

The Lord reminded me sharply of that traumatic night of 29 October 1964, and how I had gone home on furlough in 1965 and testified all over the United Kingdom to His sufficiency. It had been true. On that dreadful night, beaten and bruised, terrified and tormented, unutterably alone, I had felt at last that even God had failed me. Surely He could have stepped in earlier; surely things need not have gone that far. I had reached what seemed to me the ultimate depth of despairing nothingness. Yet even as my heart had cried out against God for His failure and my mental anguish taunted me to doubt His very existence, another reasoning had made itself felt.

'You asked Me, when you were first converted, for the privilege of being a missionary. This is it; don't you want it?'

Events had moved so fast: everything seemed to happen at once. Pain and cruelty and humiliation had continued in an ever-growing crescendo, yet with it, a strange peace and deep consciousness that God was in charge and knew what He was doing. Odd thoughts and phrases and impulses broke through, and later on were woven together to show the inner meaning of the events of that night, but it had not been orderly, in a way one could set down on paper or explain in a lecture.

'These are not your sufferings: they are Mine. All I ask of you is the loan of your body.'

Again the overwhelming sense of privilege, that Almighty God should stoop to ask of me, a mere nobody in a forest clearing in the jungles of Africa, something He needed. They had called Him 'a worm, no man'. I said I wanted to be identified with Him, yet did I really want to be a worm, trodden on, spurned, ignored? No! Yet this was the privilege He offered, the privilege of being a missionary, His ambassador, identified with Him among those whom He wanted to serve.

'You went home and told everyone that I was sufficient at that moment, in those circumstances. Isn't this true now, in today's circumstances?'

I tried to say: 'But of course, Lord. You know it's true.'

'No', He quietly rebuked me. 'No. You no longer want Jesus only, but Jesus plus...plus respect, popularity, public opinion, success, and pride. You wanted to go out with all the trumpets blaring, from a farewell-do that you organised for yourself: with photographs and tape-recordings to show and play at home, just to reveal what you had achieved. You wanted to feel needed and respected. You wanted the other missionaries to be worried about how ever they'll carry on after you've gone. You'd like letters when you got home to tell you how much they realise they owe to you, how much they miss you. All this and more. Jesus plus ... No, you can't have it. Either it must be "Jesus only" or you'll find you've no Jesus. You'll substitute Helen Roseveare.'

A great long silence followed—several days of total inner silence. At last I managed to tell Him that with all my heart I wanted 'Jesus only'.

I went back to Nyankunde, sobered and humbled, and completed preparations for Philip and Nancy's arrival. They flew into Bunia airport early on Monday morning, 13 August 1973. It really was marvellous to welcome them and drive them out to Nyankunde, watching them drinking in the beauty of our hills and views across the valley. The tempo of events really sped up now, as we had only six weeks together before I was due to leave for the United Kingdom: six short weeks in which to hand over, in orderly fashion, what it had taken twenty years to create, and in which they were also to learn as much as possible of the Swahili language.

After three days locally, meeting everyone, seeing over the Nyankunde village, getting a quick bird's-eye view of the whole, collecting the necessary residence cards, opening a bank account and acquiring driving licences, we set off to drive to Ibambi and Nebobongo. It seemed right to introduce them the hard way to African transport problems! Within the first fifty miles we met our first major mudhole with an 8-ton lorry firmly entrenched across the narrow, one-track road. Surrounding crowds lined the route and watched interestedly. No-one offered a hand, but everyone offered advice. A local church group pushed us through and enabled us to reach our immediate destination only two hours late. On Friday, the second day of our trip, the 300 miles took from 4.30 a.m. to 11.30 p.m., and involved the negotiation of some ten mud-holes of varying intensity, length, and depth, but of unvarying nerve-racking interest.

Saturday we spent at Ibambi, meeting missionaries and national church leaders, and welcoming Nancy and Philip into the family. On Sunday we went to a local church, some 30 miles north-east of Ibambi, and spent a wonderful day with over 1,000 local Christians, gathered under a palm-frond shelter and overflowing it in every direction, worshipping God. The singing was wholeheartedly African. The crowd ebbed and flowed; children trotted in and out; chickens and goats wandered around unhindered and unnoticed. The sun beat down. Older men tended to doze after noon in their deckchairs, till a rousing hymn jerked them back into active participation. Different groups of children or women or youth took part with specially-prepared items. Several different speakers, using any one of the three main languages of the area, took turns in exhorting the crowd. There was no formal direction to the service, and yet all was obviously controlled and orderly. It certainly was an experience for anyone's first Sunday in the tribal areas of inner Africa.

On Monday we started our week at Nebobongo, the first of many for Philip, my last after twenty years of 'belonging'. Eleven of our paramedical workers had gathered, from as far afield as Malingwia, 250 miles to the north-west, and Opienge, the same distance to the south. The workers had cycled in, some taking as much as five days to reach us. This was their welcome to their two new doctors; it was a week of refreshment, medically and spiritually, with daily teaching sessions and demonstrations. And it was to be their farewell to me.

Each day was full and varied. It was evident that we would not achieve all that we had planned, but we did our best. The pervading spirit of joy and harmony made work a pleasure. The whole team pulled together. The desire to learn and profit from the week was in evidence right from the start: everyone put all they had into it, to make it a great success. I was tremendously happy. These were my people: I was one of them, accepted by them. Each day the soreness grew at the thought of tearing oneself away, leaving them, and starting to make a new life again elsewhere.

Particularly was this so where John Mangadima was concerned. For twenty years we had worked together. Of course there had been ups and downs, times when he maddened me, times when I irritated him, even times when we doubted and distrusted each other but we'd come through, and were now very closely knit in spirit. My deepest joy in leaving was to know that John was appointed as assistant medical director to Philip Wood, for the running and supervision of our medical services in our church area. I had prayed and worked so hard for that. He had a Yamaha motorcycle to enable him to visit all our hospitals and dispensaries regularly, and I couldn't suppress a grin as I watched him setting off to Ibambi, with all the aplomb of one who had owned it all his life.

One afternoon, as he and Philip were operating together in the theatre, I had entered his office to glean a few facts before coming home. He had come in while I was there, peeling off his surgical gloves. 'Hi, Doctor. What are you doing in here?

'Oh, just copying down a few facts and figures to tell folk back home.'

He leant over my shoulder and saw the last line I had written: 372 major operations in 1972 with only six surgical deaths.

'Oh, Doctor, don't bother with things like that. Just tell them that nearly 200 people found Christ as their Saviour through the medical services last year.'

I turned and hugged him, my eyes filling with tears of joy. And God said pretty plainly: 'Isn't My way better than yours?'

The journey back to Nyankunde the following Monday was more cruel than usual. At 5.30 p.m., after an extremely good thirteen hours of driving, we came upon the king of mud-holes, 400 yards of a churned-up sea of mud, at some places more than 6 feet deep, already with several large transport-lorries involved. It was 3.30 a.m. when Philip and Basuana eventually struggled through, to join Nancy and myself at a small village up the next hill. We'd gone ahead on foot, to dry out and rest after the first gruelling five hours of effort. We eventually dragged wearily into Nyankunde at midday, ready to start straight into a new school year the next week.

It was a little strange, as the first Monday morning in September dawned, when Philip and Nancy went down the hill to college at 6.30 a.m., and I realised that I really had handed over. It was theirs now, not mine. There were still many ways to help them in the remaining three weeks, particularly in the office and in language-study. We made the most of every available hour.

Suddenly, my last weekend was on me and I could hardly bear to consider all that was involved. On the Friday, the missionary family had arranged a farewell party for me. It was very touching. All my special African friends were there, as well as all the missionaries. Speeches were made. I felt choked and too full up to say much, and I knew it was sincere and not just laid on for the occasion.

On Saturday afternoon, the Africans had a party for me down at the college. When I arrived at five o'clock and was led through the waiting crowd to the top table, I glanced round and saw all my friends of the past seven years, masons and plumbers, tailors and cooks, office workers and teaching staff, church elders and choir members, printers from the local press and gardeners from the school allotments. My eyes filled with tears as I sensed the love in their welcome to me.

A goat had been cooking over a spit for the past twenty-four hours, and Philip duly carved it. Food poured in, in steaming dishes and bowls from the kitchen, served by first-year students. Chatter was soon flowing in the usual free, happy way of Africa as everyone ate their fill. Two ludicrous skits followed from staff members and brought roars of laughter. Then the small group of third-year students who had returned after all the sadness of June, and who had asked to be taken back into college, had sung for me words they had written themselves, basically asking me to remember them as my sons who loved me, and to let God blot out from my memory the sore wound they had tried to inflict on me in their stupidity. Again, my heart was strangely moved and touched.

Philip made a short speech in Swahili, his first public usage of the language, much to everyone's delight, thanking me for all the service to the college over the past seven years. By then I had scribbled down all the thoughts that I wanted to express to everyone, in groups and individually, to say thank you to them for all their love and friendship over the years.

'Now it is over to you,' Philip concluded, addressing the more than sixty African guests. 'If you have anything you want to say, now is your chance.' Turning to me, he added in English: 'Not you; you just wait a bit.'

Then they started. For two hours it went on. I don't know how many spoke, probably more than twenty of them. I don't remember much of what was said. I cried: it was very, very moving. One I remember especially, but many others were like him: Nyelongo, our mason.

'You don't remember, Doctor, but one day when we were building the main school block, I was late for work. I was scared: roll-call was over and you had already gone into school. When you came out at eight o'clock you came straight over to me and asked how my baby was. I didn't even know that you knew I had a baby!

'The baby is very sick,' I told you. 'Where is the baby?' you asked.

'Back at home.'

'But why not in the hospital?' and you sounded irritated. 'We can't afford the hospital card and care,' I replied.

'Then you really were mad! You went straight up the hill to your home, got into your Land Rover, came charging down on to the building site and shouted to me to get in. I'd never been in a car before. You told me to direct you to our village, but no car had ever been to our village before. You didn't seem to care, and we went, jolting and bumping over the mountainside. I called my wife and collected the baby, and you took us all to the hospital.'

I guess his child must have been very ill, as he said I told him not to return to work till we saw whether his child would live. He probably missed three or four days' work. He continued his story:

'At the end of the month, I came with the rest to be paid. I was trying to pluck up courage to ask you to spread my debt over several months, rather than take my whole month's pay. When you called my name, you passed me my wage-packet like everyone else. I just stared at you in unbelief. Then

I rushed round the side of the house, laid the money out on the ground and counted it. It was all there.

'I ran all the way home. I called my wife. "Look, look, our money is all here. She hasn't taken any off, not even for the days' work I missed, let alone for our baby's care and treatment."'

'We cried. Then we knelt down, and we suddenly realised all that you and Basuana meant when you told us day after day of God's love: and we asked God then and there into our hearts and lives and have followed Him ever since.'

I drew a deep breath as he sat down. I was deeply stirred. I wouldn't be surprised if, when I made up the wage-packets that month long ago, I had simply forgotten that Nyelongo owed money! I'm like that. But God had not forgotten. He used that little, almost insignificant, event in our daily relationship—not through a Sunday preaching engagement, but just an ordinary work job—and He had brought about His purposes, and I had merely been one of the links in the chain. This was it. This was what Evangelist Agoya had said to me years ago at Nebobongo; it was what Basuana had said to me much more recently here at Nyankunde: 'We can't all be the last link in the chain.' Being the last link may bring public acclaim and a sort of popularity: but being willing to be any link, however inconspicuous, brings happiness and lasting joy.

The question returned in my heart: 'Has it all been worth while?' As others testified, my mind strayed round the north-eastern region of Zaire to our many regional hospitals and rural dispensaries. I pictured our many graduates working singly or in pairs, in far-off places, putting into practice all we had taught them. I began to count them, mentally ticking them off on a list. Tokpo and Ezo at Malingwia; Balani at Poko and the lovely small hospital he had built himself, loved and respected by everyone; Anizanga at Nala; Angola at

Gamba. There was Jacqueline van Bever at Betongwe doing an excellent job; Sengi at Ibambi, Boloki at Buambi and Tahilo at Opienge. Then of course at Nebobongo, the whole team with John Mangadima, Asea, Namuniabangi, and Bundayi. Way down to the south, Basetea had gone with his wife and children as a missionary nurse to another tribal area and culture. Each name conjured up a face and a story. I could think of each one through his schooling, his problems and difficulties, his first job after graduating, his settling down and now becoming a really valuable member of the medical team. Many had had their teething troubles, some had had to undergo fairly severe church discipline, but they had come back the stronger and more reliable. There were so many of them. Not only those in our own church area, but in each of the various church regions: Ngonda at Aba, Rabama at Todro, Rasereka and others at Oicha, Mukwesi and others farther south in the Ruanguba area, Mandro doing dentistry at Itendeyi.

My heart thrilled as I continued to tick them off. There were the two whom we felt were called and set apart as future staff members for our training college, whom we had been able to send for further education, Mandaboy to be a nursing tutor, and Madrato possibly to be a doctor if he could procure a place at university.

Then I remembered so many others who weren't nurses or medical workers, but who had been very much in the team since the beginning. Basuana had been such a good, close friend through nearly twenty years; Benj Gandisi the same. Church elders and pastors everywhere: Ndugu and Tamoma, Agoya and Taadi, too many to name—had become such close friends that I never even thought of them as black or any other colour. They were just those I loved, and I realised, as perhaps never before, just how much I loved them and was going to miss them when I left and went back to Britain.

The evening drew to a close. I wended my way up the hill to my little home, as Philip and Nancy drove some of the folk back to their homes, and I suddenly knew with every fibre of my being that these twenty years had been worth while, very, very worth while, utterly worth while, with no room left for regrets or recriminations.

Afterword

I love Helen Roseveare's honesty. Some Christians believe that we should only tell stories of spiritual victory to build others up. Helen was not one of those Christians. She freely wrote about her own insecurities, temptations, and even her sin, but she did it in a way that didn't glorify or excuse ungodliness.

Helen was like a patient with an ailment. There were often times when she could tell something was wrong in her soul—perhaps she felt discouraged or jealous or anxious. She would bring her heart to the Lord and let him reveal the source of the distress. If it required repentance, she would repent. Then, ever the teacher, Helen would take what the Lord had shown her and show it to all of us, like a medical professor showing his pupils an interesting x-ray so that they will learn how to spot a cancer.

Helen's gift for teaching drove the second phase of her career. She didn't intend to become an itinerant speaker, but the more Helen spoke, the more invitations came in.

It would have been easy for Helen to become puffed up over ministry success. Three times she spoke at Urbana (twice to over 17,000 students), sharing a stage with famous Christians like Billy Graham, Elisabeth Elliot, and John Stott. Yet just as Paul was given a "thorn in the flesh", God allowed Helen to be plagued by feelings of depression and self-doubt. After Urbana 81, Helen wrote, 'I went home again from an astoundingly wonderful convention, with many students making a public response to the challenge, only to find that nothing had changed for me.'[1] As much as she hated her frequent seasons of despondence, she realised that they kept her dependent on the Lord, reminding her that 'the surpassing power belongs to God and not to us' (2 Cor. 4:7 ESV).

The itinerant life is not an easy one. In addition to the stress and frustrations of travel, transience made sustaining friendships difficult. Helen would stay with a host for a few days, enjoying spiritual comradery over late-night, soul-searching conversations, and then she might never see her new friend again. She writes, 'Hundreds of people would gladly have been my friends, but there was no time to develop friendships. I found that each day I had to try to forget yesterday's people, in order to relate to those of today.'[2]

When humans live in permanent transience, it is natural to close off from deep relationships as a form of self-protection. We can become like a sticker that loses its stickiness after being pulled off and repositioned too many times. But Helen resisted closing herself off from the people she met on her travels. She listened to the stories of those who hung around to talk to her after a meeting. She chose to be vulnerable with them, sharing her own struggles, and as a result, the Lord worked through many of these conversations to heal her own hurts and to answer her own doubts.

It was during this second phase of ministry that Helen did most of her writing. Her first two books had only told a small fraction of her experiences in Africa. Some of her most memorable stories are told in the quartet composed of *Living Sacrifice*, *Living Faith*, *Living Holiness*, and *Living Fellowship*.

---

1   See later in the volume: *Digging Ditches*, p. 530.
2   See later in this volume: *Digging Ditches*, p. 459.

Although she never lived in Africa again, her spiritual and relational experiences there fueled her writing and speaking ministry for the rest of her life.

—Betsy Childs Howard

Digging Ditches

CONTENTS

PROLOGUE

'Make this valley full of ditches!'
The words almost sprang out of the page—I knew God had spoken. But did I really want to hear? I had asked him to give me just such a clear word, a 'Thus saith the Lord' type of word, to guide me into the next stage of my journey. But now that He had spoken, I was almost afraid to hear His voice.

I was lying in a hospital bed, following two major operations within a week. I had just completed a nine-month tour of deputation meetings in the USA for my mission (WEC International) following 20 years of missionary service in Congo. Halfway through that tour, which included over 400 public meetings (school assemblies, church youth groups and Sunday services, university Christian Unions, and women's meetings), in over 20 different states, as well as six weeks in Canada, I found that I had a lump (a tumour). It was early in February, a Thursday morning of a busy week. I managed to control my thoughts and go ahead with the meetings already arranged for that day and the day following. Saturday was a free day to prepare for several engagements on the Sunday and during the coming week. I asked my host and hostess if they would be kind enough to leave me on my own for a while. I knew I had to find peace in my own heart to continue the tour, knowing that medically, others would consider that I should go for help. I was very conscious that if I backed out, and asked to go home for treatment, it would cause enormous difficulties for those who arranged the tour. The publicity, arrangements for meetings, transport, and hospitality for the whole four months would be thrown into confusion.

That Saturday morning, 7th February 1976, I read my morning portion from the Scriptures, then I read Daily Light and prayed. I simply laid it all before the Lord. What did He want me to do? As I re-read the Scripture passage, I sensed God speaking His peace into my heart. Reading through the Bible in a year, I had reached Exodus 1 to 3 that morning. Many years before, God had spoken to me clearly through Exodus 2:9, when Pharaoh's daughter charged the mother of the baby Moses, found in a basket in the reeds at the river's edge, to care for the baby—her own baby!—with the promise: 'Take this baby and nurse him for me, and I will pay you (I will give you your wages).'

In 1954, when I had been in Congo (at that time, the Belgian Congo) just sixteen months, the mission committee asked me to move our fledgling medical programme from Ibambi to Nebobongo, a then disused leprosy colony seven miles up the road. I was terrified at the mere thought of what such a move would mean—all the responsibility of developing the village, as well as starting again all that was involved in developing a health service. I felt angry with that committee, feeling they had been thoughtless towards me, and I almost rebelled. Seeking the Lord's direction at that time, my morning reading had been in Exodus chapter 2. And the Lord said, 'This fledgling health service is your baby. Take it, and care for it in My Name, and I will see that you lack for nothing of which you have need.' I moved out on that promise, and the Lord never failed me through the many turbulent years that followed.

Now was He saying to me, 'I have a new baby to entrust to you. Will you trust Me?' Then I turned back to read again the verses in Daily Light for the 7th February, and I read: *'One of them, when he saw that he was healed, turned back and with a loud voice, glorified God, and fell down on his face at His feet, giving Him thanks: and he was a Samaritan. And Jesus said: "Were there not ten cleansed? but where are the nine? There are not found that returned to give glory to God, save this stranger"* (Luke 17:15-18).

I looked up the passage in my Bible and read the following verse, which said: *'Jesus said to him, "Rise and go; your faith has made you well"'* (Luke 17:19). It was all part of the story of ten leprous men who came to Jesus for healing. All ten had been *healed*, but just one turned back to thank the Lord for His healing, and that one was made *whole* by faith, and through giving thanks. In my heart, I knew that God was speaking to me, into my immediate situation, and I accepted, understanding that I was to continue with all the tour of meetings, to say nothing to anyone of what I feared to be going on in my body, and, actually, to think no more about it for the time being. In other words, God would look after my need for physical healing, but, more immediately, He would give me spiritual wholeness as I trusted and thanked him. He would indeed 'pay my wages' each step of the way ahead.

I rejoined my host and hostess later that morning with peace in my heart and was enabled to accept the first two of God's challenges, even if I did not manage to think no more about it! Two months later in the tour, when taking a week of meetings among university students in Chicago, I became feverish and unable to keep any food down. My mind worked overtime and I presumed that I had secondaries from the rapidly growing lump. This did not prove to be the case and I probably had a sharp attack of flu. I was enabled to keep almost all my engagements, despite two weeks of feeling rotten and very weak. Eventually the tour ended and I returned to the UK, where I rang my brother-in-law, the medical superintendent of a general hospital in the west of England. A medical check-up resulted in immediate admittance to hospital and then surgery. Initially thought to be benign, a simple local excision was carried out. But further laboratory sectioning confirmed that there were malignant cells present. So three days after the first, I underwent a second operation.

I was now recovering. What had the Lord for me? Would I really recover, or merely have a few more years in which to serve Him on earth? What could I do for the Lord in that time? What was His plan for my life? I was not unduly worried. I had had four months to accustom myself to the situation. In fact, I had already begun to think in terms of a three-year appointment to a job that I felt I could manage, so as to be fully occupied in the Lord's service as long as I had strength to do it. After that... well, I was willing to wait till that time came and trust Him to see me through any difficult years that followed. I actually wrote to the missionary team in Congo, when I first knew I had a lump and that I might not have much more time to serve the people, to suggest that perhaps they would give me the privilege of going back to them to serve in a new capacity, training African pastors, using French as the medium for teaching rather than Swahili, so that they would be more highly regarded by the authorities. I received no answer to my letter.

After coming round from the anaesthetic, I asked a nurse to open my Bible for me at the marker, and to prop it up on the bed table. I prayed, and asked the Lord to speak to me very clearly. Then I saw that the marker was at 2 Kings 3. How could God ever speak to me, in a meaningful way, through that Old Testament passage? I knew the story. I had taught it at the students' college in Congo not so very long before.

'Lord,' I prayed, 'I really need a "Thus saith the Lord" so that I can stand on Your Word for the next stage of my life.'

However, despite my doubts, I started to read. The chapter relates how, following the refusal of the Moabites to pay the annual tribute they owed to King Joram of Israel, he joined forces with the kings of Judah and Edom and marched south, presumably along the western border of the Dead Sea, to come round to the southern end of the territory of Moab, in order to attack the Moabites, hoping to take them by surprise. When the combined armies reached the River Arnon, expecting to refill all their exhausted water supplies, they found only a dried-up river-bed! The soldiers were ready for mutiny. The three kings, having discussed the situation, called for the prophet Elisha and told him to ask his God what they should do in this emergency.

The Spirit of God came upon Elisha, and God spoke to him: *'Make this valley full of ditches.'* Furthermore, God told him that although they would neither hear wind nor see rain, He would fill the ditches in the valley with water.

That verse, **'Make this valley full of ditches'** started with the words, **'Thus saith the Lord'** or, in the modern version: *'This is what the Lord says.'*

As my eyes moved down the page, and as I approached verse 16, I stopped and prayed that the Lord would make me willing to hear what He wanted to say to me. I was scared. I knew the story, and now I could see a 'Thus saith the Lord' coming. What would it mean for me?

As soon as I read it, even without going on to read the rest of the story—how the soldiers did as God said, and made the whole sandy river-bed full of ditches; how, during the night, God filled the ditches with water; how, in the early morning light, the Moabite army on the mountain-top to the north saw the rising sun reflected in the water and, presuming the ditches to be filled with blood from fighting between the Israeli and Judaean soldiers; how they had swarmed down the mountainside to plunder the camp, and how the Israelite and Judaean armies fell on them and brought about a resounding victory—I knew that God had spoken to me.

'Make this valley full of ditches.'

'This valley' must mean the present circumstances of my life, and so much had happened that year. My dear mother had died. I had just completed an exhausting nine months of touring and speaking in the USA and Canada. That week I had had surgery for cancer. It seemed unlikely that WEC would allow me back to the mission field, at least initially. Life felt very uncertain. It was indeed a valley situation.

'Make ... it ... full of *ditches*.' I was not being asked to dig a Suez Canal, just a multitude of small ditches, each one individually important. Was God asking me to live a day at a time, and do each small task as it arose without asking for one long-term goal? Those soldiers in the Bible narrative could have revolted and refused to dig mere ditches. 'It's not what we trained for! We have no proper tools! It's beneath our dignity!' But in fact, they appeared to have obeyed. Of course, without the ditches the water that God wanted to send would have been wasted; it would have soaked without trace into the sandy riverbed. The ditches were essential to contain the promised blessing.

If God asked me to do tasks for which I felt I wasn't trained, tasks that appeared to be much less strategic than all that had been achieved in the past twenty years of medical service in the Congo, was I willing to trust Him and go ahead, one step at a time, doing whatever He chose to ask of me, day by day, even without any apparent long-term goal?

Suddenly it all seemed very insecure. For twelve years, as director of a small hospital in the great Congolese forest land, I had had a clear-cut daily programme, well-defined responsibilities, a measurable task for which I was accountable. Again, in later years, as director of a college for African paramedical workers, my job had had clear limits, a specific goal, a tidy programme. Even when I first came home to help care for my invalid mother, there had been a regular daily programme, and others had always been available to help as needed. But now, the box in which I felt God was asking me to live seemed very open-ended. To whom would I be accountable? How would I know, each day, just what was asked of me? Would I be financially supported? Hundreds of questions raced through my mind, yet the Lord's words were clear and unequivocal: '*Make this valley full of ditches*' **and**, with the command, came the promise: '*This valley will be filled with water!*' He enabled me to say, 'OK, yes, Lord!'

For many years after I became a Christian, I yearned for the mountain-tops, for experiences of God's glory and power, of His enabling and blessing. The story of Caleb (in Joshua 14:6-14), who, at the age of 80, asked Joshua to give him the hill country as his inheritance, despite all the savage inhabitants and obvious difficulties, stirred me. Caleb was said to have followed the Lord wholeheartedly. That was what I wanted to do. Caleb was sure God would give him all the victory he needed to achieve his goal, and I knew I wanted to trust the Lord in the same way. Basically, I wanted to live on the Mount of Transfiguration!

During the first twelve years at Nebobongo, we watched God do some amazing things. The small village had grown up and expanded around the church. Pastor Agoya, and his wife Taadi, worked tirelessly amongst the nursing students, the hospital patients, and their relatives. Yandibio transformed the primary school, teaching some 170 children in four grades. Mama Damaris cared for orphaned babies with endless love and patience. Mangadima and I trained twelve male students every year to be paramedical workers who carried the main load of an ever-expanding hospital. When qualified, they staffed some ten small rural hospitals and forty or fifty dispensaries and clinics. Thousands of patients were treated every year, hundreds undergoing urgently needed surgical interventions. Mud and thatch buildings were slowly replaced by brick ones with permanent roofing. All our young people became enthusiastic members of our Campaigner Clan. Students played football with energy (even if not with a great deal of knowledge of rules!) and all ages joined together in a church choir.

We were a happy family. God graciously sent revival into our midst during the early years together, and that cemented our relationships one with another. There was little or no consciousness of colour differences. We shared all we had and grew together spiritually through many difficulties and frustrations, as well as through the good times.

It is true that there were some gravely ill patients whom we could not help, empty shops that could not provide needed building or school supplies, a broken down truck that taxed our ingenuity to keep it on the road. There was always the urgent need to respect the national people and their customs, whilst seeking to train them in good medical practice, and the urgent need to understand and keep industrial law as we handled workmen and nurses, on minimal finances. Then there was the urgent need to keep healthy, despite carrying an enormous workload and heavy responsibilities. Yes, there *were* difficulties and frustrations, and so many urgent needs. But we grew spiritually through them all, and the times of joy and blessing outweighed the problem times.

In 1960, handing over control of the country from Belgian officials to Congolese nationals caused enormous hardships and much misunderstanding. Foreigners were often barely tolerated. All leadership needed to be passed to nationals, even when there was no-one trained to carry such responsibility. There was mutiny in the national Congolese army, a breakdown of all communications, emptying shops and an almost total lack of supplies of food or medicines. Yet we worked our way through another four years of mounting difficulties, and God once again wonderfully undertook for us.

Suddenly, in 1964, we were engulfed in civil war. Guerrilla soldiers took over and cruelty reigned. Thousands were killed senselessly. Infrastructure was needlessly destroyed. Schools had to close. Hospitals could hardly cope with the influx of the seriously wounded, with minimal stocks of anaesthetics or antibiotics. Yet through the whole 18 months of mindless tyranny, the church grew. Many congregations more than doubled! Christians took every opportunity to share the gospel with terrified villagers and marauding soldiers alike. 'How is it you are not afraid?' they were often asked, by the amazed population. And they were quick to share the Good News of Jesus Christ on each occasion.

After five months of captivity I, along with most other missionaries in our area, were rescued and flown to our home countries to recover. During the ensuing 14 months, I wrote *Give me this mountain*, the first part of my autobiography, that tells my story up to that moment in 1965. And the discipline of writing helped to clear my heart and mind of the trauma of the months of captivity.

At last, news trickled out that the National Army, strengthened by fifty mercenary soldiers (mostly from South Africa), were liberating our area. Peace was slowly being restored and letters began to come to us from our local African leaders. Would we ever consider going back to help them recover from the devastation? It was so thrilling to realise that they *wanted* us back, that the way was opening up to make our return possible. We heard that 'everything' had been destroyed: buildings, equipment, supplies, hospitals, schools, and homes. We hoped they were exaggerating. Could we face the mammoth task of reconstruction, knowing that it could all happen again? My excitement became tinged with doubts. Could I mentally and spiritually stand up to the strain of all that would be involved in returning? Had I known all that the next seven years would include, I might well have chosen not to go. But God mercifully hid the details from our eyes! And He filled us with His peace and the assurance of His protection as we returned.

During those 14 months at home the Lord started to re-focus my heart from the ever-deep desire to live on the mountain-tops, to the realisation that God's work is mostly done in the valleys, doubtless spurred on by the vision given on the mountain but, in practice, turning that vision into reality in the valley. When we returned to Congo in 1966, we found the rumours were basically true. Rebel forces *had* destroyed 90 per cent of all we had built at Nebobongo in the previous twelve years. It was clear that we would have to re-build and start all over again. But then came the surprising direction to leave Nebobongo and go 450 miles to the east, to re-start the work in the valley at Nyankunde.

At Nyankunde, on the foothills of the Ruwenzori mountains, above the treeline and out of the endless forest, there were huge views and a much better climate. Five missionary societies agreed to join forces and start a new, larger, better-equipped hospital, with a government-recognised college to train national medical and paramedical workers. Dr Carl Becker, a seasoned Africa Inland Mission (AIM) missionary, and I had dreamed of such a joint venture for several years. Suddenly, it was as though the civil war with all its destruction had precipitated a fulfilment of the vision. Dr Becker would run the hospital and the multiple medical services that would be involved, and I would run the training college. The team grew around us. Three or four other doctors joined us, several American and Swiss nurses, and eventually one other English nurse/midwife tutor. The government encouraged us to go ahead and develop the work, though no-one was willing to put their signature to an official document! Richard Dix and his team made bricks and put up buildings. Dr Becker and his team saw and treated nearly 1,000 outpatients every day. And I, with a small team, taught student boys from all over the north-east of Congo and Rwanda to become the medical-evangelists who were so urgently needed. But this did not happen overnight!

The land we were given was an overgrown valley, rough brambles and wild elephant grasses growing out of a thick layer of black mud! Dr Becker had his vision already fairly clearly in his mind and heart. Waving his hand up the valley he told me I could have some four to five acres of it to develop the college. I paced it all out, stuck flags in the four corners then clambered up the hillside and looked down on 'my' valley and asked God to give me a vision of the college rather than just a vision of a valley full of mud. By modern radio and ancient bush-telegraph, we sent out messages to invite students, both men and women, who had finished at least one year of secondary school education, and who had a desire to serve the population in medical work, to turn up. The first group arrived in early August 1966—expectant, yet also suspicious. Some were proud and a little disdainful, others were shy and a little fearful.

Where was the college they had come to join? 'Over there', I answered, as nonchalantly as I could manage, waving an arm up the mountain slopes. And the dormitories? 'Also there', I declared. As they realised that there was no college and no dormitories... 'You build, I'll teach!' I challenged them. It took them 24 hours to take in my preposterous suggestion that they should take their shirts off, clear and weed, dig and shovel, cut down trees, build, roof, and thatch their own school, village, classrooms, dining hall, and dormitories. But eventually they agreed, and together we did it. In October 1966, we started classes. Two years later, and every year afterwards, a group entered for government exams, passed, and were awarded the coveted certificates.

Of course, during the next seven years, there were exasperating situations, when students pitted their strength against mine. They wanted better meals. 'OK, provide your own!' I told them. They wanted better subsidies for their fees. 'OK, I'll withdraw what I put in every week, and you can find your own!' Once or twice, the rebellion was more serious, and it took all our skill and prayers to bring them round to accept God's discipline, as well as His love and grace. There were frustrations, as when the needed roofing nails did not come in time to complete the roof before the rainy season started, and when paint eventually arrived from the 'city', some 500 miles west, with three of the twelve tins filled with water. But slowly, our valley turned into a well-respected, government-accepted college. Our vision became a reality.

Then I began to realise that I owed it to my brother and younger sisters—all married with teenage children—to take my share of the responsibility of caring for our dear mother. At the same time, my own physical strength was severely tested by several bouts of tropical fevers. Besides that, my nervous energy was running low, so often tested as it was by mindless bureaucracy or sometimes brutal harassment. The Trades' Union was always ready to pounce and cause unpleasantness if a workman complained of wrongful dismissal or some such thing. Soldiers stopped us every 10 or 12 miles on the road to town to 'inspect' our vehicle or our paperwork. Students became less and less prepared to obey 'foreign' leadership and threatened to report us to the local authority over almost anything that displeased them.

I had been nearly seven years at Nyankunde, helping to build the college, writing all the course material for classes, caring for 72 young men each year, as we trained them to take their place in the emerging health service in north-eastern Congo. Was it, perhaps, time to take a break? But how could I go home and leave the college without a director, the government having legislated in 1966 that only a medical doctor with ten years experience in the Congo could be accepted as director of a nurses' training college? Much prayer was made, then my mission agreed to my taking an extended furlough if someone could be found to replace me at Nyankunde. Just then two things happened! The government changed its insistence on the ten years experience in the Congo clause, and two recently married doctors, Philip and Nancy Wood, applied to WEC to work at Nyankunde. God's amazing and perfect timing was displayed once again!

I left Congo at the end of September 1973, and came home to the UK to help care for my mother for as long as she needed me. We holidayed together in Cornwall, and we were given rooms on the ground floor of our WEC Headquarters, near London. Many were willing and able to help me to care for Mother in the way she deserved. She and I were both happy and rested. The mission asked me to take a certain number of deputation meetings for them, particularly to challenge university Christian Unions and church youth groups with the enormous needs of two-thirds of our world to hear the gospel. And the Lord graciously blessed in these. At the same time, I wrote *He Gave Us a Valley,* the second part of my autobiography.

Then the invitation came from USA Mission Headquarters to go and take a series of meetings for them, all over the States and Canada. After prayerful consideration, and discussion with my mother, mission leadership, and my brother and sisters, it was agreed that I should go. In September 1975,

I left for that long tour on the other side of the Atlantic. Nine days after my arrival in USA, my brother rang to tell me our mother was dying. She died on the tenth. I was not there. My heart felt bruised. Why had I left her? I had returned from Congo in order to be with my mother when she needed me. If God knew He was taking her home, why did He allow me to leave her just then? Somehow I was enabled to keep going through the tour. Then, early in February 1976, I discovered the lump. I had to come to terms with the fact that this might well signal the end of my missionary involvement. What next? At that moment, still in the USA, I received the annual report from the church in our part of the Congo, in which the leaders spelt out their need of a missionary to train their pastors, using French as the teaching medium. Previously, all teaching had been in Swahili or Bangala. Having written to the church (without explaining my reasoning) to offer to fulfil that need for a three-year term, I received no answer and the silence hurt. I felt unwanted, almost rejected. Years later, I heard that they *had* replied, and were surprised that I never wrote again to them. Their letter had gone astray.

Throughout eight years in training (1945–53) and the first twelve years in Congo (1953–65), I prayed to God that He would give me this mountain! Then seven years back in Congo at Nyankunde (1966–73) and two years at our headquarters caring for Mother (1973–75), He taught me that His work is done down in the valleys. 'He gave us a valley!', and now He was saying, 'Make this valley full of ditches!'

So I was to learn to go deeper down, to 'dig ditches', that were often unseen and unrecognised by others, but which God promised to fill with blessing for others. My first instinct was, 'OK, God, I'll dig you a Suez Canal!' but that was not what He asked for! My Lord wanted just daily, small obediences; He wanted me to do whatever needed to be done next, without needing to be thanked or recognised, without a pedestal or a halo. Some might even question my continuing right to be called a missionary as I had no particular sphere of service and no proper job description. Was I willing to be insecure, perhaps lonely, often away on travels with unknown people? Fortunately He did not fill out the picture too much at the start, or I might well have backed off! Had the Lord told Moses at the time of the vision of the burning bush all about the ten plagues and Pharaoh's obstinacy, and all about the grumblings and complainings of the Israelite people, possibly Moses would never have accepted God's call to go back to Egypt and deliver His people from the cruel hand of the Egyptian oppressor. No, God just told him at the outset that He was sending him to lead His people to the promised land. That was all. And that vision of the end of the story kept Moses going when the way seemed hard and long.

'You dig the ditch daily: I will fill it daily.'

So the next stage of my life's journey was established on that promise. That it might not be easy, that there might well be heartaches and deep problems on route, I was well aware. He did not promise me a bed of roses without thorns. But He did promise me that others would be blessed if I would obey and trust Him.

1

Digging a Ditch at the Missionary Training College

For more than twenty years of my life, my mission had always been there, as it were, in the background of my thinking, in the person of my field leader in Congo, as well as all the staff at our London headquarters. When I went home on furlough, my mother was always there. There had always been somewhere to go, whether in Congo or in the UK, a home where I was loved, respected, wanted, and where I had a sense of worth, a job to do, and friends to support me in doing it. Now I suddenly felt adrift. What would God have me do?

Three months after my surgery in June 1976, I went to the WEC Home Staff Conference, asking if there was a specific job that I could do for them, a niche into which I could fit. There was considerable discussion, in public from the floor, and in private at the Executive Committee meeting. Then two suggestions were made to me. Firstly, would I write a book for the mission, to supplement *The Four Pillars of WEC* that Norman Grubb had written more than ten years previously? The four pillars, as we called them, were four doctrines on which the mission stood, in its ministry to the unreached peoples of the world. These pillars were sacrifice, faith, holiness, and fellowship. Everyone knew that I had not been exactly enthusiastic about the booklet, *Four pillars of WEC*!

Sacrifice—all of us in WEC agreed that only by following the Lord Jesus Christ, who gave His very life that we might be saved, could we possibly be used by God to bring others to a knowledge of sins forgiven. But were we, the missionaries who served in WEC, actually living sacrificial lives? I, for one, wasn't. I always had sufficient to eat and to wear, a home, a car (of sorts!), and all needed possessions whilst in Congo. And I was always (almost always!) happy, surrounded by many faithful friends. I had to ask myself where the sacrifices in my life were?

Faith—we all agreed that only by the exercise of faith in the power of the preaching of the living Word of God could we reclaim lost people from the lure of the pleasures of this world and exhort them to put their trust in the Saviour. But were we actually exercising that faith? Were we seeing a local church built up in all the lands where we worked as a direct result of such faith? We trusted the Lord for material needs, and for our health, yes, but were we seeing people saved, being brought to the foot of the cross and rejoicing in the assurance of sins forgiven? For twenty years in Congo, I had spent almost all my time with Christians, training them to be evangelists, it is true, but not myself actually reaching out to the unsaved. Was I exercising faith to see a local church built up where God had placed me to work?

Holiness—again, we all agreed that our Lord Jesus Christ was altogether holy, 'without sin', found to be faultless even by Pilate. But could we, His followers, claim to be like Him? If we did not reflect Him in His spotless loveliness, how were others ever going to be drawn to Him, and rescued from a life of imperfections to a life of holiness? We knew we should be holy, but we also knew we were not. Even on the mission field there were squabbles and jealousies between us. Sometimes during my twenty years in Congo, I felt so conscious of being unholy, I wondered what right I had to be called a missionary at all!

And then **Fellowship**—we all agreed that none of us, working alone, could ever achieve what needed to be done in order to build a church in every remaining unreached people group. We knew we had to work in fellowship with each other, and with all others who had the same objective. But were we really seeking to behave like that? Had we not still our barriers, and pride in being ourselves? Were we not still unwilling to become merged with other groups, even though they had exactly the same goals as ourselves? And was our understanding of the concept of fellowship only one of methodology, and not actually a biblical principle? The fellowship that we know to exist between the three Persons of the Trinity—one of mutual submission and promotion—was that characteristic of all of us in WEC?

I just couldn't accept the booklet, *The Four Pillars,* as an actual, real expression of what we missionaries in the WEC family were like. And I had spoken out fairly bluntly and said so!

'Write us another book,' the WEC International Leader said to me, 'that will express these four basic principles in down-to-earth practical ways, by which we can measure ourselves!' That was one job they offered me.

Then secondly, the conference suggested that I should go to our WEC Missionary Training College (MTC) in Glasgow for a year, to give me a chance to make a full recovery from all the various traumas I had gone through, before they considered a more permanent assignment. While at the college, it was suggested that I might help Chrissey Bachelor in the office, particularly with regard to the closing-down accounts. The college was due to close at the end of that academic year. Not that I knew a thing about official account-keeping! I had kept the accounts at Nebobongo for twelve years, and at Nyankunde Nurses' Training School for seven years, but those accounts would hardly have been accepted by an auditor! Using school exercise books, one side of each page headed 'IN' and the opposite page 'OUT', every transaction was meticulously entered. Each page was then carefully balanced, the money being kept in a row of empty Quaker Oats' tins, neatly labelled 'Hospital', 'Nurses', 'Wages', 'Truck', 'Leprosy work', etc. This was a somewhat 'Heath-Robinson' method, it is true, but it seemed adequate in the primitive area where we lived and worked. But now, in the UK?

So I travelled north to Glasgow, where I was warmly welcomed by staff and students, if a little hesitantly by some. How would I fit in? I was older than most of the staff, and all of the students. Would I want to boss them? That was when I first began to feel lonely. In all the years since I had become a Christian I had never experienced loneliness. I had always been so busy, always surrounded by so many companions, always on the stretch to accomplish the task in hand. Now, how would I fill my time? I didn't merely want them to find me a job to keep me occupied, if the job didn't really need doing. I needed to sense that I was needed.

Because I was part of the college staff, and they were short of lecturers, I was asked to take two courses in the MTC curriculum: a two-hour class each week with all the students, to survey world missions, and a weekly class in the Book of Isaiah, with the small group of students who were sitting for an external Diploma in Biblical Knowledge and Christian Theology. I enjoyed the preparation needed for these lectures, but I still had a lot of time on my hands. I asked to attend Dave Burnett's lectures on Christian Theology to the Diploma students, Flora Gibson's lectures to the same group on John's Gospel, and Hywell Jones's lectures on early church history. This all included study work, the writing of essays, and eventually taking the Diploma exams with the students. I was quite excited by the challenge.

But still I had time. I was not used to that, and I found I didn't like it. I tried to help Chrissey in the office but felt pretty ignorant as I didn't understand 'double-entry system' and such like terms. And the fact that closing-down accounts of a non-profit-making organisation had to be presented in a particular way if they were to be accepted by the auditors made the task even more daunting. So I went to evening classes at the local technical college to study accountancy. That really stretched me and I enjoyed it.

However, underneath all these little bits and pieces of activity, there was a gnawing feeling that this was all somewhat superficial, a filling-in-of-time. Not that I was unwilling to be a gap-filler, if that was what the Lord wanted of me for that year, but in comparison to the previous 20 years, it all seemed unnecessary, a little unreal, and of no eternal value.

Before going to Glasgow, I had been invited by Dave Howard, Director of the Triennial Missionary Conference of the Inter-Varsity Christian Unions in the United States of America, to be one of the speakers at what is known as the Urbana Conference. The title that year, 1976, was 'Declare His Glory among the nations.' John Stott was to give the four Bible Studies on the Biblical basis of missions. Various challenges highlighting the needs in differing parts of the world were to be presented by well-known international speakers. Elisabeth Elliot was to direct the students' thinking on how to find the will of God for their lives, and then I was asked to speak on 'The cost of declaring God's glory to the nations.' Billy Graham would follow with a clear challenge to all those young people, offering them the opportunity to respond to God's voice. Then the last day would be given to thinking about 'How do we move forward? What do we do next, in order to follow through with our response to this challenge?'

To say I was very nervous, as I sought to prepare a twenty minute presentation, would be a gross understatement! I knew there would be 17,000 students there, as well as representatives from over 100 missionary agencies, some of the best known missionary speakers from all over the world, Bible college and missionary training college faculties and a host of such like people. And I was deeply conscious of not being in the same league. I was not an experienced public speaker, nor a missiologist. Why had I accepted Dave's invitation? I asked myself. God reminded me that I accepted because I believed that this was God's will for me at that time. If it was God's will, why was I so terrified? Could I not trust God to give me the word He wanted me to share with those young people?

Then, during the October half-term weekend at the college, I was invited to Birmingham, to speak at Shirley Baptist Church. On the Saturday evening, they asked me to speak on 'Why does a God of love allow such suffering?' This referred mainly to all that our group of missionaries, as well as the Congolese Christians, went through in the Congo civil war in the 1960s. I shared as fully and openly as I could, including the fact that anything that we suffered was as nothing compared to what our Lord Jesus Christ suffered for us, and how He helped us all to see suffering as a *privilege*—something we shared with Him, what the Bible calls 'the fellowship of sharing in His sufferings'. In fact, God reminded me of how, just a quarter of an hour after I first came to realise, as a 19-year-old, the wonder of the fact that Christ Jesus died for my sins, a wise and godly man gave me the verse: '*I want to know Christ and the power of his resurrection and the fellowship of sharing in his sufferings, becoming like him in his death, and so, somehow, to attain to the resurrection from the dead'* (Phil. 3:10, 11), he had prayed for me, 'Perhaps one day God will give you the privilege of sharing in the fellowship of His suffering'. So my whole Christian life started with the assurance that to suffer for the cause of Christ was to be considered as a privilege, not merely as the price of service. The family at Shirley Baptist Church took me up on the thought of 'privilege rather than price', and, on the Sunday evening, I was asked to speak on this. As I prepared for that meeting, the Lord really spoke to my own heart.

God reminded me that my call to missionary service, in what was then the Belgian Congo, had been through Isaiah 58:1-12, which ends with the sentence *'You will be called the Repairer of Broken Walls.'* The word used in the Swahili for 'the Repairer' is really 'a gap-filler', the same word as is used in Ezekiel 22:30 *'I looked for a man among them who would build up the wall and stand before Me in the gap .. but I found none.'* God's call to me was to be a gap-filler. Was I not now willing to fulfil that calling or did I want something bigger and better? Did I want a job description that others could read and understand, or was I willing to be in the background and do what needed doing, even if never thanked? And I suddenly saw this as *privilege*, not price! So many of the things that we think of as price in a missionary's life (giving up of home, culture, language, rat-race, salary, being married and having one's own family, pension, whatever) is truly privilege. It is the amazing privilege of being identified with our Lord Jesus, who had nowhere to lay His head, and had to borrow a donkey, a penny, and a tomb.

After the evening service, several members of the congregation came to thank me for being God's mouthpiece to them, to rebuke them for grumbling at the 'price' to be paid, and to urge them to rejoice at the 'privilege' of sharing with Him. And my heart was filled with joy! How good of God to have graciously spoken *through* me to the blessing of others, when He was busy trying to speak *to* me at the very same time! Then the Lord clearly told me that this was the theme I was to use at Urbana: the cost is only another way of saying the price—and the price is actually the privilege!

I went back to college and sought to put this into practice, to see each small task as a privilege, no matter what others thought. At least with my lips I could state that these were privilege rather than price, but I knew my heart wasn't really in the exercise. I had no real joy in the life I was living. To a degree I was submissive to the leadership, in that I fulfilled each duty with meticulous care and no longer grumbled. But what about the Scripture that says: 'I delight to do Thy will, O my God!' (Ps. 40:8)? In my innermost being, I was not rejoicing, let alone delighting. Instead I was daily hankering for the past. I longed to go back to Congo, to take up my responsibilities again at either Nebobongo or Nyankunde, to be stretched and fulfilled, to be happy and satisfied. I was feeling increasingly useless in my new role.

This hankering for the past led to doubting the present. Was I still listening to *God*'s voice, and only His voice, to direct me, or was I now dependent on the voice of the Mission? Was I staying at home as a gap-filler because *God* wanted to give me a new direction, or because I was afraid of the soldiers, harassment, nervous tensions, and everything that welled up in my mind when I seriously thought of going back to Congo? Then there was that unanswered letter in which I had offered to go back despite my fears. The lack of an answer from the African Church in Congo made me feel that they were not ready to welcome me back. That hurt. It led to a sense of rejection. To be honest, I knew I had not always been popular with my missionary colleagues as I had often been too outspoken. And I knew that others felt I had been too keen to trust, and hand over leadership to, National Christians. But I thought I was acceptable to the African Church. Did they really not want me back?

Over and over again, the word spoke to me about living one day at a time. I was so aware of all the present tense activities of God, whose Name is 'I am'. Had He not promised Paul: 'My grace *is* sufficient for you, for my power *is* made perfect in weakness'? Flora brought this out when she was teaching us from the 'I am' statements of the Lord Jesus Christ in John's Gospel. 'I *am* the Bread of Life' 'I *am* the Good Shepherd'. These are in the present tense to remind us that God is all of the great 'I am' statements right now, to meet our needs right now, whatever they are. They are present day promises to equip us for the present day. I had to learn that God was all I needed to enable me to throw myself wholeheartedly and unreservedly into my present commitments, without comparing them with past achievements or possible future activities.

God enabled me, at least at that time, to take hold of this challenge and to throw myself into all the daily tasks to which I was assigned with renewed energy *and joy*. I actually became quite proficient in account-keeping, which was specially useful as Chrissey was having a bad time with arthritis. Flora slipped a disc in her back and I was available to help her. In fact, I spent a lot of time in her room, taking her meals, doing what I could to help her to rest, as well as studying for the upcoming end-of-year exams. Lecture preparation with the students was really rewarding and helped me feel back in my stride. God graciously blessed as I took my eyes off myself and what I wanted or felt, and fixed my eyes back on Jesus and all He had done for me.

In between all the other activities I was trying to begin jotting down thoughts towards the book I had been invited to write, starting with the first pillar—sacrifice. Slowly, the general outline of what I believed God wanted me to write began to take shape. I realised that each 'pillar' was likely to turn into a small booklet on its own rather than be a chapter in a larger book. The ministry at Shirley Baptist Church in November of that year and then Urbana in December—especially the thoughts God put into my heart regarding 'Price or Privilege?' (or 'the Cost of Declaring His Glory')—became my starting-off point: how God needs to whittle each one of us, like forming an arrow from a rough branch by removing the flowers and leaves, the side branches and thorns, even the bark itself, everything that would render the arrow less than useful—so that He can use us as He choses. We so easily see the whittling process as the *price* we have to pay to become what the Lord God plans for us, but in actual fact, it will eventually be seen as the only means by which we can enjoy the full *privilege* that He longs to give us.

That was how the Lord enabled me to present His truth at Urbana during the Christmas holiday. It was a shattering experience, standing there before that mass of students, in the huge assembly hall of the University of Illinois. John Stott encouraged me by saying, 'Don't look at 17,000 faces, just look at someone in the front row. All the rest are repetitions!' His words of wisdom helped me through. After I spoke there, using a huge visual aid that our WEC Canadian Headquarters made for me, I looked forward very much to hearing Dr Billy Graham speak. Every time he had been to the UK since his first mission in 1953, I had been unable to hear him as I was in Congo. So that evening I managed to secure a front-row seat among those reserved for speakers and seminar leaders, and sat with pen and paper, ready to listen intently to his message to those students, hoping to learn from him how one could present a meaningful challenge for world missions to the student world. Billy Graham stood—he was such a humble and unassuming man and I could see him clearly. Then, overwhelmed by the relief that my own message was now over, I fell asleep and never heard a word! On my way home after the conference, I took my visual aid with me—a six-foot long artificial branch of forsythia, with huge green leaves and bright yellow flowers made of polystyrene, and enclosing a gigantic arrow, fitted with a pointed end that showed up on X-rays as a potential weapon. At each customs checkpoint I had to explain the reason for carrying such a thing with me!

The college year back in Glasgow was drawing to a close. The final accounts were presented and accepted by the auditors. Thank You, Lord! The group of students who sat the Diploma examination all passed, some with distinction. Thank You, Lord! Several of the students, at the end of term, testified to having heard the Lord's voice clearly directing them to their future spheres of service through the World Mission Survey lectures. Thank You, Lord! Chapter one of the booklet on sacrifice had taken shape, and Flora, who read it for me, was excited by it. Thank You, Lord! And even as I write this page, many years later, I have just received an e-mail from someone who wants to meet me, an assistant professor at a university in USA, who says that she first heard me at Urbana in 1976, at which time she was deeply blessed by what God gave me to say. How utterly amazing. Thank You, Lord!

Were these all 'ditches' successfully dug and then graciously filled by the Lord? If so, what was the next step to be? As I looked back and praised God for all His wonderful undertaking for me, I could see that my twenty years of service in Congo might have been essential training for the present sphere of service. So much that occurred during the nine-month tour of meetings in the USA the previous year, and then at the college, could not really have impacted others if I had not been through the training school of the previous twenty years in Congo. That was fairly easy to say, but the inference was not so easy to accept. Was the present preparing me for the next tomorrow? And if so, what was it to be?

Dave and Anne Burnett would have loved me to go with them to the London headquarters of our mission, where they believed God would have them start a new Missionary Orientation Course (MOC), to serve all evangelical missions in the preparation of their candidates. But I just did not feel any rise in my spirit towards this. I was willing to go, should WEC feel this was the right place for me, but I was not excited by the thought of such an assignment. Actually, I helped the Burnetts pack up the college: library books, missiological records, various teaching aids and materials, as well as desks and chairs, dining room furniture and equipment, bedroom furnishings—everything moveable!—into hired vans, which Dave and others drove south to our mission headquarters. We talked and prayed about his vision for the future, and his definite need of others to come alongside him to put it all into practice. But still my heart did not rise to the challenge.

Should I take some further training in order to be of more use to Dave, or to some other similar project in WEC? Or was I to continue in a speaking ministry for them, as a roving deputation worker on full-time home assignment? I felt so insecure in this latter role. I did not feel that I was adept at relating to other people. I was not what people called a natural communicator, however much my heart beat for missions.

During the summer holiday, I went as a leader to a Girl Crusaders' Union (GCU) 'camp' in Scotland. They had hired the Aberlour Boys' Prep School for two weeks, where sixty girls (10 to 17 year olds) from all over the UK were brought together, with some twelve leaders (mature Christian women, appointed to leadership in one of the many weekly Bible classes in Scotland, England, Wales, and Ireland), to enjoy a first-rate holiday with games, outings, and activities in a

Christian environment, with daily prayer times and Bible studies. I was an Assistant Leader with GCU before I first went to Congo, and was invited back into the ranks to help in the task of 'handing on the baton' to the next generation. It was a marvellous camp, and certainly reassured me that one of the special ministries God had entrusted to me over many years was teaching His Word and challenging young people to a wholehearted devotion to Jesus Christ and obedience to that Word.

How was this going to help me find direction for the next phase of my life's journey? All I wanted was to please God. I did not want to please myself, nor merely fill in time. But how was I to be sure what I should be doing? Before my mother's death, she and I thought about the possibility of my teaching in one of the UK's Bible Colleges, and certainly my joy at being in the teaching ministry—both at the Missionary Training College throughout the year, and again at the GCU Camp in the summer—made me think again about this idea. One such college had actually invited me for an interview, with the suggestion that I join the staff for a year. That would have given me a settled place, a clear 'job description' and security. Was that what the Lord wanted?

'Please, God,' I prayed earnestly, 'I need a clear word from Yourself.'

And the Holy Spirit reminded me that He had spoken clearly, just the previous year, 'Make this valley full of ditches', and He indicated that the task was not yet completed. So I waited to see the next step.

2

DIGGING A DITCH
ON THE DEPUTATION TRAIL

I spent a lovely two weeks after the GCU Camp at Aberlour, with my friend Patricia and her mother, at a country-house hotel in Morayshire. The weather was perfect. We visited many of the surrounding beauty spots in northeast Scotland, including looking down on Balmoral Castle. We walked on hillsides and on beaches. We watched salmon jumping in the Dee and had time to reflect, refresh, and renew for the upcoming year. Patricia and I met each other through the GCU summer camp at Aberlour the previous year. With her mother, she had offered me to share their home, near Belfast in Northern Ireland, whenever I needed a base from which to work. So now, on holiday together, we prayed about what God would have me do in the coming year, but had no specific guidance.

At the end of August, I had been invited to take part in the Bangor Missionary Convention in Northern Ireland. On the Thursday evening, speaking to a packed congregation on the privilege of being one of God's ambassadors (2 Cor. 5:17–21), I was suddenly deeply conscious of His overruling power and presence. At an after-meeting that same evening, some 200 young people were prepared and willing to be challenged about how they could be involved. I remember stripping a lovely rose to create an arrow (the same illustration as I had used at the Urbana Student Missionary Conference in USA the previous winter, but in miniature!) and an intense, almost audible, silence settled over them.

I pulled the flowers and leaves off the rose. It looked like wanton destruction, but in the other hand I held up an arrow. There was nothing wrong with the flowers and leaves. In fact, they were essential to the life of the rose. Without them the rose could not breathe, feed, or reproduce. But they would be a hindrance to the functioning of an arrow if left on the branch. Would we allow God to strip us, even of good things in our lives if, by doing so, He could make us into instruments more useable in His service? If He asked us to forego the right to well paid jobs and future security, to marriage, having a family and our own home, to advancement in our professions, or to popularity or general success, could we say 'Yes' to the Lord and trust Him to mould us into the patterns He has planned for us?

I cut off thorns and side branches. There was nothing wrong with these for the rose, but they certainly wouldn't help the balance of the arrow. Would we allow God to strip off our 'rights': our right to order our own lives, to decide our life's partner, to choose our jobs and places of work, or our right to be considered, to have our opinions asked when decisions were made that affected our own lives, or even our right to own and possess the basic necessities of decent living conditions? Were we willing to *throw off everything that hinders and the sin that so easily entangles*: the sins of impatience, a critical spirit, the need to justify ourselves and our every action, the sin of being unwilling to be falsely accused and misunderstood? Could we hand all this over to the Lord and trust Him entirely with complete control of our lives? I spoke to myself as well as to the others present.

But the bare stem I held in my hand—devoid of flowers and leaves, stripped of thorns and side branches—was still recognisable as the branch of a rose. I took a knife and whittled away the bark. Had even the bark to go? The bark gave the rose its individuality; it made it recognisable for what it was. The bark protected it from rain and sun. But now the shaft left in my hand, polished and smooth, could be seen to be useable as an arrow. Would we allow God the right to invade our innermost beings, to strip us naked of ourselves, so that others looking at us would see only Jesus? Were we willing to give up our right to be ourselves in order to be wholly identified with Him, and so available to Him for whatever He wants and plans for our lives?

We stayed late that evening, talking and praying with individuals … and I simply knew that God was saying to me, 'This is the work I want to do through you. The fact that you do not consider yourself to be a communicator is good; you will trust Me and leave Me to do My own work. The fact that you are uncomfortable in this ministry, feeling that you are not trained for it or particularly good at it, is partly why I have chosen you. You will always know that any blessing that results will not be to your glory, but will be wholly Mine.'

I had most of September to think that over and to pray about it, until I came to a somewhat reluctant agreement that I would do what God was asking me to do. Part of my reluctance lay in the fact that I was still hankering after a return to Congo. Was I willing to simply lay that at God's feet? Pat and I received a copy of *Parables of the Cross*, one of Lilias Trotter's books, for a Christmas present that year. I had long loved Trotter's books, but all my copies were destroyed in Congo in the rebellion of 1964. One of the paragraphs in *Parables of the Cross* is headed 'Death to Lawful Things is the Way Out into a Life of Surrender.'

There is a painting of three buttercups: one just a bud beginning to open, a second is half open, and the third and central one is fully open, with the sepals folded right back. 'Look at this buttercup,' wrote Lilias, 'as it begins to learn its new lesson. The little hands of the calyx clasp tightly in the bud, round the beautiful petals. In the young flower their grasp grows more elastic—loosening somewhat in the daytime, but keeping the power of contracting, able to close in again during a rainstorm or when night comes on. But see the central flower, which has reached its maturity. The calyx hands have unclasped utterly now—they have folded themselves back, past all power of closing again upon the petals, leaving the golden crown free to float away when God's time comes.'

Had I learned the buttercup's lesson yet? Would I take my hands, once and for all time, off every part of my life and leave God completely free to do with me and through me whatever He chose? Or was I still in the phase of partial relaxing of my grasp, with power to take things back again when the going got tough? I wanted to say 'Yes!' to God, with complete abandonment, with nothing held back. And yet, I so easily took back and took hold again when I felt insecure or fearful.

I was invited by our WEC Scottish representative, Roy Spraggett, to go to Scotland for a tour of meetings with him, quickly followed by a week of meetings across the north of England, and then down to Bristol and South Wales for two weeks. I crossed over to Scotland by ferry, with my small car, and headed out into the unknown with a vengeance! Roy was a wonderful and understanding companion and he quickly realised my sense of insecurity. As we drove to a meeting, he would quietly quiz me about the topic on which I was going to speak. If I hesitated, uncertain between two different approaches, he would draw off the road into a parking area and suggest we prayed together. After committing the next meeting to the Lord, he often suggested what he felt might be the best way to present the challenge of missions to that particular group. Then we would think it through together until I sensed a quietness in my spirit, that this was truly the Lord's way. The meetings were enormously varied: a church youth group, a children's talk in the morning service, a women's coffee morning and a valedictory service for one of our Scottish missionaries going out to Chad. I was amazed at how the Lord was able to speak through us to each different age group, and to people of completely differing backgrounds.

From Scotland to the north of England, from Southport in the west to Doncaster in the east, we travelled and we spoke. Again, there was the continual stretch of being willing for any situation at a moment's notice, including speaking at a Communion service on the Sunday, and a women's evangelistic outreach meeting on the Tuesday, ten minutes at a school assembly—where the children had never heard of WEC—followed by forty minutes at a WEC regional rally, where everyone was already deeply involved in missions! Then I drove south to Bristol, and across into South Wales from Newport to Swansea, where my programme included a radio interview, meetings in a Bible college and two sessions in a huge comprehensive school. It was wonderful to share in a packed midweek meeting in Heath Church, Cardiff, and another in Mount Pleasant Baptist Church, Swansea.

Throughout that month, I seemed always to be packing my suitcase and moving on. I slept in a different bed almost every night, and met with new people every day. Hundreds of people would gladly have been my friends, but there was no time to develop friendships. I found that each day I had to try to forget yesterday's people, in order to relate to those of today. The pace was fairly unrelenting. In between meetings, if there was ever a spare minute, letters had to be written to thank very kindly and generous families for their hospitality.

And, if there was yet another gap in the programme, I tried to complete the manuscript of *Living Sacrifice*, the first of the series to present WEC's four pillars.

It really was all a little breathtaking. I managed four days at my new 'home' with Pat and her mother, on the outskirts of Belfast, but even these days included four meetings! Then I was off to Dublin for a packed week, then back to thirty-six meetings in the following four weeks. Thank God for a quiet Christmas at home, to look back over those three months, and try to evaluate and to look forward, and try not to plan! All I knew for certain was that God had undertaken in an amazing way. I was quite certain that I could never, never have taken all those meetings in my own strength. But I did begin to wonder if God really meant me to keep up such a pace. Then a few letters began to come telling of this one and that one who had been blessed or challenged at the meetings. So I had dug another ditch and, unknown to me, unseen and unheard, God graciously filled it with life-giving water.

Others wrote, and I sensed an underlying urgency as though the writer wanted to say something or ask me something, but was hesitating—trying me out, perhaps, as to whether they could trust me or not. My replies, thanking writers for their letters and offering friendship, were always written by hand lest type-written letters—this was before the days of computers or emails—would make people suspect there was a secretary involved, and therefore no absolute privacy and confidentiality. Then a second letter often followed in which the writer unburdened her heart, and sought counsel and spiritual help. Such correspondence began to take more and more of my time, but seemed to be very definitely part of God's planned 'ditches' for me.

Early in January, I was on the south coast of England for a weekend of meetings. On the Wednesday that followed, I drove 400 miles north to Durham for an evening meeting at the university. It started to snow, and the journey was not an easy one. I was running short on petrol by the time I reached the university car park, and I asked the Lord that, should the secretary of the meeting give me a gift, that it should please be in cash and not a cheque, as a cheque wouldn't buy me petrol. At the end of the evening, I *was* handed an envelope—but it contained a book-token! *That* wouldn't buy petrol either. Driving south the next day, I used every penny I had to put petrol in the car, and prayed that God would somehow get me to London! The next evening, I stayed with Roger Carswell and his family in Garforth, and spoke to over 300 working folk in a small crowded hall. At the end of the evening they emptied the offering box into my handbag. What a heavy weight of coins! Bless their hearts; they more than covered all my needs from Worthing to Durham, and back again! I was humbled and amazed. In my quick judgement—looking at the outward appearance and not the heart—the Garforth group had not appeared to be in a position to supply my needs. But God knew otherwise. This was a lesson I was to learn many times in the ensuing years. While I was to ask God to supply my needs, I was not to work out how He would supply them. I didn't have to tell God His own job, and He never let me down. There was always what was needed, just at the time it was needed.

Back again in the south for a week of meetings, I became sick with flu. Leaving the home where I was staying on the south coast to drive to Hildenborough Hall, I met heavy snow, traffic diversions, hold-ups, as well as accidents. And all the way I felt more and more unwell. I tried to telephone the people who were expecting me in Sevenoaks, to say it was very unlikely I would get there by 7 p.m. ready for an evening meeting. But the telephone lines were down. Struggling on, I managed about three miles in half an hour. Should I turn back to the south? I asked myself. That is what I saw others doing. But I knew that the people where I had stayed the previous night had other guests coming that day, and it would be very inconvenient for them to have me, especially as I was becoming increasingly unwell. I was upset, and not sure what I ought to do. Sticking at it, I crawled up a long winding icy hill—slithering and skithering—when suddenly there was no more snow. The sun came out and there were no more cars, as most people had turned back! I managed to reach my host's home by 8 p.m., very weary, pretty sick, and full of apologies for being so late, only to hear that they had cancelled the meeting because of the weather. I was beginning to learn that God amazingly undertakes in all sorts of situations and I don't need to panic. I had all the tender loving care I needed in that home for the next three days, until I was really fit enough to move on to my next engagement. How good God was to me!

However, that attack of flu left me with quite severe laryngitis, and no voice. I drove on to Kings Lynn where I was to speak in the large and lovely Anglican church in the morning and to an after-church rally in the evening. They had one of the most sophisticated sound amplification systems I had ever spoken into, one that multiplied my faint whisper until it filled the whole church! Once again, God graciously turned a difficult moment into one of praise to Him.

From there I went to a whole week of meetings in Oxford University, and then home to Belfast for four weeks to prepare for a month of meetings spanning the United States. There were over forty public engagements booked, and we had to cover over 2,000 miles by car. The Easter weekend services were very uplifting and the six Bible colleges were all very challenging. But I remember especially one evening when I met with some 400 university students in the Twin City Bible Church, in Urbana. I had been asked to speak to the subject 'The Cost of being a missionary', probably by a student who had heard me speak to the subject at the Urbana Conference the previous year.

As I entered the lecture theatre and made my way down to the front, I noticed two girls sitting together, about five rows from the front on my left. One of them seemed much too young to be a student, and there was something strange about the way she looked at me. I wondered if she was blind, appearing to look in my direction, but not actually seeing me. I gave my talk, basing my thoughts on the four letters, C—O—S—T, and illustrating, as I had done in Bangor, by stripping a rose to make an arrow. Part way through my presentation, I sensed the Lord 'nudging' me to tell, in a little more detail than usual, what I had suffered on the night of the 28th October 1964, when the guerrilla soldiers captured me. I shared how they struck me over and over again with the butt end of their guns, how I fell and they kicked me, breaking two or three of my back teeth, how they dragged me to my feet and forced me back to the veranda of my home and how the brutal leader raped me. I passed over this as quickly as I could, but shared with those students how God spoke to me in my distress, asking me to '*thank* Him for trusting me with such an experience, even if He never told me why.'

At the close of the meeting, I went up to the back of the hall to speak to students as they left. Then I returned to the front to collect my Bible and notes, and there were the two girls waiting to speak to me. The older one asked me if I had time to speak with her younger sister. 'She was raped six weeks ago, and since then no-one has been able to help her. She will not speak to any of us: her family, our doctor, our minister at church, no-one.' I turned to the younger girl and looked straight at her. She stood up, and slowly began to come towards me. Then, suddenly, she ran at me, threw her arms round my neck and burst into tears. We sat down together, and slowly she unloaded, sharing all that had been bottling up inside her for the six weeks since the horrifying incident. She ended by saying, 'No-one told me that I could **thank** the Lord for trusting me with this!' We prayed together, and thanked Him for His love and grace towards us, for all He has done for us, and then for trusting us. When God could have saved us from the horror, He actually trusted us to go through the ordeal *with Him*, so that He could use the experience later to help others. We cried together, hugged each other, then I said goodnight to the two of them.

Later that evening, I thanked God again for letting me know, at least in some small measure, the why of that long-ago night in the Congo. God didn't have to show me why He allowed the ordeal; I had accepted it all from His hands unquestioningly. But now I knew that at least one young girl had been helped to come to terms with the shock, *because* I was enabled to share from my own experience. Thank You, God! The fact that the Lord 'nudged' me to share that particular incident, that particular night, when it was not part of my prepared notes, also amazed me at His great goodness. If only we would trust Him utterly to overrule in every situation.

There followed two months at home—a welcome break, with only a few local meetings. During that time I worked hard, trying to complete the manuscript for *Living Sacrifice*. I had sent the rough draft to our WEC International Office for their critical evaluation, and was now working on the grammar and 'polishing' the presentation. The way in which people reacted at so many of the meetings, both in the UK and also in the USA, helped me to word some things differently, or led me to leave illustrations out or develop others. The book began with a realisation of the great sacrifice made by our Lord Jesus Christ, the very Son of God, when He died on the cruel Cross of Calvary, for *my* sins. There is no sacrifice that I can ever make that can ever come near to His sacrifice.

In fact, every effort on my part to respond to His great love to me, to thank Him for all He has achieved by His death that I might know forgiveness of sin, can only be seen as *privilege*. That my Saviour should not only save me from the guilt and penalty of my sins, but that He should then invite me to be His co-labourer, to work with Him and for Him in His worldwide vineyard, that others might come to a knowledge of salvation—that is just tremendous privilege!

How can we show God that we love Him? How can we express our thanks to Him for all He has done for us at Calvary? *'Whoever has my commandments and obeys them, he is the one who loves me'* (John 14:21). And what are His commandments that I should seek to obey? *'Love the Lord your God with all your heart and with all your soul and with all your mind and with all your strength,'* and *'Love your neighbour as yourself'* (Mark 12:29-31). I set out in the book to explore whether, of my 20 years of missionary service in Congo, I could conceivably testify that I *had* loved my Lord with *all* my heart, mind, soul, and strength. I was horrified to realise how often I failed to do this, and recognising the failures really helped me to see what should have been done on many, many occasions.

In the introductory chapter of *Living Sacrifice*, I shared a story of how our village of Nebobongo had been invaded by thousands of weaver birds that destroyed our palm trees, stripping the fronds to make their nests. We challenged the primary school children, telling them that for every dead weaver bird brought to us we would pay them a penny. The children loved it! They stripped our bright yellow acacia trees to make arrows, and then set about killing birds by the dozens! But to destroy the pest, they had also destroyed the beauty of our acacia trees. Yet at the same time, they had saved our palms and their maturing nuts that provided our essential oil for food. Was the 'gain' worth the cost? From there the book developed, seeking to underline the essential truth that any apparent cost on our part is more than compensated by the enormous privilege our Lord gives us as we serve Him and put Him wholly first in our lives.

Having sent the manuscript to our WEC International Leadership for their criticisms, I waited a little fearfully. Was this the sort of book they wanted me to write? Would they understand what I was trying to say? Then I received a shattering invitation to attend the six-yearly conference of all our WEC Mission leaders from all home bases and from all fields worldwide AND to give one of the presentations on the 'Four Pillars' at a morning devotional session. I was deeply humbled. I am not a leader in our Mission and I was almost overwhelmed at the thought of being at their conference. When I arrived at Kilcreggan House in the West of Scotland, where we were all to meet for three whole weeks, I sought out any job I could do to be helpful: assisting the official Conference Secretary in taking notes, making cups of tea, helping in the kitchen, preparing vegetables and washing up, helping some of our national brothers from other lands to find their way around, anything that I could do to help me justify my presence among them all! In between times, I went over and over the notes I had prepared for my presentation on 'Sacrifice'.

The day before the meeting, I asked the head gardener for a rose—or any suitable branch—with which to illustrate my talk. I explained to him that my visual aid needed flowers, leaves, thorns, side branches and bark. Arriving in the hall early the next morning, I saw in front of the podium, a HUGE floral display of rhododendron. It was truly magnificent, covered with glorious blossoms and glossy leaves. But as I looked at it in awe, I realised that I could not possibly break off a branch in the middle of my talk. It was far too massive. So I set to, sawed a branch off, and then stuck it back on with adhesive tape. When I eventually cut it off during my talk, with a small penknife, it looked comparatively easy! As I stood there, with the branch in my hand, and almost nonchalantly started to pull off the flowers and then strip off the leaves, there was an audible gasp of horror—especially from the men!

'What are you doing? That is wanton destruction of a thing of great beauty!' Then a deep silence settled over the whole group as they began to see the relevance of the visual aid to the message. Were we, as a mission, prepared for, and willing to accept, the deliberate laying aside of beauty in our plans and programs, in our abilities and even our visions, if God showed us this would lead to the fulfilment of His plan and purposes? There were tears shed. There were many inner battles fought, and yet throughout that day God wrought a deep new inner peace in many hearts as we allowed Him to lead us to the point of saying, 'Yes, Lord, whatever it costs!'

During that time of conference, we heard news of the fearful massacre of thirteen missionaries and their children, including a baby, in Zimbabwe, and we all prayed, 'Lord, if that had been me, could I have said "Yes" to You?' In the weeks that followed, we heard something of the blessing amongst the national children in the school where those missionaries had been teaching. We saw that God had asked them for the ultimate sacrifice that He might complete His work in the hearts of some of the older boys and girls there. Humanly, one was tempted to ask, 'Is there always a price to pay for blessing? Has God the right to demand that of those missionaries and of their families back home?' But the Spirit pressed us to look through the immediate to the ultimate. Those missionaries were all now in glory; their work was complete. And some of our group, in the prayer time that followed the announcement of this news, voiced all our thoughts. 'Dear Lord, help us to see that the stripping of the rose results in the formation of the arrow as an instrument in Your hands to perfect Your will.'

At the close of the Mission's Conference, I had a few further meetings, then most of September was spent back at home. That allowed me time for prayer and refreshment, and for preparing three months of meetings that had been lined up, meetings that would keep me travelling and speaking until the following Christmas.

3

DIGGING DITCHES IN PREPARING MESSAGES AND BUILDING UP RELATIONSHIPS

By the autumn of 1978, the preparation of the manuscript of *Living Sacrifice* was completed, ready for submission to the publishers. Meetings went on, much as previously, including ten days at Aberlour at a GCU camp for schoolgirls, and a very welcome summer holiday. With nearly 80 public meetings booked for the three months up to Christmas, it was essential to take time for prayerful consideration of how I could present the missionary challenge in different ways. Each day of my summer break I sought to pray through the meetings of each day of the upcoming tour. But I didn't always know ahead of time what any day would bring forth. Sometimes I arrived at a meeting expecting teenagers, to find the children were all primary school age, or a meeting I thought was for women turned out to be a mixed congregation.

The first time this happened, in 1975 in America, it taught me a tremendous lesson about trusting the Lord for last minute guidance. I arrived at a church one Sunday morning at 10 a.m. expecting to give a short twenty minute devotional message to the whole congregation. The pastor met me, and explained that the first hour, from 10 a.m. to 11a.m. was Sunday School, and asked if I would be willing to speak to the senior group? I knew I was expected to say 'Yes', but my mind raced, trying to think which of my prepared messages would be suitable. I flicked through my file, and picked out the notes on a message for senior teenagers, with three African stories to illustrate the dangers of sex, drink, and drugs.

I was ushered into a room for the Senior Sunday School class to find myself surrounded by some thirty senior citizens, all white haired and very welcoming! I nearly died. I had not understood the American use of the term 'Sunday School'. My choice of message, to put it mildly, seemed somewhat unsuitable. But God graciously came to my rescue. The lady leading the meeting asked them all if anyone had any special requests for prayer. When no-one responded, she handed the meeting over to me, and I said, 'Yes, I have a request for your prayers, please.' Then I shared with them how, that very week, my dear mother had died. As I spoke, I broke down and cried, and all 30 of those men and women cried with me. Then I shared with them my mother's testimony, and all she had meant to me. Later, when we went to the main sanctuary, I knew that scattered among the large congregation there were thirty dear men and women praying for me in a special and understanding way.

On another occasion, three of us left our WEC Headquarters in Philadelphia at about 5 a.m. on a cold and snowy morning, to drive to a Women's Breakfast on the East Coast. Based on some experience in the UK, I expected the women attending the meeting to be on their way to work, and so prepared a message based on the testimony of one of my African friends, Damaris, a lovely gentle person, who radiated the love of Jesus in all her work as a midwife at the Nebobongo maternity unit. Damaris really lived a Christ-like life, as described in 1 Corinthians 13, a life of practical, meaningful love. When we eventually arrived and entered the golf-club, we found ourselves surrounded by a very—

what shall I say?—elite and sophisticated group of some 200 ladies. Seated at the top table, and looking round, I felt that my story of a simple African working woman just wasn't right. I surreptitiously opened my file and started looking through it for more suitable notes for this particular group. I pulled one such out, but still wasn't convinced that it was right. I slipped it back into the file, and looked for another one. My two WEC companions were watching me from their table in the hall, and they began praying that the Lord would give me His peace as they realised my obvious confusion. Then a lady was asked to sing a solo, and she sang—most beautifully and with deep conviction and meaning—a setting of the thirteenth chapter of Paul's first letter to the Corinthians!

I took out the notes I had prayerfully prepared before coming to the meeting, asked the Lord to forgive me for hesitating, and gave the simple talk that He originally prompted me to give. And, of course, it was just right for that group of ladies. When would I learn to trust the Lord, and His leading, rather than my own feelings? And how gracious of Him to give me that clear confirmation at the critical moment!

Another similar sort of lesson had to do with numbers, because I had to learn not to play the numbers game. I had a phone call once, inviting me to a large city in USA, to a church weekend conference where I would have the opportunity (as I thought the voice said) of speaking to 12,000 teenagers. I actually had another meeting booked for that same weekend, a Mothers' Union in a local church, where I could expect some 30 or so to attend. I managed to rearrange the timetable, and flew to the States for the weekend of meetings in Detroit, where I met with around 1,200 people, some of whom were teenagers, and where, by and large, they were not prepared for the challenge I felt I should give. It was a difficult and rather unhappy time, with no apparent response.

I had fallen for the temptation of believing that 12,000 teenagers were more important than thirty women. In fact, the voice on the phone had probably said twelve hundred, and I had misheard and misinterpreted, and so jumped to a wrong conclusion. But God spoke to me clearly, following that experience, telling me that HE was in charge, and that booked meetings were not to be changed for later invitations. He could control the timing of invitations, and in His eyes every single person was as important as any other. Number counting was not to be taken into account. I'm not sure that I have fully learned the lesson yet, but I do understand the principle involved.

One of the meetings I was invited to taught me a clear lesson in preparing material to present to others. The headmistress of a school for over 200 severely physically handicapped children in South-east Belfast, invited me to speak at a morning assembly to all the children and maybe almost as many staff. 'Please bring them a missionary challenge!' My mind was shocked. How does one present a *missionary* challenge to young people, some unable to control hands or feet, some tied to beds for their own protection, many in wheelchairs?

Then a small local event occurred. Belfast was struck by a series of electricity power cuts. Every household brought out, or went to the stores to buy, hurricane lanterns, oil, and matches, in order to cope with the emergency. Our lantern was pretty ancient—battered, cracked paint, lost handle— but it did not leak. I polished up its glass, filled it with oil, and brought it into service. Our next-door neighbours bought themselves a shiny new lantern. Seeing it gave me an idea, and I asked them if I could borrow it on the day that I was to go to the school. Both lanterns were cleaned, filled with oil, but only one glass was polished; the other was painted with shoe-black!

At the school, with the help of a match, I lit the first lantern. It shone brightly. The light went in from outside, was fed by the oil, and shone out unhindered. I explained how every one of us can be like that lantern—a shining light for the Lord Jesus, as we invite the Light of the World to come into our lives, our bodies, and to shine through us. Then we compared the two lanterns. Given the choice, which one would we choose? I suggested that we needed to light them both, turn off all the lights in the hall, and see which one gave us the best light to read by. Under cover of the darkness as the lights were turned off, I removed the shiny clean glass from the good lantern and replaced it with the blackened glass. Then I lit both lanterns, and those children who were able to point, all pointed to the old and battered lantern as the one giving the best light. When the lights were put back on, they all saw that it was the battered old lantern that was the best to read by, not the new and shiny one as they might have expected!

'Children, it doesn't really matter what the outside frame of the lantern looks like, so long as the light is inside, the lantern filled with oil, and the glass polished. If your heart is filled with the love of God, you can shine for Him wherever He puts you, even if people think your body is a bit battered. You can be more use as missionaries where you live than those with perfect bodies whose thoughts and actions make their glasses so dirty that the light cannot shine out!' How good of the Lord! I had to learn to trust Him to give me the inspiration, as well as the physical strength that I needed for each day, for each meeting.

I left for Canada and the USA, for ten weeks of intensive travelling, with a rather different emphasis from the previous tour. This one was not so much one-off meetings and moving on, but rather several meetings in one place to the same group of people over a weekend. To me this appeared to be a more constructive way of building real contacts and conveying several aspects of the missionary needs of the world and the many methods available to meet those needs. It also gave a greater flexibility in accepting strategic opportunities. I visited seven Bible colleges and university campuses across Canada, and then eight across the USA, with four or five meetings at each. In between these there were ten or more women's outreach evangelistic meetings. During this tour, God helped me to develop a message on 5Ws as a way of presenting missionary challenge—the why? where? what? who? and which? of missions.

The 'Why?' brought before us God's compassion for the world in all its need, and His command to us 'You give them something to eat' rather than send them away hungry (Mark 6:32-37).

The 'Where?' gave an opportunity for a survey of world need, using a large flannelgraph map of the world, and blocking in the huge area of Muslim influence through North Africa, Middle East, Turkey, Iraq, Iran, Afghanistan, Pakistan and down through Malaysia and Indonesia; the Hindu block in the sub-continent of India; the Buddhist and Confucianist block through Thailand, China, and the Far East—thus bringing into focus the 'ten-forty window'. This is a rectangle formed by a line drawn 10 degrees north of the equator, through the Pacific Ocean, back along a line 40 degrees north of the equator, and closed through the Atlantic Ocean, a window enclosing two billion of the least reached peoples in the world, those most needing missionary endeavour.

The 'What?' gave occasion for testimony regarding what is involved in 'being a missionary': knowing the Lord Jesus as our own personal Saviour, laying everything aside for the privilege of serving Him, being willing to do anything He asks of us (from building a hospital or being brutalised as a prisoner of war, to being a behind-the-scenes secretary), and accepting that the cost involved is 'worth it' because the Master we serve is 'worthy'.

The 'Who?' lent itself to a direct challenge to every Christian to become more deeply involved in mission than ever before in the realm of giving, of going, and supremely of praying, that we must all allow God to 'stir us' profoundly if His task of reaching every creature in every ethnic group throughout the whole world, with the gospel of redeeming love, is to be achieved.

And then fifthly, the 'Which?'—by which means will this be achieved (or 'How?'): by a willingness to allow God to strip us of all that hinders, to fire us with His compassion and love, to fill us with His vision. This was, of course, a quick survey of all that was written in *Living Sacrifice*.

During this tour, I began scribbling thoughts down towards *Living Faith*, the next book in the Four Pillars series. My thoughts began to focus in on the 'Who?' It was at a WEC Easter Convention in London that God first began speaking to my heart along this particular line. That year, the Annual Convention Meeting was held in Westminster Chapel, where nearly 2,000 people poured in. The morning was spent fixing banners to all the galleries, bearing such slogans as 'Up! for this is the day!', 'Now then, do it!', 'Go into all the world and preach the Gospel' and CT Studd's motto across the front, 'If Jesus Christ be God and died for me, then no sacrifice is too great for me to make for Him.' It was an exciting day, but, for those of us asked to take part, somewhat intimidating!

I remember that the Chapel had just recently been recarpeted with a lovely deep blue pile carpet. And I was using, as a visual aid, a pot of white gloss paint, a paint brush and a rough piece of wood. Several of my friends prayed earnestly, not just that the message would be acceptable, but possibly more importantly, that I would not drop the paint pot! Starting from '*Stir up the gift of God*' (2 Tim. 1:6 KJV) and ending with '*And they came, every one whose heart stirred him up, and every one whom his spirit made willing, and they brought the Lord's offering ...*' (Exod. 35:21), and largely based on the old Keswick hymn, 'Stir me, O stir me, Lord ... Stir me to give, to go, but most to pray ...' (by Mrs A. Head). There were three challenges. The first was to those of us who should be the 'givers' (of cash, yes, but even more importantly, of our talents, our children, our so-called rights), to others of us who could be the 'go-ers' (be it to far away places, cross-culturally, to as yet unreached people groups, or to our near neighbours, often quite as spiritually needy), and thirdly, to all of us, to be the 'pray-ers', to pray without ceasing, to turn every moment and situation of our daily lives into knowledgable prayer, persistent prayer, believing prayer.

I didn't drop the paint pot or splash the precious blue carpet! But I did manage to paint the brown wood white, challenging us all to allow God to stir us up (as old-fashioned paint needed stirring before being used), and to apply us where and how He chose when He knew we were ready. Our task is to be wholly available to Him, and He is responsible for the changes wrought in the hearts of those He is seeking to reach with the gospel.

This message became more and more part of me, and led me to think out the basic message of the next book along those lines—as the application of Faith—faith to give as, what and when God wants, faith to go wherever He directs and, above all, faith to pray, without losing faith if the answer does not come at the moment or in the way that we wish or expect. As I prayed over this, I became more and more convinced that our faith must not depend on the answer to any of those challenges. If we pray earnestly for something specific, and it does not materialise, this must not shake our faith. God may have answered 'No' or 'Wait!' He knows best what we need and when we need it, yet He does desire us to ask Him for it. The struggle to define faith made the writing of the prologue very difficult. What is faith? How is it obtained? How does it work? I kept putting it off, as I developed each of the other chapters.

One Sunday on the tour, I spoke three times in Memphis. At about 11 p.m., I caught a plane to Dallas, where I had to change on to a larger flight to Los Angeles. It was midnight as I walked into the small terminal building for local planes, and everyone else on the plane seemed to know exactly what they were doing and where they were going. I tried to ask one or two people where I should go for my connecting flight, but all were too hurried to help me. Suddenly the lights dimmed as that part of the airport closed down for the night! There was no-one about, just myself, forlornly holding tightly to my briefcase. A cleaner suddenly came up the stairs to collect a cardigan she had left behind. 'Please,' I called out to her, 'Can you help me?' I explained what I wanted. 'Yes,' she answered, 'you need to catch an orange train across to the main airport. Go across there to the elevator. Go down to the first floor then turn right. Go to the bottom of the corridor, turn left, and you will reach the platform. Be sure to wait for an *orange* train!' and she was gone.

I made my way across to the elevator. It was pitch dark inside. I found the buttons, and pressed the bottom one for ground floor. Arriving there, I pushed one button higher than the bottom one I could feel, to go back to 'first floor' (having completely forgotten that Americans call ground floor first floor!). I then turned right. But at the bottom of the corridor there was no left turn! I stumbled back to the elevator, and went back to ground floor, realising my mistake. Precious time was going. My flight to Los Angeles was almost due for take-off. I eventually found my way to the platform but between me and the platform there was a grill, and the only way through it was a turnstile that needed a 'quarter' to release it and give me entrance. I did not have a quarter (American equivalence to a 20p piece).

How was I to get through? I hurriedly unpacked my briefcase, pushed all the bits and pieces, including my Bible and file of notes for up-coming talks, under the grill, flattened the briefcase and squeezed it under. Then I climbed the grill, squeezed through between the top and the ceiling, dropped down the other side, refilled my briefcase, and just then a train came in carrying an orange light! I was glad no-one caught me in the act and I trust the USA will not feel I cheated them of a quarter. Clambering on to the train, I hoped it would go fast! It was empty except for me. Arriving at the end of its journey into a fully lighted area, with crowds of hurrying people, I suddenly heard my name called over the loud speaker.

'How do I get to where I need to be?' I gasped, somewhat incoherently, to the first official-looking person I could find. Then, following the directions, I ran ... and made it. The doors of the waiting plane shut behind me as I entered it!

We reached Los Angeles, where I was met by a missionary couple on home assignment from Indonesia, in the early hours of the morning. Together we searched for my luggage, but it had *not* made the flight and was doubtless still sitting in Dallas Airport. They drove me out to Biola University (where I was to be ministering all week, in the student missionary convention) and they left me with the porter who said he would take me to my room. We walked across the compound, he let me in to one of the girls' dormitory blocks, and told me I was in Room H. Making my way down the dark corridor I found the room, went in and switched on the light, only to find an empty room. There was a bedstead but no mattress, let alone blankets or bed linen! I nearly burst into tears. I was tired, hungry, lonely, minus my luggage, and uncertain of what the week had in store for me. I probably dozed off, but wakened at the first sound of people in the corridor outside. Slipping out, I asked, rather sheepishly, 'Can anyone help me, please?'

This was met by an almost stony stare, which seemed to say, 'Whoever are you? and why do you need help?'

'I arrived during the night', I tried to explain. 'I am your missionary speaker for this week, and my luggage has not come. Could anyone possibly lend me a toothbrush and a comb?'

It must have sounded very stupid and lame. The girls certainly didn't leap to attention to do anything for me, though one did produce the requested articles. When they went for breakfast I followed them. In the dining hall I paused at the registration desk to explain who I was and immediately things began to happen. I explained to the lady who came to help me, and to give me an instruction sheet for the week, that I had arrived during the night, but that my suitcase had failed to come with me. And I mentioned that there was nothing in Room H. She was horrified and said this would be put right at once.

After breakfast, I managed to get to the first meeting where I was to speak to the 1,000 girls gathered in the big hall, on 'Why Missions?' The day wore on till bedtime when I found my bed made up, and a towel and some soap laid out for me. Exhausted, I fell into a deep sleep. Next morning, on the way to breakfast, I met some of the same girls I had spoken to the previous morning.

'Has your suitcase arrived yet?' they asked.

'No!' I laughed. 'While I am still wearing these clothes, you'll know it hasn't come!' And suddenly, their attitude changed.

'Come back with us after breakfast', they said. We went back to the dormitory together, and they showered me with gifts: night attire, a clean blouse, a nice skirt, and one girl brought me a teddy-bear for my bed!

Then they confided in me: 'We just didn't want another missionary to come and talk at us! We had all determined not to listen to you, and not to help you. But yesterday's talk got under our skin. And you were so uncomplaining, even when we had meanly emptied your room of all basic necessities. When you asked us to lend you a toothbrush ... that was the end!' We all roared with laughter together. Suddenly, I found I was accepted, one of them, and it all happened because I had lost my luggage!

Was God trying to teach me not just to *say* that I believed in Romans 8:28 *'We know that in all things God works for the good of those who love him, who have been called according to his purpose'* but actually *to believe* it. Even lost luggage can be part of God's overall purpose ... if I am willing to see it that way.

The luggage eventually turned up, just in time for me to leave with it the following Monday morning for Columbia Bible College. Over the years, I have been to CBC many times, and I love every visit. They packed my three days with eight or more opportunities to speak, including talking to the girls in their sitting-rooms. As usual, their questions included 'How did you cope with being single?' And they were a bit nonplussed when I said that singleness is a privileged gift from God, and one that was to be accepted with both hands. Then, surprisingly, the men asked me if I would share with them. 'Why should you talk to the girls and not us?' they wanted to know.

'What do you want me to talk about?' I asked.

'The same as you talked about to the girls!' they replied.

Well, we did discuss some fairly deep questions, particularly relating to the sufferings that our group of missionaries underwent during the Congo Rebellion of the 1960s. I shared some of the horrific stories of what others suffered, especially of one married man, tied to a tree, who was made to watch those wicked men rape his wife. 'How does one *then* obey the commandment: "Love your enemies"? What does that command mean in that sort of context?' I asked. I pray that none of those men will ever have to face such a situation, but should it ever occur, maybe they are a little better prepared to deal with it.

Throughout the ten weeks, there were ten women's outreach meetings. I always shrank from these, saying that I was not naturally an evangelist. That may sound strange coming from a missionary. But all my ministry in Africa had been with Christians, teaching them, building them up in their most holy faith, training them to be evangelists. We always said that all our college graduates were 'medical evangelists', but I myself had very little direct contact with unsaved people. Of course, most of the patients in our hospital were not Christians, but the problem there for me was one of language. We could have twelve or more languages spoken in the wards at any one time, and most of my medical work had to be done through interpreters. I could certainly take ward prayers through an interpreter. Our hospital chaplain, Agoya, was an excellent interpreter. But he was also an excellent evangelist, so it always seemed better that he preached in the wards, while I taught the students.

Now I was faced with the challenge of presenting the gospel, not now to simple nationals in a primitive part of Congo, but to sophisticated, well-educated people in the western world, most of whom had heard the gospel before, and either rejected it or neglected to make a response. This was a different ball-game.

Slowly, over the first three years of deputation ministry, a particular presentation took shape for reaching out to women in these evangelistic efforts, remembering there would be non-Christians there, as well as young believers and probably also mature servants of the Lord. As so often in other situations, I used a flannelgraph to hold their attention—a bicycle wheel, with all its spokes and the hub and the outside rim. The *hub* represented Christ, utterly essential as the pivot around which all else moved. The *spokes* were ourselves, each in our own individual place, rightly related to the hub, and 'well-oiled' to assure smooth running. The *rim* represented each one's little bit of world. The spoke was needed to put the hub in touch with its bit of world, transferring the strength and power from the hub to the rim. When the wheel was moving fast, the hub and the rim could be seen, but the spokes became a blur. Were we willing not to be noticed or thanked, so long as the hub remained related to the rim?

The whole talk was based on Paul's words to the Christians at Colosse: '*Complete in Him.*' Are we complete *in* Jesus, or incomplete because we have never accepted Him and the wonderful salvation He offers us? Do we run like an un-oiled bicycle, all creaking and rusty, what I called a cr-cr-Christian, always grumbling and complaining! Or are we like a well-oiled bicycle, running smoothly, uncomplaining, even in the face of difficulties? It has been amazing how graciously God has blessed that message in so many different places. I never cease to wonder at God's power to inspire in us new ways of presenting the precious, age-old gospel, to meet the needs of all people everywhere.

4

Digging Ditches in Australasia and in Dealing with Hurts

At the close of 1979, *Living Sacrifice*, the first of the series of four books that I was attempting to write for WEC on the mission's Four Pillars, was actually published, and it was an exciting day for me. I sensed that God was telling me to keep on with the writing ministry, even in the midst of all the speaking engagements. I confess I had no training whatsoever in the techniques of writing, but many friends helped in getting the manuscript ready for publication. The initial scribbling of the proposed contents of each chapter and the overall format was not particularly difficult. But the long process of checking, cutting out, filling in, spelling, construction of sentences and paragraphs … I found that tedious. Had friends not kept me at it, I would probably never have completed the project. But now it was published and I could turn my mind more fully to *Living Faith*, the next in the series.

I was preparing for a four-month tour of Australasia, from January to April 1980, visiting from Townsville in North Queensland, south to Tasmania, across to New Zealand, westwards to Adelaide and Melbourne, and eventually to Perth. The tour was arranged by three groups planning together: the InterVarsity Students' Christian Unions (UCCF), the Christian Women's Clubs International (CWCI), and my mission, WEC International. Then something occurred. With hindsight, it would be easy to say that the devil was not happy, either with the publication of *Living Sacrifice* or with the planned tour of meetings and all the people who would be challenged. It was not so easy to see things like that at the time.

Someone with whom I was staying in the autumn misunderstood my meaning in a certain conversation we had together, and sadly this person was convinced that I had lied. I gave assurance that not only had I not said what I was believed to have said, but I had not even thought along those lines. I was sad that this friend did not seem to know me well enough to know that I would not lie. And I was hurt by the accusation, possibly more deeply hurt than I realised. I was, of course, afraid that the statement that I had lied would spread rapidly, at least among our mutual friends, and just as the book *Living Sacrifice* was going on sale. I wanted to stop this and to clear my name, to proclaim my innocence of this particular offence.

Then certain events from the past came forcibly back into my mind. During my first year in Congo, I shared the home of my field leader and his wife, Jack and Jessie Scholes. They were like parents to me, helping me to settle in and learn the language and customs of the country. During that year, Jessie became very ill with Black Water Fever and I nursed her for three months. One day, while resting in my room for the midday siesta, a knock at the back door roused me. I slipped my feet into bedroom slippers, and quietly went to open the door, hoping not to waken Jack and Jessie who were also resting. A visiting missionary from another village had come to visit Jack. I gave them both a cup of tea, then left for my afternoon clinic.

During the following week, a letter came from that visitor to Jack. Having read the letter, he sent for me to come to his study, passed it to me, and left me to read it. There was a suggestion in the letter that, to a casual observer, my presence *in bedroom slippers* in their home at midday might be misinterpreted as Jack was also resting there. The inference was that there could be a wrong relationship between us. My immediate reaction was one of furious indignation, not that *I* was under suspicion, but that *Jack* was. Jack was the most godly person I have ever met. His life reflected the loveliness of Jesus, and I simply could not bear that anyone could possibly suggest that he might have done or thought anything improper towards me or anyone else. I felt the letter should be destroyed and utterly ignored!

Jack came back into the study, and I burst out, with all the indignation that stirred in my heart. He waited quietly for me to finish my outburst, and then, taking the letter from me, spoke quietly and gently. 'No, Helen,' he said. 'To tear the letter up and ignore the implied criticism is simply one way of declaring "we are innocent", one way of self-vindication.' Hardly listening to his further explanation, I said: 'But we *are* innocent! The inferred criticism is grossly unfair and untrue!' 'I know, I know,' Jack agreed patiently, 'but "Vengeance belongeth to the Lord!" We don't have to vindicate ourselves. Leave the Lord to work that out in His own way and time. Wouldn't it be better if we found you another house to live in, and so silence any such implied criticism, whether true or untrue?'

It was beyond me! I felt such a course of action was tantamount to agreeing that the accuser had a point. But I accepted Jack's suggestion, believing strongly that he always spoke prayerfully and with much deeper wisdom and maturity than I had. I left their lovely home and went to live in a couple of rooms in what was known as the Guest House. I went over and over Jack's reasoning, asking the Lord to help me accept and believe what he had said. I looked up all the Bible references about taking vengeance and about self-vindication.

Starting with 1 Peter 2:21-23:

> *To this you were called, because Christ suffered for you, leaving you an example, that you should follow in his steps. "He committed no sin, and no deceit was found in his mouth." When they hurled their insults at him, he did not retaliate; when he suffered, he made no threats. Instead, he entrusted himself to him who judges justly.*

I then turned to Deuteronomy 32:35, and to where this is quoted in the New Testament in Romans 12:19-21:

> *Do not take revenge, my friends, but leave room for God's wrath, for it is written: "It is mine to avenge; I will repay," says the Lord. On the contrary: "If your enemy is hungry, feed him; if he is thirsty, give him something to drink. In doing this you will heap burning coals on his head." Do not be overcome by evil, but overcome evil with good.*

The more I read and prayed over these words, the more I saw that Jack lived them. But I found it unbelievably hard to want to give myself wholly to implementing them. Certainly from that time on, it was implanted deeply in my heart and mind that 'Vengeance belongs to the Lord'. That must mean that we are not to indulge in self-justification.

Shortly after that episode, there was another occurrence that underlined the principle involved. Ninety miles south of Nebobongo, on the other side of the gold-mine mountain range, there was a small forest village where WEC missionaries had laboured for many years to establish a church among the WaBari people. A couple there were expecting their first child. It had been arranged that I would go to stay with them and see the young wife safely through the birth. However, I then had a sharp attack of malaria, complicated by jaundice. Jack sent a runner to Buambi, to tell the couple the situation and suggest that they make their way north to Nebobongo, where the mother could be given all the care she needed. A somewhat abrupt reply came back, stating that they had no available means of transport, and reminding me of my promise to be available to them. Jack discussed this with me and I agreed to go. But I was angry as I considered their response was selfish, as they seemed to have given no thought to what that journey would mean to me, still weak from three weeks of sickness.

Jack knew exactly what was going on in my heart, and he remonstrated with me. 'I want to ask you to do something— not for me, not even entirely for yourself, but chiefly for Christ's sake. Go to them. Do all you can for them AND do not make too much of your illness. Just die to yourself, Helen, and the Lord will bless you. If you can accept that to this young couple down there in forest-land, your delay has caused distress and anxiety, God will help you go to them in humility and to ask their forgiveness for causing that distress.' Is this what the Bible means by 'going the second mile'? Somewhere, deep down in my heart, a chord had been struck though my rebellious anger sought to stifle it. I suppose I knew Jack was right, but I did not want to acknowledge it. I wanted the right to be angry and to proclaim my innocence of any implied accusation of negligence of duty.

God won that round. He taught me, and I learned slowly. That God did not always allow us to defend ourselves (or even each other) in certain circumstances, seemed hard to me, particularly if someone had clearly been wrongly accused or misjudged. Christ, for my sake, was misunderstood by His closest friends, and falsely accused by His enemies, yet He made no effort to defend Himself. '*As a sheep before her shearers is silent, so he did not open his mouth*' (Isa. 53:7). Was

I willing to so love God, with all my heart, that I would give up loving myself, and my reputation, and the importance of what others thought of me?

Sadly, I was slow to learn, and God in His patient mercy was willing to teach me the same lesson over and over again. Many years after this episode, when I was working far away from our mission area, at Nyankunde, an inter-mission medical centre, one of our WEC missionaries from Nebobongo visited me, partly for her own need of medical care, partly for a break from her heavy work-schedule. On her return to our WEC area of service, she reported to Jack 'certain goings on' at Nyankunde, that she had heard of, in which she understood that I was involved, and which seemed to her definitely contrary to our WEC principles. Jack wrote to me for clarification, and I was hurt. Should he not have trusted me, and known that I would not contravene a basic biblical principle in my service to the Congolese, even if others around me felt that it was in order for them to take the line of action that was being criticised? And anyway, why hadn't the missionary spoken to me first, to clarify whether I was involved or not?

My 'hurt' very easily turned to anger. I wrote a sharp letter to defend myself, to criticise the other missionary's action, and to expose Jack's lack of faith in me. Sadly, that was self-justification on a fairly large scale! But wasn't that reasonable action to take? However, I did not have peace in my heart, and I struggled for several days over the issue. At last, I wrote another letter of apology to Jack for the anger in my heart that prompted the first one, but I hadn't dealt with the anger in my heart towards the other missionary.

Not long after this, Jessie had to bring Jack to Nyankunde for major surgery and they stayed in my home. I had the opportunity to love them and serve them, as they had done for me 20 years earlier when I first arrived in Congo. It was a privilege. They were just so loving and uncomplaining. Jack was found to have cancer of the head of the pancreas, and there was little the surgeons could do for him except relieve the immediate cause of pain. I nursed him for a month, until he was able to return to Ibambi for his last few weeks before he died. During their stay with me, we talked through all my reactions to the accusation levelled against me. Jack gently assured me that he had never doubted my integrity, but had merely sought to give me the opportunity of an honest and simple explanation of the misunderstanding that had arisen, an explanation that he could then have shown to the other person. Why could I not learn? '"It is mine to avenge: I will repay," says the Lord.'

Yet again, years later, as I mentioned in the prologue, when I wrote to the Congo leadership, offering to return for three years to teach in the pastors' school, and I received no reply, I was hurt. Throughout the years the Lord had sought to teach me that, when I am 'hurt', I can be fairly sure that 'I' have got in the way of God's dealings, either with me or through me to others. If my 'I' was truly crucified with Christ, and I was truly indwelt by Jesus, He may indeed be *grieved* by wrongdoing, or false accusations, or misunderstandings by others who should have known better, but He will not be 'hurt'.

In 1979, when I was accused of lying by someone who should have known better (as I thought), just as I was preparing to leave for a long tour of meetings on the other side of the world, I was hurt once again. As I sought to commit the matter to the Lord, all these past occasions welled up in my mind. I knew God was saying to me, yet again, in His infinite patience, 'Trust Me. Leave the whole affair with Me.'

As we approached Christmas, this person rang my friend Pat at home, and asked her how she could continue to be my friend, knowing I had lied. Pat was ready to jump to my defence. When Pat and I had discussed the whole situation previously, I explained as nearly as I could what had actually occurred, and the conversation we had had. Really it was not hard to see how a misunderstanding could have happened, but the person was unwilling to concede there was any possibility of a misunderstanding, remaining adamant that the conversation was remembered verbatim. There was, therefore, no room for any explanation. The letter I sent asking for forgiveness if I had given any cause for misunderstanding was rejected. It was not accepted as a valid apology because it contained no acceptance of the fact that I had lied.

Pat accepted unquestioningly my explanation, and was assured that I had not, either intentionally or unintentionally, lied, but simply that something somewhere had been misinterpreted and misunderstood. So, when the phone call came complaining about my attitude, and my unwillingness to apologise, Pat was ready to leap to my defence. 'No, Pat, please don't!' I remonstrated. 'We must leave it to the Lord. We must not justify ourselves, nor can we justify one another. Vengeance belongs to the Lord.' Somehow, it is easier to accept that for oneself, but much harder to accept it for a loved one. It hurts so much more when someone you love is falsely accused. That is what Jack Scholes tried to teach me all those years ago: I could not defend him, any more than I could defend myself.

I packed and left for Australia with this unresolved burden in my heart. When I arrived at our WEC headquarters in Sydney, I was told there were a few more meetings booked than had been on the list they had sent me. Of immediate importance was a series of meetings at Canberra University, for the executive members of all the University Christian Unions across the length and breadth of the country. They always met together in early January for teaching and fellowship to prepare them for the ministry of the new year.

Michael Baughen was to give a series of five or six Bible studies on prayer, and I was asked to give three addresses of missionary challenge. I spent the weekend trying to sort out my material and prepare for those very strategic meetings with some 200 students.

Arriving at the Canberra University Campus, I found I was sharing a very nice duplex with Michael and his wife in the other half. At the fourth of his Bible studies, when he was speaking about praying for those who hurt us, persecute us, or hate us, I sat at the back of the auditorium thinking, 'Well, I don't have anyone like that. I don't hate anyone', when suddenly the whole recent 'saga' leapt into my mind.

'Lord, this person may have accused me falsely, but I don't hate!' I tried to say. 'Do you pray for this person?' the Lord nudged me. 'Well, no, I don't.' Could I? I didn't want to think about it, but I couldn't get the thought out of my mind. No, I did not pray for this person, and because of what had occurred, I did not really want to. I slipped out of the meeting during the singing of the last hymn and went back to our apartment to wait for Michael. I needed his help to deal with the self-righteous attitude in my heart. I boiled a kettle, got a tea tray ready for the three of us, and waited. Eventually there was a knock at the door, and a second-year engineering student was there. I brought her in and gave us both tea, presuming she also wanted to talk to Michael.

'Sorry Michael is so long in coming', I said to her. 'Is there anything I can do for you?' 'Oh,' she said, 'I haven't come to see Michael, but you.' I was embarrassed at having kept her sitting there waiting. 'Sorry,' I said, 'what can I do to help you?' 'No,' she replied, '*I* don't need anything, but I felt the Lord wanted me to come to ask you if I could do anything to help *you*. All this week you have looked so unhappy!' Amazed and humbled, I began to share a little bit of what was causing me such unease, and about which I was indeed unhappy.

And as I talked to her, suddenly I realised what God was trying to say to me. I almost laughed! 'Thank you, dear', I blurted out. 'I think I understand what the Lord is trying to say to me!' She obviously didn't, and I attempted to explain. When we were captured by guerrilla soldiers in the civil war in the 1960s, we never really felt hatred towards them. Even when folk asked us how could we forgive them for what they did to us, we were honestly puzzled by the question, as we had not thought in terms of needing to forgive them. We had known they were not Christians, that they urgently needed to be saved and to be forgiven by God (not us). In a way, that had been an easy lesson to learn and had left no particular scars.

But now, I believed the Lord was inviting me, in some very small measure, to understand a little more fully what the fellowship of sharing in His suffering might mean. Had He, our Lord and Saviour Jesus Christ, not been betrayed by one of His closest friends, one of His inner circle, when Judas kissed Him in the Garden of Gethsemane? And one outstanding factor in the trial scene leading up to Christ's crucifixion was that He, the Son of God, made no effort to resist or to justify Himself. Rather, we see the perfect fulfilment of what Peter says of Him:

> To this you were called, because Christ suffered for you, leaving you an example, that you should follow in his steps. "He committed no sin, and no deceit was found in his mouth." When they hurled their insults at him, he did not retaliate; when he suffered he made no threats. Instead, he entrusted himself to him who judges justly (1 Pet. 2:21-23).

I don't think that lovely young student really followed all that I was trying to say, but I thanked her earnestly for coming to see me and for obeying the Lord's prompting. After she left, I went to my room and wrote a letter to the person concerned, asking forgiveness for having harboured hard feelings, and also for anything in our conversation that fateful evening that could have made possible the misunderstanding of what I was actually trying to say. I was about to stick the aerogramme up and address it, when I was assailed by an urgent sense that something wasn't right. In fact, I was convinced that I was not to send the letter. Why ever not? I was so sure that I would have peace of heart once the letter was written. I felt I could almost be joyous at last for the first time in three months! Now what was wrong?

I sat and prayerfully re-read what I had written, and the Lord enabled me to realise that this very letter was a subtle way of surreptitiously vindicating myself. The person concerned had no idea that I had hard thoughts, or that I felt that they were in the wrong about what had occurred. I was feeding such thoughts in my letter in order to vindicate myself. In other words, I was practically saying, in a veiled way, that I had no reason to ask for forgiveness as I considered myself free of fault, that no-one had any real justification in demanding me to seek forgiveness from them. That may sound extraordinarily convoluted reasoning (and grammar, but that is to preserve the anonymity of the person concerned), and I certainly hadn't thought it all out like that. But I came to see that was the implication of what I had written, and I knew God was asking me to tear up the letter, and not to send it. I tore it up, and then I had an intense consciousness of peace.

That was the beginning of a long and fairly exhausting but very exciting tour of meetings. From the beautiful capital city of Australia up to the heights of the Blue Mountains to the Keswick Conference Centre for a youth convention, with four meetings of 800 young people. It rained almost all weekend, and the convenors were thrilled. Because of the heavy rain the young folk came to all the meetings (it was dry in the hall!) instead of going off walking or playing ball games in the grounds. I can still remember how delighted I was when a crowd of them responded to the challenge to be willing to go wherever the Lord might call them.

From there I travelled north to Townsville in Queensland, and was it hot! The dry heat, touching on 40 degrees centigrade, was something I had never experienced before. At the morning meeting in the Salvation Army Hall all the fans were going in an attempt to make it bearable. Folk started coming in, some having travelled huge distances to get there. I was trying to find a way to fix my flannelgraph visual aid so that it would not be blown off the board by the air currents from the fans when, suddenly, there was a power cut! Certainly the flannelgraph was happy, but the heat in the hall was almost unbearable, especially as we slowly packed in nearly 300 people. Bless them, they endeavoured both to sing and to listen. Then, as suddenly as it had gone off, the power came on again.

Through Rockhampton, I travelled to Brisbane then south to Tasmania, and seven meetings with the students at our WEC Missionary Training College. One afternoon, as I was driven by a friend on the college staff to see the locality, we passed through places with wonderful Cornish names. My friend didn't know that I was of Cornish origin, and I could hardly believe I wasn't home again! Then we came to a village, in the centre of which there was an old wooden building with its name proudly carved in a wooden beam, 'Roseveare's Inn'. I was told that one of my ancestors had come across with the first convict ship to Hobart in the south of the island to open an inn to serve the prison warders on their days off!

Following a women's meeting one morning in Ulverston, a lady asked me over the luncheon, 'Did you notice the mirror in ...'s room?' and she named the child in whose bedroom I had slept that night. Strange question. I thought a moment, and replied, 'Quite honestly, no.' I had noticed all the toys, dolls, teddy-bears, and numerous creatures with wobbly eyes, but I could not recall the mirror. What was special about it, I wondered? I went back to the same home the next evening, and I looked carefully, but really there was nothing special to note. Puzzled, I pondered why the questioner had asked me about it. Then a line of thought came to me, and I believe the Lord was opening my eyes to a new perspective.

When we look in a mirror, we don't really want to see the mirror at all, but our image in the mirror. In fact, we probably only notice the mirror itself if it is dirty—splashed with toothpaste or misted up—so that we cannot see our face clearly. God wants our lives to mirror the loveliness of the life of Christ. We, as Christians, want others to see Jesus in us rather than looking at ourselves. In fact, if people notice us, and remember us in any detail, it almost certainly means that we have been in the way of their seeing Jesus. Any sin, any 'dirt' in my life, will hinder others seeing a clear reflection of Jesus.

As I thought this through, I was reminded of a lovely illustration of this same truth, from my early days in Congo. I had been invited by one of the church catechists to cycle with him to visit a native gold-mine in the southern mountains. Doubtless that was illegal, in those colonial days, and so well-hidden from public view. Arriving in the crater area, where all the palm trees had been cleared away, we saw this lake of boiling gold. Men, stripped to the waist, pouring with sweat, stoked the firing holes of an underground kiln. The worst impurities had already been drained away and this was the final purification method, the 'blowing off' of any residual impurity as exploding gas. To one side, there remained one solitary palm tree.

'Why the one tree?' I asked.

'I'll show you!' and the guide crossed over to the solitary palm, shinned up to the top fronds, and called out to a colleague, 'Haul!' I then noticed a liana-rope stretching from the top of the palm tree to a tree stump on the opposite side of the lake of molten gold. As an African hauled on the rope, the palm tree, with our guide precariously hanging on, bent down over the surface of the lake. 'OK!' and the helper slowly released the rope: the palm stood up erect, and our guide came down and crossed to us. 'What on earth were you doing?' I gasped. 'I am the watchman,' he explained. 'So what?' I demanded. And then came his explanation—so simple, so amazing—though I have never checked its scientific veracity.

'When I look down from above, while there are any impurities left in the gold the boiling surface is continually erupting in vast exploding bubbles, and I can see nothing clearly. But when the gold is absolutely pure, when I look down from above I can see the unruffled reflection of my face because the surface is completely still!'

As we cycled back home, I thought through that picture and realised that God is purifying our lives by continually stoking His kiln, to keep our inner selves, as it were, boiling. When the process is complete He will be able to see the unruffled reflection of His face in us. Isn't that the same as saying that the surface of my mirror must be absolutely clean so that others see Jesus, rather than me, when they look at me?

5

Digging More Ditches in Australasia and Dealing with Suffering

From Tasmania, I returned to Sydney for one night in the airport hotel, before flying over to New Zealand. But by the time I disembarked in Auckland, I knew I was sick. I really felt wretched. Actually, I often became airsick on flights, but this seemed worse than usual. It turned out to be the beginning of ten miserable days, possibly as a result of a mild form of food poisoning. The lady who met me and took me to her home to have tea before our first meeting was immensely patient with me. She had prepared a wonderful feast for my arrival but I was completely unable to touch it. Somehow we struggled through the five booked meetings with over 400 women at the CWCI Auckland Convention. I guess Mrs Betty must have been glad when WEC collected me! The whole of the next ten days became a blur; I just managed to stay upright for the duration of each meeting before having to lie down until the next one. I travelled south through North Island, across to South Island, and as far as Dunedin then back again to UCCF meetings in the University of Auckland and missed all the beauty of that wonderful land, but just managed not to have to cancel any booked meetings.

When I eventually reached the Stanwell Tops Convention Centre in New South Wales, I felt well again and able to cope with the programme. It was following a women's convention in Belgrave Heights, near Melbourne, that the next 'ditch' had to be dug. Some 2,000 women gathered in the large canvas hall for their annual gathering, prepared to hear God's Word and to be encouraged for the next year of service for the Master.

At the end of the Saturday morning session, as I was leaving the tent to make my way across to the dining hall, a little lady sitting in one of the pews, lightly touched me on the arm. 'Would you have time to help me?' she whispered. I felt guilty at having been in such a hurry that I had not really noticed her. Sitting down, I smiled encouragingly at her. 'Five months ago,' she started, 'my two-and-a-half year old son was drowned in our family swimming pool.' I immediately felt choked up; I could just feel her pain. I put an arm round her and waited for her to continue. 'My "Christian" friends told me to praise the Lord', she said. And as she spoke, I felt a rising anger in my heart. How could anyone speak like that to a young mother in the midst of her grief, possibly with guilt feelings too? Maybe they had left the gate open or some other such thing? I just knew that my loving heavenly Father would never have demanded praise from her in those circumstances.

'And when I could not praise God,' she continued, 'they told me I must have sin in my heart.' I cried out to God, asking Him to tell me what to say to this little mother. 'Not in the future, Lord; I need Your help right now!' But all that came into my mind was a sudden clear picture of the night I was taken captive by the guerrillas in Congo, nearly twenty years before. What was the connection? Why did the Lord remind me of that night in these circumstances? I knew that God had spoken to me that night in several different ways, but what exactly had He said? 'Please, God,' I prayed, 'tell me clearly now. What do You want me to share with Marge?'

As I was forced at gun point along the corridor of my home, there at Nebobongo, in 1964, the Lord told me that those evil men were not beating me, but seeking to beat Him in me. All He was asking of me was the loan of my body. Then He had seemed to add, 'Can you thank Me?' God was not asking me to thank Him for the evil; we never thank God for evil. We only thank Him for what He gives us, and He never gives us evil, even though He may permit us to go through evil. 'Can you thank Me for trusting you?' He seemed to ask. What an amazing thought! I can understand *me* trusting *Him*, but I had never thought of Him trusting me. So 'Can you thank Me for trusting you with this experience, even if I never tell you why?' was what the Lord had put in my heart and mind to share with those students at Twin City Bible Church in Urbana, just two years before!

I thought back quickly to that experience. Not only had it been terrifying and horrific, but also amazing and humbling, in the middle of that long-ago night, as I came to realise that God, who could have stopped the situation developing, who could have taken me out of it all, who could have prevented it going on, actually chose to trust me to go through it with Him as some part of His greater plan. It had seemed as though He was trying to reassure me that someone would be blessed, somehow, somewhere, at some future date. I had managed to stumble out, 'OK, God, though I don't understand how anyone can be blessed by this nightmare.' I was so sure that we were all going to be killed, and that no-one would ever know what we had suffered first. 'But if this is part of Your wonderful overall plan, Lord,' I prayed, 'yes, I thank You for trusting me to go through it.' Immediately, despite the pain and horror, there was an immense peace, right in the midst of the terror and pain.

I shared a little of all this with Marge, and asked her if she could thank God for trusting her with this tragic event, even if He never told her why. At first, she seemed to shut off from me; it seemed such a preposterous suggestion. It was almost as awful as those who just said, 'Praise the Lord!' But it wasn't. It was subtly different. Rather than being a blind, almost meaningless, use of words, it was actually a thought-out statement of faith, that God cannot deliberately inflict evil on us. He has promised to give us all good and needful things out of His glorious riches in Christ Jesus. But if He, Almighty God, believes we are ready to be entrusted with a deeper level of sharing in the fellowship of His sufferings, that we are ready to trust Him utterly when everything seems to cry out against such a trust, then yes, we can thank Him for trusting us in such a manner, and so allow Him to guide us through the pain.

Eventually Marge reached through the darkness of her grief, and she prayed through her streaming tears, 'OK, God, I don't understand You. I don't see where there can be blessing in this. But I want to thank You for trusting me with this tragedy.' We hugged each other and we wept together for a short time, then together we thanked God for the restored peace in our hearts. Three years later, when I was back in that part of Australia for more meetings, I stood in the doorway of a Baptist church shaking hands with people as they left. A lovely, bright-faced lady came towards me, her hand outstretched. 'You don't remember me, do you?' I certainly did; it was Marge! 'I've prayed for you every day for the past three years', I assured her.

Then she told me the sequel to that story. Marge returned home from the convention in March 1980, to share my words to her with her husband. At first he did not want to hear. But eventually the day came when, together, the two of them knelt together and said, 'Thank You, Lord, for trusting us with this tragedy. Please work out Your perfect will through it.' They then knew a wonderful inner peace. Later that very week, Marge told me, 'a child ran out of a garden lower down our road, and was killed by a passing car. The parents were not Christians. In fact, they were of another faith. But because they saw how we had been helped to come to terms with the death of our son, they let us comfort them. During these past three years, first the mother, and now also the father, have come to faith in Jesus!' I praised the Lord with her. How gracious of Him, that He should let us see and understand at least something of the 'Why?' So many, many times in the succeeding years the Lord has given me opportunities to share that word from Himself with others: 'Can you thank Me for trusting you with this experience, even if I never tell you why?'

It was also during that first tour of meetings in Australia that I was asked repeatedly by women, 'Why does a God of love allow such suffering?' I took it that they meant 'Why did God allow you missionary women to suffer the appalling brutalities and savagery that you went through in the civil war in Congo?' Hadn't we given our all to serve Him? 'Why didn't He protect you?' they asked. I felt there was almost an implied criticism of God, as though He had treated us badly in allowing us to go through a certain amount of suffering. I began to put my thoughts on paper in order to seek to answer this searching question. This exercise proved to be a tremendous blessing to me. As I have shared these thoughts with many other groups in the past twenty years, I have seen God bless so many so richly, often liberating them from feelings of bitterness or hardness of heart towards God, and also from the syndrome of 'pity me' which can so easily blight our spiritual lives when we let it take over.

It seems to me that the question, 'Why does a God of love allow suffering?' is a contradiction in itself. It is *because* God is a God of love that He allows suffering. When we think back to the beginning of all things, we know 'God is.' That ever-present-tense God created humans to be His friends, who would love, worship, and serve Him. If we are to love Him, we have to be free to choose to do so. Love by compulsion is not true love. The very fact that He created us with the freedom to choose to love Him means that we had to be free to choose *not* to love Him. God knew that some would do just that. So He was faced with the awful dilemma of how to bring someone back into relationship with Himself, someone who had freely chosen to break that relationship. So (as I understand the Scriptures) before God ever created us, He planned our redemption. He knew from the start of time there would be the necessity for His beloved Son to die in our place.

From earliest time, in the Garden of Eden, man was given a simple command to obey, in order to show that he chose to love God. At the same time, he was told the consequence of disobedience, disobedience that would show that he loved himself more than God: *'The Lord God commanded the man, "You are free to eat from any tree in the garden; but you must not eat from the tree of the knowledge of good and evil, for when you eat of it, you will surely die"'* (Gen. 2:16-17).

So God ordained from the start of life that: *'The wages of sin is death'* (Rom. 6:23). Man chose to disobey that first simple command, and so deserved to die physically and to die spiritually, to be separated from God eternally. God knew that the only way of redeeming man was for someone to accept man's deserved wages in his place; that is, for a substitute to be found to die instead of man. But that substitute would have to be without sin, otherwise he would have to die for his own sin and would be unable to die for the sin of others. But who was there without sin? *'For all have sinned and fall short of the glory of God'* (Rom. 3:23). In fact, earlier in the same chapter, we read, *'There is no-one righteous, not even one'* (Rom. 3:10).

The only One without sin is God Himself. So God planned for His own beloved Son to become flesh and to dwell among us men, in order to die in our place, as our perfect substitute. God *planned* the death of His Son *'before the creation of the world'* (Eph. 1:4). Why? He did it because He loved us! It was because of His love that God Himself suffered for us. God actually planned His own suffering because of His deep love for us. True love always leads to heart suffering: *'For God so loved the world that He gave His one and only Son, that whoever believes in Him shall not perish but have eternal life'* (John 3:16).

I can think of so many examples of this. True, they are only pale reflections of God's great love and intense suffering as His only Son became sin for us, *'so that in Him we might become the righteousness of God'* (2 Cor. 5:21). Hugh, a seventeen-year-old student nurse, recently saved, who was willing to give his life to protect me from death at the hands of rebel soldiers, because he loved me. Then there was Pastor Agoya, who was brutally beaten up, when blows were aimed at me, during those same days. And there was a missionary's teenage son, who saw his father savagely murdered by gunmen, who prayed that evening, 'Father, forgive the soldiers who shot my daddy. They did not know what they were doing!'

In each example, it is because of love that the victim is willing to suffer. A mother yearning over a teenager hooked on drugs, or a wife knowing that her husband has failed to gain merited promotion because of his Christian testimony, would not suffer if they did not love. So when I faced the horror of the shame and the cruelty of the guerrilla soldiers, and God whispered to me, 'Can you thank Me for trusting you with this experience, even if I never tell you why?' He made it possible for me, by His overwhelming love, to accept the suffering. The amazing thought that He was offering me the privilege of sharing in some tiny way in the fellowship of His suffering was tremendous. Even at the time, even in the midst of the pain, God actually gave me His peace. And He took away from me, straight away, any desire to question Him or to ask, 'God, why?' I don't honestly think we can answer the question, '*Why* does a God of love allow suffering?' But we can accept from Him the enabling not to ask the question!

There have been opportunities to share these thoughts many times in subsequent years, and not just using the phrase, 'Can you thank Me for trusting you with this experience?' as though it were a charm or mantra, but sincerely moving through to that level of trust in our heavenly Father that can bring complete deliverance and peace. I remember one night at a Bible college in Central Canada, when I was on an extensive tour of meetings right across Canada, from Vancouver, British Columbia, in the west to St John's, New Brunswick, in the east, arranged jointly by Nell Maxwell of 'Women Alive' and my mission through our headquarters in Toronto. A very distressed young lady came to my room one night about 11 p.m. after a public meeting in a Bible school in Saskatchewan, asking if I could help her. She told me that, as a young teenager, she had been raped, and that she had been helped by her family and their doctor to 'accept' the trauma. She had done so, to the best of her ability, and sought to put the matter behind her. Quite recently, she had married a good man, 'but I cannot bear for him to approach me! I freeze. The whole past rises up and frightens me! Can you help me, please?' she sobbed. 'I accepted the past, but I can't get rid of it!'

In those sort of moments, I feel like Joseph before Pharaoh, or Daniel before Nebuchadnezzar. 'No, I'm not sure that **I** can help you,' I said, 'but I know One who certainly can!' It was in this lady's repeated use of the verb 'accepted', that I sensed the problem lay. When we 'accept' bitterness or hurt or any other wrong inflicted on us by another person, we may lock the skeleton of the incident into a cupboard, and try to lose the key. But in the cupboard, with the skeleton, there is also a small grain of blaming God. When we unlock the cupboard, take out the skeleton, and looking straight into the eyes of our loving heavenly Father, thank Him for trusting us with the experience, even if He never tells us why, then He can free us completely from the pain, and remove from our heart even the tiniest grain of 'blaming Him' for having allowed the experience to occur. It is impossible to blame God at the same time as thanking Him!

As we moved through the planned tour of meetings in Australia in 1980, there were one or two lovely experiences that God allowed to encourage me to know that *He* was in charge, and that I could trust Him each step of the way. I think it was in Port Lincoln we had the first of the day's meetings at a women's rally, with the CWCI. I shared with the ladies, using the flannelgraph of the bicycle wheel, starting by explaining how I had come to know the Lord as my own personal Saviour through seeing a bicycle wheel padlocked to iron railings outside a church in Cambridge, when the thief had stolen the rest of the bike! Then years later, in the heart of Africa, having stopped for a coffee break on the long 300 mile journey from Kampala (Uganda) to Bunia (Congo), I was accosted by a herdsman, with the request, 'Are you a sent-one to tell me of something called Jesus?' Having shared the Scriptures with this man, with the use of the Wordless Book, I had the enormous privilege of pointing him to Jesus and explaining to him how he could accept the Lord as his Saviour. We prayed together and his face filled with a new-found joy.

As I went back to my car, an African cyclist passed by on his way to the local market, with a huge head of bananas on the carrier. At that precise moment, the hub of the front wheel of his bicycle gave way, and the man fell off. Man, bicycle and bananas spread across the road. Together we helped him up, repaired his bicycle, restored the bananas to him, and saw him on his way. I then turned to the herdsman, and told him *my* story of the bicycle wheel, padlocked to iron railings, that had been the start of my journey to salvation. The herdsman loved it. Africans are very quick to see and appreciate such picture language. And I drove away on my journey homewards, thanking God for His infinite goodness in making me stop at that particular clump of bushes, to meet with that particular man that particular day.

Having shared this story in the morning meeting at the Port Lincoln Women's Convention, everyone went back to their homes for their midday meal. When they returned to the town hall for the afternoon meeting, one group was brimming over with excitement, longing to share with me— and anyone else who would listen!—an amazing event. As they were walking home that midday, suddenly they had seen, bowling down the high street, unaided and alone, a bicycle wheel! Whether its hub was intact or not, I do not know! They just couldn't believe their eyes. But it really reinforced the story they had heard only that morning, and they said, 'We shall never forget that illustration!'

It was nearly at the end of that four months' tour that I reached Albany, in the southwest of Australia. At the rally there I was presented, not only with a beautiful bunch of flowers, but also with a very special gift that I have treasured ever since. It is a lovely little presentation box containing a silver spoon specially fashioned as a Kangaroo Paw, the emblem of the state. The spoon had been crafted by a master silversmith as a presentation gift for the Queen. But, I was told, they always make two on such occasions in case anything goes wrong with one of them, and I had been chosen as recipient of the second! I felt so enormously honoured that I have never used the spoon. It is still in its lovely presentation case. That was such a lovely climax to my first visit to the other side of the world.

At another meeting during a further visit to Australia three years later, in a large church with many university students in the congregation, I challenged them to ask what was holding them back from accepting the Lord's call to missionary service. At the close of my message, the pastor again challenged them all to ask what was holding them back from responding to the Lord's invitation to commit their lives to full-time service for Him. He made a few suggestions such as, to the girls, 'Are you asking the Lord to let you get married first?' and to the fellows, 'Can I just complete a second degree course first, so as to have added security for my future?' Then he said, 'As we sing our closing hymn, if you are willing to give that 'thing'—whatever it is, that is holding you back from total commitment to God—to Him, then would you just come forward as we sing? Don't tell me what the 'thing' is, but be willing to tell God, and to hand it over to Him without reservation!'

As we sang the last hymn, and a few came forward to the front, I watched three young girls sitting in the front row at my right. They appeared to be about fifteen, thirteen and eleven years old. The middle one looked as though she would have liked to come forward, but did not. As the service closed, I went down to speak to her. But the three saw me coming, and bolted out of a side door! So I sat down where they had been, and turned to speak to the ladies in the row behind. One of them was quietly crying. I spoke to the others first, and then turned to her and asked if I could be of any help.

As she spoke, the lady's voice told me at once that she was an American rather than an Australian. She and her husband had gone to Australia a year before as missionaries to the aboriginal peoples. 'We have two daughters', she said. 'The 15-year-old has fitted straight into her new school and is enjoying our new life here. But the 13-year-old ...' and her voice trembled. With tears flowing, she continued, 'She has completely changed her character. She is tearing our family apart. Even at school she is causing trouble. We just don't know what to do to help her!' Then she asked me, 'Are we wrong to force our children to follow us, even though we are so sure of our calling to be missionaries here?' Then she added, possibly by way of explanation, 'Back home, we lived on Grandma's farm, and she had a horse.'

I was unsure how to answer the question she had asked, and as I was praying for direction, two of the three girls arrived at the end of the pew. I just guessed that one of them would be the thirteen-year-old. I greeted them both, 'Good evening!' One said a polite, 'Good evening!' The other said, 'Hi!' The first was obviously a local Australian girl, the second an American. I chatted for a moment with the Australian, and then turned to the American. 'You don't belong here, do you?'

'No!' was the short, sharp answer. She had no intention of being drawn into conversation. I tried again, 'It's not easy living in someone else's country, is it?'

Again, an abrupt 'No!'

We carried on a monosyllabic conversation for a short while, and I was beginning to feel frustrated, unable to break through her resistance. Then the pastor sent someone to call me to go to the back of the church to talk to some students. A short time later I returned to the church to collect my Bible, and the 13- year- old met me in the aisle. 'Was I too young to come out tonight?' she asked me bluntly.

'No! Did you want to?'

'Yes!'

'OK,' I said, 'Let's go out together now.' So we went together to the low steps at the front of the church and knelt side by side. 'You just tell the Lord Jesus what it is that you want to give to Him', I encouraged. There was a silence, and then she began to sob. I repeated my suggestion and waited quietly. Then, with tears running down her face, she burst out, 'My horse!'

'That's lovely, dear', I said, suppressing any surprise. 'Let's just give the horse to Jesus.' We prayed together, as she gave her beloved horse to the Lord.

With a radiant smile, through her tears, she turned to me and said, 'My mum and dad aren't half going to be pleased. I've made their lives hell!'

'And now are you determined to change that?' I asked.

'Yes! Yes indeed. I just want to make their lives heaven, and to help them to be the missionaries they want to be!' She was just 13, but she had known what she was holding on to that was spoiling her life and making her family so unhappy. I wonder how many of us have hidden 'horses' in our lives that we don't want to give up to the Lord.

6

DIGGING DITCHES AMONGST UK SCHOOLGIRLS

There had to be a tremendous switch in gears before the next year of ministry started. The Girl Crusaders' Union (GCU) approached WEC International, my missionary society, to ask if they would 'lend' me to them for a year to head up what they were calling, a 'Forward Movement'. GCU came into being in 1915 during the First World War, when a group of ladies became burdened for schoolgirls they saw, especially on Sunday afternoons, wandering aimlessly on the streets with no-one apparently caring about them. Encouraged by some Christian men who, a few years earlier, had started Crusaders—Sunday afternoon Bible classes for schoolboys—they took the plunge and brought into being the GCU. The idea caught on, and in a very short time classes opened all over the south of England, then in the north, across into Ireland, up to Scotland and eventually in Wales. A council was formed to safeguard the aim of the union, which was to teach the Bible in such a way that girls came to a knowledge of the Saviour and grew in their faith into mature Christian women. A badge could be earned by attending ten classes, and a Bible was presented to any girl who attended a further fifty classes. A regular magazine was started and Easter and summer camps organised. Interclass activities and sports days attracted more girls to join. Women were only appointed to leadership of these groups after being interviewed to be sure that they truly loved the Lord, knew Him personally as Saviour, had a good grasp of the Scriptures and knew how to present biblical truth in a way that girls would be drawn through them into an assurance of personal salvation.

During the first sixty years of its existence over 150 Classes were opened, with a total membership of over 5,000 girls. A Bible correspondence course (Lones) had 2,000 girls actively taking part, and 1,500 ex-Girl Crusaders had joined the Associate Fellowship as prayer partners, and over 700 girls had attended the Easter and summer camps. On average one ex-Girl Crusader every month had gone overseas to preach the gospel in a missionary capacity. The union was thriving.

But in the 1970s and 1980s, like so many other Christian youth organisations, numbers were dropping. Groups were fewer and smaller, and it was proving harder to gain and keep Leaders. The Central Council, after much prayer, decided to launch a 'Forward Movement Year' to increase the public image of the GCU, to explain to the parents what the union was seeking to do for their girls, to challenge each girl in every Group with their personal need of salvation, and to present a clear missionary challenge to all those girls who truly loved our Saviour. Would WEC lend me to them for that year? After prayerful consideration, the British home staff of WEC International agreed to this suggestion. Their Leader, Robert Mackey, led a dedication service in GCU Headquarters to launch this special effort. That same evening we had our first meeting, a seniors' supper with thirty senior girls from London Groups.

For me, the mental switch involved in changing from preparing material to present to university students, church congregations and women's meetings, to thinking in terms of schoolgirls—from six-year-olds in primary schools to 18-year-olds, taking their final exams in secondary schools—was not exactly easy. Very little of the material I had used in the previous five years was applicable to this new task. Also the difference between speaking to a school assembly of five-to-seven-year-olds, and seeking to communicate meaningfully with a roomful of sixteen-to-eighteen-year-olds, was enormous, far greater than the differences between the various groups in the previous tours. The Lord gave me a lovely bright yellow Fiat 127 for the year's work, and it became very well known all over the UK. Girls made maps, marking in all the GCU groups in England, Scotland, Wales, and Ireland and, using a small model of my yellow car, they followed my progress week by week. At the same time as this Forward Movement Year was launched, I was trying hard to complete the preparation of the manuscript of *Living Faith* for the publishers.

Two camps in the summer holidays, both in Scotland, with Bible studies and missionary challenge talks to the girls, and morning devotional talks to the leadership, helped to get my mind attuned to the task ahead. That October we started in earnest, with forty meetings all over Scotland in the first month. Everywhere I was given such generous, loving hospitality by leaders. Everywhere girls came and listened well in their various group meetings. Every now and then a public meeting was arranged to introduce a wider audience to the work of the GCU, and to encourage other parents to send their girls to our weekly groups. Three meetings were arranged on successive Monday evenings for 'Teens and Twenties' in the Glasgow area. Some sixty young folk came each time and seemed very receptive to a missionary challenge: the world we live in today in all its need; the God we love and worship in all His power to supply that need;

ourselves, the means God graciously chooses to use to channel His supplies to meet that need.

Visual aids were definitely part of the plan of campaign. Several times, using the letters G—C—U—'God' in His great grace on one side of the board, 'Us' in our sinful and selfish need and lost to His saving power, on the opposite side, and the 'Cross' of our Lord Jesus Christ, the only way to bridge the chasm between us and God, a chasm caused by our sin. As Isaiah says: *'Your iniquities have separated you from your God.'* At other times, I used a large flannelgraph presentation of our GCU badge, and built it up. The white background represented God's standard of holiness. The big red Cross reminded us of our Saviour Jesus, the only Name by which we can be saved, and the four small crosses spoke of our response to His saving grace—to say 'No' to all that displeases Him, and to say 'Yes' to all that pleases Him. Finally the golden border reminded us that our Lord and Saviour is now seated in heaven, preparing a place for us and praying for us.

I was invited to speak at the Scottish Scripture Union Camps' Reunion in the midst of that month, and someone helped me to paint a large flannel background depicting Mount Everest and the way that explorers attempted to climb to the top. Using the four letters C—O—S—T, we followed that pathway, from the base camp (the need of Conversion to start the upward journey), up the icefall to the advanced camp (by Obedience to the map, and to the instruction book, wearing all the correct gear such as goggles and crampons). Then we traced the long haul in the shadow of the mountains to the assault camp, be it by means of Sacrifice or Service, even when the way seemed long and tedious, and when, at times, the final peak was hidden from view. And then, with our eyes on the goal, we looked at the last slog up to the summit, the wonderful Triumph when we finally reach the glory of the Lord's Presence. The responsiveness of those four hundred youngsters was so exciting, and that means of sharing God's challenge for wholehearted commitment to Him became a very popular presentation.

In Dundee we had the first of many subsequent weekends, from a Friday evening through to the Sunday afternoon. I used a flannelgraph of a lantern to illustrate the truth of Christian living. The frame of the lantern was used to point to our bodies in which Jesus wished to live. The wick, clean and long enough to carry the oil to the light, was used to portray our thoughts and minds. The glass, clean and without a crack, through which the light could shine, reminded us that our actions, our lifestyle, had to be consistent with our testimony. The oil that had to fill the lantern was a picture of the Holy Spirit with whom God fills us when we come to Him for forgiveness of our sins. And the LIGHT, being the Lord Jesus Himself, who comes into our lives when we open the door and invite Him in! Again, we were all humbled and awed at the gracious working of the Lord in the hearts of the thirty girls who were there that weekend.

There were special meetings, some for Leaders, others for parents or interested friends, and a number at church youth fellowships. Variety was the order of the day! With all the travelling involved, being available to chat to folk in the homes where I stayed, and writing letters before and after meetings, there was very little time for preparation of new material. I soon realised how essential it was to have time dedicated to such preparation between each section of the tour.

My work that year with GCU involved over 400 meetings and 24,000 miles of driving! I know it was very exhausting and yet, at the same time, strangely exhilarating. There were moments when things were far from easy. Some years previously, GCU had had another similar year with Miss Cicely Radley, a lovely, gracious lady, leading it. Reports of that year were impressive by their visible results. Many girls joined the groups, several in all parts of the country signified that they had heard the call of the Lord in their hearts and responded to Him, and some women went forward willing to become group leaders. Somehow, it wasn't quite so obvious this time … and I began to feel a failure. I knew perfectly well that we should not compare ourselves with others, and the results were all in God's hands, not ours. But nevertheless— perhaps particularly when weariness was the order of the day—I was caught in the snare. Then in the November, after a hectic four weeks in the London area followed by a time in south Wales, I heard that Pat's mother had to go into hospital for major surgery, just at the very time when Pat was moving home. And I wasn't there to help.

Someone who came to one of the open meetings told me after it that she had heard the same message a month before when she came to hear me in London. Did I only have one message? I nearly broke down and wept. 'What do they expect of me?' I cried out to God. There were two or three meetings every day, and in some places the same people turned up at several of these! Then I had a meeting with sixth-formers in a large girls' school, about 180 of them crowded into the room, and I had thirty-five minutes to speak to the subject, 'Can God really cope in the twentieth century?' followed by forty minutes of animated discussion.

Yes! Indeed Yes! God can cope in all situations, whatever the understood need. His power is the same today as it was 2,000 years ago when He worked such wonderful miracles in the days of Jesus Christ. And at that moment I sensed God's smile as He rebuked me for bothering to compare myself with another Christian worker, for questioning His timing about my not being at home when I felt I was needed there, and for reacting when someone indicated disapproval at hearing the same message twice. All that was necessary was that I knew I was in the centre of His will, seeking to please Him and trusting Him moment by moment. I had really no right to waste time feeling sorry for myself or getting angry with God. Had He not taught me several times in the past that it is all *privilege* to be invited by Him to have even a tiny part in His programme of reaching out to others?

There were many challenges during those months. One group celebrated its fiftieth birthday; another was a get-together of GCU Associates who were all senior citizens. Then there was a special meeting for parents where one father told me, 'I wouldn't send them if they were boys!' From that I gathered that, although not a church-going person himself, he was scared for his two daughters in today's world and wanted us to give them moral standards that would protect them from all that would assail them in the years ahead.

Prayer days with Leaders were specially blessed to my heart. I often shared with them thoughts from a sermon we had heard in our own church on the word '*Philotimeomai*', which apparently only appears three times in the New Testament, and which means 'Consider it an honour' (although often translated quite differently in our various modern English versions!). In 2 Corinthians 5:9 we read, '*we make it our goal to please him.*' In other words, if I realise what an honour it is that God condescends to be pleased with anything I do for Him, I will surely struggle to please Him at all times. Nothing will be too much trouble that is pleasing to Him. In 1 Thessalonians 4:11 '*Make it your ambition to ...*' Paul goes on to remind them of all he taught them about being Christ-like, about living lives that truly portray Jesus to others. If I realise that God allows me the inestimable honour of reflecting the loveliness of Jesus to others by living a Christ-like life, surely I will indeed study to portray Him more perfectly, more accurately? In Romans 15:20, we read: '*It has always been my ambition to preach the gospel where Christ was not known ...*' Should that not be my greatest desire, to strive to preach the gospel wherever the Lord sends me? If I realise what an honour it is to be entrusted with His precious gospel, I will leave no stone unturned to share Him with all whom I meet.

As we went through these thoughts together, with times of prayer between each, we asked God to make His Word alive in our hearts. These days it is so easy to have other ambitions and desires and motives than simply pleasing Him. How necessary it is to be willing to check out everything by this one standard: does it, will it, please God? Again, we were all very conscious that 'what you do speaks so loudly that we cannot hear what you say'. And we asked God to search deeply in our hearts and to reveal to us if there was anything in our daily lives that was spoiling the image of Jesus so that others could not see Him reflected in us. We earnestly wanted an ever-increasing willingness for the Spirit to 'conform us to the image of God's Son', to sanctify us and make us clean mirrors of His glory. Thirdly, we looked at our willingness—or lack of it—to buy up every opportunity to preach the gospel. How easy it often was, when it came time for the weekly group meeting, to feel 'Oh, no, I just don't want to go out to teach those girls!' or just to feel 'Can I not have one afternoon free to myself? Does it have to be *every* week?' And we asked God to deal with that part of our nature that shrank from total involvement in this task of preaching the gospel and teaching the girls committed to our care.

I always felt renewed and enabled to keep going after one of the days of prayer that were woven all through that year of ministry. How good of God to organise it in such a way! He knew my need, and He met it before I really became conscious of it.

It was back to Northern Ireland in December, for meetings that included a residential houseparty for some senior girls, two carol services, and three meetings in

Belfast with 'Teens and Twenties', and a Camps' Reunion, with ninety girls from all over the Province. Their excitement was infectious, and really was a rebuke to any feeling of weariness or wondering if what I was doing had any eternal value.

Just after Christmas there was a Union-wide Camps' Reunion in London with over 200 girls in attendance. That was marvellously exciting! Girls who had first met at the summer camps met up with each other and chatted away twenty to the dozen. All sorts of camp-like activities took place in different rooms: crafts, team-games, even sweet-making. Then there was a Bible study for each age group before a magnificent tea, which was followed by 'the Challenge'. The talk, based on the word 'F-O-R-W-A-R-D', was illustrated by an enormous painting of a £100 note. I actually had a £100 note in my hand—a red note that the Northern Bank graciously 'lent' me in exchange for ten £10 notes that I 'lent' to them! On one side of the giant imitation note we attached the letters F, O, and R in turn— and we reminded ourselves of all we had learned in our groups and at camps throughout the past year: **F**orgiveness of sins, if we confess and trust in the blood of Calvary; how we must be **O**bedient to all God's commands that we read in the Bible, to show Him that we love Him; and how we can **R**ejoice in hope, knowing we are saved and kept by His Spirit. It was summed up in the phrase 'Christ died **FOR** us.'

Then we turned the huge note round and attached the letters W, A, and R. We are saved to do WAR against the devil and all his wiles, to overcome all his subtle temptations, and to stand up for Jesus 'no matter what'. We are to **W**itness with our lips; we are to be **A**pproved workmen, acting as Christians every day; and we are to **R**each out to others, telling them about our Saviour. In fact, we are to '**WAR** a good warfare!'

Having looked at each letter in turn, and thought about where each one of us was in our own Christian lives, we realised that God was challenging us to go forward with Him. We held the note up, while a helper shone a light through from behind it, and the girls saw a large **D** in the 'blank' watermark space. D was for 'Now then, **DO** it!' (1 Chron. 28:10, 20) was our final challenge, that we should go out into our everyday lives—at school, at home, when studying, when playing, wherever—and live for Jesus, seeking to 'please Him' in all the little details of life, as well as in the great big decisions that have to be made. That was our message to the girls and to us.

In the weeks that followed, letters came in from leaders of many of the groups in different parts of the country, from Tiverton in Devon, from Cardiff in Wales, from Harrogate in the north of England, and from groups around the London area. All these shared with us conversations they had had with their girls during the journey home about what they had enjoyed most about their day in London. Many shared how the Lord had spoken to them personally, and how they really wanted, by His enabling, to go **forward** in their Christian lives, asking the Lord to help them every day to be pleasing to Him. Our hearts were thrilled by God's gracious goodness to us in allowing us just a glimpse of what He was doing in girls' hearts. And that certainly gave me fresh courage to keep going into the new year.

Another Leaders' Quiet Day for those in the London area re-awakened in all of us a deep desire to go forward with God, to grow in grace and in knowledge of our Lord and Saviour Jesus Christ, and in an ever-increasing determination to be available to serve Him every day of our lives. We looked at the principles underlying revival in Scripture, concentrating on a passage in 2 Chronicles, from the close of chapter 28, where King Ahaz shut up the house of God and turned to the worship of foreign idols, into chapter 29, when Hezekiah *'did what was right in the eyes of the Lord'*. During sixteen days he cleansed the temple, carrying out all the accumulated filth that had gathered, then re-established, the sacrificial services. And in chapter 30 he gathered everyone together to 'return' and to 'submit themselves to the Lord their God.' We read *'The Israelites who were present in Jerusalem celebrated the feast .. with great rejoicing!'* By the close of that day we all sensed a renewal in our hearts and spirits, and an increased hunger and thirst to be pleasing to our God.

After a month of meetings in and around London and the Home Counties, the tour took me to the south coast, to Lansdowne, Ferndown, Wentworth, and Bournemouth. Several school assemblies brought a new challenge. We compared ourselves to civil servants, who can use the letters O-H-M-S (On Her Majesty's Service) on their letters instead of stamps. Only, as Christians, the letters stand for 'On **His** Majesty's Service'. We are called into the high profession of being God's civil servants, willing to be sent anywhere at any time, willing to do any job our Sovereign Lord King asks of us, and always knowing, without a shadow of doubt, that He will be wholly responsible for us—not just for stamps on the envelope! It was such a joy to share with them stories from my twenty years of missionary service in Congo, to illustrate how wonderfully I had proved this true in my own experience. He never fails us. He is always there, and always able, whatever the need.

From the south coast, I travelled up to the Midlands of England, for another Leaders' Quiet Day. We worked our way through the three chapters of the prophet Joel, seeing the exceptionally severe plague of locusts, wave after wave, in chapter 1, as a picture of all the wickedness of our day. We thought of laws that encourage immorality, lack of discipline in schools, industrial unrest, those who proclaim a post-

Christian era and that God is dead, the insidious attitude of 'what do I get out of it?' that pervades everything, the ceaseless demands for 'my rights'—until eventually nothing is left, anarchy rules and the soul withers away.

But this terrible picture is immediately followed by a call to repentance. Should the condition of our world not drive us to our knees? There is no other way out. A devastating fire in the midst of overwhelming drought had destroyed any possibility of recovery. They were surrounded by unutterable devastation. This led to a trumpet call to WAR against sin, to repentance, and to believing prayer.

Chapter 2 brought us to see the forebodings of the prophet. He saw the invasion of the locusts as a forecast of the anarchy of the last days. There is the inevitability of doom, the irresistible force of destruction as we read the prophet's description of the mighty army drawn up against them. Then in verse 11, the startling phrase: '*The Lord thunders!*' reminds us that He, and He alone, is at the head of the army at the last day. And the Lord's plea to us: '*Return to me with all your heart!* ' He wants us to plead with those around us, in His Name, as His ambassadors. '*Rend your hearts! Repent! Return to the Lord!* ' God challenged us. Were we awake to the awful responsibility laid on us to warn the girls committed to our care? A holy God must judge all sin and condemn all that is not according to His will. Dare we be silent? Once again, there follows a trumpet call to worship in repentance.

In our third session together we looked at the Lord's answer, and how precious are His promises! They are as real for us today as they were in the days of Joel. God's power had been doubted, His honour impugned, and His people reproached. Is it not the same today? Some say that God is dead! Others insist that God can't cope! And on television they make a joke of anyone portrayed as a minister. In Joel's day God was jealous for His great Name's sake. He *had to* intervene, and

He will yet intervene today. He promises complete and total relief from starvation, ridicule and oppression, and all with the wonderful purpose *'Then you will know that I am .. the Lord your God!'* (2:27).

There follows an even more wonderful promise of not only material blessings, but also spiritual blessings. We must repent and be transformed, made conformable to the mind and will of God. He promised a great wave of spiritual revival. This began at Pentecost, at the birth of the church, and will find its fulfilment in that great and dreadful Day of the Lord *'... when everyone who calls on the name of the Lord will be saved!'* (2:32). I believe we all prayed that day with renewed earnestness for the lost, the mockers and the rejecters. We prayed that we would be found available to God, more than ever before, available to be His ambassadors to all those to whom He sends us, to warn them and pray for them.

I travelled on from there to Sheffield, Leeds, Harrogate, and Bridlington. There were some tremendous meetings: youth rallies and school assemblies, as well as church services. Each one was important; each one was different. Then I went over to Dublin, to a packed week, before returning home for a week to prepare for a hurried trip over to Canada for a weekend women's convention that had been arranged before the GCU tour was planned.

That took me to the final straight of this marathon. Throughout June I was to re-visit every place to which I had been during the year, and the GCU leadership was to organise 'rallies' in central places, where we could, by God's enabling, bring the challenges given throughout the many smaller meetings, to a head. Our prayer was that girls would come to the place of commitment, and step out with the Lord into a life of obedience. We started in Belfast then went across to Scotland where we held meetings in Dundee and Glasgow, before travelling south to York and Sheffield. The title was 'At the Crossroads'. One GCU Leader's husband had made us a superb visual aid—traffic lights, that actually worked! **Stop**—and listen to what God wants to say to you. **Caution**—there are so many dangers and pitfalls if you don't obey. **Go**—go forward with your hand in God's hand, trusting Him and His Word, obeying Him and enjoying Him, and the Lord will go with you every step of the way.

It was a tremendous month with eighteen rallies in all, and we wept many times as we saw the Lord at work in girls' hearts and lives. The final thanksgiving service in London at the end of June was a most humbling yet uplifting time, as together the leadership worshipped our Lord and Saviour and gave all glory to Him for anything that had been achieved during the year.

7

DIGGING DITCHES IN THE SLOUGH OF DESPOND

*L*iving Faith was published in 1980, and appeared to be well received. I needed to begin thinking seriously about the preparation of *Living Holiness.* There was only one important public commitment in the immediate pipeline, as I had been invited back to Urbana, to the Student Triennial Missionary Conference in Central North America in December 1981. The title for the whole conference was 'Let every tongue confess that Jesus Christ is Lord', and Eric Alexander was to lead the four Bible studies. As in 1976, the conference sought to challenge the 17,000 young students who would gather there for their Christmas holidays, with the *needs* of the 3,000 million still unreached people in our world, and with the fact of our *privilege*, as well as our responsibility to be available to God to meet that need. The theme of my particular talk was to be 'The Spirit's Enablement'. That seemed to fit well with the slowly forming thoughts about the next book on holiness.

But there were other matters of more immediate concern, matters that were distressing me. During three months at home in the autumn of 1981, I became assailed by feelings of failure, of doubts, of insecurity. It was probably incomprehensible to others. I looked like a very self-confident, capable sort of person. In the world's eyes I was what others would have called 'successful'. But serious doubts began to assail me. Was I in the centre of God's will? Why was I not back on the mission field when I knew how urgently doctors were needed, when I had the language already and understood a good deal of the culture and the thinking patterns of those in Congo? Was it *my* choice to be in a fairly cushy job, where there was no danger, no real sense of sacrifice, in which I was always treated with a red carpet, looked up to, even sought after? Alongside all this, there was a nagging fear of being a failure. Did I really represent WEC? Why did my prayer life not match up to the desperate world needs with which I sought to challenge others? And at moments, especially after a tour of meetings, I could almost lose the assurance of my salvation. Was it only head knowledge and not heart experience? Verses such as: '*so that after I have preached to others, I myself will not be disqualified for the prize*' (1 Cor. 9:27) nagged at me.

I had written in my Christmas prayer letter (1981/82) 'I am enjoying the privilege of a year to "*come apart for a while*", to be quiet with the Lord'. I was living at home, seeking to be a normal member of a family and of our local church, writing hundreds of letters as a ministry instead of merely as a necessity, studying and praying without specifically preparing messages for public meetings and without deadlines. WEC had both counselled me, and agreed with me, that it would be wise to take on no more public engagements until September of 1982, when they, at WEC headquarters, would co-ordinate my programme, thus helping me to avoid the over-booking that had tended to overwhelm me during the previous three or four years.

But underneath all that, mostly unknown to WEC or others, there was turmoil in my heart. I simply could not share my deep heartaches with anyone. I tried once, but felt immediately that the person to whom I wanted to unload recoiled and drew away from me. Then I nearly panicked.

So many people seemed to look up to me and respect me as a strong Christian, but if they knew the tempestuous battle raging inside my heart, would I hurt them? Would it shake their faith?

There were moments when it was so dark; I felt such a load of depression. I almost feared I was going to have a complete nervous breakdown. It was probably the result of what is commonly called burn-out (nervous exhaustion) from keeping up what some people thought was an unreasonable pace for so long. But knowing that did not help me to handle the problem. Sometimes it was like a crippling nightmare. Nevertheless, in the midst of it all, I *knew* that God *was* there, and that He *was* in control. I *had* to learn to trust Him utterly, to rest in Him and to cease from my own struggling. Besides everything else, I was suffering nightmares, re-living the horrors of the civil uprising in Congo, even though it was by then almost twenty years distant. I cried out to God for His mercy, for His deliverance. A small group of people prayed for me every evening, and one of the things they prayed for was that the Lord would give me calm sleep.

Then God seemed to say to me, 'Are you not willing?' And I sensed He was saying, 'This is a small price to pay if others are blessed by your testimony, if others are brought to see that I can preserve them in the midst of war and harassment and brutality. You have to re-live the experience as you speak of it or others will not sense the reality of all that occurred. And the greatest thing that occurred to you was that you had My peace in your heart even in the midst of the storm!' So was I not willing to suffer the nightmares? Was it perhaps, for me, the *'thorn in the flesh'* that Paul had prayed three times to have removed before God told him to accept it, not to pray to be delivered from it, and to receive the deep truth of that wonderful promise: *'My grace is sufficient for you, for my power is made perfect in weakness'* (2 Cor. 12:7-9)?

Through all of this, I was also struggling to know what God would have me share at Urbana. I was led to Judges 7, to the wonderful story of how Gideon was chosen by God to lead the people of Israel against the hosts of Midian, and of how God chose and equipped His crack regiment to go against the forces of evil. The *subject* of the Urbana convention was, surely, each individual student as a potential missionary in the hands and the purpose of God. The *object* was undoubtedly those people in the world, estimated at that time to be 3,125 million, still in total ignorance of the Saviour. There had to be a *verb*, and obviously that could only be the indwelling of the Holy Spirit, making it possible for the subject to relate to the object. The subject, each one of us, needed to be a clean vessel, filled with the Spirit of Christ: '*We have this treasure in jars of clay to show that this all-surpassing power is from God and not from us*' (2 Cor. 4:7). But if the vessel, filled with the water of life, stays at home, how can it satisfy the thirst of a dying world?

Not only that, but as I looked more carefully at how God equipped His army, I saw *empty clay jars* covering smoking flax, and trumpets to terrify the scared enemy. The clay jar was there simply in order to be smashed so that the flax would flare up as a beacon of light. As we allow God to smash us (our ambitions, our selfishness, our pride, our rights) the Light can stream out to a needy world. As the woman in Mark 14 smashed the alabaster jar of very expensive perfume and the fragrance filled the whole house, was I willing (am I still willing?) to be smashed—utterly poured out, nothing held back—that others may be blessed?

How can anyone say 'Yes!' to such a demand? Our 'yes' is only by the indwelling Holy Spirit. He alone is the enabler. He is indeed the Spirit of Christ, who was Himself the first and greatest of all missionaries. Jesus left His Father's glory to come from heaven to earth in order to die. He made Himself of no reputation, even becoming a slave. He put obedience to His Father's will before everything else. Was He not indeed a perfect *clay jar*, willing to be smashed that I might live?

'Am I willing to be like-minded?' I had to ask myself—to give up my rights, e.g. to be married, to have a family, or a job, or security, to let go of my reputation and to become wholly submissive to my heavenly Father's will? Would I actually be willing to die if that would enable God to reach dying men and women with the gospel? How could I ever reach such a standard? I could do it only as I asked the Holy Spirit to create such an attitude within me, making me 'like-minded to Christ'. He, the Holy Spirit was, and is, willing to move heaven and earth on my behalf to conform me to the image of God's holy Son, so that others will see only Christ in me, and not me myself. But without doubt, this has to involve a death to self. For years I have called this 'the crossed-out I life' of Galatians 2:20. '*I* [the ME who lives in me] *have been crucified with Christ and I no longer live, but Christ lives in me.*' Like the smashed clay jar in the Old Testament, or the smashed alabaster box in the New Testament, the contents— the light, the fragrance—could then stream out to the world in need.

When addressing the students at Urbana that year I touched briefly on the appalling need of the two thirds of our world out beyond the furthest reach of all missionary endeavour, still waiting to hear, for the very first time, the Name of Jesus. Then we looked at what seemed to me to be even more shattering than the plight of those millions, the apparent apathy of the Christian Church. I talked about the need of every missionary-sending agency for men and women sold out for God, in an abandonment of love '*to serve him without counting the cost, or seeking for any reward, save that of knowing that we do his will*' that was so overwhelmingly apparent.

But again, I asked, who can possibly give such devoted service? Only someone indwelt and ruled by the Holy Spirit of God can do that. He, who was the *verb* of the conference, the third Person of the Trinity, can enable the clay jar to be willing to go, and to carry, and ultimately to be smashed in order to release the Treasure to those in need. It was easy to identify with the thousands of young hearts who were questioning, 'Is it I, Lord? Are you really calling me to go? How can I be sure?' We thought briefly of the faith needed by the twelve apostles when the Lord Jesus gave each of them half of a bread roll and told them to go to the waiting multitudes and feed them. The bread only started to multiply after the apostles began to obey! God didn't fail them. His grace was sufficient for the need. Five thousand were fully fed and many basketfuls of leftovers gathered up.

I testified to how the Lord kept us in peace during five months of captivity in the hands of ruthless and unpredictable guerrilla soldiers. And my God is their God. He kept me; He can and will keep them as they step out in obedience. One aspect of the wonderful ministry of the indwelling Holy Spirit is to transform us into the image of Jesus, and to make us *'more-than-conquerors'* (Rom. 8:28-39). He can enable each and every Christian to accept every detail of our lives from the hands of a loving Father with thanksgiving (Phil. 4:6), even in the face of suffering, misunderstandings, frustrations, and even in the face of death.

I went home again from an astoundingly wonderful convention, with many students making a public response to the challenge, only to find that nothing had changed for me. In fact, things were worse. I now *felt*—oh, that verb again!—I felt a hypocrite. Those 17,000 young people were willing to be challenged by God to full-time missionary involvement, no matter what the cost, through *my* testimony, and here I was in distress, crying out to God to meet me at the point of my need. I even feared that I might not really be saved. At times Pat must have been so aggravated by me; I was so stupid! God had just blessed in an enormous way. Who did I think I was? Did I really think I could have influenced that vast crowd in my own strength? Of course it was all of God, so why did I question whether I was saved or not?

But this reasoning, however reasonable, did not help me. I really could not explain myself to myself or to anyone else. It was just a deep inner unrest and fear, a sort of emptiness, a sense that I had lost touch with God. I still read my Bible every day. I tried to pray, but I felt (!) that my prayers were helpless. I taught every week at a mid-week women's Bible class at our church and I taught a group of schoolgirls every Sunday afternoon in our GCU group. I said the right words—I was even sure that they were the right words—but they did not reach through into my own heart. *'What a wretched man I am!'* Paul cried: *'Who will rescue me from this body of death?'* That is what I felt like crying out. I was desperate for a deep, meaningful encounter with God. I taught assurance to others; I knew the right Scriptures to quote. But when I said the same Scriptures to myself, they did not bring me the comfort I yearned for.

As I turned my mind to preparing the manuscript of *Living Holiness*, I was absolutely sure that God's standard for each one of His children was that they should be holy *'as He is'* (1 Pet. 1:15-16). Equally, I knew that I myself had not reached that standard. Yet the Bible clearly states: *'Without holiness no one will see the Lord'* (Heb. 12:14). With all my heart I wanted to see the Lord. How could I attain to that standard of holiness? It wasn't only then, as I sought to prepare to write a book on holiness, that this hunger took hold in my heart. No, I remember clearly, how many years before, at Nebobongo, when faced by an outbreak of smallpox, isolated in my home for several weeks of quarantine, I first read Bishop J.C.Ryle's book *Holiness*. It captured my imagination and filled me with a great longing, a hunger after true holiness. Holiness was surely what God planned to work in each one of us by the transforming grace of the Holy Spirit, making us into the image of His dear Son. This ongoing ministry of the Spirit would doubtless take a lifetime to bring to any sort of fulfilment.

Then, as I continued to pray over the subject, I realised that at times of revival the Spirit achieves that ministry in a person's life almost overnight—the life-long process appearing to be speeded up. If I studied the work of the Spirit during some of the mighty revivals in church history might I see a pattern of what the Holy Spirit desires to do in each of our lives? I acquired every book I could that recorded revivals during the past 150 years in Canada, Scotland, Ireland, Wales, and the Congo, from 1854, through 1904, to the 1920s and on to 1954. I read and re-read the records until a certain pattern began to emerge. Each of the accounts of revival started with an overwhelming conviction of sin leading to godly repentance. As each convicted and forgiven sinner came to realise more fully what Christ had done for him at Calvary the love of God flooded over him, filling his heart with an intense desire to learn more of his Saviour through the study of the Scriptures. This in turn led on to an ever-increasing desire to obey every command that was written in Scripture so leading to godly lives, lives lived in an attempt to tell God how much His people love Him. And through that conscious obedience to the Word, came a wonderful willingness to serve others. Jesus, when He washed His disciples' feet, told them to serve each other as He had served them. Humility and the willingness to serve at all times, without asking, 'What do I get out of it?' became the hallmark of holiness.

These seemed to me to be four steps in the transforming work of the Spirit in our hearts, making us *'holy as he is'*:

conviction of sin, overwhelming love, meaningful obedience, and humble service. They do not necessarily come in that order. At some stages in life's journey one or other takes on the more important role, and it is not always easy to know where one ends and the next begins. In fact, I saw these four steps as the steps of a galloping horse. All four are essential. The horse will limp or fall if it tries to gallop with only three legs, but it is often well nigh impossible to see the order in which its legs move. So it is with the quiet, steady, inner work of the Spirit in each Christian life bringing us to holiness. Yet, even as my mind was grasping these thoughts, my emotions remained in turmoil. At times I felt a lonely coldness, as though I had altogether lost touch with the Lord. How could I pull myself out of my 'slough of despond'?

By the following September, I was back on the road again. I had several meetings in the Inverness area of Scotland before going to Switzerland for a month filled with over forty meetings, mostly spoken through an interpreter. What joy it was to be amidst the fantastic beauty of that land, from Lausanne and the lakes of the west, to Interlaken in the Bernese Alps, to wake in the early mornings to see the sun touching the JungFrau with a rosy hue, to enjoy the sound of sheep-bells, and see the myriad of tiny flowers in the meadows. What an extraordinary month that was! Everyone was so kind to me, so welcoming, so encouraging. Then I returned to the UK and another forty meetings in universities and Bible colleges throughout the length of the land. Once again, God graciously poured out blessing. Yet still the unrest in my own spirit remained. I read my Bible daily. I prayed. I prepared talks and sought to be pleasing to God. But the peace and the joy of such service were not there.

As mentioned earlier, in 1983 I went again to Australia. One of the themes during that two-month tour was 'God is at work in His world.' Using a large traffic sign that warned motorists of road works ahead, I commented on how frustrating these signs can be when traffic is brought almost to a standstill and there is no sign of any workmen or any activity! Does God want to put up His sign 'Road works ahead' in many countries all over the world, but is hindered from doing so because there are no workmen available to Him?

At the final houseparty the leader asked a group of some twenty of us to be available at the close of each meeting to counsel any who stayed behind afterwards. I was very nervous of this, as I did not feel that I was in a sufficiently positive Christian state myself to be able to counsel anyone else, but I acquiesced to his request. At the end of the main meeting that morning a number of people stayed in their seats after others had left. We sat quietly waiting. Then the leader asked me to go to a lady halfway down the marquee. I went and knelt beside her, and waited. The lady was sobbing, and obviously in distress. 'Can I help you?' I asked quietly. She turned to me with such a blank look, almost of agony and helplessness. 'I am the wife of a pastor,' she sobbed, 'but I have lost my assurance of salvation!' Then she poured out such a sad story of past usefulness and blessing compared to present emptiness and failure, and all seemed to hinge on one word, 'I don't *feel* ...' As she shared with me, it just seemed as though she was describing exactly where I had been for the past year or so. 'Can you help me?' she pleaded.

'I think I can!' I almost laughed. It was suddenly all so clear. I remembered when I was first saved, hearing teaching at a CSSM beach mission, using a simple flannelgraph representation of a train with an engine, a tender, and a coach. They were labelled Fact, Faith, and Feelings. The train came to a sharp bend in the tracks and Feelings fell off. Feelings nearly pulled Faith off, but Fact puffed on, strong and unaffected. The *fact* of our salvation is unshakeable.

Christ died on the cross of Calvary for our sins. If I confess my sins, God is faithful and just to forgive me my sins, and to cleanse me from all unrighteousness.

Together we looked up these verses (1 Cor. 15:3, 1 John 1:8-9) putting our fingers on them in the Bible, and there was the *fact* of our salvation. Yes, we acted in *faith* when we first came to believe these wonderful truths for ourselves, but that faith had not saved us. The fact of Christ's death saved us. And even if our faith failed, that could not alter the fact of Calvary. As for *feelings*, they come and go, they fluctuate; they do not stay the same two days running. Feelings are quite unreliable as an index as to whether I am saved or not.

'Yes,' she said, 'I can see all that, but ... God no longer speaks to me. I am not able to feed on His Word as I used to.' And the Lord brought into my memory a simple story I heard somewhere, likening our heavenly Father to a gardener. He had three women working in His garden. During the day, He came into the garden to see them at work. He passed by the first woman, saying nothing. He stayed a short while with the second, encouraging her to keep on. Then He spent a long time with the third, sitting down and talking gently to her. The following day almost the same thing occurred. At last, the first woman could not contain her distress any longer. 'Why do You not stop and talk with me?' And the Lord smiled at her, 'But I know your love for Me. I do not need to comfort and help you as I do the other two!'

Even as I shared this with that dear woman, I was conscious of the Lord smiling at me, and saying, 'Are you listening?' The comfort wherewith I sought to comfort another had turned back to me, and I was comforted! That evening, I *knew* that God had put into my heart the reassurance that I had *felt* I lacked. I knew all was well. The doubts were an attack of Satan to seek to stop me in the ministry the Lord had entrusted to me. My longing to *feel* good, to *feel* saved, to *feel* needed, was to be exchanged for a deep realisation of His unspoken love, His outpoured grace. I cannot say that the doubts have never sought to assail me again, nor that I have never become distressed by lack of feelings, but I do know with quiet assurance that His peace in my heart is due to the *fact* of Christ's death for me and has nothing to do with my *feelings*. I prayed earnestly for that dear woman, that she too might have found release from the enemy's attack and a new joy in her service for the Master, a joy unrelated to her feelings.

It was shortly afterwards that the Lord had to speak to me again along similar lines. I had been eight years in this roving ministry, living out of a suitcase, travelling all over the English- and French-speaking worlds, challenging men, women, and young people to put Jesus first in their lives, to trust Him utterly, and to move out into a life of obedience to Him in every detail. But still deep in my heart was the niggling doubt as to whether this was really what God had chosen for me, or if it was merely an opt-out of my own creating? Should I be responding to the challenge and go back to Congo to serve as a medical missionary again?

I had the opportunity to go to Portstewart in Northern Ireland to the annual 'Keswick Convention' there, staying in a caravan with a lovely Christian lady companion. And I pled with God to meet with me during that week, and to speak to me so clearly that this problem could be finally dealt with. Just before the first evening meeting, I met a young friend in the car park, a missionary on her first home assignment. She was having a problem knowing, with complete assurance, whether God wanted her to remain in the UK to care for her ageing parents or go back to the mission field for a second term of service. I spoke to her briefly, assuring her that should she need to talk and pray over her problem with anyone, I would consider it a privilege to be available to her. But I tried to make it very low key, as I certainly didn't want to butt in where I was not wanted.

By the Thursday evening I was just yearning for God to speak to me. My own problem was as big as ever—to stay here or to go there? Please, please, God, speak to me clearly, I yearned. And I sensed that it would be that night that God would meet with me in a definite way. As we drew into the car park for the evening meeting, there was my young friend. 'I need your help, please!' she said. And I shrank. Dear God, please not tonight. You were going to speak to me at this meeting! But, as I had offered to be available, we got into my car and I drove us out to a parking lot on the headland looking out on the Atlantic Ocean.

After making us each a cup of coffee, I asked my friend how I could help. She poured out all the tussle that was going on in her heart, the apparent pros and cons on both sides of the problem, and the heart cry to hear a word from God giving her clear, unmistakable guidance. 'When you first went out to the mission field, did God give you a verse of Scripture to stand on?' I asked. Yes, indeed He had, and she shared with me how the Lord had guided her so clearly. We went over this two or three times, from different angles, to re-assure her of the clearness of her original guidance.

'Let us look at Isaiah 30:21: *Whether you turn to the right or the left, your ears will hear a voice behind you saying, 'This is the way: walk in it!'* When will you hear a voice re-directing you into the right way?' I asked. 'Only when you turn *out of the way,* turning to right or left! But if you remain *in* the way, the Voice does not have to speak again. God has not rescinded the calling He gave you; He has not pointed you in a new direction so He does not need to give you another word!' Immediately my friend was filled with joy and with a consciousness of the peace of God. She just knew, without a shadow of doubt, that God had spoken to her.

Having driven her home to where she was staying, I returned to our caravan annoyed with God. I had been so sure that He was going to speak to me, to meet my urgent need of guidance, that very evening. But the evening meeting was now almost over, and I had neither reassurance nor peace. I lay on my bed, got out my Daily Light, and argued with God: 'Why have You not spoken to *me*? You have given my friend peace and joy, why not *me*?' As I read Daily Light, it was as though God said to me, 'I have spoken to you, but you are not listening.' I read the words again. 'God, You say You have spoken to me, but I have not heard. Please, speak again!' Then I was brought into a state of conviction: 'Do you think that you were speaking to your young friend out of your own cleverness, out of your own mental deductions? Surely, I was speaking to her through you. She listened but you didn't!'

I went back over all our conversation together that evening and suddenly my heart was filled with light. Yes, God had clearly given me a word from Himself in 1972, telling me to prepare to leave Congo in order to go home to the UK to nurse my dear mother. WEC, my mission, had agreed when I shared this with them. I came home from Africa to the UK, and was with my mother for two years. Then Mother died, somewhat unexpectedly, although all our family knew how fragile her hold on life had become. Thereafter I was asked to do deputation work for the mission, nine months of it in USA, before—as I thought—returning to Africa. During that time I became unwell and needed surgery to remove a malignant cancerous tumour. While I convalesced, I was asked to continue doing as much deputation work as I reasonably could. Asking God for a clear word of direction at that juncture, he said: *'Make this valley full of ditches.'* Again, I knew it was God's voice, and accepted this word as His direction for my immediate future.

Since which, through eight years of deputation travelling and speaking, daily 'digging ditches' (many of which God graciously filled with water, blessing many young people), I kept on asking Him for another word, for further direction. Could I not trust what He had already said? Was I mistaken? Had He not meant what I had clearly understood Him to mean when He spoke to me through 2 Kings 3:16?

That evening God spoke to my missionary colleague through what Isaiah wrote in 30:21. He reminded her that if we turn out of the way of His will, either to the right or to the left, we will hear a voice behind us, prompting us to come back into the way of His will. We had together concluded that the corollary of that was that if we *are* in the centre of God's will, we will not hear the voice, as we will not need re-directing, or called back into the right way. Was I listening? I had heard God's voice, and passed His message on to my friend who had heard, listened, accepted, and received with joy the Word of God to her heart. But was *I* listening? Apparently not! As I lay on my bed in the caravan that evening, God spoke right into my heart, and I *knew*—at last—that I *was* where He wanted me to be, doing what He wanted me to do. Why had I taken so long to heed God's Word?

More recently I have been corresponding with a dear young friend who, six years ago, was in a terrible accident which left him a helpless paraplegic, in a wheel chair, totally dependent on the help of his wife and others, frequently in pain, and distraught with the frustration of the whole situation. I have kept all our emails to each other over the past four years. His latest heart cry reads, 'I am literally totally in the dark. My prayer life and my heart for Jesus seem to continue to dry up. I don't think that I am being a hypocrite but feel that to pray, confess His truths ... is done in the flesh. ... I feel that my grace period has ended because it has been going on for six years, and I'm beginning to get some of Job's friends' responses (when I broach the subject with other people)...'

I have just written back to this dear sufferer, and I believe my reply may well have been born out of this chapter. For that reason I reproduce it here:

> You spoke of your 'dark night of the soul' experience ... your whole world turned upside down ... and all the past (knowing who you were and what you were supposed to be) has been stripped away, 'and I don't know what I am supposed to do or be.' Let's start there. Basis: God is in charge and in total control. Nothing can touch you except He allows it. And He only touches you with the tenderness of touching the apple of His eye. For a time in our Christian lives we 'go along', growing, developing, knowing who and what we are ... and then God sees that we are ready for a radical and total change. We may have begun to rely on who we are and what we do ... and God says, 'No! Rely wholly and only on Me.' So He appears to strip away all the props, all the known things, all the known and accepted 'feelings' that go along with our Christianity. It seems dark—even frightening—insecure—what's the point? And God is wooing us into Himself, independent of everything else. We have to put our hand in His in the darkness, seeing nothing, possibly even understanding nothing—but simply trusting. He cannot do us harm. He will never hurt us pointlessly. But if He strips us of all we know, all we hold dear, all that is certain, it is because He wants us to be wholly His. He is a jealous God. He will not share our love and service and worship with another. And if He sees that even a tiny scrap of self-pleasing has crept into my service; if He knows that I am beginning to rely on my being able to do what He wants me to do, and not wholly on His being able to do what He wants done even when I cannot ... then He must strip me of myself, of my dependence on my

ability, even of my apparent ability to know Him, and share Him with others.

Does all that sound like nonsense? Yet in my heart it is making sense to me. As He strips away all of myself, and my self-reliance, He is actually making me into the clay jar He wants to indwell. He is ridding me of anything and everything that He sees could hinder the free flow of the Holy Spirit to others. I was just reading Acts 8 an hour ago, preparing Bible study notes for our little group at church, and seeing how He (the Holy Spirit) ordered Philip away from the region where he was being mightily used, possibly at a time of revival, and leading him into a desert place ... a lonely road ... to meet one lonely African eunuch, probably a proselyte to the Jewish faith, but still basically a despised foreigner, on the fringe of temple worship because of being a eunuch. But God, who had set the scene, took Philip into it, and he was able to buy up the opportunity and preach Jesus!

Going back to your letter—you have said, 'It's one thing not to know His purposes for my life, but quite another matter not to know what He wants of me.' No, no! That is the next step in the darkness. We do not have to know anything except that He is El-Shaddai—He is the great Almighty Creator God who loves me and loves you, and in some amazing way, who has chosen us to be part of His programme. He does NOT have to explain to us how or when or in what way. We just HAVE to rest in Him, in unquestioning trust. Let Him have YOU, all of you, all your thought processes, all your desperate desire to understand, to know the meaning of this whole protracted process. Stop hankering to know what He is not choosing to explain to you yet. Oh, how relatively easy to write that, but how infinitely harder to put it into practice. Give over to Him the impatience; give over to Him the longing for the joy and peace of the past. Just let Him be the ALL for you in the present.

You say, "I beg the Lord to heal me or let me know if paralysis is to be my life." Then you say He doesn't answer you. He does, dear, but you are perhaps not entirely willing yet to hear His gentle whisper ... and possibly others keep on feeding other desires, which contradict God's gentle answer. I sense that He does not wish to heal you—He could, and if you press Him hard enough, He yet may—but I sense that is not His highest will for you. Psalm 106:15 (KJV) is frightening: *'He gave them their request, but sent leanness into their souls.'* Take your hands off. You feel that all is virtually lifeless now ... no! That is not so. It is just that the life has gone down to a deeper level. It is real LIFE, life in Him, life that is no longer dependent on feelings, or seeing answers to prayer, or knowing that you are being used etc. You say, "I long for a personal relationship, but there seems to be no-one there." Oh, but He is right there! His love surrounds you, upholds you, envelopes you—but it is FACT, not feelings. In that glorious day when we shall see Him face to face, and we shall weep at His beauty, He will at that instant fill us with an amazingly sweet knowledge of Himself, and a deep quiet shattering realisation that, Yes! He had been just there all the time!

Dare I lovingly challenge you, are you hanging on to the desire to be healed? You have asked Him for His best for you, and if He knows that this pathway through the darkness is overwhelmingly more wonderful than mere physical healing, can we together embrace that and accept that we must go at His pace? ... We dare not race ahead of Him, nor lag behind. Yes, dear, you (and I) are seeking to pray for others, to serve others—we long to be light and life to a dark and needy world—but do we want to do this in our own chosen way, in a way that seems to make sense to us? Can we trust Him to do it through us, even when it seems to make no sense?

I read on through your letter—being like John the Baptist... and the disciples when others all left Jesus ... and then you go on to liken yourself to Job (even though you don't actually name him) when you say, "I despise the day I was born." Job at the end of his testimony came to accept the almighty greatness of God as the most real thing in his life, despite all the circumstances, and he realised that we simply cannot understand the mind of the Almighty with our little puny human minds. But we can accept. Accept His will. Accept His way and His plan. Even accept the dryness, and the sense of loneliness, lostness. Do you remember when the Brook Cherith dried up? Elijah was where God told him to go, doing what God told him to do, yet the Brook dried up. And God knew that it would dry up! It didn't dry up because of any sin in Elijah, or any failure of obedience. Not at all! It was just part of God's perfect plan. When Jesus told the disciples to cross over the lake (Mark 4:35), He knew that the furious squall was going to blow up, and that they wouldn't be able to cope. And it wasn't because of anything they had done wrong. It was part of the fulfilment of the will of God (Mark 4:40-41). Is that where we feel we are? Terrified! But Jesus was there in the boat with them. And He is in your boat and mine, and He will never leave you or me alone.

'I do not know if anything I have said—or could say— will actually help you, but I just pray that God will break into your thought processes and help you simply to say "I accept!" no matter what.

Jesus is able, and He is the ONLY ONE in whom to trust. There is no other way, no other god, no other Name given among men in whom we must trust for our salvation. May He fold His arms around you and give you His peace—even if you don't feel it!

And what I wrote to my young friend, I seek to apply to myself.

8

Digging Ditches Hither and Thither

In the summer of 1983 I was invited to speak at a conference in Eastern USA, at what I understood to be an American 'Keswick Convention', a week of biblical teaching on spiritual holiness and our individual responsibility to walk with God in our daily lives. The Ben Lippen property was partly owned by Columbia Bible College, and partly by the Billy Graham Organisation. I felt honoured to be asked to take part, and expected to speak at one meeting, giving a challenge to full-time cross-cultural missionary service—in what we used to call the Missionary Day at Keswick Conventions. Arriving there two days before the conference was due to start, I was flabbergasted to learn that I was expected to speak each day of the week, giving the daily Bible readings as well as the missionary challenge. I had twenty-four hours in which to prepare!

It was an amazingly hot week. The sides of the marquee were rolled up, but as the air was so still this barely helped to reduce the temperature. Crowds came for the week's convention, including a large contingent from Augusta, Georgia, with a number of medical consultants and students among them. I confess I felt overwhelmingly inadequate for the situation, not least because I had no messages prepared. Until then, my deputation ministry had been almost entirely 'one-off' missionary challenge meetings. Now I was invited to give a series of Bible studies with no specific mandate as to subject matter!

At that time I read right through the Bible in each year, and my daily reading that weekend was in Jonah. I was immediately reminded of my last months in Congo, some ten years previously, when the students of our Nurses' Training School accused me of mishandling college funds. That was a shattering experience. At that time (also in July) I was, once again, reading the Book of Jonah. God had spoken to me—eventually, when I was willing to listen to Him—on my third reading of the book! Subsequently, when at the WEC Missionary Training College in Tasmania, the students and I worked our way through the Book of Jonah, chapter by chapter, looking at the biblical principles of guidance, of prayer, of knowing and giving God's message to the people to whom we are sent, and of our own relationship with God and with His message. Unfortunately I did not have any notes with me of those meetings, but I sensed that that was to be the theme for the week's meetings.

I spent that Friday night before God on my knees at my bedside and with an open Bible before me. 'God's prepared Message', His Son, our lovely Lord Jesus, the One who died for our sins, who was buried and rose again on the third day for our justification, became once again the central pivot of all I longed to share. Oh, for the grace of God to so share Him with others that they would see His infinite beauty and indescribable worth!

Throughout the Sunday the Lord helped me to clarify my thoughts as I prayed my way through the message for each day of the next week, focussing on God's preparation of His messengers, using the phrases 'the Lord *prepared* a great wind and a violent storm' and 'the Lord *prepared* a great fish.' By implication 'the Lord had *prepared* a great city', and 'the Lord *prepared* a weed, a worm and a scorching east wind.' To what wonderful lengths the Lord is willing to go to make us what He wants us to be! And how stubborn we can be, resisting the pressure of His loving hands, as He shapes and re-shapes the vessels He is making! I was so blessed in my own soul as I worked on the details of each talk, and thought through the Lord's abundant goodness to us each step of the way.

During the week I was asked to suggest a missionary project for their weekly love-offering. My heart was full of the urgent needs of our little hospital, deep in the forests of North east Zaire (as it then was, Democratic Republic of Congo today). They needed to replace all the mud-and-thatch buildings with permanent structures, to stock the pharmacy with medicines that could only be procured with hard currency from outside the country, and to fund bursaries for student nurses and medical auxiliaries. I had an album of photographs of the hospital, from our earliest buildings in 1953 up to the time of my last visit in 1973, with pictures of the teams of male nurses and girl midwives. Everyone was interested, and they asked many searching questions. At the Thursday devotional meeting a love-offering was taken up. On the Friday, they presented me with a cheque—I nearly fainted. It was in five figures. I had never, ever received such a gift before. I cried. I simply did not know how to express my gratitude to them all. I could just picture the faces of both missionaries and Africans at Nebobongo when they heard that people thousands of miles away from them cared so much as to pour out such a gift to help them. It was indeed overwhelming!

After the Friday evening meeting, and all the many goodbyes to such a lovely group of people, I remained at the conference centre over the weekend, in order not to have to

travel on the Lord's Day. What I had not previously understood
was that the Ben Lippen Centre ran several consecutive weeks
of conference throughout the summer, and on the Saturday
the next group arrived, as did the speaker. I had the joy and
privilege of sitting in the meetings and being spiritually fed
all day Sunday as a member of the congregation.

The speaker was none other than Richard Halverson,
at that time the Chaplain of the United States Senate. He
was such a godly gracious Christian gentleman and I was
privileged to sit and talk with him on the Saturday. He gave
me a signed copy of his newest book *The Timelessness of Jesus
Christ*. Everything he said, everything we talked about, all
centred on Jesus Christ and His great relevance to the needs
of the world of our day. To hear him speak of Jesus Christ
warmed my heart. Even in his very tone of voice there was a
deep love for the Saviour. His life obviously revolved around
Him. The Lord was totally central, pivotal to this godly
man's existence.

At that time the second great Lausanne Conference of
evangelical and missionary leaders had just taken place. There
was great pressure, especially from third world countries,
that missionary service should include social services, and
not be restricted to the straight preaching and teaching
of the Word of God. It became the starting point of a new
phrase that stressed the importance of the need for a *holistic*
approach in presenting the gospel. Warning lights flashed
in my mind and heart. It was not that I disagreed with aid
programmes and caring for the whole person, especially
in crisis situations. But I feared that these would take over
and squeeze out the ministry of the Word. I had known this
battle during my twenty years of service in Congo as a doctor,
where we were always surrounded by need. The never-ending
lines of sick people needed care, and the work of the hospital
filled almost every waking moment, but I was out there in

Congo in order to point people to the Saviour. Was my main ministry being squeezed out of existence by the urgently-needed humanitarian ministries? It was hard work to keep the priorities right. We strove to maintain the first hour of every day for Bible study together in the church building. Now it appeared possible that all missionaries were going to be pressurised to do more, not less, on the humanitarian front, and as a direct consequence they would have less time and energy to spend on the preaching and teaching of the Word of God.

As I talked with Richard Halverson, and possibly began to air this fear, he said something I have never forgotten: 'When there is an international disaster, all the isms (not just Christianity, but also the communists and the atheists, the secularists and the philanthropists) rush to help. But there is one job that only Christians can do, and that is point people to the Saviour they need. That is our unique privilege, to show people the way to Calvary, to repentance and forgiveness of sin, and the deep inner joy and peace of knowing salvation from the hands of a crucified Saviour.'

I have just read Halverson's book, looking for where he expressed what he and I discussed on that long-ago Saturday, and a discussion that confirmed in me the urgent importance of maintaining the preaching of the gospel as the priority in my life. When I came to the eighth chapter, entitled 'As I have, I give' based on the story of the healing of the crippled beggar at the Beautiful Gate of the Temple (Acts 3:1-11), I found what I was looking for:

> One of our problems is that we have many deliverers of good sermons, and few preachers of the gospel. In the final analysis, preaching of the gospel is what the church uniquely offers the world, and this is that which the world stands ultimately in need of. Let us not sacrifice the gospel for any other message, however

relevant and practical it may seem to be, for in so doing we are giving the crippled beggar a coin, when we might raise him up to his feet to walk and leap and praise God!

I thank God for keeping me at Ben Lippen Conference Centre for those extra two days after my own time of ministry was completed, in order to meet and have fellowship with this wonderful man of God around the Word of God, refocusing my heart and mind on the task the Lord had commissioned me to undertake in His Name.

I returned home excited and with a new conviction of direction. Shortly afterwards, I had the privilege of two weeks of ministry at our WEC Conference Centre in Scotland, and in the second of those weeks we centred our thoughts on Jonah. I began to realise that my ministry was to change from one-off meetings to a more Bible teaching emphasis, with a series of meetings at one place, giving opportunity for a deeper approach to the biblical challenge to missionary service. That autumn I spent six weeks in Canada, travelling from Vancouver in the west right across to St John, New Brunswick in the east. Women Alive and WEC arranged the tour together. It included ten women's conferences, with three or four meetings at each, eight Bible colleges (we studied the Book of Jonah together at most of them!), and ten different churches, as well as several high school assemblies!

In each venue there was more than one meeting, and I certainly found the ministry more meaningful and probably more likely to produce long-lasting results in lives. However, once home in the United Kingdom, during the six weeks leading up to Christmas, it was back to the one-off ministry, a very tiring, rapidly moving, apparently less productive method of challenging young folk to full-time commitment to serve the Master wherever He chose to send them. Then it was on to the United States again for eight weeks with over

100 specific meetings, not counting all the private talks, interviews, and counselling sessions. There was no doubt in my mind that, humanly, I could not keep up the pace much longer, and yet God was blessing! Why did I grumble? Why was I not content to allow God to direct as He chose? What did it matter if I was tired and/or lonely? Was Jesus Himself not both tired and lonely when He lived on earth?

During that tour the Lord led me to put together some thoughts on 'Motivation to Mission.' I was so conscious that many of the talks and challenges I gave, particularly in Bible colleges throughout America, were not apparently having the impact on young lives that I longed to see. The overwhelming cry of all missions was for full time career men and women, sold out for Jesus, ready for whatever cost might be involved, prepared to go anywhere that God directed, no matter how dangerous or difficult. Yet despite a great number of people being engaged in deputation ministry the cry was still the same. Missionary societies were not receiving the candidates they longed for.

I usually presented young people with what I believed to be a vivid description of world need, using a countdown system to enlarge their vision and understanding of the **CONDITION** of millions of people in our world today. Over **ten** hundred million teenagers, largely in the great cities of the world, desperately need to hear the Good News of a Saviour who loves them, and can deliver them from the problems of loneliness, worthlessness, drink, and drugs. **Nine** hundred million Muslims, many of them becoming increasingly fanatical, follow a fundamentalist agenda of shari'ah law, with a deep-dyed hatred of the Name of our Lord Jesus. **Eight** hundred million atheists, who claim to live in a post-Christian era, where they have no time for, nor need of, God or a Saviour, believe that Christians are living in cloud-cuckoo-land. **Seven** hundred million Roman

Catholics, many of whom believe in the virgin birth of our Saviour, His sinless life, His death on the Cross, do not understand that they can know Him personally and have direct access to God by prayer in His Name. **Six** hundred million Hindus, with all the intricacies of the caste system and thousands of gods, have no power to live a godly moral upright life. **Five** hundred million Buddhists, seeking to live moral lives according to a strict code of ethics, are without the enabling power of the indwelling Spirit of God. **Four** hundred million Protestants, who should know the truth, so often live inconsistent lives, denying the very standards of the God in whom they claim to believe. **Three** hundred million isms represent all those who worship at the shrine of the occult and/or the black arts, as well as all the cults and sects that abound today in ever-increasing numbers. **Two** hundred million—a startling figure—of born-again, Bible-believing Christians, who have put their trust in the Lord Jesus Christ, often seem to be so indifferent to the plight of those outside their fold, doing almost nothing to propagate the spread of the gospel among the two-thirds of the world who have still never heard the gospel. And I concluded by holding up a large **ONE**, and asking 'Are you the ONE to whom God is speaking today, seeking to challenge you to go and become part of the fulfilment of His great commission to tell the gospel to people of every ethnic group?'

Having heard me politely enough, they thanked me for going and challenging them. But how many responded and actually moved out of their comfort zone to train and to go to another people group, another culture, another land, to preach and teach the Word of God? No, I came to realise that just knowing the actual condition of the world in its great need is apparently insufficient to move people to take action. What then would motivate them to go and act?

I thought about the **CONTENT** of the gospel. Surely as we meditate on all that God has done for us we must be moved with compassion to do something about those other sheep that Christ wants to bring into His fold? Our God so loved the world that He gave His only Son, so that by believing in Him, men should not perish but should have everlasting life (John 3:16). God is not willing that any should perish, but that all should come to repentance (2 Pet. 3:9). I had reminded young folk that there is no other Name given under heaven by which men can be saved, only the Name of Jesus. There is no other way, no other name, no other method than by conviction and repentance of sin, by believing and acceptance of God's free gift of eternal life through the merits of the death of His Son at Calvary. I know that God is holy, altogether holy, and that He must therefore condemn sin. We are all sinners, and therefore deserve only judgment and eternal death. But by the grace of God, He offers us forgiveness and restoration into friendship with Himself. I love Cecil Frances Alexander's hymn, 'There is a green hill far away', in which she says:

> There was no other good enough,
> To pay the price of sin:
> He only could unlock the gate
> Of heaven and let us in.

Christ died for our sins. He is the only true, sufficient and satisfactory Substitute to take the death that I deserve, so that by accepting His death in my place I might receive His righteousness: *'Look, the Lamb of God, who takes away the sin of the world!'* (John 1:29).

And with all that certainty in my heart, I know equally well that those without Christ are lost, that they are going to a Christless eternity. The Bible gives us no right to believe anything else. As we read in Psalm 19 and in the first chapter of Paul's letter to the Romans, God has made it possible for all to know Him, so that men are without excuse who choose not to know Him. But knowing all this—the fact of man's lostness, God's outstretched hand of love in Grace, the availability of salvation to all men—young people still did little or nothing. However yearningly I presented them with, and reminded them of, these truths, by and large they simply did not respond to my appeals for action. Neither the knowledge of the world's condition, nor the knowledge of the content of the gospel was apparently sufficient to motivate them into action on behalf of the lost.

What else could I do? I sought to share with people the need to obey the specific **COMMAND of Christ** to us, as His disciples, to: *'go and make disciples of all nations, baptising them in the name of the Father and of the Son and of the Holy Spirit, and teaching them to obey everything...'* (Matt. 28:19-20) that Christ commanded us. This has been God's purpose for His Christian people since the beginning. God promised Abraham that if he would pack up and leave his home city of Ur of the Chaldeans, leaving all that he knew of culture and customs and language, to go to a place that God would show him, He would bless him, make him a great nation, and that all the families of the earth would be blessed through him.

Matthew 28:20 is a **COMMAND**, not a vague request! If Jesus Christ is Lord of my life, I have a 'must' placed upon me. It is no optional extra, no matter of choice. There comes an implicit urge in my heart, along with this explicit command to go to tell others the gospel. Jesus said: *'As the Father sent Me, I am sending you.'* He was sent from heaven into the world of lost sinners. He came to seek and to save the lost. Jesus came to serve us, to be a slave for us, willing to die for us. That is the where, why, and how of the Father sending the Son. And Jesus says that He is sending us in like manner.

Will we then go? Yet once more I discovered that even this clear command was insufficient to actually move people to leave their comfort zone and go to wherever God would send them to reach the lost. What **will** motivate Christians to obey, to care, to go to the waiting millions? I asked myself over and over again.

As I prayed about this problem, and wondered just how to present the challenge in such a manner as to drive folk to respond in a positive way, I became convinced that it was only as '*we have the mind of Christ*' (1 Cor. 2:16). When God the Father sent His Son into the world, to be born the Babe at Bethlehem, to grow up into manhood among all the sin of this earth, Jesus came. He obeyed His Father. Jesus did only those things that His Father commanded Him. He spoke only the words that His Father put in His mouth. He sought only to be pleasing to His Father, and to fulfil His perfect will. At the close of His three years of ministry, after His death and resurrection, the Lord said to His disciples: '*As the Father has sent me, I am sending you.*'

As we have the mind of Christ, that is, the very **CHARACTER** of Christ, we shall do as He did, think as He thought, obey as He obeyed, submitting always to God's perfect will. In the Garden of Gethsemane Jesus prayed to His Father: '*Not my will, but yours be done*'. Is that my prayer every day of my life? Should it not be the prayer of all our hearts? Paul said we were to be like-minded to Christ, having the same attitude to life as He had, '*who ... made himself nothing, taking the very nature of a servant, being made in human likeness. And being found in appearance as a man, he humbled himself, and became obedient to death—even death on a cross*' (Phil. 2:5-8). Have I the very mind of Christ? Do I exhibit the very character of Jesus Christ in my everyday life? Can others, looking at me, see a true reflection of Jesus, as in a mirror?

The more I prayed about this, the more convinced I became that as the **character of Christ** takes possession of each one of us, then, and only then, the **command of Christ** *will* become the great priority in our daily lives. This, in turn, *will* make it possible for the **content of the gospel** to compel us into action to share Jesus with other people, even as the **condition of the world** *will* drive us to tears and to prayer.

I gave this series of thoughts on 'Motivation to Mission', based on 1 Corinthians 2:16, '*We have the mind of Christ*', at the WEC Public Rally, at the start of another tour of meetings in 1984, and the mission staff were tremendously encouraging to me. They sensed God's hand upon the presentation that evening, and saw its effect as it challenged many young people to commit themselves to whatever God had in store for them. So this particular line of thought became one of the main messages in my ministry during the next two or three years. Somewhere along the line, Dave Howard, one of the main forces behind the Urbana Conference in those days, heard me give this particular challenge. The facts are that no amount of knowing the dire condition of the world and its desperate need of the gospel will, of itself, move believers to take action. Being deeply conscious of the content of the precious gospel that is entrusted to us to make known to all men is, sadly, insufficient, of itself, to drive us into action. Even concentrating on the direct command of the Lord Jesus to all of us who truly love Him and have put our whole trust in Him and in His sacrifice on Calvary, to go to all peoples, all ethnic groups, throughout the world and to proclaim the gospel to them, even this appears insufficient, of itself, to motivate to action. Christians are so gripped by a defensive mechanism to protect themselves from hurt that they just will not take the risk. What then will actually motivate us to obey our Lord and Master? What will motivate us to take seriously the fact that all men outside of Christ are lost and are going to a Christless eternity? What will cause us to weep over the frantic state of the world today, sliding ever more deeply into a morass of sinfulness and wickedness, deliberate godlessness, unbelief, and error, calling black white, and mishandling the Word of God? Only as we are indwelt by the Holy Spirit, allowing Him to change us into the likeness of Christ, truly giving us the 'mind of Christ' that we might think as He thinks, love as He loves, weep as He weeps—only then will we be motivated to move out, as Christ left heaven to become flesh and dwell among us. Only then will we be willing to be spent and not count the cost.

Dave got in touch with me in 1986 and asked if I could go to the next conference, at Christmas 1987, and give this particular message there, to challenge the thousands of Christian young men and women in universities across America at that time. The main thrust of the conference that year was to be on outreach ministries in urban districts, and God's concern for those in the great cities of the world. When I arrived at Urbana, I was amazed when Ajith Fernando stood to lead the four Bible studies, and opened up at the Book of Jonah! They were exciting studies, and showed so relevantly God's concern for Nineveh, the greatest city of that particular time, full of cruelty and wickedness, not at all unlike the great mega-cities of today.

Then four different speakers took us to different great cities of our world and clearly laid in front of us their appalling needs. Two or three of us followed with passionate pleas for the students to listen to God's voice, and to heed the yearning in His heart that none should perish, but that all should be called to repentance, and to make their response. There was a tremendous response. All over that huge auditorium, students stood. Some were in tears, others looked excited, and some seemed almost stunned. Everywhere there was a deep sense of doing business with God.

9

Digging Ditches—a Renewed Emphasis

In 1986, just ten years after the Lord clearly spoke to me through 2 Kings 3:16, '*Make this valley full of ditches*', I looked back to evaluate the passage of those years. The initial emphasis had been on '*this* valley'. My mother had just died, I had undergone radical surgery for cancer, WEC was not planning to send me back to Congo and the Missionary Training School where I was to teach for one year was about to close down. Everything had looked very bleak. It was truly a valley experience after the mountain top that, in hindsight, the previous twenty years of work in Congo had been.

Then, slowly, the emphasis changed to the '*ditches*'—not a Suez canal, but just small, possibly insignificant ditches, perhaps with no apparent reason, and often with no apparent result. Their digging might well involve blistered hands and a sore heart. So began ten years of deputation meetings all over the English-speaking world, some evangelistic and others more specifically missionary-orientated. Some were challenges to service within the ranks of WEC, but many were more generalised in nature. I also became more involved in ministry in my local home church, in various Bible teaching ministries and in sharing with lonely and hurting individuals. Three books were completed in the series on the 'Four Pillars' of WEC.

Now, though I knew that I did not need a new directive from the Lord, I was keen for a word of confirmation that I was still in the centre of His will for me. The ten years of continual travelling and public speaking had brought considerable physical weariness. Writing three books, in between journeys and ministries, had caused some mental weariness. A fairly large correspondence and a growing involvement in a counselling ministry, as well as the preparation for all the speaking engagements, resulted in quite a degree of spiritual weariness. Ten weeks of flu, followed by a minor slipped disc episode was almost the last straw.

Yet at the same time, four weeks of meetings in Finland followed by ten days in London were an exciting climax to the year. It seemed that so many were helped, challenged, stirred, and/or encouraged through those meetings, as well as through some newspaper articles and television interviews in which I took part. I was deeply humbled at the Lord's graciousness to me. When attending our British WEC Staff meetings, where I was going to ask the Leadership to pray with me about the possibility of re-direction in my service, I was invited to speak at the morning devotional session before the day's business started.

'What shall I share, Lord?' And the word came clearly: 'Make this valley *full* of ditches!'

'But,' I remonstrated, 'they have heard that message over and over again from me!'

'You haven't finished yet', the Lord said patiently. 'The valley is not yet full!' So I accepted the Lord's gentle push to keep going, digging more ditches. And during that week, it was suggested that I should write the story of the first seventy-five years of WEC as a seventy-fifth birthday present for the mission for the next year, 1988.

That launched me into an amazing year of research. The three books I had just finished were all basically autobiographical, and needed very little research other than reading books on the matter in hand, and discussing with others who had been present at certain occasions to check the accuracy of my memory. I mostly knew the subject matter at first-hand. This was different. I wrote to many missionaries all over the world, from all different age groups, to ask for incidents from their different fields of service. I collected all the magazines from the WEC archives: British, American, and Australian, from the earliest days until the present times. I unearthed every book that had been written by a member of the mission from 1913 onwards. And I started to devour the information available.

At the same time I spoke at several meetings in Canada and Belfast, Finland and in the USA, that had been previously booked. And there was no let-up in my correspondence responsibilities. It was quite hard to make adequate time available, in reasonably large blocks, to do all the reading that needed to be done. But the research proved to be amazingly stimulating and exciting. I re-read all the early biographies of WEC men and women: C.T.Studd, Alfred Buxton, Edith Moules, and others. I became immersed in the magazines. Letters and cassettes from all over the world arrived, telling anecdotes and stories of the early days. Soon I realised that I was going to have an enormous quantity of material to draw on for one short book, and that the problem was going to be what to leave out as much as what to put in!

I started scribbling. After two or three months, I felt the book beginning to take shape, though not, perhaps, as I had initially expected. What was evolving was very short chapters, two to three pages at most, one for each year of WEC's life story, just to highlight some special feature within each year. The whole book would probably be some 150 pages long. The title *Living Stones* became apparent, as it was a potted-history of the *people* who made up the story, each a stone in the construction of the whole building. As Peter says: 'You also, like living stones, are being built into a spiritual house, to be a holy priesthood, offering spiritual sacrifices acceptable to God through Jesus Christ' (1 Pet. 2:5).

Then I saw another pattern emerging. The early years were all bringing to the fore the principle of *sacrifice* as the essential factor in missionary service. The next group of stories, following the death of C.T. Studd, the founder of the mission, underlined by the principle of *faith*, that no meaningful missionary programme could be effective unless underpinned by faith. Looking forward, I could see that in the third period of time, from the mid 1950s onwards, *holiness* had to become the most important element. And I knew instinctively that from 1970s onwards the most stressed of our 'Four Pillars' was *fellowship*. The story started with one man, with a vision for one country, using one particular manner of service. As it unfolded, it became the story of nearly 2,000 men and women, and countless nationals, in over forty different countries, using every conceivable method of presenting the gospel.

I wrote a rough draft of the first ten chapters, plus an overview of the whole, and sent it to our WEC Publications Committee to see how its members would react. They were not happy, certainly not excited! Apparently this was not what they felt they wanted, or what the mission needed. We wrote to and fro; we phoned each other, and eventually I travelled across from Belfast to London to discuss the matter face to face. I then met with the British leaders and asked their help to sort the matter out. I felt I knew what God wanted me to do; the members of the Publications Committee knew what they wanted, and we seemed to be poles apart.

I had to travel to Canada for two weeks of meetings, and it was suggested that I let the matter lie until I returned. By then, another person had been approached to produce the special book for the seventy-fifth year of the WEC. I was hurt, probably more deeply hurt than I at first realised. I really couldn't even pray about the matter. I was hurt, and felt I had the right to be hurt. I didn't want to pray about it, as I feared God would speak to me about my attitude!

Over the years, I have said to others, 'When you feel hurt, stop and pray.' As I have already written 'hurt' means that self is very much alive, and striving to get back on the throne of my life. If Jesus really indwells me, I ought not to be hurt. I may well be grieved at the behaviour of others, or by certain events, but not hurt. Hurt is a symptom of self. If I let the Lord have His rightful place on the throne of my life, He will handle that which causes the hurt. Oh, yes, the Lord had clearly taught me this on more than one occasion. But here I was, caught up again in the same difficulty. It seems that it is almost easy to say these things to someone else, but I did not want to say them to myself. Even though I had learned their truth so clearly in the past, I now had to learn it all again for myself.

While I was in Canada, at a Women Alive Conference at Waterloo University, I shared with nearly 2,000 women our need as Christians to be holy, '*to be holy as he is*', to be clean instruments in God's hands, based on 2 Corinthians 4:7: '*We have this treasure in jars of clay, to show that this all-surpassing power is from God and not from us.*' We looked at the four thoughts that God put in my heart when writing the book *Living Holiness*: repentance, love, obedience, and service, as three steps to *inward* holiness, in order to offer *outwardly* holy service to others. God blessed that message in a very marked way. I was humbled and awed at His gracious goodness.

Now, as I faced the hurt in my heart, I knew I needed to repent of it. I knew it came out of my pride. I felt I could cope with this new book in a God-honouring way, and I was not really willing for anyone else to tell me how to do it. I guess

I was proud of having been asked to write it in the first place and I was so sure that God had given me the inspiration as to how to tackle it. Consequently, I wanted to prove I was right. What a mess! 'I' was certainly in charge of my thoughts by that stage. 'Helen, give in and let Me control this situation', God said. It wasn't as easy as that. I had dug my heels in and I wasn't going to give in without a fight. 'Helen, you're fighting Me', He said in my heart. Of course, I knew God was right, but I still wanted to prove my point.

I had various local meetings during the month of May, and then back to WEC headquarters for our British staff meetings. The leaders discussed the whole matter with me again, and I agreed to leave the book on the back burner till the summer was over. I was going to Finland for the Lahti Conference of the Evangelical Church in early July, and needed time to prepare for a series of five Bible studies there. God was graciously giving me breathing space, time to step back and cool off. He is always so patient and kindly towards us when He knows that deep down in our hearts we honestly only want to please Him.

The conference in Finland was a wonderful encouragement. Again I was led to take 2 Corinthians 4:7: *'We have this treasure in jars of clay, to show that this all-surpassing power is from God and not from us'* as the basis for our thoughts. Using the well-known chorus, 'Spirit of the living God, fall afresh on me; break me, melt me, mould me, use me ...' and we added a fifth verb, 'smash me.' As I spoke the words, the Lord was working in my own heart. 'Listen to Me, Helen!' he said. Was I willing for Him to continue His gracious work in my life, to make me more like His holy Son, our Lord and Saviour Jesus Christ? Every part of me wanted to cry out, 'Yes! Yes, Lord. Please go on. Don't listen to me saying, "Stop! Stop! I've had all I can take." Please, God, remember only that I sincerely asked You to take my whole life in every part, and to fill me with Yourself, and to work on me until others could see only Jesus in me, and not me myself!'

Back home again, and faced with the incomplete manuscript and piles of books and magazines all over the floor of my study, I could not run away from the situation. 'Dear God, what are You trying to say to me? Please help me to understand!'

'Helen, for whom are you trying to write this book?' That seemed an easy question to answer.

'For WEC, Lord', I told him. 'I just want to thank them for all they have been to me, and done for me, over the past forty years.'

'Then you are doomed to disaster', came the loving response, clear as a bell in my heart. And it was accompanied by a sudden strange reminder of a scene from my candidate's days at the old WEC headquarters in south-west London, near the old Crystal Palace. I had just started my six month trial period for me to test the reality of my call to serve for the rest of my life in the ranks of WEC, in acceptance of their principles and practice, promising loyalty and obedience to those over me in the Lord, wherever I might be sent. It was, at the same time, a time for WEC to test me, as to whether they felt happy with the reality of my call, my willingness to submit to direction from the leadership, my physical, mental, and spiritual health, my reaction when put under stress, my understanding of what full membership in the mission would entail, and my unquestioning support of their faith attitude for the supply of all needs.

The first job I was asked to do was to wash out and clean the floor in the girls' toilet area. I scrubbed and polished number one area, and had just moved to number two to do the same there, when someone came in to use number one. She had muddy shoes on, and the floor was still wet. When she left, I moved back to number one and re-cleaned it. At the same time, someone came into number two ... and so started a kind of ping pong action between the two areas! I was reduced to tears, and frightened of failing to complete the very first job I was allocated. I would be a failure! I wouldn't gain the coveted title 'missionary'!

My senior missionary came in and stood looking at me for a moment, then realised I was crying. 'Helen, what is wrong?' I explained the impossible situation, that I simply could not complete the cleaning process under the presenting circumstances. 'Helen, who are you cleaning these floors for?' she asked.

'For you!' I ejaculated. 'You sent me here!'

'Then Helen, you will never succeed. You should be cleaning them for the Lord's sake. And He saw the first time you scrubbed the floor. That,' she said, pointing to the new mud recently carried in on the shoes of one of the girls, 'that is tomorrow's dirt!' I laughed at the memory! It was as clear in my mind as though it happened yesterday. And here was the Lord trying to teach me the same lesson again. Why was I so stubborn, so slow to learn? 'Do each task for Me, and let Me handle the problems that arise', the Lord seemed to be saying.

Accepting that WEC was unlikely to publish this particular manuscript, but that God was encouraging me to complete its preparation, I started again into the work of writing the book, with renewed vigour, and actually with renewed joy. Every chapter was a challenge. All the reading proved to be so exciting. It opened up vistas of the history of our mission that I had known nothing about previously. In 1924, for example, there was the amazing story of Fenton Hall among the Guajajara Indians, and how he died seeking to reach them with the precious gospel and without a murmur of complaint against God. His last recorded letter ended with the scribbled words, 'Yes, I *will* rejoice, *rejoice* in the Lord and in the God of my salvation.' Then, in 1925, there was a letter received from Rolla Hoffman, an American missionary, who had just gained access to Herat in western Afghanistan, telling of the overwhelming need for more workers, not only for the desperate medical needs of thousands, but even more because of the shattering spiritual darkness of those same people: 'Come over and help us!'

Jock Purves was one of those who responded, and he wrote amazing letters describing trudging through mountain passes, traversing narrow ledges overlooking precipitous cliffs, wading through ice-cold rivers, until at over 15,000 feet high, he could look down into Baltistan, 'a land without Jesus Christ; a land whose people have not yet had the Bible translated for them; a land largely unknown and unexplored.' Jock could see the shattering need of Afghanistan, Tibet, Russian Turkestan, Central Mongolia, Nepal, and Bhutan, all without a single missionary: 'Oh, it is shameful! Oh, Lord God, for Jesus' sake, send forth the labourers into the harvest! Millions of souls—and no reapers—not even sowers yet!'

There were so many thrilling stories of missionaries like Pat Symes, who, in 1928, started the work in the Republic of Colombia, of Alec Thorne in Spanish Guinea and Sam Staniford, along with Fred Chapman in the Ivory Coast. All these pioneers endured opposition and persecution, yet there was always a note of triumph in their voices! There were stories of the opening up of so many home bases for the recruiting, training, preparing, equipping, and sending out of reinforcements, and for the tremendous task of prayer support in every area, and of keeping the 'over-timers' supplied with prayer fuel month by month. Somehow, I guess, I had always taken these ministries for granted. They were in place and working relatively smoothly by the time I joined the mission. Now I saw a little of the price that had been paid to establish the work.

Then I reached 1940 in my reading. For each new chapter I read carefully through all the material I had gathered about that particular year. I then went back and read it all again, asking the Lord to highlight what He wanted me to write about. Sometimes this was easy; sometimes it demanded a third reading to discover a wee jewel tucked away in a small, almost unnoticed paragraph at the bottom of a page! But that year, 1940, the story was clear: it was the account of Bessie Fricker of Portuguese Guinea!

'Bessie, a fair blue-eyed scrap of humanity, used to forage around market stalls ... for damaged vegetables ... scrag ends of meat ... to feed six hungry mouths at home in London's East End', I read. And then followed the story of her conversion, through four fantastic years of patient Bible teaching, her dogged determination through three years at Bible School, knowing she had been called to be a missionary, and eventually the account of her going out to Angola to begin to study Portuguese, for her eventual entry into Portuguese Guinea. She suffered endless setbacks and hindrances and fought a lonely battle against the 'hierarchy' who were sure a woman—a *mere* woman—with difficulties with the language, would never be able to deal with government papers and legal requirements. Despite all obstacles, she did go eventually!

Bessie wrote, 'I know that God can look after me, and will; all that matters is to do His will! I go alone—yet *not alone*—I go with Him!' As I read forward through the ensuing years, there came the slow, almost painfully slow, story of victories in that land, where there is now a national church with national church leaders and evangelists, all because one woman dared to believe God and obey Him.

There were stories of the start of various new ministries to help to preach the gospel to all peoples: the birth of the Christian Literature Crusade, Radio Worldwide, the Gospel Broadsheet Ministry, the Leprosy and Medical Crusade, and others. Then there was the tremendous research ministry of Leslie Brierley (husband of Bessie Fricker-that-was).

The 'book' was rapidly taking shape. The next problem was to find someone willing to publish it for me. Two friends read the first draft, and both encouraged me strongly to go ahead and not give up halfway. I got in touch with my editor, with the publishers who had accepted the manuscript of my previous three books. She asked to see the manuscript, but sounded very dubious over the phone. 'Mission history is not exactly popular reading!' she warned me.

I realised that publishers took a risk. They did not want 5,000 books sitting on shelves instead of selling. All Christian publishers were saying the same things, that people no longer read as in the past. To print an edition of less than 5,000 was not good economic sense, but to print that number and fail to sell them wasn't sense either! Could I assure them I could sell 5,000? I swallowed hard. I was sure I could sell 500, but 5,000? However, God had pressed me into writing this book for His Name's sake, so could I not trust Him? Yes, *I* could, but would the publishers accept that reasoning? They were hardheaded businessmen.

I travelled to London to meet my editor. We sat in a restaurant, not far from the BBC headquarters, and drank endless cups of coffee while she toyed with the manuscript. I explained the structure—it was pretty obvious, but I had to say something to persuade her. She liked the idea of emphasising the four pillars and could see that it really was not history, in the ordinary sense of that word. She agreed that she had enjoyed what she had read and been stirred by it. But ... we always seemed to come back to a 'but'. She honestly doubted if she could persuade her bosses to publish the book. However, she took the draft manuscript with her, and I returned to WEC headquarters, and eventually home, to start the job of polishing the script. This always takes me longer than writing it and I tend to get very impatient with the detailed working-over of every paragraph, every sentence and every phrase—to be sure the right word has been used, the right emphasis given, as well as acceptable grammar!

Then the letter came. 'No,' said my editor, 'I'm sorry but the publishers do not think they can take this on at this time.' I rang her. 'At this time,' I said, 'do you mean you might take it on at some other time?'

'Well no, not really. I warned you that a history of a missionary society is not exactly popular reading these days.'

'May I come back to you?' I asked.

'Yes, by all means.' I went by myself to pray over the whole affair.

'God, I really felt You wanted me to do this book. I have been conscious of Your help and encouragement over and over again as it has developed. You taught me to take my eyes off what others thought, and to keep them on You and what You want. I have tried to do that, and it has been exciting! God, I honestly believe that You have made this book such that many people, who haven't previously been so, may be excited for mission. Has it just to die now?'

What if I offered to underwrite the production of 5,000? I wondered. Would the publishers accept the other 5,000, to make a 10,000 print run? Could I actually do that? Eventually I rang my editor, and asked her, 'If I had someone underwrite 5,000 copies, would you accept and print 10,000?' She had no idea how to answer. This was outside her remit. 'But,' she said, 'there is a Board Meeting on right now. I will go and put this suggestion to them and see what they answer. I'll ring you back.' I prayed earnestly for the next hour. I only wanted to be in the centre of God's will. I did not want to push open a door if He wanted to close it. The phone rang. 'Helen?'

'Yes.'

'The Board want to know who this benefactor is?' Silence. 'Helen, is it you?' I just could not answer. 'Helen, the Board says they cannot allow you to do this. They will print 10,000, and together we will trust the Lord to sell them!' I cried. How good God is!

I worked flat out over the next two to three weeks to complete all the corrections and submit the final manuscript to the publisher, who was going to have the book ready for the start of the next year—our mission's seventy-fifth anniversary year! I was asked to supply names and addresses of all outlets that I knew would promote sales. I wrote round to every bookseller that I had ever had dealings with and beat up all the support I could. The book, *Living Stones* came out, was distributed … and sold! Before the year was out, we had a further 5,000 printed. Write-ups in almost all the Christian press were so encouraging. Letters came in from all sorts of people, telling how they had been encouraged and challenged. Several missionary societies wrote to say that they were also promoting it to their people. Yes, God was good.

Most importantly of all, there was no bad feeling between WEC and me. The mission had not felt led to accept and print my book, as they had already accepted another manuscript for the seventy-fifth anniversary. God did not let me have any sense of self-vindication in the excellent sales of *Living Stones*. Rather, He showed me that His way was best. As a large publisher produced it, He had organised that it reached far more widely into the general Christian public than would have been possible if it had remained an in-house job. Really God rebuked me for my lack of faith in Him in those difficult early days of writing *Living Stones* and reminded me constantly that His way is always best, if only I will wait for Him to show what that way is instead of pressing on with my own ideas. The book that WEC themselves produced was truly blessed and used of God in our own ranks. Had God not moved me out of the way, that second book might not have been written!

During the last few months of that year, whilst the book was at the printers, I had another tour of meetings in the United States, and I was so much freeer and more relaxed, more able to rest in the Lord and to enjoy the ministry. Four studies at Bryan College, ministry at First Alliance Church in Atlanta, Georgia and then at Toccoa Falls Bible School allowed opportunities to begin to focus on the fourth pillar, *Living Fellowship*. Thoughts began to centre on the relationship between the Three Persons of the Trinity, as our perfect example of true fellowship—submission, servanthood and a willingness to suffer—with three symbols from the life of our Lord Jesus Christ: the yoke of submission (Matt. 11:28-30), the towel of service (John 13:1-17), and the cup of suffering (Mark 10:38, 14:23, and 36). I was beginning to become excited at the thought of tackling this last book to illustrate our WEC pillars.

Digging Ditches and
'Mama Luka Comes Home!'

For twelve months during 1988 I was invited to tour through England, Scotland, Holland, Australia, and Canada, specifically to challenge young people in university Christian Unions, youth groups, Bible colleges and churches with the urgent need of two-thirds of the world to hear the gospel of redeeming grace. I was to discuss with them what such a challenge entailed and how they could train for their part in the fulfilment of the Great Commission, and what a life-long commitment would involve. All the study and reading I had done in the previous year into the history of WEC, with its principles and practice, aims and vision, fired me up for this.

At the same time, my mind was just beginning to turn to the fourth book on the Four Pillars of WEC, this one on Living Fellowship. I started thinking about this as I wrote the final quarter of *Living Stones*. But I knew it was going to take me some time to develop those few thoughts into an understandable book on what biblical fellowship was honestly about, as a *principle* for Christian living rather than merely a *methodology* of working together in teams.

I had the privilege of leading a Quiet Day for prayer and personal reflection at the Birmingham Bible Institute. There were three sessions of Bible study, prayer, and meditation, during which we thought about those three symbols in the life of our Lord. The first is in Matthew 11:28-30: '*Come to me, all you who are weary and burdened, and I will give you rest. Take my yoke upon you and learn from me, for I am gentle and humble in heart and you will find rest for your souls. For my yoke is easy and my burden is light.*' The **yoke**—that heavy, unwieldy, wooden bar that holds two oxen together when ploughing—looks like an instrument of torture rather than something that is light and brings rest, until we remember that unresisting compliance to the pressure of the yoke makes possible a sharing of the load that more than halves the weight involved. The ox suffers no pressure sore on its neck if it keeps in step with its partner and does not seek to turn to right or left. In other words, the yoke causes no pain when the ox works with it in quiet submission. So as we agree to be yoked to Christ—what an indescribable privilege!—submitting to Him in unquestioning obedience, He takes far more than half the load and guides us to plough a straight furrow.

The second symbol we turned to was the **towel** with which Jesus girded Himself when He stooped to wash His disciples' feet at the supper in the upper room (John 13). At the end of the practical lesson that He gave them, Jesus said: '*Do you understand what I have done for you?*' ... '*You call me "Teacher" and "Lord," and rightly so, for that is what I am. Now that I, your Lord and Teacher, have washed your feet, you also should wash one another's feet*' (v14). We are to serve one another as He serves us. There was a job to be done. They all knew that there was no slave to wash their dusty smelly feet before they partook of the meal, but not one of them was prepared to take the necessary action until Jesus Himself rose and took the towel. He saw a job needing to be done and did it quietly. He didn't stop to discuss whether it might be beneath His dignity, or demeaning to His status. He took off His outer garment, twisted a towel around His waist, got down on His knees and went round the circle of men with a bowl of water, washing their feet. That was true service. Are we willing to serve one another like that, without discussing our merits or place on the social ladder, or what esteem we will gain by doing it? True service does not count the cost.

Our third symbol was the **cup.** In Mark 10, as Jesus and His disciples were on their way to Jerusalem, the Lord sought to prepare them for what He knew lay ahead, for his betrayal, condemnation, mocking, flogging, and crucifixion. At that moment James and John seem to have butted in and asked to sit on the Lord's right and left hands in His glory! Jesus must have looked at them, both sadly at their inability to understand what He was saying, and compassionately in His willingness to help to prepare them for the immediate future. *'Can you drink the* **cup** *I drink or be baptised with the baptism I am baptised with?'* He asked them. Surely Jesus was thinking of the intense agony and suffering that lay ahead of Him, the cup that He was preparing to drink to its dregs on our behalf. Shortly afterwards, in Mark 14, during the course of that last meal together with His disciples, Jesus took the **cup**, gave thanks, and offered it to them: *'This is my blood of the covenant,'* He said, and they all drank, thinking of it as a cup of fellowship. A few hours later, thrown on the ground in the Garden of Gethsemane, agonising in prayer, Jesus cried out to His heavenly Father: *'Father, everything is possible for you. Take this* **cup** *from me. Yet not what I will, but what you will.'* Again, the **cup**—but not the cup of fellowship, rather the terrifying cup of suffering—the cup that our Saviour drank in its entirety that we might be saved.

Those 'cups' are one and the same. Yes, it *is* the cup of fellowship, but it is *also* the cup of fellowshipping in His sufferings. Wasn't that Paul's amazing prayer, as he languished as a prisoner in Rome: '*I want to know Christ and the power of his resurrection and the **fellowship of sharing in his sufferings,** becoming like him in his death*'? Are we willing to pray such a prayer? Are we willing to actually desire to share in Christ's sufferings as He continues to suffer for millions in our world today who are still outside His Kingdom? Can I ask God to help me begin to feel, as Christ feels, for the lost, the unreached, and the hurting peoples of our world in all their need? Jesus feels for their need of physical and material goods, yes, but far above and beyond that, He feels for their need of the gospel.

That day at Birmingham Bible Institute was an immense blessing in my own life. The Lord spoke to us clearly through His word, through these three word-pictures—the yoke, the towel, the cup—and the realisation that these three are each part of the deep biblical meaning of 'Fellowship'. The three Persons of the Trinity are a tremendous portrayal of true fellowship, submitting to each other, serving each other, and each willing to suffer in order to bring about the wonderful plan of salvation.

Through that year this theme became more and more real in my heart. It seemed to meet me wherever I went, during a marvellous day with the girl leaders of the Young Life Movement in northern England and another at a Bible college in central England, during a tour of meetings in Australia and at our own Mission Conference Centre at Kilcreggan in Scotland, even as I travelled in Canada and North America the Lord spoke to me on that same theme. Each time He prompted me to share it with others, it seemed to develop and shine more brilliantly with an increasing radiance.

That May Bank Holiday I spent at High Leigh at our GCU Annual Leaders' Conference, and whilst there, I was asked if I would consider writing a small book for them, for *their* seventy-fifth anniversary year! My natural instinct was to say 'No!' I had just finished working on a similar book for WEC, and the thought of doing all that research again made me shrink. But I had been a member of GCU for forty years and they had all prayed for me so intently during the months of captivity in Congo, this was probably the least I could do to say 'Thank you!' for all their love and care and prayers. So I obtained from GCU Headquarters in London all the early magazines and annual reports, copies of ever so many letters, especially those written to our large missionary family.

At almost the same time, I received a letter from my friend, Crawford Telfer, a Christian young man who was devoting his life to making videos for missionary societies all over the world, to help them promote their need of more workers and of more prayer support. 'Would you ever consider going back to the Congo to make a film to promote "mission" on a broad background?' he asked. Letters, phone calls, prayer, and discussions followed as I sought to enter into Crawford's vision of what he was seeking to do. Without much difficulty we all agreed to 'give it a go.' Crawford had previously made a short 20 minute video of an interview between Margaret Collingwood and me at her home in Bristol. Margaret was an experienced radio worker and interviewer, and Crawford invited her to accompany us to Congo to do this proposed one-hour video programme.

Preparations began in earnest. Tickets were booked for our flight to Nairobi from Heathrow. Arrangements were made for our stay in Nairobi, where we were to collect visas to enter Congo, and obtain permission to film there. Our flights to Bunia and on to Nyankunde and Nebobongo to do the filming were planned. All the vaccinations and immunisations, paper work, the gathering of needed finance, the packing of the minimum of clothing so that all our allowed weight could be given to the filming equipment, had to be seen to. Eventually we were ready to go.

It was to prove an extraordinary month for me, and for each of the others in our party of four. I had been away from Congo for fifteen years. Would everything have changed almost beyond recognition? Would I remember the language? Would I recognise my friends? All those years I had hankered to go back, but now that the opportunity had come I was afraid. Would it work? Would it expunge the longing to return, and give me a better acceptance of my present ministry, or would it just increase my desire to go back full-time? Would I be able to do what the team wanted—not to act, but to re-live the past—so that they could make the film they envisaged? There seemed to be 100 unknowns. I was deeply grateful for Margaret's supportive friendship as she sought to enter into all my apprehensions and fears, yet at the same time to give me the reassurance I needed that this really was part of God's programme.

Everything went according to plan from the moment we were enabled to put through all our grossly overweight equipment without being charged a penny! We were given such a warm welcome in Nairobi, and our applications for visas for Congo went through more smoothly that I had dared to hope. At last, we were on the final leg of the journey, from Nairobi, via Kampala, to Bunia. At the small airport at Bunia, faced by the official inspectors who were prepared to open every bag and case and to charge us as much as they could, suddenly there was the big smiling face of one of the Africans I worked with all those years before! He had heard on the grapevine that I was coming and came down to greet me. We were waved through without a case being opened! So to Nyankunde.

The shock of seeing over 1,000 people at the airstrip to greet us—all singing, all waving bright bunches of flowers—of being swept off my feet into a huge armchair on the back of a truck, and being driven slowly around the whole village, every path lined by cheering crowds, took my breath away. School children, workmen and their families, nursing students, were all there, and the warmth of their love overwhelmed me. We spent a week there. I was invited to speak every day to different groups—in French, Swahili, and English—including at the opening ceremony for the new college year for the nursing students! I just never knew what would be next. We were feted continuously, taken out to meals in different homes every day. And somehow, between it all, we filmed. We had to remember that this part of the film was to be at the end of the final version, so I had to say, 'Like we saw at Nebobongo,' or some such phrase, from time to time, even though we hadn't yet been there! They filmed in the home, in the church, in the local village, and in the College. At the end, we had to climb the local mountain for the final shot. I had never climbed it before, even when I lived there!

From Nyankunde we flew on to Nebobongo. We had to stop at Wamba for three or four hours while the filming crew were taken to Nebobongo ahead of me to prepare to film our arrival! Here again, in Wamba, a tremendous welcome awaited us. Everything in the village stopped. 'Mama Luka (my African name, from Luke, the physician in the Bible, and Mama, as they call every older woman) Mama Luka has come back!' went up the cry, and folk poured across to the pastor's home to see for themselves! I shook hands, smiled, hugged, greeted ... I suppose several hundred people, plus a couple of hundred school children. And would I please speak to them from the Word of God? All through that month, I had to be ready every day for impromptu speeches and Bible messages.

Eventually it was time to fly on to Nebobongo. The whole family was down at the airstrip. I wept. The joy was almost more than I could cope with. One of my dearest friends, Mama Damaris, already in her late seventies, was the first to greet me. Deep love shone out of the eyes of her dear wrinkled face. My colleague John Mangadima was there, almost in tears at the sheer joy of reunion, as was my house lad, Benjamino, ready with a glass of cold water. He was always considerate of my slightest need. Tall Samuel was there, at the back of the crowd. 'Asobeinobambi!' I exclaimed. He beamed, 'Only you ever remember my real name!' The ranks of school children sang a special song that Yandibio, faithful schoolmaster for over thirty years, wrote to greet me. And, of course, it was accompanied by excited banging on the native drums! Yes, I cried. It was just so wonderful, more than anything I had dared to imagine. And my Swahili came back as though I had never been away. We seemed to pick up conversations just where we left off fifteen years before. I was home, and I knew it.

We then started an intensive week of filming, firstly at Nebobongo itself, in the hospital, outpatient clinics, my old home and down at the leprosy care centre. Later on, at Ibambi, we interviewed other missionaries and national pastors, and attended a packed Sunday service. There were probably 2-3,000 people crowded inside the building and another 1,000 sitting on the ground outside! Pastor Ndugu, dear saintly man, probably in his mid-eighties, interpreted for me as I shared the Word of God at the morning service. We visited the village of Adzangwe to see a rural dispensary in action—one of the forty-eight that had been opened up within a fifty-mile radius of Nebobongo. It was thrilling, not only to see that the nationals were continuing all the work that I had some part in starting, but also to see how that work had been improved and grown.

One evening the crew wanted to film part of the harrowing story of what occurred in that very house 25 years before, when cruel guerrilla soldiers broke in during the night and I suffered brutally at their hands. I was not to be part of that bit of the film as the crew, out of kindness and consideration, felt it would be too much for me to cope with. I went to bed, actually in the back room of the house. But of course, I could hear them ... and I relived that dreadful night. Suddenly something inside me snapped. I just couldn't bear any more. I rushed out to them, and they were all very distressed and felt guilty when they realised how it had upset me. But actually, it was God's hand of blessing. That 'snap' proved to be the final healing of the hurts of that long-ago night, hurts that I had not really realised were still there. But that night God enabled me to hand it all over to Him, and to cease to harbour even a grain of bitterness.

Eventually, after sixteen hours of filming, Crawford knew he had all he needed to make the video. So Margaret and I left on a whistle-stop tour around all the other WEC/church outposts throughout the Northeastern province of Congo. Mission Aviation Fellowship (MAF) flew us everywhere, and the welcome poured upon us at each stop was unbelievable. At Malingwia we had three meetings in the day and, from the outset, we sensed in a peculiar way the presence of the Lord with us. A number of young men came forward to give their lives to full-time service for the Master. It was both moving and humbling. At one church, where we stopped unexpectedly, the people gathered round us in obvious distress. We had arrived at a critical moment in a church conference, where there had been a difference of opinion between leading men. They were in deadlock. Those dear people allowed us to minister in the Name of the Lord. And in a very precious way God poured in healing oil, and there was brokenness on all sides. We stopped in at another mission/church centre at Lubutu for re-fuelling and, once again, a crowd gathered down on the airstrip and there was opportunity for a quick word of encouragement. The missionary there, who is involved in translation work, said it was just the Lord's perfect timing. How gracious God was to us!

We flew on to Mulito—our most southerly visit—to an area where Maud Kells worked for years building up the church, Bible school, hospital, leprosy care, and primary school work. Again, we were privileged to minister at the opening of a new care centre for leprosy patients, and in the evening to the whole church including the Bible School students. It was thrilling to see how the work had grown, and all that was being accomplished so far from outside help of any kind. And it was as we were flying back to Nebobongo that the Lord first began to speak to me about the possibility of writing this book. He even gave me the title—'*Digging Ditches*'!

It was time to go back to Nebobongo and Ibambi district for our last few days, and I was invited to meet with all the pastors gathered at Ibambi. We were quite a small group, and they ministered to me, encouraging me to stay true to the Word, with my eyes fixed on Jesus at all times. They reminded me of certain biblical truths, such as Romans 8:28: '*We know that in all things God works together for the good of those who love him, who have been called according to his purpose*'. They had no doubt that I loved our Lord Jesus, and that He had called me into my present ministry. Then they thanked me for having become a member of their church family, there in Congo, and for submitting to their church discipline through my twenty years amongst them. They thanked me for 'treating them with the respect of a child for its parents', as well as for all the various ministries, medical, material and above all, spiritual.

Then the pastors asked me to kneel and they laid hands on me, prayed for me, and committed me to the Lord 'and to the ministry amongst English-speaking people worldwide to which He has called you'. In effect, they said to me, 'Go as our missionary, from our church, to all churches everywhere, to preach the gospel and to tell people of the great need of the world to hear and respond to the gospel.' Suddenly, at that very moment, I was filled with an overwhelming sense of peace—deep inner peace—from God Himself. The doubts that had plagued me on and off for so many years, as to whether I was in the centre of His will or not, whether I ought to have returned full-time to Congo rather than accepting a new direction for ministry within WEC, whether my present 'job' was an easy cop-out compared to facing the demands of front line missionary service—suddenly all these fears were put to rest, at least temporarily! It was not that the Lord had not spoken clearly to me on this matter before—He had, as at the Portstewart Convention some ten years previously—but I had allowed the same doubts and fears to surface again. But at that moment, in the meeting with the pastors gathered at Ibambi, God again gave me His assurance that I was doing what He had chosen for me to do, and it was just so wonderful to realise that my African family knew it too. They did not begrudge me my present work. No, not at all! Rather they sent me back into it with their blessing, as 'their missionary'. My sending church was there in Congo and the rest of the English-speaking world was my mission field!

Our last days in Congo were filled with seeing people, encouraging them, and catching up with their news, as well as Bible teaching and preaching on every possible occasion. It was as though they just could not have enough. Then a very sweet thing occurred, almost like 'the icing on the cake'. I had been slightly conscious that some of the ex-patriot missionary family had not been exactly as welcoming as we might have expected when we first arrived. I vaguely sensed that they were afraid of my obvious popularity with the Africans, though I could have told them that such popularity grows ten-fold after one has left! When I lived amongst them I was no more popular than anyone else. But there was just a fear in some hearts that, maybe, I had come to show them how the job ought to be done.

In the last two days before we left, three different groups/ households invited me to join them in their homes for coffee or for a meal, and at each they asked my forgiveness for any lack of warmth in their welcome when we first arrived. I was deeply touched by their honesty and willingness to put things right. We prayed together and wept together. And I think in each instance, we entered into a new and deeper relationship of oneness in our Lord Jesus.

Home again. The month had flown by. We had covered hundreds of miles, met with thousands of people and spoken at thirty three 'official' meetings, and ever so many unofficial ones! We brought back a fantastic number of photographs and completed sixteen hours of filming that had to be condensed into a one-hour video presentation of those wonderful twenty years of ministry in the hinterland of Congo.[1]

For most of the following six months I stayed at home, basically in order to get on with the manuscript of the book for GCU. But at the same time I hoped to become more part of my local church family. I had the privilege of weekly meetings with ten young people, firstly studying the Ten Commandments and their relevance for us today, then eight studies on biblical theology based on the Creed (as used in Anglican churches). And I also enjoyed leading a weekly Bible study (mostly for women) through John's Gospel. In the summer I went for ten days to Holland, to the WEC Missionary Training College, with a group of senior GCU girls, for a working holiday. We all enjoyed the challenge of scrubbing, polishing, varnishing furniture, cleaning windows and making new curtains, of turning out a garden shed and re-vamping it, and of clearing a patch of ground and preparing a new vegetable garden. Interspersed between

---

1 'Mama Luka comes home'—by Crawford Telfer and avaialble from CTA, Christian Television Association, wraxall, Bristol BS48 1PG, UK (email: info@cta.uk.com).

all these activities we had time for visits to local beauty spots and tourist attractions, and seven Bible studies based on Mark 10:45: '... *even the Son of Man did not come to be served, but to **serve**, and to **give** his life as a ransom for many.*' We took as our motto, 'Serve and give' (rather than 'be served, and get')! It was a truly wonderful holiday and we all felt we had met with the Lord in a new and exciting way.

The need to concentrate on writing the book for GCU was becoming increasingly urgent as it had to be finished and in print for January 1990. It was quite exacting work. Writing autobiographical books does not demand too much research, only a good memory and God's wisdom to know what to leave out (quite as much as what to put in!). But writing a history of any organisation demands a great deal of researching of all available material, and then putting such material together in a way that others will be inclined to read it.

Over several months I had read and re-read all the available material. Now began the job of sorting, and planning the structure for the book. Letters had to be written to everyone to be mentioned in the book, gaining their permission, and asking each one to verify the accuracy of what I proposed to include. Meetings had to be arranged with the various people in the text—older retired leaders, the new leadership and headquarters' staff, camp-leaders, and associate members— all needed to have the opportunity to check the accuracy of their particular input into this history. Suitable photographs had to be found and a title chosen. The cover for the book had to be decided. I really had little idea of all that is involved in producing a book! Until then, all I ever did was write the text and then others handled all the countless jobs involved in turning the manuscript into a printed and published book.

But at last *On Track* was ready! It was an exciting day when we saw it piled on the bookstall at the annual GCU business meeting, ready to be bought and, hopefully, to be given away as Christmas presents![2]

---

2 'On Track'—available from GCU Headquarters, 31 Catherine Place, Westminster, London SW1E 6EJ.

11

DIGGING DITCHES IN
VARIOUS NEW SITUATIONS

For twelve months during 1991 I stayed, for the most part, at home and concentrated on writing *Living Fellowship*, and on becoming more fully part of my local church and of our local GCU fellowship. I certainly enjoyed the quieter pace, and having more time for Bible study and prayer. I remember taking a series of Bible studies with a group of ladies, associates of our GCU family in the Lisburn area, on the Tabernacle, using this to illustrate the keeping of our daily tryst with the Lord—our own personal times of worship—as well as of public worship in church fellowships.

Another line of thought had been developing in my heart. I woke very early one morning with a verse of Scripture imprinted in my mind: *'Then the fire of the Lord fell!'* (1 Kings 18:38). I lay there in the dark meditating on that verse and bringing back into my mind its context. The 'Then' at the start of the verse challenged me to think through what occurred before this verse to make possible the falling of the fire of the Lord. I lay quietly thinking of Elijah, the shepherd boy, who was probably brought up in a God-fearing home and taught much of what we can read today in the first five books of the Bible. Angry at the state of his world at that time, so far away from godliness and obedience to the Ten

Commandments and living with idolatry and promiscuity on all sides, might he have challenged Jehovah with His own words? *'Be careful, or you will be enticed to turn away and worship other gods and bow down to them. Then the Lord's anger will burn against you, and he will shut the heavens so that it will not rain and the ground will yield no produce, and you will soon perish from the good land the Lord is giving you'* (Deut. 11:16-17).

'God, why don't You do something? Why don't You stop the rain as You said You would?' And did God say, 'OK, Elijah. You go and tell King Ahab that that is what is going to happen?' And Elijah obeyed God and went. (1 Kings 17:1) In my mind, I thought through the next chapter, how Elijah fled from the anger of King Ahab and hid in the Cherith ravine where God fed him with meat brought daily by ravens. Then the brook dried up and God told him to go to Zarapheth to a widow lady. Elijah obeyed and went. There the widow lady took him in and cared for him until the end of the years of drought. Through all that time, Elijah was doubtless learning deep spiritual lessons from God, lessons of absolute dependence on God alone and not just on His blessings, but also about the importance of immediate, unquestioning obedience to the Word of God without demanding explanations, and about the ability of Almighty God to undertake and provide for and protect His servant, no matter what the situation.

God then sent him back to King Ahab to challenge him. Elijah obeyed and went, even though he may well have had fear in his heart. Did Ahab not hate him and blame him for all the ills and tribulations that had fallen on the people due to the three years of drought? There follows the remarkable story of chapter 18. Elijah told Ahab to summon all the people including all the prophets of Baal to meet on Mount Carmel for a public contest—450 prophets of Baal versus Elijah, the prophet of the Most High God.

'*How long will you waver between two opinions?*' Elijah challenged them. '*If the Lord is God, follow him; but if Baal is God, follow him*' (1 Kings 18:21). Then Elijah called for two bulls to be brought, one for the prophets of Baal, one for himself: '*Let them cut it into pieces and put it on the wood but not set fire to it.*' The prophets of Baal were to call on the name of their god, and Elijah would call on the Name of the Lord: '*The God who answers by fire—He is God!*' After the prophets of Baal had done all this, and cried unavailingly to Baal for fire, Elijah had to act. This seemed to me to be the beginning of the conditions necessary for the fire of the Lord to fall. First he had to rebuild the broken-down altar of God, then to kill the bull and cut it up ready for sacrifice. The wood had to be arranged on the altar, and after that he even demanded that the people pour on barrelfuls of water, until the whole sacrifice was soaking wet. Then he prayed and God answered with fire, fire that fell from heaven and burned up the sacrifice, the wood, the altar, and all the water in the surrounding ditch!

Today we long to see God '*rend the heavens and come down*' in revival blessing, to answer by fire, burning up all the dross, all the selfishness, all the offered sacrifice, and convincing the people of His power and of His willingness to save those who turn to Him in repentance and with faith. What are the conditions that we possibly need to fulfil so that Almighty God may act? Surely we need to repair the broken-down altars, to confess and repent of our own waywardness and our stubborn self-will, our lack of faith and prayerlessness, whatever and wherever we have allowed 'things' to come into our lives that seek to take over and displace our Lord Jesus from His rightful place as King.

Then we have to kill and cut up the sacrifices. We have to offer our '*bodies as living sacrifices, holy and pleasing to God*' (Rom. 12:1)—our very selves. We need to put our 'I' on the altar, our right to ourselves. Oh, that I would honestly seek to enter into Paul's wonderful statement: *'I have been crucified with Christ and I no longer live, but Christ lives in me'* (Gal. 2:20)! That requires death to self in all its forms: self-esteem, self-consciousness, self-justification, and our desire for a good self-image. Everything has to go that has to do with pride (where the middle letter is 'I'!), what I want, what I get out of it, and always thinking that I know best. Jesus said: *'If anyone would come after me, he must deny himself, take up his cross daily and follow me'* (Luke 9:23). We need to deny our-SELF and enthrone Christ.

Why did Elijah demand that people pour water over the altar and the prepared sacrifice? Was it so that no-one could suspect him of cheating? He had not hidden some smouldering flax in the midst of the firewood, hoping for a change in direction of the wind in mid-afternoon to fan it into a blaze. The fire of God had to fall from above. It could not be worked up from below. It must be clearly seen by all to be *God's* fire, and not his. God demands absolute honesty and integrity; He will have nothing to do with guile or hypocrisy.

Elijah was so sure that God would indeed answer his prayer with fire from on high that he was willing to pile on the difficulties. Then he prayed—publicly—in a loud voice: *'O Lord, God of Abraham, Isaac and Israel, let it be known today that you are God in Israel ... Answer me, O Lord, answer me, so these people will know that you, O Lord, are God ...'* (1 Kings 18:36-37). There was nothing self-centred, nothing to justify or glorify himself in his prayer. And Elijah expected God to answer! *'Then the fire of the Lord fell!'*

In the years that have followed since that morning meditation, the Lord has led me to this passage many times, and always He has so graciously blessed me through it. God showed me that He had prepared Elijah through chapter 17 before He could trust him with the fantastic victory of chapter

18. Was I also willing for that continual preparation of heart and life that enables God to trust me to be His co-labourer in His vineyard? Do I allow God to train me daily to rely wholly on Him, and not on myself or even on His blessings?

But then the Lord led me on another step to look at the next chapter, 1 Kings 19. Here we see Elijah fleeing for his life, terrified by the angry Queen Jezebel. He told God he had had enough. All he wanted to do was die. I just felt I understood exactly where Elijah was! He was going through what I call 'the backlash'. After great spiritual blessing or victory, when humanly one would be expected to be over the moon and full of rejoicing, so often there comes an almost overwhelming sense of failure, of uselessness, and even of depression.

The amazing thing is to realise that God understands this! God did not rebuke Elijah for this reaction, but rather He sent an angel to him to supply him with '*a cake of bread ... and a jar of water*'. Elijah needed a meal. After his continued journey to Mount Horeb, and a night spent in a cave, the Lord called him out into His presence, and spoke to him— not in the wind or the earthquake or the fire but in a gentle whisper! How gracious and tender is our Almighty God! So God sent Elijah back again with a fresh commission and a fresh enabling to put that commission into practice.

God began to show me that chapter 19 was as much part of the preparation for the victory of chapter 18 as the events of chapter 17 had been. Before God was able to entrust to Elijah the huge victory that occurred on Mount Carmel, not only had He trained him in obedience and trust, but also God knew He could trust him to come through the backlash that would follow. I have found this a tremendous comfort myself. God did not prevent the backlash occurring, nor did He wait until Elijah was so perfected that no backlash would occur. No. God, who created us as humans, who are therefore capable of reacting to the backlash after great events, does not condemn us for so reacting, but meets us at our point of need and provides us with '*a way out so that you can stand up under it*' (1 Cor. 10:13).

The following spring, I had the privilege of another ten days of ministry in the United States, starting at Nanibijou, a wonderful conference centre on the west of Lake Superior, down to Augusta, Georgia, in the southeast of the States. Sharing mostly from the almost completed manuscript of *Living Fellowship*, the Lord also led me into a fairly detailed study of Paul's second letter to young Timothy, possibly Paul's last letter from his prison cell in Rome. I enjoyed sharing this study with a most receptive congregation in a huge Presbyterian church in Knoxville, Tennessee, at their annual missions' conference. Each year at this conference the church ask the invited speaker to speak to encourage any missionaries there on home leave and also to challenge the congregation to consider their level of involvement in the world missions' programme—as those who give to support those who go, or as those who could go to swell the ranks of those proclaiming the gospel on the front lines, or as those who should get behind them in meaningful, regular, informed prayer. They gave me the overall title 'Fanning the flame!' from 2 Timothy 1:6, and that led me to study how Paul set about passing the torch on to young Timothy, and therefore how we should be seeking to pass the torch on to the next generation of younger Christians.

As we started out in 2 Timothy 1, we looked, firstly, at God's plan to meet man's need, a plan that involved a group of argumentative, vacillating disciples being sent to 'go and tell' the Good News to all peoples, to every ethnic group, without partiality or favour. There was no other plan. There was no other Name, given under heaven, by which men must be saved! The Lord Jesus is **the** way, not just one of many ways. And, however frail and weak we may feel, we have to be sure that God's Spirit of power, His Grace in the Lord Jesus, plus the sufficiency of the Scriptures are the divine resources that He gives to each of us, both to preserve His church and also to spread the gospel throughout the world.

Paul challenged Timothy (chapter 2) to be strong, to endure hardness, to strive, and to labour so that God's plan to meet man's need might be met. This is equally true of each one of us today. God's power to meet man's need must surely be the indwelling Holy Spirit. It would seem possible that young Timothy was almost willing to throw in the sponge. It may have been in his nature to keep a low profile and to opt out of suffering. Maybe he was finding the whole task of mission too big to cope with. Then the aged Paul wrote him this letter to encourage him: '... *join me in suffering for the gospel, by the **power** of God!*' Paul didn't minimise the difficulties that Timothy would meet. In fact, he told him bluntly that any who would live as Jesus wanted them to would inevitably suffer and be persecuted. 'Keep going, son. I'm in the same boat, and I'm not ashamed of it!'

The God who has saved us, called us to be holy, and sent us out to proclaim the gospel, has given us *the* Gift (not merely a gift!) of the indwelling Holy Spirit. The Spirit gave Paul zeal for the work even though he knew there was a price to be paid. Paul always had a goal in view, and he pled with Timothy not to drift but to trust God to keep him whatever sufferings might be involved. All he had to do was to commit himself wholly and unreservedly to Him. All God asks of us is to preach Jesus and to be unashamed of Him. He is our message; He is the Good News, '*the power of God for the salvation of everyone who believes*' (Rom. 1:16).

Paul challenges young Timothy, and so us, to be strong in the grace of Jesus Christ, enduring hardship as a good soldier, uninvolved in every type of self-indulgence and pleasing our Commanding Officer at all times. He challenges us to fulfil all the rules for entry into God's Olympics—intensive training, self-denial, no cutting corners—and therefore assures us of the victor's crown. And He challenges us to work hard and diligently even through disappointments, just as a farmer works with no days off but in the expectant joy of harvest. The servant of God must study hard to know the Word thoroughly so as to 'plough a straight furrow', not be drawn aside by distractions, and able to withstand all false teaching. We are to keep our eyes focused on our Saviour, the Lord Jesus Christ. In all things and at all times we are to be Christ-like in our actions and words, in our attitudes and motives. Just as He came 'to serve and to give' so is that to be our sole purpose.

In chapter 3 of Paul's second letter to Timothy, we saw that the facts of the world in Timothy's day were just as they are today. The wicked seemed to be flourishing. But Paul continues: 'You, however...' and reminds Timothy of his own testimony, and his one goal: 'to present everyone perfect in Christ.' And what did Paul get for all he gave? The list is almost unbelievable. He suffered ill health, loneliness, and misunderstandings. He was beaten, stoned, put in the stocks, and had to endure false accusations. Most of us, faced with such a challenge, might well say, 'No-one in his right senses would choose **that!**' Yet Paul knew from the day he was saved on the road to Damascus what to expect. He knew that he would suffer in his service for God. Had not God shown 'him how much he will suffer for my name' (Acts 9:16)? Are we prepared, in our day and generation, to so fall in love with Jesus that we are able to call all such suffering a **privilege?** We have to make the choice with our eyes open. Do we want riches here or hereafter? Then the living Word is liberated 'so that the man of God may be thoroughly equipped for every good work' (2 Tim. 3:17) to which God longs to call us. We need be afraid of nothing except failing Him. He will never fail us!

And then finally in chapter 4:2, Paul charges Timothy, God's servant: *'Preach the Word!'* Study and stick to the Word. Everything else is secondary: *'... faith comes from hearing the message, and the message is heard through the word of Christ'* (Rom. 10:17). Paul warns Timothy—and so all of us involved in God's service—to keep his head! We must not be sidetracked or caught up in lesser issues, even in good things. The one job that only we can do is to preach the Word with endurance when mocked, with patience when all seems fruitless, and with love when we are criticised or ignored.

If we do this and stick at it our Lord and King promises the crown of righteousness. And what a triumphant ending to the letter! The elderly apostle Paul, in prison, awaiting death, said: *'... so that through me the message might be fully proclaimed and all the Gentiles might hear it. ... The Lord will rescue me from every evil attack and will bring me safely to his heavenly Kingdom. To him be glory for ever and ever. Amen!'* (2 Tim. 4:18). What a wonderful encouragement for timid Timothy, and for all God's servants today everywhere in the world! All we are called upon to do in order to discharge our responsibility is to preach the Word, that the message might be proclaimed (2 Tim. 4:2) wherever God sends us and whatever the circumstances.

The following year, after sharing these thoughts in Knoxville, I had the wonderful opportunity of going to Poland to minister among the Campus Crusade for Christ workers from all over Eastern Europe. Once again we worked our way through these same four chapters of this last letter Paul wrote before his martyrdom. They grew on me and excited me. Each time I shared them the Lord showed me new things and new ways of presenting the truth.

Then, almost unexpectedly, the Lord led me in a new direction in ministry. I was invited to go to Hong Kong, and from there on to Singapore, to minister in our WEC home bases, and at churches and youth rallies, Bible schools and seminaries in their areas, and to promote the whole concept of missions—that our God is a missionary God! It certainly was very exciting to see over 1,000 young Chinese Christians and, a week later, hundreds of Singaporeans almost sitting on the edge of their chairs listening eagerly to the challenge as though they had never heard it before.

That was the start of a specific ministry to visit and encourage our WEC personnel at many of our sending bases. I had already had this privilege in the USA and Canada as well as the UK, but now there were invitations to visit France, Switzerland, Germany, and, a little later, Mexico! Each visit was interwoven with ministry arranged by and through the University Christian Unions, and also various women's outreach programmes. I had just begun to feel that, after twenty years 'on the road' it was time to begin slowing down, but how could I say 'No'? While the Lord continued to give me reasonably good health, daily fresh visions of Himself, and ever-deepening joy in the study of His Word, I felt constrained to keep on keeping on.

A sudden call to help out at Bethany Fellowship in Minneapolis, at their annual 'Deeper Life Convention', where the booked speaker (a pastor from Bosnia) was hindered by the war in his own country and unable to obtain a visa, helped me to re-focus. God blessed me so much through that week of seeking to share His Word, not so much as a direct challenge to missionary involvement, but rather as a call to true holiness of living in our ordinary everyday lives. I began to see that such a presentation of biblical truth would, in itself, lead to missionary challenge without having to verbalise such. Surely as the desire to live more and more like the Lord Jesus and to be more and more like Him grows in our hearts, He will move us forward into ministry without anyone having to spell it out! Missionary service is so much on the heart of God the Father who sent His Son into the world to die for us, and God the Son who sent us the Holy Spirit to indwell us and empower us for service, and God the Holy Spirit who sends us into the world around us to show forth the love of God.

The trip to Mexico was unforgettable. There was the sheer vastness of that mighty city and the desperate contrast between the 'well-to-do' side and the 'do-without' side. The welcomes I received at the Union Evangelical Church for the first weekend, and then by the WEC family on the other side of the city, were very touching. And I was given liberty to minister to different groups. One was a group of some seventy five missionaries gathered together from all over the city for encouragement. Another was a congregation of over 300 on the Sunday morning. Then there was a whole day's retreat with our WEC family at which we concentrated together on the importance of 'being' Christlike, even before 'doing' godly activities. At every meeting God had to touch my heart and speak to me, before I could pass on His Word to others. It was humbling, sometimes exhausting, but always exhilarating!

From Mexico I flew, by an amazingly circuitous route, back to Knoxville, to Cedar Springs Presbyterian Church, for a missionary weekend. And their loving welcome was like an oasis to my thirsty soul. The unbelievable privilege of speaking to over 1,000 at each of two Sunday morning services really was a refreshment and an encouragement for all that lay ahead in that particular tour in the United States.

My Christmas prayer letter to all my loving supporters sums up that year: 'One particular thought has recurred many times during this year. It is summed up in a quotation from Robert Murray McCheyne, '*My people's greatest need is my personal holiness.*' That is to say, no matter how biblically accurate and doctrinally sound my regular teaching, if my daily life is not lived in accordance with, and in practical outworking of, the theory, the latter will fall on deaf ears. I realise that that is only one side of the truth, but it was a side that the Lord emphasised to me over and over again at that stage in my own journey. And I began speaking more and more on that theme.

My heart was being thrilled, as God continued to direct my ministry to bible teaching, without my being narrowed down to one particular emphasis. I had the joy of a week of teaching in our own church, on the 'Whys' in the life of our Lord Jesus. Why was He born of the Virgin Mary? Why was He, the Holy Son of God, baptised? Why did He do so many miracles, and yet often say 'Tell no-one!'? Why did He have to be crucified on the cruel cross of Calvary? Why did He rise again? Shortly afterwards, when invited to speak at our GCU Annual Leaders' Conference, we thought through the biblical concept of worship. A quotation from a former Archbishop of Canterbury, William Temple, had come into my hands, and certainly enriched my own concept of worship: '*For true worship, we must: (a) quicken the conscience by the holiness of God, (b) feed the mind with the truth of God, (c) purge the imagination by the beauty of God, (d) open the heart to the love of God, and (e) devote the will to the purpose of God.*' On several occasions in the following months I had the opportunity to go through those five points as five steps to be taken into the fullness of worship.

Then there came an invitation to go to another mission's annual field conference and to be with a lovely group of thirty dedicated missionaries, all working in a very hostile and difficult climate. They had come apart for a time of refreshment and renewal, for a period of sharing and praying together. What a privilege to be with them! They were so hungry to see a breakthrough in the barren lands where they served, and so willing to pay any price needful to see this come about. Morning by morning we thought through the training Elijah needed before God could entrust him with the mighty outpouring of fire from on high on Mount Carmel. And each evening we meditated on the last verse of Paul's letter to the Corinthians: 'The **grace** of our Lord Jesus Christ, the **love** of God, and the **fellowship** of the Holy Spirit, be with **us all**. Amen.' It was so good just to take unhurried time to ponder on the amazing grace of God in sending Jesus into the world to die in our place, to save us from our sins. We thought of the love of God, that despite us being His enemies and choosing to ignore or disobey Him, He so loved us that He gave His only-begotten beloved Son to die for us. And we were blessed as we thought of the fellowship that He offers us with the Godhead, by filling us with the indwelling Holy Spirit, the very Spirit of Christ.

In 1997, my friend and colleague, Pat, and I had the wonderful joy of sharing in another of our WEC Fields' annual conferences, when we spent time every morning and evening meditating on John's first letter. It was probably written to the scattered Jewish Christians through what is now Turkey, believers harassed and with a sense of foreboding and fear of the persecution about to fall on the young churches at the hands of the Roman tyrants. There was so much in every paragraph of that letter to speak to our own hearts. There was teaching to encourage, warn, and support us in times of persecution, loneliness, or apparent fruitlessness. So many of our Christian brothers and sisters in that land were under stress, being watched daily, often being threatened, never knowing from what side the next attack would come. It was amazing to stand alongside them and enter a little into their heart-agony and yearning.

Pat was invited to share with them on the theme 'Coping with stress'. As she prayed and prepared this message beforehand, the Lord led her to the realisation that it is really *learning to live in the presence of stress*, rather than learning how to cope with it. Her words were so blessed to all of us. She also based her thoughts on the story of Elijah, especially the later episode after the victory on Mount Carmel, when Elijah fled from Jezebel because he was afraid of being killed. He felt weary, discouraged, and a failure despite the enormous victory (or more likely, because of it). Pat then led us through three basic steps, or essential principles, in learning to live in the presence of stress. Firstly, there is the detachment of prayer. Secondly, there is the discernment of priorities, and thirdly, the discipline of pain. Each part was illustrated from Scripture and from the writings of others, such as a poem by Amy Carmichael of Dohnavur:

'Hast thou no scar? No hidden scar
   on foot or side or hand?
I hear thee sung as mighty in the land,
I hear them hail thy bright ascendant star
   – Hast thou no scar?'

Pat illustrated so simply, and yet with such telling reality, that we must accept all that the Lord allows to come into our lives. Another of Amy Carmichael's poems reminds us that 'In acceptance lieth peace.' Is it not indeed a privilege to be invited by our Lord to share in the fellowship of His sufferings? Not only should we accept this, but we should also embrace it.

At the close of that year, as I wrote my Christmas letter, once again I felt a wave of discouragement despite all the blessing of the year, and there had been many. Although I knew I was very tired, I allowed the feelings of discouragement to make me wonder if I was still in line with God's perfect will for my life. I dreaded that I might just keep going out of habit, even if I was no longer in His will. One morning I asked God for a specific word of fresh direction for the in-coming year. My reading that morning was in 2 Chronicles 15, and verse seven seemed to jump out at me. *'But as for you, be strong and do not give up, for your work will be rewarded.'* How gracious of the dear Lord! I knew I was to press on towards the goal of pleasing Him, day in and day out, preaching the Word in season and out of season. But I also knew that I had to learn not to be so easily swayed by feelings. It is easy to say that to others, but I was so slow to learn the lesson myself—allowing myself to feel self-pity, to feel insecure, to feel that what I was doing was self-pleasing, even self-indulgent, rather than pleasing to God.

I re-read the notes of Pat's words to those missionaries on 'Learning to live in the presence of stress' and felt convicted by how little I had really learned of this lesson myself. To acknowledge that my life was stressful—not because of danger or open opposition, so far as I was personally concerned, but rather because of the sheer pace of living, travelling, meeting with so many people, of other people's expectations, and of seeking to be always ready to fit into any and every situation that arose—was probably half the battle. Having done that, I had to honestly commit the whole to God in believing prayer, seeking His help to set realistic goals for the in-coming year (which had to include learning how to say 'No' graciously!), and accepting His plan even if there was pain involved, realising that it is a privilege to be invited by the Lord to share in His sufferings for this sin-sick world and the desperate need of millions to hear the gospel of His redeeming love.

12

Digging Ditches from East to West, from North to South.

The next few years were filled with conferences involving many different nationalities, and with four or five Bible studies at each conference. It really was very exciting. How good God was to give me His word of encouragement to keep on keeping on, and not to grow weary in His service, whether I saw results or not. And throughout the travelling it was amazing how many individuals came up to me to thank me for some word given during the past *twenty* years, 'a word,' they would say, 'that was just for me'. Often they said that they were where they are now because of the challenge of God to their hearts at that time. Though I shouldn't have needed such encouragements, how gracious of God to give them to me to help me keep on keeping on.

It was a very humbling experience to be invited to different WEC sending bases as well as several different Annual Field Conferences to minister a word of encouragement and challenge to our often hard-pressed missionaries, some in situations of considerable danger and/or loneliness. I had been to our WEC families in Hong Kong and in Singapore in 1992 and I went again two years later, together with my friend Pat. We enjoyed such lovely fellowship in the homes of our missionaries and were excited to see the tremendous potential among the young life in both areas. A youth meeting, with over 1,000 teens and early twenties, sat 'eating out of our hands' as we shared the challenge of the unreached millions around the world still waiting to hear the gospel for the very first time. Churches were packed Sunday by Sunday, mostly with young folk, often with very young pastors seeking to lead them on in the Christian faith. They seemed so vibrant; it was as though they were just waiting for the challenge to personal involvement in overseas cross-cultural missions.

Then there was a second visit to Mexico City with its teeming millions. It was a huge joy to speak in a new 'indigenous' church in the centre of the city where there was already some 3,000 members, and where they had started their own Bible school to train national pastors. They were praying that one in every ten students would be called of God into overseas cross-cultural ministry. It was a great opportunity to share with those particular students, basing our thoughts on Luke 5:1-11: (a) the crowd following Jesus representing the needy world 'out there' desperate to hear His voice, (b) the huge catch of fish, representing God's power to bring to birth a church in every people group in the world, and (c) Peter, the reluctant disciple, whom God chose to 'need' for the fulfilment of His purposes. Were we willing to say 'Yes' to the Lord's call to *'launch out into the deep'* (Luke 5:4 KJV) to *'let down the nets'* in what we might think of as the most unlikely place at quite the wrong time of day, and to trust Him to know best? He who made the fish knew exactly where they were, and how they could be caught! What an encouragement to us, the often reluctant 'fishers-of-men'!

After an amazing three-day church retreat focussing on the **grace** of God, who invited us to accept—who entrusted to us—the responsibility of telling others of His love and almighty provision for all our needs, I then had a lovely day with our WEC family. There were around twenty of us, and we thought together of the beauty and loveliness of our Lord and Saviour Jesus as the Treasure, and of ourselves as the jars of clay (2 Cor. 4:7). He moulds us, prepares us, and fires us in order to send us wheresoever, and for whatsoever. There were precious times of personal chatting together through some deep problems and seeking His grace to be willing to be 'fired' as He saw fit and needful.

Each year there were so many opportunities to talk of our Lord Jesus, of the grace of God, and of the unbelievable wonder of being called into His service, at Bible schools across America and Britain, and at churches and women's groups at home and abroad. I well remember spending time preparing three Bible studies on Moses, based on Hebrews 11:24-27, He *chose* to suffer, '*to be ill-treated along with the people of God rather than to enjoy the pleasures of sin for a short time.*' He *chose* to believe. '*He regarded disgrace for the sake of Christ as of greater value than the treasures of Egypt.*' And he *chose* to endure. '*He left Egypt, not fearing the king's anger; he persevered because he saw him who is invisible.*' The time spent in preparation was such a blessing to my own heart! God actually gives us the privilege of making those choices as His Holy Spirit in us draws us to obey Him, and as we are willing to choose to suffer (if needs be) in obeying His will, rather than going with the crowd. If we are willing to choose to believe in Him and His goodness and in His almighty power and ability to keep us whatever befalls, rather than being drawn away to trust in this world's goods and glory, then God will bless us. If we are willing to forego a settled income and the option of promotion; if we are willing to keep on keeping on even in the face of opposition or apparent failure or fruitlessness, then God will bless us, fill us with His peace, joy, and His enabling. What a wonderful God we serve!

There was a small Christian fellowship in Cornwall (the county of my roots, as my American friends would say!) where we had five tremendous sessions together facing the challenge of missions worldwide, under the old titles 'Why?' 'Where?' 'What?' 'Who?' and 'How?' Then I was invited to East Germany not long after the fall of the Berlin Wall for a 'Deeper Life' conference of workers of Campus Crusade in Europe. Once again, the Lord led us to the ministry of Elijah on Mount Carmel, but I sensed Him changing the emphasis from the extraordinary event they all saw when the fire fell from heaven on the prepared sacrifice, to the meticulous preparation in the heart and life of Elijah, making him a 'fit instrument' in the hands of the Lord. It was also very humbling to meet up with nationals of Eastern Europe, so long separated from us by a wall of man's making, and to sense their deep love of the Lord. No amount of persecution or threatening had been able to extinguish the spark of holy fire. I was given a beautiful gift at the close of the conference, a gift that I have treasured ever since and that is brought out every Christmas. It is a hand-carved manger scene under an arch with five candleholders. Beautiful in its simplicity, it is also amazing in the delicacy of its workmanship.

That was followed by a trip back to the USA for ten days packed with meetings, including three days at the Nanibijou Conference Centre, where I have made dear friends over the years. There were many there who had been deeply hurt and whose minds were bruised by a sad occurrence in the church fellowship to which they belonged, and I was specifically asked to minister to the question, 'Why does a God of love allow suffering?' This was the question that I had been challenged to answer years earlier when in Australia. God led me then to realise that it is *because* He **is** a God of love that *He* suffered for us, and that now He invites *us* to share in His sufferings. As then, so it is now. We did not actually come up with an answer to the initial question, but rather we reached some understanding of the unquestioning acceptance of a life of sharing in the fellowship of His sufferings. If we love deeply we can expect to suffer deeply as well.

And so to Africa! Pat and I were invited to Malawi, where my youngest sister and her husband taught in the secondary school at Livingstonia. Robin and Frances were deeply involved in the restoration of the church building that had been started by Dr Laws, a Presbyterian missionary, early in the 1900s, but had sadly never been completed. We had played a small part in encouraging folk to give financially to this project. So when it was nearing completion, we were invited to go out for the dedication service. This certainly was a very different kind of ministry. What a beautiful country Malawi is, right there in the heart of the vast continent of Africa! We were given a royal welcome and we enjoyed every moment of our time there. The church was packed for the dedication with two separate choirs of younger and older singers. All the workmen who had been involved in the restoration and building programme were there, as were visiting Presbyterian missionaries and leaders from other parts of Malawi. I was invited to say a few words of spiritual encouragement. I spoke on the fact that God is more deeply desirous of the completion of building His temple in the hearts and lives of His people, even than in the bricks and mortar building in which we were sitting (1 Cor. 3:16). There was a hush over that huge congregation and we sensed a willingness in some to be challenged to put God first in their lives.

For all my travels over the years I had never been to mainland China. However, I *was* invited to minister at the Easter Convention of Chinese students studying at various universities in the east of the UK. As so often, I found it very humbling to see the intense interest of over 100 young students as we worked our way through 1 Corinthians 15:1-11. On Good

Friday, *'Christ died for our sins'* (15:3) reminded us of all His death means for us and to us. He died as our substitute: 'in my place, condemned, He stood'. We sought to take a new grasp of the wonder and magnitude of the gospel, reminding ourselves that there is *'no other name under heaven given to men by which we must be saved'* (Acts 4:12). On the Saturday, when our subject was that *'He was buried'*, we thought of the more than two billion people in our world today who are still waiting to hear the gospel, considering not only their geographic distribution but their needs, and the countless opportunities we have to meet those needs. On Easter Sunday, *'He was raised on the third day'* was the glorious truth we studied. We revelled in the marvel of the resurrection, worshipped the Lamb in many glorious Easter hymns, and sought to realise afresh something of what His resurrection means to us. It is our ultimate assurance that Christ dying for us on the cross was acceptable to the Father as our propitiation. On the Monday, we thought about the various appearances of the Lord after His resurrection, first to Peter and the Twelve, then to the 500 brethren gathered together and to James, and lastly, to Paul in that wonderful meeting on the road to Damascus. From that meeting Paul, a completely changed man, went out to *'carry God's name before the Gentiles and their kings'* (Acts 9:15). Are we prepared, we asked ourselves, to be completely changed, re-created by God in the likeness of our Lord and Saviour, and sent out by Him to witness to all peoples? The responsiveness of those young people was almost overwhelming. They were indeed 'prepared vessels', ready for the challenge.

Immediately following that weekend, I went to the headquarters of the Overseas Missionary Fellowship (OMF), to meet up with a selected group from GCU: Ruth Hodgson, a leader from Glasgow, and four young university students: Elaine from Northern Ireland; Rachel, the daughter of missionary parents working in Thailand; Hannah from a university in the Midlands of England; and Maddy from Wales. We were there to prepare for 'the experience of a lifetime!' as one expressed it, after our summer excursion. We were going together as a team to Thailand and Vietnam to experience what it means to 'be a missionary', in as far as that is possible in six short weeks! These two countries were chosen for their contrasts. One is an 'open' country, but with little response, the other is a supposed 'closed' country where, in fact, there is an eagerness to hear the gospel.

We had two days of orientation and teaching to seek to prepare us for living in another culture, amidst a people of another language. It was a good two days. We got to know each other a bit, and began to gel together. We thought of various aspects of how we should behave in the two countries we were to visit, seeing ourselves as servants of the people, and being willing to learn from them as well as longing to pass on to them the truths of the gospel. I shared the 'five vowels of Christian discipline—specifically in the life of a young missionary': A, accepting the authority of those over us in the Lord, in the main without questioning; E, enjoying the experience as a gift from God, and seeking always to help each other and our host missionaries to enjoy having us, by thoughtfulness and helpfulness; I, the essential need to cross out our individuality, our 'I', as in Galatians 2:20, so that it may truly be said of each one of us, '*I have been crucified with Christ and I no longer live, but Christ lives in me*'; O, obeying all orders promptly, knowing that those who have been there for years know better than we do how we should behave in certain situations—such as the advice we had been given about the clothes we should or should not wear; And U, be understanding, slow to criticise but quick to listen, and to seek to enter into the lives of those we were there to serve— missionaries, as well as nationals. When we return home, we noted, we were to be quick to express appreciation, and very slow to express criticisms, knowing that God would give us understanding hearts as we asked Him.

On the 15th July 2000, we were ready to leave the UK and to launch out into the deep, not without trepidation, yet full of excited expectations. From our meeting together at Heathrow airport, and the celebration of Maddy's birthday (she was the youngest member of our team) to the day, six weeks later, that we said our goodbyes to each other, again at Heathrow airport, it was indeed a fantastic experience. We were all so conscious of the prayerful upholding every day by a veritable army of supporters from each of our six families, our home churches, and the GCU family throughout the UK. And we were almost overwhelmed by the generous kindness of our hosts. The stretched, and often overworked, team of OMF missionaries in both Thailand and Vietnam were marvellous. We were met at Bangkok airport and driven north by Eunice Burden to Lop Buri, the OMF language school and centre for initial orientation of new missionaries. They allowed us to take part in some basic lessons in speaking Thai. The girls really worked at this and did well. But my ears and tongue were simply not as quick as theirs!

Snippets from my diary of the visit might have read, 'Down town shopping... finding our way around by maps rather than by enquiring... eating in local cafes... coming to terms with sticky heat... the privilege of sharing with all the local OMF personnel... taken further up-country to the OMF medical centre at Manorom... touring the hospital and local village... further privilege of sharing with the team of doctors and nurses, and then of speaking at the local church.' Everywhere we walked we saw idols of the Buddha, and we could feel the heaviness of spiritual darkness. We moved to Uthai, to stay with Jan Trelogan. Once again a generous welcome awaited us. Jan moved out of her bedroom, so that Ruth and I could enjoy that comfort, including the fan to cool us down in the hot sticky nights (just as Eunice had done for me in Lop Buri). Then started the 'service' that we had come for—teaching English in an enormous state secondary school, with 1,800 pupils in ten streams in each of six years! How we thanked God that Ruth was a seasoned teacher and knew how to encourage the four girls to prepare for and deliver their teaching! None of the rest of us had much idea. By the end of ten intensive days the girls were just beginning to enjoy the experience.

The four girls lived in Thai homes, ate Thai food, and travelled on the back of motorbikes in true Thai fashion! They taught several classes a day to all the different age groups, made many friends and really began to integrate into the local culture. At the end of our time at that school we were treated like royalty. Presentations were made to each of us by the principal, before the whole assembled school. A party in the school and another (including a karaoke of 1960s Beatles' songs!) with staff members at a local hotel were some of the highlights before we moved on to our next assignment, with our hearts overflowing with praise to God for all His abundant goodness to us.

During the time that Ruth and the girls were teaching at Uthai, I had the opportunity to travel over two hours further north to Tak, to spend three days with our WEC family at yet another minifield conference. There were many opportunities for ministry and encouragement to the whole group, in smaller groups, and to individuals, as well as in the small but vibrant local church. Once again I was filled with an awed sense of humble worship at God's condescension in allowing me any part in such a ministry. As we saw and sensed the enormous difficulties of presenting the gospel in a country soaked in Buddhism, with the attendant threat of a sense of failure, of fruitlessness, of 'is it really worthwhile?', the Lord led us all to concentrate on the fact that it is HIS work, not ours. He calls us to a life of holiness and trust, a life lived in the belief that He is fulfilling His perfect plan, even if we cannot see how. As I mentioned in the last chapter, the words of McCheyne had become very meaningful to me in the previous year or two, 'My people's greatest need is my personal holiness.' We are called to reflect the Lord's beauty through our lives as much as through our words, and God will use this in His own perfect time. 'We have this treasure [the lovely Lord Jesus] in jars of clay', but those jars need to be absolutely clean, fired, and filled, so that the overflow may be seen by others.

On travelling back to Bangkok, once again we were welcomed by the OMF personnel at their guesthouse. We had two days to relax and refresh, to see the sights of Bangkok, and to go out to lunch with Ruth's brother in a smart downtown hotel, where eating rice was thankfully not mandatory! There was also shopping and the celebration of Rachel's birthday! Then we flew on to Vietnam to be met at Ho Chi Minh City airport by two OMF missionaries. As everywhere, they put themselves out to welcome us and help us settle into yet another new situation. We were to stay at Lan Anh Hotel right in the tourist area of the city. As our four lovely rooms had air conditioning and en suite bathrooms, we had ample opportunity to scrub our filthy feet after frequently being barefoot (in accordance with local culture) in Thailand!

On the Sunday, we walked together along the bustling street to church, passing hundreds of small shops crowded with vendors and their tricycles, and noisy with the roar of motorbikes. It was a large airy building seating some 400 people. The congregation was celebrating the seventy-fifth anniversary of missionaries from the Christian and Missionary Alliance founding the work in Vietnam in 1925. There were to be three services that morning to accommodate the over 1,000 members. Several choirs, of every age group, led the worship and the singing was beautiful. We heard an excellent sermon by the senior pastor, on Numbers 21:4-9, the remedy for being bitten by a fiery serpent was to look up to the image of a serpent, made by Moses, and raised on a pole in the centre of the Israelites' camp, in accordance with the Word of God. The teaching was so clear. It was wonderful to have fellowship with local believers in such an open and unharassed way, though no foreigner may today take any part in the leadership of the church in Vietnam. We heard that there are some twenty other similar churches throughout Ho Chi Minh City. This was all such a contrast to what we had seen in the Buddhist stronghold of Thailand, and so different from our expectations.

Throughout our three weeks in Thailand, Ruth led our group each day in prayer for what lay ahead of us, and in Bible study in Mark's Gospel, with notebooks that she had prepared for us beforehand. In Vietnam it was my privilege to lead that daily prayer time, and we started a Bible study on how God changed Simon into Peter. I think each of us had times of feeling very much like Simons, and of asking God to complete His work in us, His work of making us into Peters.

Each day we enjoyed eating out at a local restaurant/café. A good meal of rice and pork, with a large milk shake made from local fruits, cost the princely sum of £1! We went shopping in the market and managed to pick up lots of small souvenirs to take home. The girls made use of a local 'internet cafe' to send and receive e-mails. We had a wonderful outing to the Mekong River and a boat trip across it to a coconut plantation where we watched the process of extracting all the goodness from coconuts and the making of coconut sweetmeats. Then we saw the shells being carved into ornaments for exporting.

One of the OMF missionaries tried hard to find a 'way in' to a local school where we could teach English, but this was not as easily arranged as in Thailand. We had to be patient. But then came the news that we could go to a small private school for 15 to 30-year-olds wishing to learn English. It was a conversational arrangement rather than a formal classroom situation. The 'students' were at all stages, from some who knew practically no English at all, to a couple going on to university, who already had a fairly good grasp of basic English. All six of us were to be involved, with Ruth very definitely our coordinator-cum-leader! I wrote in my diary that evening, 'I dread to think how we would cope without Ruth. She just *is* a teacher, and so patient with us, willing to guide, help and encourage us!'

During our first evening at the school, we broke up into small groups and got to know each other. We shared, as far as they were able to understand, about our homes and ourselves. Then we played games using the little English they knew. From then on it was to be more intensive! We prepared dialogues, taught a little bit of grammar, engaged in conversational pieces, and made up a story about shopping involving the prices of fruit and vegetables. Maddy and I worked together with five students of 'middle ability'. All groups were taught in the same small room, and Maddy and I did not find this easy. Everyone talked loudly and laughed a lot. It was not exactly the best atmosphere for serious teaching. Each evening we spent an hour or more thinking out what we would teach the next day, preparing material, photocopying crosswords, maps, word-searches, block-busters, noughts and crosses, choruses—anything to increase vocabulary and encourage our students to try out their English.

At the end of our ten days with them, we all gave each other a fantastic farewell party! The school director, with his own class of students, plus three other members of staff at the school, joined us. We had a hilarious time. Everyone joined in and seemed to enjoy themselves tremendously. Speeches were made, presents given, certificates presented, and then came the 'eats'—in a mixture of Vietnamese and European. Having eaten, photos were taken, addresses swapped and quite tearful goodbyes said. There was genuine emotion on all sides, including a letter from one of the staff (unable to come to the party) saying that our presence had made 'this school a different place'. She thought 'it must be your God.'

Although our time at the school was ended, we still had another exciting adventure ahead of us. A Christian travel agent organised a trip up-country into the mountains, to DaLat, with a group of students (most of whom were not Christians) who all wanted to improve their English. Two leaders (at least one of whom was truly a Christian) and thirteen young people aged from fourteen to twenty-four years, all piled into a twenty-four-seater coach with us and all our luggage. Introductory remarks and welcomes were followed by a few songs to a guitar accompaniment, and then we all fell asleep as we drove north through a tropical downpour. Eventually we arrived at a hotel in DaLat, settled into our nice and very adequate rooms, before spending the evening together. By the time we had been for a walk, stopped at a coffee shop, and played some party games, we were beginning to know each other's names. Ruth kept everything going and under control. Two older people in the group, a boy aged sixteen and a lady of twenty-four, were definitely seeking to know more about spiritual matters and they asked about our reason for being there. On the second afternoon, despite heavy rain, we went on an excursion that involved walking up hundreds of steps, through an alleyway of stalls all selling the same 'tourist-icky' articles, across the plateau, and down the far side of the 'mountain' to a lake. Then, despite the continuing rain, we set off in two motorboats to tour the lake. At the far side, the 'driver' of our boat allowed us to disembark and clamber up a slippery, muddy hillside, where we discovered enormous models of animals: giraffes, camels, bullocks, rhinoceros, all two by two. Suddenly, as we reached the top of the hillside, we saw straight in front of us two huge statues of Adam and Eve! It was so totally unexpected that we laughed. One of the Vietnamese group who was with us, twenty-four-year-old Phon, asked if we knew who these two people were? That started a truly amazing conversation that continued, on and off, throughout the next two days, and all the way back down to Ho Chi Minh City. Phon was hungry to know all that we could tell her, not only of Adam and Eve, but also of our Creator God, and all that is written in His Book. She never ceased to ply us all with questions. Ruth and Hannah spent hours with her, and slowly her heart opened up—like Lydia's in Acts 16—to receive the Lord as her Saviour.

On our arrival back at the city, as we said goodbye to each other at the Travel Agent's shop, Phon looked straight at us. With a lovely smile, she said, 'We will meet again— if not here, then in glory!' We realised, in almost stunned amazement, just how much she had already received from God in understanding the gospel. That was truly the 'icing on the cake' for all of us. Phon's conversion was the best possible gift God could have given us as our time in Vietnam drew to a close.

We all felt so full of gratitude to God for those amazing six weeks. In our last Bible study together, we looked at John 4, the woman who met Jesus at the well, and we wondered if Phon was our 'woman at the well'—thirsty, ready, and responsive. Had we been in Vietnam because the Holy Spirit knew that we *must* go through that way in order to meet that young woman?

As I look back over all that I have recorded in this chapter, and ask myself, 'Lord, what were you teaching *me*? Have I learned the lesson?' Surely above all else, the Lord was saying, 'I am able!' He *is* in control. I don't need to panic. I don't need to tell Him what I think I can or cannot do. I can trust Him in *every* situation, even if I may be faced with totally unknown and unexpected moments. It is not for me to dictate to the Lord how I want to serve Him, nor where. He is a much better judge of that than I am. I am so full of thankfulness to the Lord for His overwhelming goodness, His enabling, His strength, and His vision, and I just want to go on going on, to know Him better, to love Him more dearly and to keep following Him to the end of the journey.

13

STILL DIGGING DITCHES –
NOT YET A SUEZ CANAL!

Immediately following my exciting trip to South East Asia, Pat and I went away for a short holiday. We needed to be refreshed and renewed, physically and spiritually, before a new year of activities began. Unfortunately, I went down with a chest infection and was quite sick. It cannot have been much of a holiday for Pat as I struggled to regain strength. But it taught me, once again, how frail we are apart from the Lord's enabling, and how utterly dependent we are on Him every day for His sustaining grace.

Back home, we were immediately into vigorous preparation for a tour of meetings of Bible schools in central and western Canada. I never cease to marvel at the Lord's grace in allowing us to minister among these keen young Christians. Some of the schools were fairly large with over 500 students and others were smaller with 150 or so. At some I was invited to minister four or five times over several days, at others once or twice in one day. Travelling between the schools sometimes involved one or two air flights or long car journeys through the prairies. But everywhere there were such warm welcomes and such intense and eager interest.

At the first college we worked our way, as on some previous occasions, through the prophecy of Jonah, looking at (a) how to find God's will for our lives, (b) the need of prayer and obedience to God if we are to know and act on His will for our lives, (c) the urgent need of the world of today to hear the gospel message, and (d) our motivation in our service— to see God glorified, and not simply to please ourselves, and certainly not to receive the praise of men.

At other colleges we spent more time concentrating on our need to be clean mirrors, reflecting the loveliness of Jesus all day every day, no matter what the outward circumstances. I shared with them that instead of asking ourselves 'Is it worth it?' when the way gets tough, and our backs are to the wall, we should ask 'Is He worthy?' There will certainly, eventually, come a day when we will be tempted to say 'No' to the first question, but the second will always bring us round to saying 'Yes. One hundred times yes!' At the last college we visited there was freezing snow on the ground, but the warmth in the students' hearts was a tremendous contrast. Five meetings were held there, from a classroom situation with some thirty to a chapel period with all 300 students. The smaller group focussed on relationships on the mission field, and the larger on the fact that the world's deepest need is to see Christ in Christians who live holy lives that reflect His loveliness and goodness.

Back home again, Pat and I received an unexpected invitation to go to visit and encourage two different groups of workers in two neighbouring countries in the '10/40 window' area of the world—probably in February of 2002. (For reasons of security these countries will not be named in this narrative.) We began praying about this request, seeking clear guidance from the Lord. Should we go or not? We did not wish our decision to be made according to the safety and/or risk that such a journey would entail, nor according to our desires or otherwise, but simply, was this God's voice to us? Meanwhile there were plenty of engagements closer to home. The list included teaching a small group of older teens every Sunday in our GCU group, a group of ladies every Wednesday morning in our church, a sizeable collection of students at a university Christian union houseparty in Wales, and an exciting group of nearly 100 young people at an outreach weekend organised by OMF in Ireland. There were opportunities in our Belfast and Coleraine University Christian Unions, various Anglican Mothers' Union meetings, and Presbyterian Women's Association gatherings.

At the same time, Pat and I together were becoming deeply involved in another ministry for our local church. Our minister, after over twenty years of devoted service, often despite ill health, had to retire. There was a vacancy. In the Church of Ireland the local congregation chooses four members as 'nominators' to search for a new minister who is able and willing to come and fill their needs of pastoral care and faithful biblical teaching. Pat and I were two of those four in our church. For six months this involved us in writing letters, visiting other churches to hear ministers preaching, and meeting with our Bishop and the four nominators he had appointed to discuss and pray over our needs.

In the midst of all this activity, in April 2001, we went together on a visit to South Africa. That in itself was quite a story! A phone call came to us a year previously, and a man's voice said, 'This is John Carter!' Who was John Carter? Why was I expected to know him? And where was he phoning from? He told me that he was ringing from South Africa, and that this call was the result of years he had spent trying to find me. Why? I wondered. He told me that, in 1964, he was one of the mercenary soldiers who rescued me from the 'Simba Uprising', (the civil war) that erupted so mercilessly in Congo that August. Something in me stood still. Did I want to be reminded of all that had taken place that dreadful year? John went on talking, saying that through that day's rescue of the ten Protestant missionaries (our WEC family, working in that part of the world at the time) and through our testimonies, our whole attitude, and the apparent lack of any hatred or anger, he had become a Christian! I could hardly believe my ears! John wanted to make contact. He wanted to meet me. But I couldn't respond quite so quickly. I needed time to take it in and to know if I truly wanted to open up the past.

Some months later, and following further telephone conversations with John and with Stuart Rising, another of the same mercenary group, we got a phone call to tell us that John, and his wife Rona, were in Northern Ireland, at a Bed and Breakfast establishment near the port through which they had arrived the previous day! We drove across and spent a day with the two of them, Rona with Pat in her car, and John with me in his hired car. We talked! We filled in a lot of history of all that had taken place in our lives in the intervening thirty years since our first meeting. When we said goodbye to them, they pressed us to accept their invitation to visit them in South Africa.

During the months that followed, John had a recurrence of a previous cancerous condition, and sadly, in January 2001, he died before we managed to visit them. But his dying wish was that we would, nevertheless, go out to visit his home. As Rona and their daughter echoed that wish we made the necessary preparations and in April we went. Met by Rona, we were driven northwest from Durban, up to her home in Hilton, near Pietermaritzburg. Interestingly enough, my own brother and his wife had lived for two years in that small town of Hilton, teaching in the boy's college! We went out to see the college one day, and took photos for me to bring home to Bob and Ione.

Rona organised a tremendous holiday for us. We went for several days on an escorted tour of the battlefields, and we spent three wonderful days in a hotel by the beach south of Durban, spending as much time in the water as out! Then we travelled to Cape Town and stayed with Rona's daughter. From there we took three bus tours in different directions to see something of the beauty and hugeness of the country. Everyone was so kind to us, and made it what one might call 'the holiday of a lifetime'!

Needless to say, on our return to Northern Ireland we had to resume our duties as nominators, looking for a new rector for our parish, meeting regularly for prayer, and reporting on all we heard, and on letters we received. All this activity came to a happy conclusion with the appointment of our present rector. We learned a considerable amount through all that was involved in the exercise, not least our utter dependence on God for His guidance and assurance each step of the way.

Then suddenly—and I suppose, for everyone, wholly unexpectedly—there was the enormous catastrophe of the 11th September 2001. All ex-patriot workers serving in NGOs in the countries to which we had been invited had to leave and come home. Initially there was no immediate expectation of a return to the countries of their adoption. So all plans were put on hold. That October, I went to Cleveland, Ohio, to minister to a group of 300 women at their annual church retreat. Once more I had such a sense of privilege. They were hungry for all I felt led to share with them. There was a great responsiveness, not just at the five programmed meetings, but also in all the private conversations and at meal tables throughout the weekend. On arriving back in the UK, there was a letter from those workers who had had to be evacuated following the 9/11 events, asking if I would consider going to London to meet with them as they were discussing and praying about their future. As I sat in on all their sessions, I was humbled—awed—to realise their total dedication to the tasks to which God had called them. All were ready to go back to the country of their adoption the moment the way opened up, and the powers-that-be in the Foreign Office agreed to it. None idly dismissed the all-too-obvious dangers, but equally, they did not major on them, and that included the mothers of young children as well as their husbands.

In the daily devotional times, we based our studies on Philippians 3:10: *'I want to know Christ and the power of his resurrection and the fellowship of sharing in his sufferings ...'* We linked our studies to each of these three phrases. Firstly, there is our personal relationship with our Lord Jesus Christ, in submission. Secondly, we have our relationship to one another, in service—as He served us, so must we serve others (John 13:14). And thirdly, entering into the suffering of God for those in our world today who are without Him—dying to ourselves that Christ may wholly dwell in us, and so feel through us, act through us, care through us.

The year 2002 brought a renewed invitation to visit our friends who had been enabled to return to their country of service, so that we could see the needs there for ourselves. We were torn. Part of me was deeply attracted and part was afraid. How could I be sure what God was saying? Could I know without doubt that He was telling us to go, and that it was not just my own inclination? Could I trust Him to undertake completely for both of us (I never considered going without Pat's companionship and encouragement!) despite the natural fears in the climate of the day? We both agreed to lay the matter before the Lord and seek a clear word of direction.

Meanwhile, I had a ten-day engagement at a Bible seminary in Mississippi to give five Bible studies at their annual public conference. I was strangely fearful. I just felt I was not the person to be filling such an important role, and that the faculty and students would all be much better trained in biblical exposition than I was. I knew that my reasoning and fears were based on the wrong assumption that God was dependent on my abilities and educational training in order to be able to use me in His service. Although I knew that was not true, once again it was quite a fight to accept God's peace, and to know that what He had put in my heart to share with those seminarians was His choice and not mine, and that He would undertake if I took my hands off and did not look for personal satisfaction in this particular ministry.

I went, and was so warmly welcomed by the family with whom I was to stay. It really was a rebuke for having been afraid. It was the same at the college. The reception of what God wanted to share with them, through me, was overwhelming. Again, I had to accept God's rebuke: 'Could you not trust Me?' Once again we thought through the story of Elijah, of how God sent him to rebuke King Ahab, then hid him and cared for him through months of drought at Brook Cherith before sending him on to the widow at Zarephath. We saw how God directed him to challenge King Ahab and all the prophets of Baal on Mount Carmel before instructing Elijah to rebuild the broken down altar, slay the bullock, set the wood and the bullock on the altar as a sacrifice, pray ... but not to put fire under the sacrifice. Then, as Elijah prayed fearlessly in front of the huge gathered crowd on the mountainside, '... *the fire of the Lord fell and burned up the sacrifice, the wood, the stones and the soil, and also licked up the water in the trench*' (1 Kings 18:38). God spoke to all our hearts about the various conditions that are necessary, today as then, for Him to send down the fire from heaven in mighty revival blessing.

During the ten days I spent in Mississippi I had the joy of ministering in various churches, including to a group of young people and in a local secondary school. But above all, I had the most wonderful fellowship in the home of those who invited me there, with their four delightful young people and two huge friendly dogs! It was a time of deep and real refreshment. How good it was of God to give me that, as well as the privilege of being His mouthpiece at the college.

I arrived home again to another communication from our friends in that faraway nameless country. Would we come to visit them in February 2003? Pat and I talked it over; we sought the Lord's face and, when we read Daily Light for that morning (November 11th), *'He led them on safely'* (Ps. 78:53), we nearly laughed out loud! The next verses confirmed the word of the first: *'I lead in the way of righteousness, in the midst of the paths of judgement'* (Prov. 8:20) followed by: *'Behold, I send an Angel before thee, to keep thee in the way, and to bring thee into the place which I have prepared'* (Exod. 23:20). What more could we possibly need? We bowed our heads, and said, 'Yes, Lord.' We sent a communication to tell our friends of God's word to us and then started preparations in earnest. They let us know what they wanted so far as ministry was concerned: four Bible studies during their annual get-together, possibly two opportunities to share with bigger groups of foreign workers at their Sunday meetings, and a Bible study for a small group of workers who were seeking to go up-country to serve in an almost unreached tribal area. Letters were written to embassy officials seeking visas in our passports. Injections were organised to protect against the most commonly-occurring infections, and clothes bought for the cold of winter and to be acceptable to the culture.

The day came when all was ready. Many friends supported us in their prayers, and none actually told us that they thought we were foolhardy 'at our age'. But sometimes the looks we intercepted told us more than their unspoken words! The route of travel had been chosen, and we set off, from Belfast through Heathrow to Germany. After a short delay, we flew on, on two more planes, to our final destination.

There our friends were to meet us! Although our luggage was grossly over the allowed free baggage weight, we were not charged a penny! The luggage included many gifts for the children from their family in Belfast, plus needed electrical tools for Martin. We had to explain at each airport check that the 'things' in our baggage that looked like firearms were actually only tools for helping our friends in their service ministries and, amazingly, we were not made to unpack a thing! Everything went through without a hitch. 'You of little faith, why did you doubt?' Was that what Jesus wanted to say to me? Just as He had told His disciples, that 'they' (Jesus and the disciples) would go to the other side of the lake, had He not clearly told us that 'we' (Jesus and ourselves) were to go over to visit our friends, and that He was sending His angel before us? Why then did I doubt?

What excitement, amidst the encircling snow-covered mountains, as we disembarked at the airport, eventually collected all our luggage, and then drove through the city to our friends' home. The welcome is hard to describe. Saying that it was tremendous does not do it justice! We realised, with a deep sense of unworthiness, that our coming truly was an encouragement to those who might well have felt discouraged at the slowness of change in that vast land of huge needs. Dear Joyce, mother of three lively young boys, made us feel immediately at home. And meals appeared like clockwork despite all the shortcomings of the cooking facilities. Even in the middle of a sharp bout of real winter weather, the home was kept warm despite problems with the heating arrangements. No one complained when the room suddenly filled with billowing black, acrid smoke, and everyone helped to patch up the leaking chimney and then to clean up the sooty mess. The giving and opening of presents appeared 'like a second Christmas' one of the boys exclaimed!

A group gathered over the next day or two, made up of a doctor from the far west of the land, a trained teacher from the far east, and those of the city itself, as well as two senior workers from further afield and ourselves from the UK. All were housed, all were fed, and all were kept warm. The informal get-together was soon underway, with hymn-singing to a guitar accompaniment, testimonies from one and another, sharing of problems and heartaches and a godly seeking of solutions. A daily study in the Word was based on the four biblical principles: sacrifice, faith, holiness, and fellowship, about which I had by then completed writing four books, and how we must all seek to see these principles worked out in our daily living experience.

Then there was a lovely time together with the small group of four workers who had their hearts drawn to serve in a remote northern region. Our friend Martin was their team leader. The team included three single women, one a doctor from the UK, another a nurse from the USA, and also a male Norwegian logistician. They had asked me to prepare some thoughts on verse nine in the Beatitudes in Matthew 5: *'Blessed are the peacemakers'* as they saw this to be one of the most important parts of their ministry in the future. We thought together of our need to accept the whole standard of all the beatitudes, and not just one isolated verse. We must know ourselves to be spiritually *poor*, unable to achieve anything in our own strength, utterly dependent on God's enabling grace. We must never cease to *mourn* over our frequent failures—our waywardness, our criticisms of others and our pride, our lack of faith and our slowness to grow up into maturity in Christ—so that we can receive and rejoice in His comfort. This must always be accompanied by a *meekness* of spirit, a humility, a knowing that we can never deserve His grace and forgiveness. And that should lead us into a deep *hunger and thirst* after righteousness, an ever-increasing desire to be truly Christlike, to be holy as he is. Such holiness will always result in a *merciful* spirit towards others, a purity of heart towards God and a purposefulness to be always pleasing to Him rather than to one another or to ourselves. Then, from that position, stems the possibility of truly being *peacemakers*—but with the realisation that such a ministry brings the certainty of *persecution*. The devil will not let us alone. He will throw himself into the battle to stop our ministry or to render it ineffective. Has not God specifically told us that any who strive to live godly lives will suffer persecution (2 Tim. 3:12)?

On more than one occasion during the fellowship of those two weeks, I used the experiences of the civil war in Congo in the 1960s to illustrate these truths. One such illustration involved the night in October 1964, when I was beaten up, when the Lord challenged me with the question, 'Can you thank Me for trusting you with this experience, even if I never tell you why?' I tried to explain a little of what this question had come to mean to me. It was as though God had said to me, 'Don't try to reason it out. Trust Me! I have a plan and purpose. I do know what I am doing and what I am asking of you in the fulfilment of My purpose. Can you not thank Me for inviting you to be part of My plan, even if you never understand the Why?' I shared my testimony of how, in the midst of that terrible night, with very little understanding of what God was actually saying to me, I managed to say, 'OK, God, if this is in Your plan, thank You for letting me be a part of it', and how, immediately, He flooded my heart with His peace despite the continuing pain and brutality.

Several months after we returned home from those two weeks we heard an amazing story. Immediately after we left, the small team went the three-day journey north and had a very successful visit of the region, setting up a small mobile medical clinic to help the people there. Around three months later, some of the team went back with their local helpers for three weeks of ministry. As they were leaving on mule-back, they were attacked by two young tribesmen who drove away their national helpers at gunpoint. They then fired shots round the girls, beat them with sticks, and forced them to climb up the steep rough mountainside, goading them on with their guns if they stumbled or hesitated. What lay ahead? Cruelty? Torture? Death?

Suddenly, local people appeared on the scene and rescued the captives. Their national helpers had gone to find others to join them and to follow the marauders, in order to bring the girls back to safety. They achieved this, and the girls were practically unhurt. But what of their thoughts? What of the mental strain of such an ordeal? How did they stand up to that? When questioned, they shared how at the beginning of the incident they had a brief opportunity to pray together, and they committed themselves to God before being forced to start their gruelling ascent. They could see by their captors' eyes that at least one of the men was capable of killing them. Indeed, they found out later that he had previously killed eight people, including some of his own relatives.

Their minds turned to one thought—as they were later to tell each other. Knowing, and almost expecting, that they might die, they felt the Lord ask, 'Can you thank Me for trusting you with this experience even if I never tell you why?' They went on to tell how they experienced no fear throughout the hours of their capture—only the peace of Christ—the Christ who had promised to be with them always, in life and in death. Isn't God wonderful? I never cease to wonder at His perfect timing, and at how He can prompt us to say what He wants said, and at just the right time. I was awed and humbled to have been a small part of that remarkable story, and I thank God for giving me the privilege of sharing with others His teaching and prompting under so many different circumstances.

Later the same year, Pat and I had a traumatic experience, and I was tested regarding the reality of my own testimony. Did I speak only from my head, or was it honestly from deep down inside my innermost being? At 2.20 a.m. one morning, I went from my bedroom across the small corridor in our home, to the bathroom. I had not put on my glasses, but I did notice a light on in the hall. Had I forgotten to turn off one of the lights at bedtime? When I went to investigate, the light went out. I stepped into the sitting room doorway to glance out the windows. Had someone's security light gone on and off? I looked, but did not notice any movement outside. Then, when I turned back, thinking to go to the kitchen and get a drink of water, I became conscious of an 'object' in the hall, and wondered what Pat had left there. Suddenly, the 'object' exploded, leapt up, hands waving, and crashed towards me. Utterly devastated, I fell back against the wall in the corridor and the intruder rushed past me and out through the French windows in the study into the dark night. He must have left them open for his getaway.

Finding my voice out of my shock and horror, I yelled for Pat to come. 'There's a man in the house!' We rang for police and the rest of the night passed in a blur. In my heart a voice seemed to say, 'Can you thank God now?' and I shrank away from the voice. For several days I would not even listen to the challenge in that question. Yet, even in my refusal to listen, I felt condemned. Was I for real, or was my testimony always past tense? For several nights I relived the horror of that experience. I could not sleep peacefully. Would the intruder come back? I wondered. We heard from the police that on several occasions in our area, where people had been 'disturbed' at night, the intruder returned some weeks later. Would that happen to us? Would it be worse next time?

When the police first arrived, I had almost triumphantly said, 'No-one was hurt!' I was sure that God had protected us, but would He protect us next time round? My mind went over and over the events; I tormented myself, and was unable to let go and relax into His grace and goodness. I just could not bring myself to thank Him for trusting me with this. Security people came and readjusted the alarm system so that it could be used when we were in the house as well as when we went out. A new lock was put on the French window in the study, and also on the back door into the garage. Banks replaced all our stolen credit cards and refunded the money stolen from them. Everyone was so kind, doing all they could to restore my equilibrium. Our neighbours gave us their telephone numbers and told us not to hesitate to call them any hour, day or night, if we needed help.

Three days after the event, my reading in Daily Light started with: '*We know that all things work together for good to them that love God*' (Rom. 8:28). I held on to that. A few days later it was: '*Beloved, think it not strange concerning the fiery trial which is to try you ...*' (1 Pet. 4:12). I prayed earnestly that I would be willing to learn whatever God wanted to teach me through this incident. Then in reading, on October 1st, from *My Utmost for His Highest* by Oswald Chambers, the text for that day was, '*Jesus took Peter and James and John with him, and led them up a high mountain, where they were all alone.*' I was challenged to rethink that prayer, to be willing to learn whatever the Lord wanted to teach me through the recent horrific incident. Chambers wrote, 'We are apt to think that everything that happens is to be turned into useful teaching—no!—it is to be turned into something better than teaching; it is to be turned into character. The [momentous moments in our lives] are not meant to *teach* us anything, they are meant to *make* us something.'

It was hard indeed to think of that terrifying moment at 2.20 a.m. on the 18th September as a 'mountain top' experience. And yet, in a sense, it was. It was driving me to re-evaluate my living, ongoing relationship with God. How completely was I given over to Him, accepting a daily dying of my self-life that He might more and more fully indwell me, possess me, control my thinking, my emotions, my reactions in every part? Suddenly it all slipped into place, and I knew that it was for real. It was not just theory or head knowledge. It really was part of becoming *'mature, attaining to the whole measure of the fullness of Christ'* (Eph. 4:13-15). I actually thanked Him for trusting me, even with this experience, even if He never told me why.

A few days later I had occasion to ring up an elderly lady who lives near us. When she answered the phone, I knew at once that she was deeply distressed, almost unable to talk. I waited, listened, and then asked if I could help her at all. Suddenly, she burst out with a terrible story of how, a few nights previously, an intruder had entered her home and ransacked it while she was visiting her husband in hospital. At times she was almost incoherent with the overwhelming sense of the violation of her privacy and peace. Gently, I told her, 'I think I understand how this event has hurt you, and how you are now feeling. We also had an intruder only two weeks ago'. There was a startled silence.

'Did you really?'

'Yes,' I replied, and I told her a little bit of our 'event'.

'Oh, so you *do* understand how I feel!' she exclaimed. We talked for some twenty minutes as I sought to comfort her *'with the comfort we ourselves have received from God'* (2 Cor. 1:4).

Afterwards I thought, Isn't God good? He had prepared me for that moment so that I could comfort her meaningfully. Had we not suffered that shocking intrusion, I would not have been able to enter so wholeheartedly into that dear lady's distress. But how slow I am to learn! God has been teaching me this truth, by one means and another, over the past forty years. Despite that I had to fight to bring myself to say, 'Thank You, God, for trusting me with this experience, even if You never tell me why.' Another ditch was dug, and another blessing poured out by our gracious God.

14

A Return Home—Will this be the Start of another Ditch?

I sense that I may be nearing the end of this particular stretch of my life's journey—not that my valley is yet full of ditches, but that possibly God has a new direction for me. As a result, I find myself thinking in present tense and future possibilities, rather than past tense and memories. However, let me fill in a little background for this final chapter.

In September 1954, fifty years ago, I started work at Nebobongo, a small clearing in the Ituri forest in the northeastern province of what was then the Belgian Congo. With a willing team of African helpers, we embarked on the task of setting up a medical service for the church in the region for which our mission was responsible. There was already a brick-built maternity centre where Florence Stebbing cared for the women, and where she patiently trained Congolese girls to be midwives. There was no hospital. But there were some small buildings for the orphan children—mostly the children of leprous parents who had been segregated to protect them from infection— who were loved and cared for by five widowed ladies. It was decided to take over their buildings and re-house the little boys elsewhere in the village. Their dormitory became our operating theatre, scrub-up room, two small rooms for male and female changing, and another room for immediate post-operative care and office work. Indeed, this became our 'theatre' (O.R,, to my American friends)!

It was in 1954 that I did my first-ever major operation there, a Caesarean section on a wee pigmy woman. The instruments I used were gifted by a widowed lady in the south of England after the death of her husband, who had been a surgeon. For the next fifty years that was the centre for all surgical procedures at Nebobongo Hospital, and many of those original instruments might still have been in use! Now it was to be all change!

Under the leadership of Dr Mola, with Mrs Mary Jean Robertson, a Canadian nurse, and a team of local workmen supervised by Berndt Lutz, a German engineer, a new complex for surgery was being constructed, new surgical instruments supplied, new equipment installed, and I was invited to go out to 'cut the tape' and dedicate the new facilities to the glory of God. It was an exciting, a thrilling, prospect! Dr Mola, our first Congolese doctor and a graduate of the University of Congo, has been in charge of the medical programme at Nebobongo for a few years, and has been very gracious in thanking me many times over for my part in establishing the medical service in our WEC area of responsibility in the D.R. Congo. He does not allow today's generation to forget that many of the present team of medical workers were trained at Nebobongo back in the 1950s and 1960s, and others at Nyankunde in the 1970s, when I had the privilege of being the doctor in charge of the teaching personnel. Now he suggested that it was time he and I met face to face!

Initially, Pat and I hoped to travel out there for Easter 2004, but the building was not ready due to all the 'unforeseen' frustrations and difficulties of any enterprise in the Ituri forest, which is hundreds of miles from stores and supplies, with roads increasingly impassable. Little by little the date was moved towards the end of the year. Eventually it was settled for mid-November. So what did God have for me to do in the months of waiting? There were weekly Bible studies at church, and with our girls on Sunday afternoons, a WEC holiday convention in Scotland at which we studied the biblical basis for true Christian fellowship in John's first letter, and the annual World Missions' Conference in Bangor. The days were full, and the Lord graciously filled us with His peace and joy.

At the Easter General Meeting of the members of our local church, I was invited to become the Church Treasurer, at least to fill in for a year. It sounded a simple enough task, taking note of all funds donated from whatever source, and paying the bills: heating, lighting, water, rates, office supplies, salaries of all staff, cleaners, and a hundred and one other expenses. But the struggle to make my accounts and monthly bank statements tally, to consistently make double-entries for all income and expenditure and to prepare simple monthly balance sheets to present intelligibly to the church committee combined to make me more and more aware of my personal insufficiency for the task!

As the weeks rolled relentlessly on, our proposed journey back to Africa drew nearer. I started reading my Bible aloud, every morning, in French and Swahili as well as in English, to get my ears accustomed again to the languages used at Nebobongo. Pat and I looked through our wardrobes to see that we had suitable cotton dresses, skirts, and blouses. We began to think about what gifts we could take out to my dear friends, things that would neither add substantially to our weight nor cause difficulties at customs.

All injections and inoculations were completed and antimalarial medicine ordered. Odds and ends to take out to my many friends were gathering on our guest room bed ... and there were only two weeks to go! The air tickets had been purchased, sterling currency exchanged for American dollars and suitcases brought down from the roof space. Anticipation was growing daily, and nervousness seemed to grow as fast!

* * *

We've been. We've returned. What a fantastic journey! What have we learned? How do we start to explain all that we saw and felt?

My friend Pat and I travelled out together and the journey was relatively straightforward, except that Pat's suitcase was left behind in London, half-filled with gifts to the Nebobongo Primary School children, and we did not meet it again until our homeward journey! The MAF plane met us in Entebbe International Airport, and took us into Congo, via a three-hour wait at Beni airstrip. Then it was on to Nebobongo on the edge of the great Ituri rain forest, arriving just before dusk to a rapturous welcome! School children, their parents, workmen, nurses—everyone waving and cheering and singing—and Doctor Mola and his brother Umo (the Senior Administrator of the medical service in our area) came forward to greet us. John Mangadima, my very first student in 1953, was there, as was Benjamin, my house-help all my years in Congo, and Mary-Jean Robertson, who was really responsible for all the arrangements and for our arrival. They were all there. We were led triumphantly the short walk up to the home that had been prepared for us for the week. I think we looked a little like the Pied Piper followed by an ever-growing excited crowd!

Outside the home, we found a welcome-banner of flowers and a row of cane chairs. And there was my dearest Congolese friend, Mama Taadi, frail and weak now, but with the same lovely smile and outstretched arms! We hugged each other ... and cried. It was just so good to be together again. My adopted daughter, Fibi, joined us. She is now a grandmother in her own rights! Then speeches began. The pastor spoke, then Dr Mola and Mangadima ... and I was expected to respond! How thrilled I was that the Swahili language returned to me as though I had never been away. I could understand everything they said, and they seemed well able to understand me.

A group of some twelve people gathered in front of us in the last glimmer of daylight. I recognised one of them, Bebesi, an excellent carpenter (really a cabinet maker) from the mid-fifties. Now lean, stooped, and grey-haired, he had come to me in the first instance due to his having developed leprosy, as did so many of my early friends. The rest of the group had all been workmen or their wives from those early days. They started to sing to us. I could hardly believe my ears! They were singing the chorus that we had had in our Campaigner Clan, ending with the motto: 'Kwa Yeye, pasipo mupaka!' (Unto Him, through and through). They hadn't forgotten! I cried. It was so tremendous to realise that all the teaching and working of those long-ago days had borne fruit that was still evident.

During the next three days we were taken round the village to see all the improvements and changes. Permanent buildings of brick or cement blocks with corrugated iron roofing had largely replaced the mud-and-thatch hospital. Yet inside, the lack of beds, equipment, and medicines was all too evident. Going to the south end of the village, we were welcomed by the primary school children—over 700 of them—with thirteen teachers, all standing on parade on the football field, and singing specially written songs in French and Swahili to greet us. Compared to the 120 children and four masters of the 1950s and 1960s, the growth was indeed impressive. But the eight classrooms, into each of which fifty-five or more children crowded each day for their classes, were still mostly mud-and-thatch with beaten earth floors and hardly any proper benches or desks. That was heartbreaking. (This is another of the projects close to Mary-Jean's heart— not just the hospital and new operating room, but new classrooms and furniture and equipment for the primary school.) The children are meant to pay a tiny sum each week for the right to be taught, but there is no money. So they arrive with a little bundle of firewood, or some other such offering for the teacher. The teachers receive practically no salary and the parents of the children have absolutely nothing with which to pay them. Yet their joy overflows. They sang to us so lustily. And as we walked into one, then another, of the classrooms we were amazed to see what was written on the blackboards. They were being well taught to a good standard.

We were then taken to the north side of the village, to see another primary school of some 300 children, and a secondary school, probably with about 120 children, in years one to four. These were private schools mainly for the children of the doctors, nurses, hospital, and school staff. But how they were able to afford the slightly higher fees I never found out. It was a local initiative to keep these parents there at Nebobongo. Without proper schooling available for the children they would so easily have been tempted to leave, to seek work in one of the towns.

Everywhere there was this strange and disconcerting dichotomy. There was orderliness, discipline, good training, and joy, but it was always alongside utter poverty, people with nothing of this world's goods, hardly enough even to live on. We came to the nurses' training school. The nurses too were all out on parade, as each of the other schools had been. There they were waiting for us, dressed immaculately in white, and singing in four-part harmony! Speeches were made, mostly in French, and that stretched me more than the Swahili. The nurses' school was better equipped than the primary schools, but their sleeping quarters were again unbelievably basic.

We were driven ten bone-shaking miles to the next village of Ibambi. This had always been the centre of the Mission's work, with its Bible School for training pastors for all the local churches, and a simpler Bible teaching centre for those who would assist those pastors, alongside its print shop, primary and secondary schools, and a large church where 2-3,000 could crowd in for services. Again we were met by the whole population of the village, all singing and rejoicing to welcome us into their midst. We were escorted round to see various new initiatives, especially a centre set up by the Wycliffe Bible Translators to train national workers. And we went to see the cemetery, all beautifully cleaned and tended, where our founder, C.T. Studd, is buried along with some six other foreigners, several African pastors, and dear Mama Anakesi, one of the very first nurse-midwives. In each place we visited, not only did they sing to us ecstatically but they also fed us— out of their poverty. Their extreme generosity was so moving that I was often almost in tears.

Then the BIG day arrived. They had erected a huge outdoor shelter with palm-frond covering, and from first light people began arriving from every direction carrying all kinds of seats, stools, chairs, and benches, until eventually some 6-7,000 were there. An enormous procession slowly wound its way up the slight hill to the enclosure. There were nurses, technicians, workmen, bricklayers, a group of pygmies, and the school children—nearly 2,000 altogether! And all the time we sang! Two choirs, duly robed, with drums as accompaniment, kept the proceedings moving. Then there were speeches from local government dignitaries and from Dr Mola, our Medical Superintendent, from the pastor and from Berndt, the German engineer who had overseen the building of the new operating theatre. After they had all spoken I was asked to bring the message to them all from the Word of God.

Eventually we were gently marshalled into order to process to the front of the new building. There was the tape, neatly prepared across the porch, and above it a sheet was hung. When we were all gathered the sheet was ceremoniously withdrawn, and the beautifully carved redwood sign was revealed to us all. Once again, I cried. In their hearts they were doing everything to honour *me* ... and I just wanted to crawl away and not be in the limelight. The new surgical unit was to be called by my African name, Mama Luka—the Surgical Centre of Mama Luka. They were humbly thanking me for having laid the foundations of today's work when I served there fifty years ago. The teaching programmes of today, so vastly superior to the small beginnings in 1954, were nevertheless seen by them to be a bringing in of the harvest of those early years of sowing and preparing the ground.

I was offered a beautiful new pair of surgical scissors on a presentation tray, with which to cut the tape. Prayer was offered, the tape was cut, and a short statement given that the building was now officially opened! And they cheered! There was an unbelievable welling up of happiness—a deep inner joy—a sense of the culmination of a long-held dream. For many it was really a moving forward into a future full of hope and anticipation with barely a thought about the difficulties, frustrations, shortages, and poverty. It may also have been a drawing of a line under the past.

As I thought back over those fifty years, from being the only doctor (and I a foreigner) with Florence Stebbing, a nurse-midwife (and she also a foreigner), in charge of everything in every department in 1954, to 2004 with doctors, well-trained nurses, technicians, administrators, a pastoral care team—all nationals—all able to carry the work forward. It really was the fulfilment of a dream, a vision, that God had given me so long ago, when I first started work at Nebobongo, of seeing all the work led by Congolese.

Among other things we did in the days we had left was visit John Mangadima's village, some five miles along an almost impassable road into the forest, a road full of pot holes and ruts swirling with mud as torrential rain fell most days we were there. John had been appointed by the church leadership to become the pastor of the Anga Church. Once there he saw the need of the people for medical care, so he built a small hospital to run an efficient medical service for the local population, including surgery and maternity care. He also saw hundreds of primary school children, with no secondary education, so he built a secondary school and employed four or five qualified teachers for some sixty girls and boys! For sheer persistent, believing faith and initiative and determination, we had rarely seen anything comparable.

Everywhere we were feted and given flowers, presented with national dress and welcomed with songs and feasts, then offered amazing gifts. In one home we were offered four live chickens with their legs tied together. We had to accept their gifts, yet our hearts condemned us for accepting anything out of their appalling poverty. How could we refuse without hurting? 'Please, we do say a big big "Thank you!" for your love and your generosity to us, but would you allow us to give you back three of the hens?' we said, and they accepted them from us. Then a man, with an amazing story, came to the house where we were being fed. Fourteen months before our visit one of my dear friends, Mama Damaris, died, probably in her nineties. And she had made this man promise to keep her one goat, care for it, until 'we', her sisters, arrived, when he was to give it to us for a welcome feast. How could we refuse? Having kept the goat carefully all that time, he now brought it to us to fulfil his promise to dear Damaris. Such love!

At last the time came for us to leave Nebobongo. The little MAF plane came for us and, as we flew up over the forest and watched Nebobongo disappear in the distance, I began to feel a chapter had ended. But I wasn't yet sure ... We then flew to Nyankunde, to the other hospital where I worked from 1965 onwards. Over the years since then a large 250-bed hospital, with over 1,000 outpatients attending daily, and supporting a training college for some seventy two students annually, had come into being. And the college trained to a higher academic level than had been possible when we started at Nebobongo. When I left in 1973 there were several Western doctors and nurses there, and the standard of the training college was soon to rise to university status under the new leadership. Known as the Centre Medical Evangelique (CME in French, the Evangelical Medical Centre), Nyankunde became well known throughout not only Congo, but also Africa.

Then in 2002, inter-tribal fighting erupted in the district. In one terrible night the work of over thirty years was destroyed. Buildings were burned to the ground, ravished, wrecked. Possibly up to 2,000 were murdered, and there were other great brutalities and horrific atrocities. Patients, relatives, doctors, and nurses were all victims. Others were enabled to escape, to flee on foot through the interminable forest to the south. After ten days of trekking they reached Oicha, another mission medical centre established by Dr Carl Becker, a renowned leprologist, who worked with the Africa Inland Mission back in the 1930s. We had a brief half hour to see something of the devastating destruction at Nyankunde, and the courage of a small group who were starting again in the burnt-out remains of the buildings.

From there we flew on to Oicha, where we saw a little of the enormous refugee camp on the one hand, and the continuing work of the hospital and nurses' training school on the other. Philip and Nancy Wood, two doctors who took over from me at Nyankunde when I had to leave in 1973, had returned to Oicha and were heading up the two wings of the ministry, the hospital with the college and the care of thousands of refugees and displaced people.

They had invited twelve or more of the 1967-1972 graduates from the Nyankunde School, when I was the doctor in charge of the training programme, to come and have an evening meal with us. After the meal (when we enjoyed a whole goat cooked on a spit!) three of the ladies, probably all in their 50s or 60s, stood up to sing to us—and they sang the first part of Handel's Hallelujah Chorus! We had learned it together all those years ago and they hadn't forgotten it! One of them imitated me as conductor, bringing in each of the voices in turn. It was hilarious! Deep inside me, along with the laughter there was a wonderful glow of comfort. God was so graciously showing me that those years—sometimes of hardship, often with frustrations, possibly loneliness—had not been in vain. How true *'Therefore, my dear brothers, stand firm. Let nothing move you. Always give yourselves fully to the work of the Lord, because you know that your labour in the Lord is not in vain'* (1 Cor. 15:58).

The following day we flew 25 miles to the south, to Beni, a large township with an airstrip, and with reasonable roads in all directions. Here Philip and Nancy had helped the medical staff to re-establish the 'Nyankunde CME' project in rented warehouses. We were greeted by the whole student body, all lined up in immaculate white uniforms, all singing in French, Swahili, and even English, to welcome us. I was presented with a magnificent bunch of frangipani flowers, golden and white (actually, superb artificial silk flowers that I managed to bring home with me). We were led into their temporary chapel accommodation where the student body and the nursing staff of the hospital, including technical and practical workers, sang to us once again. I was invited to talk to them, which I was delighted to do. I shared the three 'musts' (oughts) from 1 John 2:6, 3:16, and 4:11. As Christian young people, privileged to be called into God's service, it is so essential that our whole lives bear testimony to His saving grace, not just our lips in what we say, but our behaviour and all we do. We *must* walk as Jesus walked, we *must* die to ourselves as Jesus died to Himself, and we *must* love one another as He loved us. They were so receptive, and their bright young faces thrilled me as I saw in them the hope of tomorrow for Congo.

We were shown all round their makeshift hospital in the two warehouses that had been skilfully divided up by partitions into wards, clinics, laboratory, pharmacy, and all the other necessary departments for a modern teaching hospital. Then we were taken to see their sleeping accommodation. It was desperately cramped and with very little beyond basic essentials, but no one seemed to be complaining. They were just so grateful to God that they were alive, and that the staff was doing everything possible for them to continue their education.

At last we had to leave. Flying home, over the southern end of the Ruwenzori mountain range, the top of the mountain, which is over 16,000 feet high, was covered in clouds. I knew it was there, but it was hidden from view. Again, tears were very near as I thought how the future of Congo is indeed hidden to our view. All we hear is of warfare, rebel groups of soldiers ravaging and pillaging and harassing local populations, spreading fear and increasing poverty as they steal anything they see and want. Yet we know assuredly that there is a future for them. We have seen it in the shining faces of those young students. We have heard it in the confident voices of their church elders and pastors, and we have realised it in the persistent effort to rebuild every time their previous efforts are destroyed.

So we came home full of amazing memories, wonderfully encouraged to see the harvest of all the early years of preparing the soil, clearing out rocks and weeds, sowing the seed, watering ... and waiting. And all that we had seen and heard engendered hope, hope to stand by them as they seek to go forward, to find a way to re-establish, not only the medical service and training schools, but even more the spiritual work among all age groups in every tribe throughout their vast country. Then came the niggling desire to go back again for a longer period. Could I be of service to them, perhaps just as a grandmother-figure, someone to listen, share, pray, and teach the Word, someone who could 'be available'? There were moments when this desire almost overwhelmed me, and I didn't want to back away if by any chance it was God's voice speaking to me. I asked Him to speak to me very clearly, to show me if this desire was His will for me.

Our daily reading at the time was in the final chapters of the first book of Chronicles. I came to chapter 17, when King David, settled in his beautiful palace, suddenly realises that the Almighty Lord God only had a tent. He wanted to build a dwelling place for the Ark of the Covenant, worthy of the Lord God. He was willing to give all he had to the task. But God spoke to the prophet Nathan, who came to King David with God's message full of promises of blessing, full of encouragement of peace and victory. Nathan said, '*You are not the one to build me a house to dwell in*' (1 Chron. 17:4). David responded in a prayer of thanksgiving and worship because God had brought him thus far, and was promising him so much for the future. '*There is no-one like you, O Lord, and there is no God but you!*' (17:20). He accepted that it would be his son, Solomon, who would build the temple for the Lord. So David set about preparing all that would be needed in the task: silver and gold, bronze and cedar timbers, iron and stone. In chapter 22, David said: '*My son Solomon is young and inexperienced, and the house to be built for the Lord should be of great magnificence and fame and splendour ...'* (22:5). Then he called his son and charged him to build the temple of the Lord God Almighty. *'Now, my son, the Lord be with you, and may you have success and build the house of the Lord your God, as He said you would'* (22:11).

As I read these chapters (including David's sin through pride, thinking he could do things for God in his own strength, and his repentance and God's forgiveness) I remembered so clearly the last time I talked and prayed with John Mangadima before I left Congo in 1973. I had explained these very same chapters to him, and then we turned together to chapter 28:9 through to the end of the chapter: *'And you, my son Solomon, acknowledge the God of your father, and serve him with wholehearted devotion and with a willing mind, for the Lord searches every heart and understands every motive behind the thoughts. If you seek him, he will be found by you; but if you forsake him, he will reject you for ever. Consider now, for the Lord has chosen you to build a temple as a sanctuary. Be strong and do the work!'* David then passed on to Solomon all the plans he had drawn up, and all the supplies he had amassed for the work. *'Be strong and courageous and do the work. Do not be afraid or discouraged, for the Lord my God is with you.'* I had prayed with John, 'passed him the keys', as it were, and left him in charge of the work that I had led for twenty years. Now the Lord chided me: 'You passed the responsibility on, now do you want to take it back? Can you not trust Me in them to complete the job?' Was I now jealous to get back into the task that had previously been assigned to me, but that had been handed on to the next generation? Did I think I could do it better than they could? Was I discontent with my present job description as a digger of ditches?

Maybe God has had to prise my hands off, like the folded-back sepals of the opening buttercup, never to close again, allowing Him to have His way. Surely I can rejoice in having been allowed by God, in His gracious mercy, to see so much of the fruit—the harvest—of all the early sowing, and to see the next generation taking over and carrying on the task so efficiently, without hankering to get back into the fray. 'I've given you another task now. Be content, and trust Me!' God seems to be saying to me.

So I trust my Congolese colleagues and friends into the Lord's hands, that He will keep them, lead them, and use them despite all the apparently insurmountable difficulties that surround them. And I must keep on digging ditches until my valley is full—without regrets, without looking backwards, but rather with joy and expectation, *'waiting for the glorious appearing of our Great God and Saviour'.*

Epilogue

The Valley is Not Yet Full of Ditches!

'Make this valley full of ditches'
(2 Kings 3:16)

For thirty years, that Bible verse has been my inspiration—the word from God to encourage me and keep me moving forward in His will.

'This valley' always speaks to me of the ever-present-tense nature of our God. He is the great 'I am' God (Ex. 3:14); 'My grace *is* sufficient for you!' (2 Cor. 12:9). God has taught me over many years to trust Him for today's needs and not to be hankering for the 'good old days' and looking backwards, nor to be planning endlessly for tomorrow and the 'what-might-be' of the future. He has taught me to believe utterly that He does know and understand my circumstances—including my needs, my hopes, and my fears—and that His plan for my life takes all that into account, and brings peace. An acceptance of the fact that His will for my daily life is the best possible thing for me, does, in itself, bring peace.

The 'this valley' of thirty years ago, when God first spoke this verse into my heart, was different from the 'this valley' of today, but God is the same! Then there was the death of my dear mother and the uncertainty of my own health, the wrench of leaving Africa and the tension of trying to adapt to living in the affluent West. I had been asked to take on a roving deputation ministry for the Mission, with 'no fixed abode' as my residence. There was the realisation of endless travelling (and I suffered quite a lot from travel sickness!) and meeting up with new people every day when, basically, I am shy and not particularly outgoing. There was also the need to learn far more about the work and outreach of our mission than just what was being done in Congo if I was to truly represent WEC to others, and I was very conscious of my own inadequacy for the task. Above all, the new calling in my life was open-ended. There was no clear job description as there had been when I served as a doctor in Congo. And that caused me to fear. To whom was I ultimately responsible? I felt the need to be accountable to someone; but that was a very ill defined area in my appointment. It wasn't hard to see all of that as my 'this valley' when I started out in 1976.

But the truth of this Scripture has always to remain present tense. As the Lord graciously led me forward, step by step, to recognise those areas in my life that He wanted to change, and to allow Him to work through them with me, to bring about an ever-increasing trust in Him and therefore peace of heart, I came to see that my description of 'this valley' was bound to change.

My ability to keep abreast of changes in the mission, and of the extent of the work in many countries and situations throughout the world, was no longer really sufficient for the task of representing them. Like others, as I grow older my memory is no longer as accurate as previously, and I am fearful that I will give facts wrongly. Travelling long distances across several time zones causes much more weariness as we get older than it does when we are young, and I dread becoming a burden to those whom I visit for ministry. Yet sitting at home and doing nothing is simply not an option! I long to be found working and watching for the Lord's coming again, not just waiting and watching. There is plenty to be done nearer home in our local church and amongst young people. Am I willing for continual daily direction as to the 'where' of service as well as to the 'what'? Is this perhaps an assessment of 'this valley' for me today? When the Lord shows a task that needs doing near home, is my temptation to think, 'That can't be for me. I'm no good at that!' or perhaps, 'surely so-and-so would be much more capable than me of doing that?' Or am I prepared to allow the Lord to help me to do what He asks me to do? Am I willing to think in terms of further training, or tackling a new task with new tools, and trusting Him to teach me the 'how' during the process?

'**Make**' is a verb of activity, not of sitting down and watching others! Yet, over the years, I believe that the emphasis has changed from the physical activity of 'doing' to, I trust, a more spiritual activity of 'becoming'. Early on, during my first years as a Christian, and also when I first arrived in Congo, I clung to the verse in John's Gospel, '*Whoever has my commands and obeys them, he is the one who loves me* (John 14:21). I have always been very hesitant about saying, or even believing, that I truly loved God. I knew I should, for all He has done for me and is to me, but did I actually love Him? When I was first saved, my understanding of the verb 'to love' was limited to what I had read in cheap and rather sloppy love stories and I did not have that sort of relationship with God. So the verse that said that my obedience to His commandments was in truth a demonstration of the fact that I loved Him was a great comfort to me, and I was willing to work round the clock to obey His commands. We used to say at Nebobongo, that we worked twenty-fives hours in each day, eight days every week, fifty-three weeks each year! And I loved it. I thrived on hard work, no matter how long the hours. I just wanted to show God—to tell Him—that I loved Him. It was my way of trying to say 'Thank You!' to Him for dying for me on the cross.

Slowly over many years, the Scriptures have shown me that although it is Biblically true that only obedience to His will can reveal our love for Him, the bottom line of His will for me is that I should become conformed to the image of His Son, that I should become Christlike. My enthusiasm for activity in my service for the Master—my 'making' the valley full of ditches—has to be tempered by an understanding that He is 'making' me come into line with His vision for my life. The Master Potter is moulding the jar of clay so that it can carry the Treasure (2 Cor. 4:7). How willing am I for the pressure of His hands moulding, refining, perfecting, and making me into His vision for me? As I quoted from Oswald Chambers in chapter 13, it is not always what He is *teaching* me that is important, but rather, what He is *making* of me. My 'making this valley full of ditches' must, pre-eminently, come about as I allow God right of way in my heart and life, conforming me to the image of His Son.

Ditches—going back to the original story in Scripture, the ditches were to be dug by the soldiers in the sandy bed of the dried up River Arnon, so that God's gift of water would not be wasted, lost into the sand, but could be captured and used. Each soldier may have been ordered to dig a ditch, one metre long, 30 cm across, and 50 cm deep. How many thousands of soldiers might there have been? What a sight to see them all busy digging ditches, lines and lines of ditches! Where did they put the sandy soil that they dug out, without allowing it to fall into another man's ditch? It was not exactly the work for which they were trained, and they had not the right tools for it. But they were soldiers, and as such, they were expected to obey orders without questionings or murmurings. There was nothing to encourage them. The Lord had actually said: '*You will not see wind, nor rain*'. So why were they told to dig ditches? It was hot and tiring work. They had no water to drink. They must have felt very foolish. But as the day went on the number of ditches grew and grew.

Then in the night God filled the valley with precious, life-giving water. The ditches were filled. And in the morning everyone was able to slake their thirst, fill their water bottles, and bring their mules and other animals to drink. Furthermore, the rising sun shone down the valley from the east, and was reflected up as a red glow in the water. The enemy saw the redness and presumed it was the blood of rioting soldiers! They rushed down the mountainside to grab all the plunder they could, expecting no resistance from the Israelite army. But that army was ready for them and a great victory was won by God, due entirely to His gracious outpouring of blessing.

Ditches—God told me nearly thirty years ago that He wanted me to dig ditches, hundreds of little, often unconnected, ditches. Preaching, teaching, visiting, sharing, chatting, being available, in the main, without seeing any special blessing, these were the ditches I dug. They were the taking up of every opportunity of witnessing to God's love, by lip or by life, at meetings, in homes, sitting in an aeroplane, or waiting in an airport; whether with students, senior citizens, or primary school children; whether over the telephone or in a radio broadcast. I was not to question the where or the what of God's choice, but just to be ready and available to the Spirit, to buy up every opportunity. Each occasion was another ditch. God gave me no promise of hearing the rain or seeing the wind of His blessing; He just asked me for unquestioning obedience and absolute trust in Him with regard to the outcome.

In His grace, God has allowed me the huge encouragement—especially more recently—of hearing, every now and again, from someone who was especially blessed or heard the Lord's word of direction or came to know the next step they were to take in their lives at a particular meeting. Quite often, as they named or described the meeting, a wave of memory would come to me about how difficult I had found that occasion. Yet the Lord was at work, silently fulfilling His perfect purpose in this one life. God Himself had filled another 'ditch' with His own perfect blessing; the water of life had been given to another precious servant.

'Make this valley **full** of ditches!' But how do we know when the valley is full? How full of ditches does the valley have to be to be full? That reminds me of a youngster in our Nebobongo orphanage. As he was sent back from the line-up for lunch to wash his hands, he muttered as he turned away, 'How clean do my hands have to be to be clean?'

They are relative concepts, aren't they? Jaki's hands looked clean enough down in the shadows by the water hole, but in the full glare of the midday sunshine in the school courtyard, they looked anything but clean. The nearer we get to the sun, the more clearly we can see the dirt. The nearer we get to Jesus, the more clearly we realise the sinfulness and deceitfulness of our hearts. When compared to someone else's heart, my heart may look fairly good, or at least passable. But when compared to His utter purity, the truth is revealed and I am in no doubt of my need of His gracious cleansing.

Is it the same with being 'full'? The widow, told to bring empty jars and to pour out her meagre supply of oil, had enough oil to fill every jar until she ceased to bring another empty one. Then the oil stopped flowing. When Elisha told King Joash to shoot an arrow out of the window, it was to be the sign of Israel's victory over Syria. Then Elisha told the king to strike the ground with the arrows, and the king struck just three times and stopped, and Elisha was angry with him for stopping! '*You should have struck the ground five or six times, then you would have defeated Aram and completely destroyed it. But now you will defeat it only three times*' (2 Kings 13:19).

Is he temptation to want to stop 'digging ditches' and perhaps do something apparently more interesting, more fruitful, and more meaningful in the public eye? Yet the question is still there, Is the valley *full* of ditches yet?

May the Lord give me stickability to persevere with the task until it is completed, and not to ask for a new word of direction whilst there is still leeway in the fulfilment of the previous clear word. Did the Lord God not promise that His Spirit would speak a word in our ears saying: '*This is the way; walk in it*' whenever we turn out of the way, to the right or the left? (Is. 30:21). Surely this indicates that He has no need to speak such a word into our hearts when we keep in the way! We are just to keep on keeping on, with our eyes fixed on Jesus, the Founder and Perfecter of our faith (Heb.12:2). He will indeed hold our hand and guide us through the dark places as well as those that are full of light, the difficult as well as the relatively easy, the sad as much as the joyous. He has promised, '*Never will I leave you; never will I forsake you*' (Heb.13:5), but rather, that He will be with us to the end—to the end of the world, to the end of time, to the end of our sense of need! Wonderful Lord and Saviour!

May I be kept willing to obey His sure word to me:

'Make this valley full of ditches!'

AFTERWORD

"Has it all been worth it?" This was the question Helen asked at times, such as when war destroyed in a few hours what had taken years to build or when students and colleagues treated her with suspicion. Her final trip to Africa answered that question with a resounding yes. Helen's whole life was an illustration of Paul's words to the Galatians: "Let us not become weary in doing good, for at the proper time we will reap a harvest if we do not give up" (Gal. 6:9, NIV).

Although Helen's autobiography ends in 2004, she kept on writing and speaking as long as she was able. She continued to live with her friend, Pat Morton, near Belfast. The final year of her life was spent in a care home, and on 7 December 2016, she breathed her last.

In the introduction to *Give Me This Mountain*, Helen spoke of her life as 'a journey with one glorious goal, "that I may know him…."' At her funeral, a representative of the Girl Crusader's Union read Philippians 3:7–12, which includes these wonderfully fitting words: 'Indeed, I count everything as loss because of the surpassing worth of knowing Christ Jesus my Lord…that I may know him and the power of his resurrection, and may share his sufferings, becoming like him in his death…" (ESV).

Helen was buried in the graveyard of St Elizabeth's Church, Dundonald, the church that had been her sending base and spiritual community for 39 years.

At her funeral, her friend Roger Carswell gave a eulogy, and told a memorable story from one of Helen's trips to America.

In the mid-70s, you needed an actual ticket to travel on an airplane. Because Helen was flying around for months, she had a thick book of tickets. She stayed overnight with a pastor and his wife but needed to fly to her next speaking engagement on a Monday morning. Her hosts lived a couple of hours from the airport but were traveling that way anyway that Monday morning, and so they drove her to catch her flight. They arrived at 6 a.m. for Helen's 7:30 flight, and she told them simply to drop her off at the curb.

When Helen got to the ticket desk to check in, she discovered she had left her tickets, passport, and all her money on the bed in the house where she had been staying. Of course, her hosts were long gone by this time, and there was no way to phone them. Helen explained her predicament to the desk agent, who informed her that no ticket meant no flight. "But you've got to help me!" Helen said. The agent insisted that she could not fly without a ticket, but she asked Helen where she was going.

Helen had no idea where she was about to fly! She had planned to simply go to wherever the next ticket in her book took her. "Do you know your name?" the ticket agent asked wryly. Helen gave her name, and the agent found her reservation. But even with her reservation, Helen had no way to prove her identity. Finally, the ticket agent offered her a possible solution. If she could find someone to act as a guarantor for the flight, to cover the cost if it turned out she was not in fact the ticketed passenger, they would let her take her flight.

But Helen didn't know anyone in the city to call. She prayed for God to help her. Then she got an idea. She asked the ticket agent if she had a phone book. She told the agent to open it and look for someone with the words "Rev." beside his name. The agent agreed and opened the directory to "A." She found the first "Rev." and Helen asked her to phone him, even though it was still just after 6 in the morning.

Helen could only hear the ticket agent's side of the conversation. She explained that a woman named Helen Roseveare needed someone to guarantee her flight. Helen waited anxiously while the man responded but didn't know what he said until the agent hung up the phone. "He said he'll be here in 20 minutes."

Sure enough, the American pastor arrived as promised and asked for Dr. Helen Roseveare. He had even withdrawn some cash for Helen to take with her on her journey. She expressed her gratitude, but he said that he was the one who was grateful. Then he told her his story.

Some years before, when he was not yet a Christian, he and his girlfriend had been traveling the world. They were in Afghanistan and went to a nightclub in Kabul, where they took some contaminated drugs. Feeling very sick, they left the club and stumbled upon the British embassy. Someone from the embassy gave them a lift to a hostel, where they were given a bare minimum room. His girlfriend immediately fell asleep, but he felt awful and couldn't sleep. In the bedside cabinet, he found a book written in English. He read the book straight through and trusted Christ for his salvation.

"Helen," the pastor said, "It was your book, *Give Me This Mountain*."

Of all the pastors in a strange American city that Helen could have called for help at 6:30 on a Monday morning, God led her to call one who had been converted by her writing!

This kind of head-spinning, God-ordained provision happened over and over again in Helen's life. But Helen also faced many trials that didn't have a tidy ending or a clear purpose.

One time when she was living in Nebobongo, the thatched roof of Helen's cottage started to leak. She waited until the dry season when she knew she could expect 5 weeks without rain. Workers stripped off the thatch one day and planned to put on corrugated sheet metal the next. Helen went to sleep under the stars but woke up soaked in rain. All of her possessions, including her precious books, were drenched in an inch of muddy water. The books had been treated with shellac to prevent mold in the humid climate, but now that they were wet, the shellac made them a sticky mess.[1]

Helen believed that God allowed these hugely inconvenient trials to give her opportunities to "count it all joy" no matter what her circumstances. She knew that someday she might, in hindsight, see God's purpose, but she needed to give thanks in the present. This was not easy for her, but she did it. Her thanksgiving was interspersed with tears, but she chose to rejoice in the Lord by faith.

* * *

While rereading the works contained in this volume, I happened to be studying the psalms. For the first time, I noticed how the various themes and plotlines of Helen's life and ministry track with the themes of the psalms, even some of those that seem hardest for modern-day believers to identify with.

First, Helen regularly experienced the joy of salvation. She gave thanks to God for saving her from her sins and giving her new life in Christ. She also knew the joy of being rescued from earthly peril. Whether it was by getting her van unstuck from the jungle mud on a dark road in the middle of the night or by sending mercenary soldiers to free her from captivity during the Simba rebellion, God answered her prayers and saved her again and again.

Like King David, Helen had enemies who opposed her. After independence in 1960, Europeans in the Congo were despised and treated with suspicion. Some Africans saw no distinction between a missionary doctor and the colonisers they had shaken off. Then, during the Simba uprising, rebel

---

1   Helen Roseveare, *Count it All Joy* (Fearn, Ross-shire: Christian Focus, 2017), p. 33–39.

soldiers stole her property, destroyed the hospital she had helped to build, and beat and imprisoned her.

And like David, Helen experienced great despair. The truly miraculous answers to prayers that she saw did not keep her from feeling abandoned by God. In the same way, victory over Goliath didn't keep David from despair when he was pursued by Saul.

Human beings, even those who belong to God's people, have a terrible time believing that the God who delivered them once will deliver them again. Bible commentator, Dale Ralph Davis, describes this as the nature of believing experience: "There's enjoying the beauty of the Lord and then there's facing an unnerving emergency. The calm of faith can become the crisis of faith. And they often occur in that sequence."[2]

My life will most likely never have moments as dramatic as Helen's, but my faith follows the same undulation of highs and lows. There are times when I've seen God's faithfulness so clearly that I think I'll never doubt him again. Then some new dread arises, and I act as though God's steadfast love has run out and his promises are at an end (see Ps. 77:7).

Helen saw God work in her life again and again, but she still struggled. Praise be to God that His steadfast love never fails, even when our faith falters! Helen learned that our frailties force us to lean our whole weight on Jesus, and that this is something to rejoice in.

Helen Roseveare sacrificed a great deal for the work of the Lord, but she gained everything. She lived and died clothed in the righteousness of Christ, and she testified to His goodness all the way to the end. Her medical ministry in Africa and her teaching ministry around the world bore lasting fruit for the kingdom of God. And even now, her faith continues to speak to all who read her books.

—BETSY CHILDS HOWARD

---

2 Dale Ralph Davis, *In the Presence of My Enemies: Psalms 25–37* (Ross-shire: Christian Focus, 2020), p. 61.

Christian Focus Publications

Our mission statement
Staying Faithful

In dependence upon God we seek to impact the world through literature faithful to His infallible Word, the Bible. Our aim is to ensure that the Lord Jesus Christ is presented as the only hope to obtain forgiveness of sin, live a useful life and look forward to heaven with Him.

Our Books are published in four imprints:

◁◯✕ CHRISTIAN FOCUS

Popular works including biographies, commentaries, basic doctrine and Christian living.

◁◯✕ MENTOR

Books written at a level suitable for Bible College and seminary students, pastors, and other serious readers. The imprint includes commentaries, doctrinal studies, examination of current issues and church history.

◁◯✕ CHRISTIAN HERITAGE

Books representing some of the best material from the rich heritage of the church.

◁◯✕ CF4KIDS

Children's books for quality Bible teaching and for all age groups: Sunday school curriculum, puzzle and activity books; personal and family devotional titles, biographies and inspirational stories – because you are never too young to know Jesus!

Christian Focus Publications Ltd,
Geanies House, Fearn, Ross-shire,
IV20 1TW, Scotland, United Kingdom.
www.christianfocus.com